This Mad Masquerade
Stardom and Masculinity in the Jazz Age

Film and Culture
John Belton, General Editor

Film and Culture

A SERIES OF COLUMBIA UNIVERSITY PRESS

Edited by John Belton

GAYLYN STUDLAR

This Mad Masquerade

Stardom and Masculinity in the Jazz Age

Columbia University Press

NEW YORK

Columbia University Press

New York Chichester, West Sussex

Copyright © 1996 Columbia University Press

All rights reserved

Library on Congress Cataloging-in-Publication Data

Studlar, Gaylyn.
This mad masquerade : stardom and masculinity in the Jazz Age / Gaylyn Studlar.
p.cm. — (Film and culture)
Includes bibliographical references and index.
ISBN 0-231-10320-4 (cloth). — ISBN 0-231-10321-2 (pbk.)
1. Men in motion pictures. 2. Sex role in motion pictures.
I. Title. II. Series.
PN1995.9.M46S78 1996
791.43'652041—dc20   95-47557
                                                                          CIP

Casebound editions of Columbia University Press books are printed on permanent and durable acid-free paper.

Printed in the United States of America

c 10 9 8 7 6 5 4 3 2 1
p 10 9 8 7 6 5 4 3 2 1

For my dear Aunt Elvern and Uncle Emil

Contents

Acknowledgments

In *Red River* sage old Mr. Melville (Harry Carey) gives advice to Matthew Garth. Garth (Monty Clift) has just finished the first trail drive from Texas to Abilene, Kansas. Carey tells Clift how a person (in the film, "a man," of course) should feel at the end of a job that he "was crazy to take on in the first place." Maybe because I'm a fifth-generation Texan, fanatical by birthright, that line, about punching cows over a thousand miles, resonates with this moment in my life. This book about men—or at least, about their representation—evokes a host of feelings from me after six years of research, writing, and editing. My long-range enthusiasm for any project was tested and so were many other aspects of my life. For those who helped me bring this trail-drive of a book to a conclusion, I owe many thanks.

First, I wish to thank those who helped in the development of the ideas contained here. My students in my stardom and performance class at Emory University in 1991 were an inspiration. Special thanks to Maria Pramaggiore, Adrienne McLean, Laurie Watel, and Tina Fuller for their enthusiasm and their ideas. Gratitude to Adrienne too, for being so kind as to bring back research materials for me from the British Film Institute.

Vital to the work of shaping this book was Matthew Bernstein, who read some of the chapters in their very early forms. His astute reading of much of my writing over the past few years has made me a better scholar. My thanks to Matthew for being a marvelous colleague and the best reader anyone could ever ask for. I am grateful also to Marty Norden for graciously sharing his immense knowledge of Barrymore sources with me, a total stranger. His generosity made chapter 2 better than it was. My appreciation goes to David Pratt, who shared his research on film exhibition in the 1920s and helped turn nagging suspicions about Lon Chaney into fact. I also wish to thank David Desser, who gently prodded me at the right time and in the right way to finish.

Thanks are due to those who have encouraged me along the way and whose own work on stars or on masculinity, or both, provides a model for my own: Steven Cohan, Peter Lehman, and Krin Gabbard. I owe a huge debt to Tom Gunning and John Belton, who read the book and made it better with their cogent suggestions. Without peer for patience is my editor, Jennifer Crewe, whose enthusiastic support of this book has been crucial. The College of Literature, Science, and the Arts of the University of Michigan provided welcome support that allowed me to use the many photographs that this book needed to make its points.

This book would not have been possible without the cooperation of many libraries and archives. My thanks to the staffs of the Motion Picture Broadcasting and Recorded Sound Division of the Library of Congress, the Hoblitzelle Theatre Arts Library of the Harry Ransom Center of the University of Texas, the Museum of the City of New York, the Hertzberg Circus Collection and Museum of the San Antonio Public Library, and the UCLA Film and Television Archive. Charles Silver of the Museum of Modern Art's Film division deserves particular thanks for providing screening opportunities for many films. I owe the staffs of the Theatre and Dance Collections of the New York Public Library for the Performing Arts, Lincoln Center, special mention for their professionalism. I am also indebted to my friends and fellow USC alums—Ned Comstock of the University of Southern California Archive of Performing Arts, and Janet Lorenz of the Margaret Herrick Library of the Academy of Motion Picture Arts and Sciences, for assistance in locating important materials. I also want to thank Marie Hansen and the staff of the interlibrary loan unit of the Woodruff Library at Emory University for their cheerful efficiency and good humor in the face of my unrelenting requests. Mary Corliss and the Film Stills Archive of the Museum of Modern Art provided help in the most pleasurable part of this book: the selection of stills. Unless otherwise noted, all production stills are courtesy of MOMA. An extremely early version of chapter 3 appeared in Steve Cohan and Ina Rae Hark's anthology, *Screening the Male: Exploring Masculinities in Hollywood Cinema* (London: Routledge, 1993). An early version of chapter 2 appears as "Barrymore, the Body, and Bliss," in Roger Hillman and Leslie Devereaux, eds., *Fields of Vision* (Berkeley: University of California Press, 1995).

Finally, thanks to my two best friends, Connie and Tommy, sometimes incorrigibly interchangeable in more than just their names. From pushing me on a plane to attend my first conference, to providing a home while I wrote my dissertation, Constance Goodwin has contributed to all my professional successes. How can I thank you for all you have done for me? Likewise, there are not words enough to thank my husband, Thomas Haslett, who rarely gets enthusiastic about the films or stars I adore, but, nevertheless, patiently puts up with it all—the old movies, the writing, and me.

This Mad Masquerade
Stardom and Masculinity in the Jazz Age

With a thousand soft pictures
his memory will teem.
And his hearing is touched
with the sounds of a dream.
—Wordsworth, "The Farmer of Tilsbury"

Introduction

"We didn't need dialogue. We had faces," defiantly asserts Norma Desmond (Gloria Swanson) in *Sunset Boulevard* (1950) as she stands to watch her own youthful image flickering, veritably glowing, on the silver screen. Of course, the "we" to which she refers are Hollywood stars of America's "Jazz Age." If the faces of that "silent" era of cinema are sometimes vaguely recalled and even revived, they are, by and large, like the fictional Norma Desmond, forgotten, both by popular culture and serious scholarship.

The elusiveness of silent film stars might seem surprising since America's Jazz Age, defined roughly as stretching between the end of World War I and the 1929 Wall Street crash, has been the subject of innumerable studies by historians and students of popular culture. They have illuminated various aspects of what America's collective memory takes to be an alluring era of fascinating excess, rich in literature and art, as well as change and controversy.[1] Stereotype associates these years with flappers, fast living, and frenetic modernism, but they were richer in implication than stereotype suggests. By Hollywood's measure, they were the glory years of stardom in which the star system came into full flower.

Stars were a means of selling movies, but they also became a cultural phenomenon in the late teens and early twenties. Film quickly graduated from tentative beginnings to becoming a full-fledged national institution in the 1920s. Gaining a foothold around 1907, the process of star-making was just as quickly perfected as an institutional practice. Hollywood's adoption of the feature-length format for its fiction films in the 1910s intensified the need for players whose bodies and faces could be exploited as "identifiable figures acting on the screen."[2] By bringing famous actors from the respected venue of high-class theater (Broadway) to the fledgling medium, Adolph Zukor, founder of Famous Players Film Company (1912), and others such as Harry Aitken of Triangle Pictures, sought to imbue prestige on a star system that was already an efficient economic reality.

Nevertheless, Hollywood reluctantly acknowledged that stars had become the cornerstone of its financial success. In 1918 producer Thomas H. Ince suggested that the star system "is here to stay" because in spite of "all that is written about its pernicious effect on the new art," the public "spends its money freely and generously whenever the star is in evidence on the screen."[3] By the time of Ince's commentary, star salaries were frightening the industry, but such comments still may seem curious. From the perspective of hindsight, the emergence and rapid growth of stars as the cornerstone of American film seem inevitable. The industry's adaptation of narrative film as the mainstay of its production and its link to star-centered theatrical tradition made it so.

By 1919 (the year F. Scott Fitzgerald declared to be the official beginning of "the Jazz Age"), public fascination with star celebrities was well established. There was a marked change in the twenties with the construction of stars as public identities because, typically, a star's extrafilmic identity in the 1910s was less complicated. Richard deCordova notes that in these earlier years, star identity "merely reproduced the representations of personality already produced in films."[4] In the 1920s stars became complex creatures with "textual identities" forged across a number of films and "private identities" created by the popular press and Hollywood's promotion machines. Nevertheless, there was an inevitable conflation or intermingling of the screen persona with the actor. This conflation was necessary to construct the star persona as a marketable commodity. However, there was also some recognition in the 1920s of the need to create a distance between the actor-identity and his/her screen persona so that revelations of the private identity inconsistent with the textual/screen identity would not lead to embarrassing (or even scandalous) contradictions.

The institutional supremacy of stars in Hollywood during the 1920s took place within a system that tried to carefully negotiate how actors and actresses were presented, on and off screen. The goal was to create a most intense—and profitable—fascination among the moviegoing public. Myriad film-related mechanisms—including newspaper interviews and film reviews, trade magazine articles and fan magazines, press agent stunts and theater exhibition displays, publicity photographs and advertising for consumable tie-in products—all formed a discourse of stardom that guaranteed the widest possible circulation of a star's image.

Characteristic of a time in which everything before the public seemed subject to debate and discussion, the American film industry—and its stars—could not escape social controversy. It has been observed that the boundaries of star discourse shifted radically in the 1920s as the press became "fascinated with scandal."[5] The salaries of stars, as well as their sexual conduct and social pleasures, became high-profile news. Unable to predict volatile public reaction to changing standards of conduct (sexual and otherwise), industry-related fan magazines, however, were not eager to cover stars' transgressions. They usually maintained a family discourse of stardom emphasizing traditional romantic love rather than revelations of sexual indiscretions.[6] In spite of this standard strategy, as we shall see in chapter 3's discussion of Rudolph Valentino, the industry was not beyond courting controversy to draw attention to some of its acting personalities.

Most of these controversies are little remembered, and the fascination exerted by stars in the early years of Hollywood's star system is now largely assumed rather than realized. Most of us can only intuit the truth of Norma Desmond's declaration. We have seen too little of these faces and of their films to judge a phenomenon obscured by time, by the loss of our film heritage, and by our own historical disinterest. Our experience is limited by the cinematic equivalent of "sound bites": a film clip on television in a documentary or as part of an obituary tribute, or a usually brief mention of scandal from the decade of the "Roaring Twenties." Scholarly neglect of stardom is even more surprising. In spite of its assumed centrality to the cinema, Hollywood's construction of stars has only recently become the object of scholarly interest that seeks to do more than offer biographical description. Although there is a growing number of scholarly books about stardom,[7] the heyday of feature film in Hollywood's silent years (1916–1929), one of the richest eras of star vehicles, remains underanalyzed and misunderstood, especially when it comes to understanding why and how stars came into prominence and what purposes they served for their audiences. It is that situation that this book hopes to correct.

As the title and subtitle of my book suggest (see note 11), this study of the phenomenon of stardom has set parameters for itself in several ways. First, the study limits itself to a particular period of time in Hollywood film history, stretching from 1915 to 1930. In considering stardom within these years, my analysis focuses on the circulation of meaning created around a selected group of male stars. That focus grows out of the beginnings of this book in 1989 when I was invited to write an article on feminism and film for *Film Criticism*. With no limitation to my choice of a topic, I chose to write on Rudolph Valentino.

My interest in Valentino was a guilty pleasure, fueled by my living in Hollywood, literally around the corner from the Hollywood Memorial Cemetery where he was interred in a crypt borrowed as a "temporary" resting place from the woman credited with discovering him, June Mathis.[8] The cemetery was a regular stop on my own Movie Land tours for my friends visiting from out-of-town. In many respects, the publication of Miriam Hansen's important scholarship on Valentino allowed me to find a more respectable outlet for an interest in the star. My article was written as a response to Hansen, who had suggested that Valentino's films were organized around the expression of ambivalence that related, in a largely unconscious way, to female spectatorship.[9] I was intrigued by Hansen's work, but also disturbed by how little we seemed to know, in historical and cultural terms, about stardom as a phenomenon, and even about important stars such as Valentino. I was inspired to pursue the historical implications of his appearance as a foreign "ethnic" star within an era of American history characterized by blatant xenophobia.[10]

Out of those beginnings, this book has evolved. In it, I seek to illuminate how masculinity was represented through stars and to extend the study of stardom into the broader context of culture. I focus on four case studies of male stars who were box-office favorites during some part of Hollywood's Jazz Age: Douglas Fairbanks, John Barrymore, Rudolph Valentino, and Lon Chaney. All these stars came into prominence in film within a few years of each other (1916–1921) and, with the exception of Valentino, they were all still making films at the end of the silent era (1929).

My case studies of Fairbanks, Barrymore, Valentino, and Chaney are related by the overarching goal of explaining the relationship of these stars and the star phenomenon in general to culture and the circulation of meaning around masculinity as a cultural concept. I am also interested in how stars were pitched to and received by gendered audiences, both male and female, during this historical period. These studies may seem rather autonomous because I shift, from chapter to chapter, to different cultural influences that impacted the individual star. However, the chapters are related by their shared revelation of *transformative masculinity*, of a paradigm of gender construction that, in many different guises or "masquerades," foregrounds masculinity as a process, a liminal construction, and even a performance.

In a period associated with rapid and radical change on many cultural fronts, popular magazines, literature, and film constantly reiterated images of masquerade, of game-playing and disguise, especially in reference to gender roles and sexual relations. To many, the creation of masculinity and femininity constituted a "mad masquerade" whose impetus was modernity.[11] Within the period's extremely self-conscious negotiation of tradition and modernity, femininity and masculinity, a paradigm of transformative masculinity appears to be the characteristic element that links these stars together, in spite of their sometimes considerable differences.

If the modes or styles of masculinity represented by the four stars under consideration in this study are inevitably related, they also evidence how American masculinity negotiated various social and sexual dilemmas of the time. These included the perceived rebellion of women against sexual and domestic norms, the ethnic threat of new immigrants, and the alteration of middle-class lifestyles by modern industrial economics. With Douglas Fairbanks and the established cultural norms of masculinity as the topic of the first chapter, each successive chapter moves to a star who, it may be argued, increasingly *transgressed* those standards of normative masculinity. While the book moves along this trajectory, the reader may notice what seems to be my violation of chronology. We do not move forward in time with each chapter but retrace roughly the same period from a completely different cultural perspective that illuminates that particular star's construction.

This strategy is motivated by the assumption that we cannot understand how and why these stars functioned within culture as they did by looking only at their films as divorced from a consideration of history. If we must first go to the forgotten films of this era, we must also go beyond these film texts to the extratextual materials that were used to create stardom for the public's consumption. And we must go farther, to the broader historical field of American culture, to understand what motivated and influenced these specific stars and their representations of masculinity as well as the public's response to them.

My concern with American culture has led me to a method of studying masculinity and stardom that may seem curious to those who may be familiar with my other, theoretically oriented scholarly work on film.[12] What I am attempting to do has a theoretical aspect to it, but anyone looking for a theoretical treatise on masculinity or the psychoanalytic use of the term *masquerade* in reference to gender identity will be disappointed. A number of film scholars have suggested, following feminist theory, that masculinity is a performance, a construction of identity shaped through the repetition of positions, whether gendered, racial, or sexual.[13]

By the end of this book, some readers may conclude that my study, grounded in the specific cultural history of the period, actually confirms other, more theoretical attempts to generalize about the representation of masculine sexual identity in terms of masquerade conceived as a "performance of virility."[14] Certainly, my study's conclusions concerning

Hollywood's textual and extratextual representation of masculinity fit comfortably within Judith Butler's notion of gender as a performance in which all the signs of gendered identity "are performative in the sense that the essence or identity that they otherwise purport to express are fabrications manufactured and sustained through corporeal signs and other discursive means."[15]

Rather than theoretical generalization, I am interested in doing the historically specific "spade work" that I believe is necessary as the foundation for theoretical generalizations in film studies. Such an approach starts with the films, not as isolated entities but as texts that impact each other and become an intertextual chain. In this respect, I am assuming that the star's appearance is always being renegotiated by his audience in light of earlier films. As deCordova has aptly noted, the star "draws the spectator into a specific path of intertextuality that extends outside of the text as a formal system."[16] Obviously, film uses the gendered human body of the male star in its texts and circulates that figure and the star's persona through the extratextual discourses produced by its industrial strategies. Thus, my approach depends on analyzing the discourses surrounding stardom as an ongoing, always changing process.

However, it cannot be ignored that the star's emergence as a cultural production exceeds the limits of the cinema. As Peter Lehman has suggested, stardom and casting cannot escape "cultural assumptions about the relation between the male body and certain attributes of masculinity."[17] Extending this observation (and most important to my purpose), I attempt to fully integrate the stars into their cultural context. I am assuming that we can only know the meaning of early male film stars for their contemporary audience if we have some understanding of how culture literally and figuratively "set the stage" for that star. To achieve this, we must look at the cultural framework, both at the historical "moment" of the star's emergence as a star and also preceding his stardom, if we hope to analyze why the film industry used specific strategies for constructing the star and why an audience accepted that actor, among many, as a popular attraction.

Problems in method are raised by such an approach. How can a rather detailed study of stardom be related to an entire historical-cultural framework? How do we look at the overwhelming amount of material that constitutes culture at any given time? Rather than attempting to suggest each star's relationship to every conceivable element of American culture, I instead analyze each of the four stars in this study in relation to a specifically defined and delineated cultural intertext. By this I mean that I have chosen what I have determined by my research to be the most important cultural influence on the meaning of the star profitably shaped by the industry discourse and then pleasurably experienced by film spectators. For example, in chapter 1, I examine the construction of Douglas Fairbanks's stardom in the context of a cultural movement aimed at reforming "boy culture." This movement, exemplified by the rise of the Boy Scouts, was a widespread and influential reform-centered discourse that attempted to reshape masculinity in response to the perceived threat of a "feminization" of culture. Here I argue that only by understanding this phenomenon and its cultural pervasiveness can we understand how the construction of Fairbanks as a star borrowed directly from a contemporary discourse that sought to influence the transformation of (American) boys into (American) men.

In chapter 2 the cultural intertext that is foregrounded is the emergence of the notorious "matinee girls" of late-Victorian theater. This controversial phenomenon was thought to be the primary reason for the emergence of matinee idols such as John Barrymore. I argue that the theatrical construction of male stars for a female audience provided an important precedent for the construction of a "woman-made" masculinity for female film spectators in the 1920s.[18] Taking my investigation of Barrymore's construction as a stage star for women into the arena of film, I examine how elements of his theatrical representation of a controversial masculinity were resituated and then restructured for his presentation as a film star in the 1920s who was thought to appeal primarily to women.

In chapter 3, I look at the film star often thought to have elicited the strongest public responses in the 1920s. In "'Optic Intoxication': Rudolph Valentino and Dance Madness," I continue the previous chapter's discussion of how masculinity was constructed for female audiences in the late 1910s and 1920s, this time within a consideration of the cultural impact of dance, a form of entertainment securely linked to the unleashing of women's sexuality during this period. This chapter undertakes a detailed examination of what kind of discourse emanated from the rise of dance culture, both social and as "high art," especially in its figuring of female sexuality in relation to ethnic or racial difference. I discuss dance's influence on Valentino's construction as a star who evoked American culture's stereotypical picture of the countless "darker" immigrants who were believed to be pouring into the United States and finding their way into tango palaces for the purpose of exploiting American women. I argue that

Valentino was constructed as a star in ways that adhered closely to theatrical matinee idol tradition, but that he was also a sexually troublesome, ideologically transgressive star associated with trends already crystallized in dance.

In chapter 4, I take up questions raised by the stardom of Lon Chaney. While Chaney may seem far removed from the admirably boyish or beautifully bodied men discussed in previous chapters, his popularity suggests a logical complement to some of the issues surrounding the representation of masculinity put into play in previous chapters. His long-standing association with the "grotesque" and the "monstrous" indicates an exception to the obvious consolidation of glamour and "sex appeal" as expected elements of the Hollywood star-making process during these years.[19] In this chapter I reference the intertext of the freak show and its strategies for constructing the deviant or stigmatized social identity of "the freak." I relate these strategies and patterns to Lon Chaney's representation of the grotesque body and the male body in pain. Within the context of the sideshow's construction of often grotesque spectacle, I also consider Chaney as a star who violated the norms of stardom in his construction as an offscreen persona.

In addition, Chaney's extreme popularity in the late 1920s provides insight into gender-differentiated spectatorship since many exhibitors claimed that Chaney's fans were virtually all male. Thus, this chapter provides a counterpoint to the previous two chapters that deal with stars whose appeal was aimed at women. Chaney's stardom also provides a logical, if unexpected, conclusion to the discussion put into motion by chapter 1's analysis of Fairbanks. While both were thought to have particular appeal to men and boys, Chaney's screen persona, associated with profoundly disabled characters, suggests a rejection of boy reformers' emphasis on the possibility of physical perfection. If Fairbanks represented boyish certainty in action, Chaney represented a grotesque paternal masculinity, emotionally and physically flawed, masochistic yet also capable of destroying others.

While my use of cultural intertexts (boy culture reform, theater, dance, the freak show) may seem to isolate a single cause to the star's construction and reception, I hope the reader will be patient and defer such a conclusion. These intertexts are not meant to suggest a single determination or meaning, but instead are used to suggest how cultural frameworks often figure importantly in the creation of a star who is presold in the sense of being constructed to appeal to an audience's established interest in controversies, dilemmas, or spectacles that are already in cultural circulation. In my attempt to illuminate the process by which a star is embedded in culture and to discover why this happens, the intertext reveals the process of overdetermination and helps sort out the star's connections to other aspects of culture that may not at once be apparent.

The book is organized so that chapter 1 provides the foundation to my analysis of the historical construction of dominant cultural norms of masculinity and how those may be played upon and against in different modes of masculine representation. Although somewhat obscured by my attempt to maintain a chronology governed by when a particular star came to his greatest popularity, it will become clear that these four star studies form a pairing: Fairbanks and Chaney, Barrymore and Valentino in terms of their gender-differentiated appeal. Together, all four stars demonstrate how different modes or styles of masculinity could be popular with a range of filmgoers at the same time, even as they also suggest overlaps and, especially in the case of Fairbanks, Barrymore, and Valentino, convergence. All of them raise questions about the period's emphasis on a transformative masculinity, a conception of masculinity that seems to have had particular symbolic resonance during the early twentieth century.

Ultimately, this is a book about Hollywood's depiction of masculinity in an era in which America felt process-driven and unsure of the meaning of rapid cultural change. A preoccupation with the polarities of transformation and stasis, the future and the past, tradition and modernity underscored much social discourse. American identity was perceived as being thrown into flux. The pressure to find—or reinvent—the self appeared acute. In light of this cultural context, Hollywood stardom may offer unique insight into the creation of masculinity in a complex era. "Acting is masquerade," Lon Chaney is quoted as declaring in a 1922 fan magazine article.[20] If acting is putting on a figurative (and, sometimes, literal) mask, then was masculinity in the Jazz Age and the formative years immediately preceding it far removed from a similar strategy in the attempt to cope with changing gender and social expectations? The following chapters should help answer that question.

One

Building Mr. Pep:
Boy Culture and the Construction
of Douglas Fairbanks

> Do not get the idea that boys are going to be debased because they
> are taught to be brave and self-reliant and to defend themselves. The
> greatest danger is not that the boy will be too brutal, but that he will
> be too soft, too easily discouraged, too weak; not that men will be too
> manly, but that they will not have sufficient manliness.
> —C. R. H. Jackson, "The Moral Value of Physical Activities"
> (1909)[1]

> The Fairbanks hobby is the out-of-doors and everything that goes
> with it. The lithe, brown arm is literally as hard as oak when the rip-
> pling muscles are taut, and this bespeaks years of rigorous athletics of
> all sort. . . . The strength which the popular "Duggie" [*sic*] so fre-
> quently and picturesquely displays in most of his pictures is his by
> rights; it is his diploma from the school of strenuous life.
> —Arthur Hornblow, Jr., "Douglas Fairbanks, Dramatic Dynamo,"
> *Motion Picture Classic* (March 1917)[2]

In the autumn of 1915, American newspaper headlines were dominated by
the European war. The Bulgarian coast was under bombardment. The
British prepared to send Lord Kitchener to Serbia. And the Bull Moose
himself, Theodore ("Teddy") Roosevelt, acerbically challenged President
Wilson to create a "real defence programme."[3] With such a glut of disturbing news, it is no surprise that little advance notice was given to the
screen debut of a popular if lightweight Broadway actor named Douglas
Fairbanks. On the one hand, this was to be expected. Most major city
newspapers did not bother reporting on cheap amusements such as the
movies, in contrast to their enthusiastic coverage of first-class theater, dog
shows, and horse racing. Fairbanks's debut film, *The Lamb* (1915), had

not even rated inclusion in advertisements for the most glowing release prospects of a fledgling Hollywood studio, Triangle Corporation. It was important primarily for being part of a new strategy of Triangle boss Harry Aitken, who had signed a number of Broadway actors to film contracts. Following a model set by Adolph Zukor's Famous Players Film Company, Aitken hoped to use these actors to attract a solidly middle-class audience to the movies, an entertainment still rejected by many Americans as being of little interest and even less propriety.[4]

Unexpectedly, there was an overwhelming response to *The Lamb* and to its star. *Moving Picture World* noted "Triangle's Auspicious Opening": "Unquestionably the honors of the evening went to the Griffith production, 'The Lamb.' . . . There were moments when the audience fairly rose with excitement, which is saying something for a 'mere motion picture.'"[5] It went on to suggest an impression echoed by other reviewers: "A new star has appeared in the motion-picture constellation, a comedian who wins through interesting personality and delightful characterization, a decided relief from the raw crudities of acrobatic clowns. . . He holds the eye so strongly, and without apparent effort, that he is the whole play from beginning to end."[6] This narcissistic centering on Fairbanks, the star, would be commented on again and again over the years, but few seemed to mind, especially in these early years when he appeared to be a perfect performer for the movies. Reviewers at once suggested that the romantic-comic actor offered more than stereotyped physical slapstick. Only a few years removed from the nickelodeon era, the film industry craved the kind of commodity Fairbanks exemplified: a respectable Broadway talent whose body seemed made for movement. As his movie publicity would soon declare at every opportunity, his was movement that no mere stage seemed capable of holding.[7]

Upon his arrival at Triangle, Fairbanks's kinetic freneticism motivated supervising director D. W. Griffith to recommend the actor's assignment to Mack Sennett comedies.[8] But Sennett's slapstick was no more appropriate for his talents than Griffith's melodrama, even though few stars in the years 1916–1919 leapt more than Fairbanks. Fewer still leapt so quickly from film to film or rose with such speed from relative obscurity to become a proverbial overnight star. Beginning with the unexpected success of *The Lamb*, screens were filled with Fairbanks during the remainder of 1915 and throughout 1916. Triangle capitalized on his popularity with the release of a multireel Fairbanks feature virtually every month. *The Lamb* was followed by *Double Trouble* (December 1915), *His Picture in the Papers* (February

1916), *The Habit of Happiness* (May 1916), *The Good Bad Man* (May 1916), *Reggie Mixes In* (June 1916), *Flirting with Fate* (July 1916), *The Half Breed* (July 1916), *Manhattan Madness* (October 1916), *American Aristocracy* (November 1916), and *The Matrimaniac* (December 1916).

Fairbanks became one of Triangle's few unequivocal successes in the company's attempt to use Broadway actors to expand its middle-class market. Heywood Broun suggested that Fairbanks's screen appearances could be used as a test of whether the movies continued to be shunned because of pure snobbery: "People who think they don't like motion pictures should see Doug Fairbanks in *Manhattan Madness*. If they derive no amusement from this merry farce-melodrama they are correct in supposing they are film blind."[9] Exhibitors, told that "A Fairbanks picture sells itself," were warned also that they might "embitter" their audiences if they were foolish enough to engage the star's films in a "short run policy."[10]

Soon Fairbanks rivaled "Little Mary" Pickford and Charlie Chaplin as Hollywood film's premiere box-office attraction. Like them, he cultivated strategic career moves that enhanced his salary, but also his aesthetic control over his productions. In 1917 he left Triangle to join Artcraft, a prestigious division of Paramount. In 1919 he became one of the founders of United Artists Film Corporation (along with Pickford, Chaplin, and Griffith), a radical experiment in studio organization that eliminated moguls and made film artists into self-determining producers and distributors of their own vehicles.[11]

Patrician Peppiness and Red-Blooded Manliness

No matter what the studio of origin, Fairbanks's films of the 1910s were remarkably consistent. With the notable exception of *The Half Breed*, a serious and sensitive examination of racial prejudice in the Old West, they usually came under the rubric of "comedy-melodrama," "thrillers," or "the athletic straight comedy."[12] Collectively, they created the trademark Fairbanksian hero of the decade. He was a young man of a certain patrician quality and privileged Eastern upbringing who ran, jumped, punched, and smiled his way into and through a vigorous, "red-blooded" manhood.

Such a hero may seem deceptively simple. However, as this chapter will show, Fairbanks's model of masculinity was as complicated as the era in which he came to fame. During an era marked by fears of national and masculine enfeeblement, Fairbanks's stardom represented the fantasy of an adult attainment of many American reformers' perfected ideal of manhood, gracefully balancing moral gentility and primitive instincts, wilderness skills and genteel urbanity, boyish wanderlust and the promise of undemanding romance. Within this transitional period that led to the arrival of the Jazz Age, there was a veritable obsession with the attainment of masculinity.

In this social context, Fairbanks's stardom became Hollywood's exemplar of an idealized, boyish masculinity that cheerfully reconciled felt tensions between many of the era's contradictory impulses. Such impulses seemed to characterize the period, for these were years in which the optimism of Progressivism coexisted with the pessimism of Social Darwinism, Victorian domestic traditions were confronted with rapid changes in family and gender relations, and the adventure of aggressive militarism was countervalenced by the national pull toward isolationism. As America became an urban country (noted for the first time in the 1920 census), popular discourses, including Fairbanks's films, began to register too the tensions created by the attempt to reconstitute American myths amidst new social realities. Those myths were crucial to redefining the nature of masculinity in a society in transition. Hence, wilderness worship and nostalgia for rugged yeoman individualism might exist side by side—and even converge—with the valorization of corporate consciousness and industrial-based modernity. It is no surprise, then, that Fairbanks offered an idealization of masculine norms that foregrounds the theme of transformative masculinity and the reconciliation of "opposites," i.e., of the working and upper classes, of East and West, urban and rural, male and female.

In addressing the problematic social construction of American masculinity, Fairbanks's light-hearted films generally offer two variants to a basic formula. Sometimes Fairbanks's hero entered a thrill-packed situation that released nascent qualities of vigorous manliness, as in the early Fairbanks vehicle *Reggie Mixes In* (1916). The pampered scion of a wealthy family, Reggie (Fairbanks) is "just *fresh* from college," as an intertitle notes. Like many a Fairbanks hero, he can be found in bed, under silken covers, even as the clock strikes noon. But Reggie is due for a change. As the intertitles tell us, "Champagne and lobsters aren't always the best fare. Some folks grow stronger on beer and beef stew, if they don't overdo it." Reggie's diet changes radically after "a trifling incident." He sees a child crying forlornly as she sits on a street curb. Accompanied by his valet, whom he has dubbed, affectionately, "Old Pickle Face" (Joseph Singleton), Reggie whisks this "losted" child off in his elegant roadster. They arrive back at her home on the wrong side of the tracks. Here, in the "world of beer and beef," he sees "a new sort of girl," one who is protec-

Transposed to a "world of beer and beef" (Douglas Fairbanks and Bessie Love in *Reggie Mixes In*, 1916)

tive and nurturing rather than manipulative and materialistic like those of his own class. Intrigued by the wistful saloon dancer, Agnes (Bessie Love), Reggie moves to a nearby tenement apartment to be near her.

No sooner than he decides to become a local, Reggie faces Agnes's disdain for his cowardice. "You're afraid!" she sneers after Reggie rather adroitly climbs up a chandelier to avoid a gang fight. Forced by hostile circumstances to develop long-repressed physical skills, Reggie becomes a saloon bouncer in the neighborhood's toughest bar. In the end, he bests a vicious gang leader in a grueling fistfight and wins Agnes, who quickly adapts to his upper-class world. The description of the film as "one joyous round of assault and battery from beginning to end"[13] captures the paradox of a transformed hero who literally mops the floor with a gang leader but remains, like most Fairbanks heroes, steadfastly nonbelligerent in his aggressive physical defense of the good.

In the other major variation in his film plots, Fairbanks's character often starts out with vigorous, manly qualities, but must prove their appropriateness. This occurs with *In Again, Out Again* (1917), a typical

Fairbanksian satire on contemporary social mores. Fairbanks plays Teddy Rutherford, a "Real American" whose "belligerent ideas" in the cause of "preparedness" alienate his pacifist fiancée. No audience could mistake the character's resemblance to that self-proclaimed "good-American," Teddy Roosevelt, who spent most of 1915 berating President Wilson, a former member of the American Peace Society, as representative of those "professional pacifists . . . flubdubs and mollycoddles . . . every soft creature, every coward and weakling."[14]

Similarly surrounded by meeker men of peace or deceit, Teddy Rutherford seems to be the most suspicious resident of his New Jersey community, one made particularly nervous by the dynamiting of bootleg ammunition factories. As an innocent bystander, Teddy is almost done in by the latest bombing: the first shot of him in the film is as he pops up from the rubble with a shell casing as an impromptu hat. Teddy punches the air with his fists while he berates his fiancée's pacifist father: "Your puny, pussyfooting policies are pulling the punch out of Preparedness!" In response, Teddy's fiancee coldly rejects him. Teddy goes on a drunken and decidedly misogynistic spree. Gleefully wrecking all the consumer displays in a drugstore, he tosses raw eggs at cardboard Coca-Cola girls, tackles all the Venus pencil Venuses, and yells: "If I ever have a son, I'll never let him come in contact with a woman!"

Jailed as a "common drunkard," Teddy meets Janie (Arline Pretty), the sheriff's daughter. To his dismay, he is pardoned just when his romance with Janie has made him forget the outside world—including his ex-fiancée. But his release brings more trouble as he tries to find a harmless way to be arrested again. "I want to go back in my own little cell!" he moans. Events quickly get out of hand. Teddy is on the verge of being lynched by vigilantes before he manages to prove that he is not the bomber. After revealing the real culprit (a pacifist, naturally), Teddy marries Janie. The film ends as he surprises his bride. The Rutherford mansion is graced with the addition of a new music room. It is a perfect duplicate of the jail cell (including bars) where Janie sweetly serenaded Teddy with her "eukaleli."

Even though romance was always an important part of Fairbanks's films, by 1917 viewers had come to identify the actor with "the 'pep,' the good natured 'rough stuff,' the thrills, and *the* smiles."[15] By the end of 1918 the *New York Times* commented on the fact that Fairbanks appeared to be taking "the same character into every part."[16] Audiences and exhibitors did not seem to mind. There was obvious appeal in the thirty-something actor's uncanny ability to scale walls, take on monumental staircases in a single bound, leap-frog across the roofs of cities, and roll like a human bowling ball over the countryside. There was also something appealing in Fairbanks's attitude toward his antics.

The actor's energetic performative prowess was matched only by the good-humored intimacy he cultivated with the camera and with his audience. He was a showoff, an impulsive but not an irrational one. Fairbanks's comic-romantic characters might (as in *A Modern Musketeer*, 1917) have the audacious spontaneity to do a handstand on the edge of the Grand Canyon, but also the sense to crawl away from the edge on hands and knees.[17] At such moments, Fairbanks often gave a knowing grin at the camera. The extent to which Fairbanks's smile dominates a film's mood is evident in *His Picture in the Papers* (1916), where the most extreme of crises becomes another glorious challenge met with a grin and a gesture of anticipation (the actor's characteristic punching of the air with his fists). A fan magazine article described his oft-flashed, famous smile as: "simply the Fairbanks smile—a whimsical, mischievous, happy, nonsensical grin that lights up the whole neighborhood. . . . Of course you've seen it on the screen and you've grinned too. It's as infectious as the German measles."[18] Publicity suggested that Fairbanks (aka "Smile Boy") was "America's Greatest Exponent of the Smile."[19]

Historically detached hindsight might lead us to regard Fairbanks as a glorified gymnast, but film reviewers and social commentators saw something more in his popularity than a response merely to his graceful athletic prowess. A reviewer of *The Matrimaniac* (1916) suggested:

His magnetic personality fixes attention . . . he is compelling. . . . People enjoy his "act in one" because he represents something to them. He illustrates clearly that there are tremendous sources of energy in nearly all men which are very seldom released. . . . Fairbanks represents physical agility and temperamental optimism, and it is really the latter quality that wins. His leaping and climbing feats would soon pall if he did not perpetually demonstrate that life is good and growing better.[20]

Commenting on *Knickerbocker Buckaroo* (1919), the *New York Times* suggested that his "amazing feats" were second in delight to "his manner and personality, and the fun he seems to get out of doing things."[21] Another reviewer suggested that "more than any other actor Mr. Fairbanks's magnetism defies the cold elements of celluloid electricity and canvas and communicates itself to the audience."[22]

In a mere two years Fairbanks became the unrivaled cinematic exponent of American good humor, preternatural optimism, and physical vitality. His fans, commentators noted, seemed to include everyone.[23] Fairbanks's films were broadly pitched to appeal to men, women, and children. Adults, however, were assumed to appreciate the socially satiric situations cleverly exploited in his earliest comedies, especially those that teamed him with scenarist Anita Loos and her husband, director John Emerson. Starting in 1916, the Loos/Emerson/Fairbanks films set the standard formula and tongue-in-cheek tone for most of the star's films before 1920, whether scripted by Loos or not. Remarking on their collaborative effort *The Americano* (1917), *Photoplay* was typical in its generous praise: "Anita Loos, the demi-tasse librettist is a great help to our hero. Her frolicsome scenarios are not only immense entertainment, but they are satires more subtle than our contemporary vocal dramatists [of the stage]."[24]

The Loos/Emerson/Fairbanks films satirized aspects of contemporary American culture through the adventures of a protagonist who finds himself cheerfully coping with the problems of modern life. Exemplary in this respect is *His Picture in the Papers* (1916), Fairbanks's third film and the first of the Loos/Emerson/Fairbanks collaborations. The introductory intertitle quickly establishes the film's central concern: "Publicity at any price has become the predominant passion of the American People." The film proceeds to follow the adventures of Pete Prindle (Fairbanks), who is "the nonconformist member" of his family. Pete is an exercise fiend who leaps out of bed to wield barbells and spin Indian clubs, but his family dismisses him as an oddball because he prefers cocktails and steak to the faddish health food concoctions that his father, Proteus (Clarence Handyside), manufactures à la John Harvey Kellogg.[25]

When the prodigal Prindle announces his engagement to be married by running into his father's office and perching happily on the parental lap, the father stands up and roars: "What have you ever done for Prindle's Products?!" Unexpectedly, parental disapproval elicits patrician confidence rather than fear. Pete bounces off his father, starts laughing and patting his father's broad expanse of chest. To satisfy the publicity-mongering demands of his father, Pete must get "his picture in the papers" and gain free publicity for his father's "27 Vegetable Varieties" (including "Toasted Tooties," "Dessicated Delights," and "Puffed Peanuts"). By doing this, he will, it is assumed, secure the half-interest in the family business demanded by his future father-in-law ("another vegetarian nut") in exchange for permission to marry Christine (Lorette Blake), the meat-eating girl of his choice.

In the end Pete succeeds, but in the course of his quest he stages a spectacular car wreck, wins a boxing title, and lands in jail for pummeling two policemen. The latter try to arrest him for drifting up on an Atlantic City

Young men who put things over (*The Youth's Companion* magazine, June 1915)

beach. Pete has been compelled to dive off shipboard and swim home from a nautical adventure. He comes ashore in pajamas he thinks are entirely too "respectable" to warrant jail time. But even arrest cannot get Pete's picture in the papers—his name is withheld out of respect for his family. All of these missed opportunities for Prindle promotion are forgotten when Pete manages to rescue his father-in-law-to-be and a train from a gang of vicious kidnappers. This event is accompanied by an intertitle that coyly asks: "Ain't he the REEL hero?" At last, the newspapers provide appropriately exaggerated accounts ("1000 saved," "1500 saved," "2000 saved") to satisfy parental ultimatums and reunite the lovers.[26]

His Picture in the Papers demonstrates how, on screen, Fairbanks was confident, fearless, gallant, possessed of a radiant energy and a nonchalant effortlessness that distinguished him from his many imitators and from a host of other boyish movie heroes such as Wallace Reid, Charles Ray, Buster Keaton, Richard Barthelmess, and Harold Lloyd, whose films, in different ways, were frequently revelatory of the trials and tribulations of a youthful masculinity. It may now seem ironic that of Hollywood's many boyish heroes during the late 1910s and early 1920s, the decidedly middle-aged Fairbanks became the movies' most famous exemplar of those young American men believed to be "putting things over in sports and in business."[27] No one seemed to mind the star's masquerade of youthfulness although *Photoplay* (1917) gently kidded "the first American juvenile for the venerable years that are really his." The magazine summed up the actor's impression: "There are those who assert that he was born grinning, wearing a Tuxedo, doubling his fists and crouching for a high jump."[28]

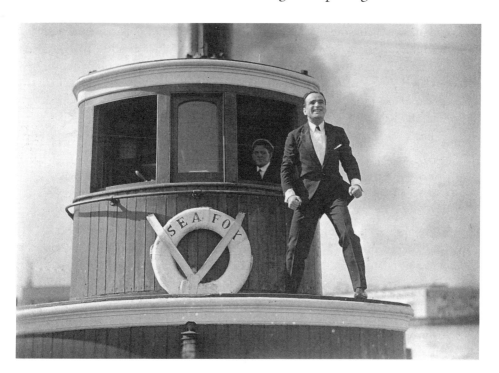

Hollywood's "first American juvenile" (Douglas Fairbanks) putting things over in *American Aristocracy* (1916)

In similar fashion as Peter Prindle, Fairbanks's other grinning-jumping-tuxedoed protagonists of the 1910s good-naturedly confronted a variety of much-discussed dilemmas and fads of modern American life: prewar pacifism versus preparedness (*In Again, Out Again*), foreign spies (*The Mollycoddle* and *American Aristocracy*), quack psychology, and the modern corporate business routine (*When the Clouds Roll By*), health reform and urban ennui (*Down to Earth*), the habits of the nouveau riche (*American Aristocracy, His Picture in the Papers*), the habits of the genteel old rich (*The Nut*), tourism and "nuts" on the West (*Wild and Woolly, Manhattan Madness, A Modern Musketeer*), as well as American interventionism (*His Majesty, the American, The Americano*).

While adults might enjoy a Fairbanks film as amusing social commentary, the chain of physical antics inevitably set into play was thought to appeal strongly to children and to make a particular impression on boys. It was said they were diving off roofs and falling out of trees in unprecedented numbers in their attempt to emulate their cinematic hero.[29] As an even more reliable measure of his success, Fairbanks not only was emulated by children but by other actors in search of box-office results. To "out-Fairbanks Fairbanks" became the ultimate commercial compliment and was used to sell as unlikely a Fairbanks rival as Maciste, "The Giant Hero of *Cabiria*" in *The Warrior*. Taciturn western star William S. Hart's Artcraft/Paramount vehicle *The Narrow Trail* (1919) was advertised to exhibitors to capitalize on the successful Fairbanks formula:

Wm. S. Hart has all the "pep," virility, thrills, and dexterity with his "hardware" that characterized the heroes of the "five-centers" and something more besides— humor, honor, optimism, and always a "straight story" that American fathers and mothers are glad to have their sons see—and go by the millions to see themselves.[30]

Fairbanks's success quickly spawned direct imitators including "rollocking [*sic*], dashing, daring" William Desmond, and male ingenue Pat O'Malley, who had "the grit and the grin, the pep and the punch of the U.S.A."[31] A photo caption of William Russell in *Motion Picture Classic* was forthright about the situation: "Now that athletic straight comedy has become a screen fixture—thanks to Douglas Fairbanks—every young actor and actorine is trying to climb aboard."[32] All these attempts to exploit the Fairbanks formula are not surprising since, by 1919, the actor was considered to be the number one Hollywood box-office draw.[33]

"And a little child shall lead them"

Even as his film characters proved their physical and moral mettle as human dynamos employing "pep," "power," "punch," and "personality" for the forces of good, Douglas Fairbanks the actor became known to all into advanced middle age as "Doug" or "Duggie." He was descriptively labeled as "Mr. Pep, "Old Doc Cheerful," "Mr. Electricity," and "Dr. Smile." Taking into account the exaggeration of Hollywood publicity does not alter the fact that Fairbanks appeared to be among the most beloved stars of the era, and with few exceptions his films were consistent winners at the box office for almost fifteen years. By 1924 he was being touted as "the most popular man in the world."[34]

His contemporaries regarded the actor as an ideal representative of vigorous American masculinity. That ideal seemed inevitably childish. A reviewer of *The Good Bad Man* (1916) praised the star's "expressive face, radiant, toothsome smile, immense activity, and apparent disposition to romp all over the map."[35] A fan magazine article of the period claimed that he once greeted a reporter by jumping over a chair, turning three hand-springs, two flips, and a somersault—all before shaking hands. Between answering questions, he might be expected to kick the chandelier, pretend to run a foot race, or put a hammerlock on an imaginary giant.[36] Frederick James Smith described "Doug" in a 1917 interview: "He is athletically rugged and distinctly masculine. When he talks you get the impression of a boy who hasn't grown up. He seems to be charged with a sort of restless energy."[37]

Smith's was not the first—nor would it be the last—description of the actor in terms befitting a child and, more specifically, a boy of boundless energy and irrepressible enthusiasm. Fairbanks's publicity encouraged such a view of the actor, so that even though he might occasionally be pictured with his young son and namesake,[38] more typically it was "Doug" who was childlike. If not shown in the middle of a leap, he was as often depicted crouched perilously high on any available piece of furniture (used also in advertisements for *Reaching for the Moon*), walking on his hands, or engaged in other daring physical gags. A *Woman's Home Companion* pictorial of 1919 depicted Madame Nellie Melba taking a break from opera to wag a finger at Fairbanks and issue a maternal reprimand: "You'd better take care and not be too daring!" To which the thirty-six-year-old Fairbanks is depicted as responding: "I'm the most careful little fellow you ever saw in your life." He then is said to have immediately gone "out and walked all about the yard on the top of a tall ladder."[39] A *Motion Picture Magazine* article of 1923, "'Kind of Crazy,'" is similar in suggesting that Fairbanks may talk as if he is quiet, restful, and sane, but in the end his words are always belied by his impulse to respond to every childish, dangerous dare, including trying to climb a ladder that is resting on nothing more than thin air.[40] Even Fairbanks's marriage to second wife Mary Pickford was constructed in the press to fit his childish persona. As late as 1927, Adela Rogers St. Johns described the marriage as the equivalent of a mating between Wendy and Peter Pan, with Pickford as the "eternal madonna—the eternal mother of the world" and Doug as "eternal youth . . . impractical, reckless, filled with enthusiasms, bubbling with actions."[41]

As a case of apparent arrested development, Fairbanks was not alone. In fact, he was but one of a number of admired and influential child-men of the era held in esteem by their peers. His most famous predecessor in representing youthful optimism and American vigor had been Theodore ("Teddy") Roosevelt. The exemplar of the neoprimitivist hero who "succumbed to Western fever," Roosevelt (it was said) cultivated a "clean, boyish enthusiasm for sports and athletic games, and . . . physical exercise," and retained "a boyish admiration for feats of physical strength and prowess."[42] It was his ability to keep boyish optimism in the face of struggles that was praised by one biographer as the secret to his popularity and no less than a "gift of the gods."[43] In spite of his privileged upbringing, Roosevelt was no stranger to tragedy. His mother and first wife unexpectedly died within days of each other in February 1884, and it was this enormous loss that sent him to the Dakotas in the autumn of the same year with the hope of achieving forgetfulness in the West.[44]

By the time Fairbanks arrived on the screen, "T.R." was staving off blindness and old age. However, the former President of the United States and Honorary Chief Scout Citizen of the Boy Scouts of America was still a national symbol of youth as well as a "youthful" symbol of the nation.[45] In "Roosevelt: A Force for Righteousness," William Allen White persuasively delineated the combination of masculine qualities that Roosevelt and, in many respects, Fairbanks represented as public figures and idealized models of masculinity:

> A life unstained by vice of any kind, a clean mind and a boyish heart, simple, confiding, and just, have combined to keep Theodore Roosevelt's faith in God and his belief in the common honesty of the common man unseared. . . . Roosevelt is not leading a double life, as his enemies secretly believe. He will not be found out; because there is nothing to find out. He is merely primitive. He has the gaiety and optimism that belong to youth, and youth is not a mere physical adolescence; it is that state of soul which men keep so long as they have not smudged their ideals and trifled with their consciences. One may be a boy at eighty, or a man at fifteen. . . . Perhaps that is the meaning of the prophecy: "And a little child shall lead them."[46]

Roosevelt's style of masculinity seemed to cut across class differences to suggest the symbolic reconciliation of modern American dilemmas and the mythic restoration of American character. That character, energetically masculine and youthful in its essence, was the subject of much discussion in the Progressive era, a time of rapid social and economic changes. Even as these changes generated Progressivism's widespread attempts to reform American economic and political institutions, they also seemed to generate a considerable anxiety surrounding the meaning of masculinity. As we shall see in subsequent chapters, that anxiety was exacerbated by the Jazz Age debate concerning women's throwing off of traditional social and sexual strictures and the resulting effect on men.

In the midst of these anxieties, Fairbanks's optimistic, performative masculinity had a capacity to make audiences feel as if they had entered an intimate and personal sphere where they, like White responding to

Practicing "Biff-bang Americanism" (Douglas Fairbanks in *The Americano*, 1917)

Roosevelt, thought themselves privileged to read something absolutely innocent and indisputably encouraging about a "primitive" child-man representing Americans as citizens.[47] Social commentator George Creel immodestly declared Fairbanks to be

what every American might be, ought to be, and frequently is *not.* . . . Men like him as well as women, and, best proof of all, the "kids" adore him. . . . And let no one quarrel with this popularity. It is a good sign, a healthful sign, a token that the blood of America still runs warm and red, and that chalk has not yet softened our bones.[48]

Photoplay declared Fairbanks to be "*the* representative American actor" whose roles "represent America and the biff-bang Americanism for which we are, justly and unjustly, renowned."[49]

Like Roosevelt, Fairbanks came to be regarded as a man in whom the primitive urges and instincts of boyhood had not died, but who reflected ideal masculine goodness in a manly way through physical regeneration and optimistic moral action. He became a cultural icon who evoked zealous commentary praising his youthfulness, his "spirit," his "personality," his amazing physicality—in short, his personification of everything little boys dreamed of becoming and everything men wished they might have retained of an idealized youth.[50] The discursive terms of this rather contradictory valorization of youthfulness are suggested by James E. West, chief scout executive of the Boy Scouts of America, who in 1924 remarked of the star:

He appeals to the eternal boy in us, the sun loving, swashbuckling, romantic boy in us. . . . If he speaks to the mature, then think with what appeal he speaks to boys, to those youngsters of ours from whom the energy floods, as over a dam, seeking an outlet? The Douglas Fairbanks of the screen talks to them in a voice as authentic as their own. . . . [These pages] give you a key not only of *the boy in the man, but the man in the boy.*[51]

Fairbanks and Roosevelt were boyish men who were admired for their much-coveted preservation of an apparent lifelong identification with a vigorous, idealized boyhood. This identification made them logical public instruments in a widespread effort at the turn of the century to redefine male agency within a changing society.

In a quest for masculine redefinition, a primary effort during the Progressive era centered on the need to guarantee masculine "character" in new generations of boys. As Jeffrey Hantover has observed in his discussion of the founding of the Boy Scouts of America: "Men believed they faced diminishing opportunities for masculine validation in the workplace, but adolescents faced immense barriers, it was thought, to the very development of masculinity."[52] Reforming the lives of boys and recapturing the romance of America's lost boyhood became an Anglo-American growth industry in the early 1910s and was sustained in the postwar years.

Despite the lighthearted tenor of most of Fairbanks's roles, they were amazingly convergent with the ideals of "character building" that believed that "manhood not scholarship is the first aim of education."[53] At the forefront of this movement to build character in boys were scouting advocates Robert Baden-Powell (founder of the Boy Scouts of Britain) and Ernest Thompson Seton (founder of the Woodcraft Indians and chief of scouts in the Boy Scouts of America), Daniel Carter Beard (The Sons of Daniel Boone and a Boy Scouts of America founder), as well as Edgar M. Robinson and Luther Gulick of the Young Men's Christian Association (YMCA) and psychologists William Forbush and G. Stanley Hall.[54] While character building was cultivated by these and lesser known "boys' workers" on numerous political, social, artistic, and even religious fronts, Fairbanks was its exemplar on the Hollywood front.

In concert with the obvious kinetic appeal of Fairbanks's films, the star's popularity was crucially dependent upon his textual alignment with this culturally pervasive discourse focused on reform and the future of American masculinity. Fairbanks's films of the 1910s almost all had at their core an imminently recognizable and important lesson to contemporary audiences: a lesson in the attainment of manhood in modern American society. Other actors (such as Charles Ray in rural comedy-melodramas, or Harold Lloyd in daring, slapstick comedies) might have specialized in portraying youthful American men, but none were identified in a serious way, as Fairbanks was, with contemporary, character-building ideals that sought a revitalization of American masculinity.[55]

While Fairbanks's vehicles of the 1920s are best known, the films that brought him to fame during the period 1915–1920 will be the focus of this chapter because of their importance to formulating postwar norms of masculinity. They established a normative standard that continued to hold hegemonic sway over Hollywood's representations of masculinity in the 1920s. Also, these films provide an overt reference to social discourse on masculinity that is muted by Fairbanks's costume or "swashbuckling" films of the 1920s. However, as we shall see, all of Fairbanks's films of the silent era addressed the construction of proper masculinity in fantasy-fulfilling terms that reverberated with the era's obsessionary quest to make men of boys and boys of men. Throughout the late teens and into the twenties, Fairbanks on the screen became the virtual cinematic embodiment of the theoretical principles that underscored a broadly based, boy-centered reform movement. Those same principles dominated discussion of American male identity from the 1880s to 1920, a period in which, it has been suggested, there was a "crucial identity crisis for the American male."[56]

"Be Prepared": Character Building for Crisis

Many scholars propose that from the late 1880s through World War I and into the waning years of the Progressive era, American masculinity was in a self-defined crisis.[57] What might be categorized as traditional masculinity (white, middle-class, Protestant) took a defensive stance on multiple fronts: at home as well as in the workplace, in the schools, in politics, and in many other arenas of public life. Changes in economic, ethnic, and demographic structures in the country were perceived as threatening mainstream values and actions traditionally used to define masculinity and manly virtues. In particular, the fear of losing traditional masculine anchors of identity, such as the gender-role validation provided by work, seemed to spur a multifaceted, nervous search for middle-class male identity in an increasingly bureaucratized, industrialized, and, therefore, "feminized" America.

Practical attempts to construct manly citizens. (*Good Housekeeping*, September 9, 1914)

Already by the 1880s, Theodore Roosevelt had warned of the need for the leadership class to seek out what he called "the strenuous life"; America's young people were growing up in a "slothful ease . . . that was creating a generation dominated by the over-civilized man, who has lost the great fighting, masterful virtues."[58] Something had to be done, Roosevelt declared, "to stave off effeminacy that is one of the dangers of nations that grow old and soft and unwilling to endure hardships."[59]

Roosevelt was not alone in his concern for "gilded youth" or in his single-minded concern with the creation of manliness in an era of perceived national enfeeblement. As defensive reactions against an effeminant modern civilization, theories of masculine development emerged from this cultural climate and led to widespread practical attempts to construct hardy, manly citizens from boys and adolescents.[60] Concern with the proper development of masculinity was the impetus for a massive reform movement intent on systematically reshaping Anglo-American masculinity. As scholars such as E. Anthony Rotundo and David I. Macleod have detailed, specialists began to emerge in the 1880s to standardize and organize boy culture in the fight against a perceived weakening of masculinity.[61] A whole generation of psychologists, social reformers, politicians, educators, and commentators in the United States and Britain theorized about the nature of proper masculinity and then became involved in massive, organized attempts to ensure its proper development among boys and youth of all classes. These new boy specialists, boy reformers, "boys' workers," and experts in the "boy problem" were involved in mapping and mastering the principles and particulars by which good masculine—and therefore, national—character might be attained.

Distinguished by a remarkable cross-fertilization of ideas, a huge body of reform-centered literature and numerous organizations for character building and boy reform had grown up on both English-speaking sides of the Atlantic. In addition, early twentieth-century America witnessed a tremendous growth in the number and size of organizations aimed at the social control of cultural patterns associated with childhood. In spite of their differences, the various United States-based systems of physical and spiritual regeneration such as the YMCA, the Boy Scouts of America, the Woodcraft Indians, and the Sons of Daniel Boone shared a defining common purpose. Ernest Thompson Seton, one of the most influential of the era's boy reformers, stated the purpose succinctly: "To make a man."[62]

Reformers like Seton believed that masculine rejuvenation depended upon influencing boy culture, those habitats and habits of boys once regarded as a spontaneous outgrowth of boys' "natural" social interests.[63] In the wake of amorphous anxieties concerning perceived social changes and masculinity, boy culture soon became a phenomenon to be researched and, more importantly, controlled. There was, it was widely agreed, a boy problem of national and even international proportions that demanded a solution if traditional masculine virtues were to survive into the new century. Character building for boys became the solution to a host of widely perceived social problems: the debilitating effects of industrialized urban life, the changing complexion of middle-class economics to consumer values, a bureaucratized and feminized white-collar workplace, and even the increasing control of women over the family.

Some have suggested that this emergent crisis or exaggerated anxiety surrounding the meaning of middle-class masculinity at the turn of the century was primarily induced by the gains women made in the public sphere.[64] Certainly, boy reform reflected the widely held belief among many Americans that the heretofore comforting differences between men and women were being reduced by changes in the workplace, in the home, and in the arena of public affairs. While many, especially those concerned with boy culture, regarded changes in gender roles and expectations defensively, others did not, and this mixed bias often stands side by side in popular discourses, including Fairbanks's films.[65]

Nevertheless, in the late nineteenth century many American men expressed a sense of being threatened by changes in gender roles and emergent social expectations. At the baseline of many of these fears were economic factors that transformed the middle-class workplace and also created a population shift to cities.[66] An increasingly bureaucratized society in a changing, post-Civil War environment endangered the traditional validating force of work for defining masculine identity. A changing national economy dictated the channeling of male middle-class vocations away from the autonomous and independent self-employment of the past. There was a new system of "command and obedience" for the middle class in contrast to the pre-Civil War situation when 88 percent of American men were farmers or self-employed businessmen. Middle-class men were expected to take up salaried employment in hierarchy-structured corporations and in sedentary white-collar jobs increasingly shared with women.[67] Not only were women perceived as invading white-collar domains of work, but new corporate structures were perceived as undermining autonomy and individuality, qualities that had been important in defining masculinity. Already in the 1870s, middle-class, white-collar work was equated with imprisonment in a corporate bureaucracy that limited manly independence and decisiveness.[68]

Even as the white middle class was threatened from above by big capitalism's corporate structure (which would become the focus of "muckraking" scrutiny), middle-class manliness was perceived as being under siege from new forces of frantic urbanity as well.[69] The erosion of traditional masculine virtues associated with work was exacerbated by threatening cultural changes associated with the influx of "darker" immigrants. As chapter 3 will detail in the discussion of Rudolph Valentino's stardom, these immigrants, many from southern and eastern Europe, were regarded with suspicion as the established, white middle class became increasingly concerned with "race suicide" as defined by eugenicists and politicized by many proponents of Social Darwinism.[70] Roderick Nash has observed that the "flood of immigrants seemed to many to be diluting the American strain and weakening American traditions."[71] It was believed that the Old World was reasserting itself in the New. The results, it was said, were obvious: the decline of democracy, the corruption of values, and the undermining of the American character.[72]

With Social Darwinism providing even more fuel for an ethnocentric Americanism focused on these overdetermined factors, much anxiety centered around the preservation of traditional white, Anglo-Saxon-identified, Protestant, middle-class-identified masculinity. While not all the central tenets of the ideals of middle-class masculinity promoted by character-builders were new, newly realized pressures made many believe that the passage into male social and sexual identity had been made more precarious than in the past, especially within the context of the industrialized environment of the cities. In a commentary typical of the era, Norman E. Richardson and Ormond E. Loomis described the problem in a pro-Boy Scouts of America tract of 1915:

Time was when he [the boy] grew up under the careful tutelage of his father. . . . Now conditions have changed. Congested city life, which has increased with our industrial development, has thrown the boy on the street. . . . No longer does he have the same opportunities for healthy recreation or clean companionship that gave him something daringly, but harmlessly, interesting to do. . . . To check this awful waste is a serious problem.[73]

By the mid-1910s a boy reform discourse based on these observations and intent on character building permeated almost every facet of mass culture in the United States. Although never a static entity, the relationship between boyhood and manhood took on unprecedented significance in the United States. The very process of turning boys into men was perceived as being imperiled as never before.

Sunday School Morality and Muscular Christianity

In the late 1880s the foundations of this boy-centered reform moment were established within a broader cultural response to emergent social pressures. As one historian has suggested, "Men embraced boyhood at the same time that they were learning to value savagery, passion, and the embodied manhood of the athlete and the soldier."[74] A physically centered masculinity, a "cult of the body," emerged in the 1880s with an emphasis on muscular physical development achieved through boxing, organized sports, and athletics. The muscular male body became the last refuge of middle-class manliness as traditional institutional supports defining masculinity appeared to collapse the distinctions between the masculine and the nonmasculine, the latter defined increasingly as feminine rather than as simply childish.

In its simplest incarnation, masculine virtues associated with the cult of the body were used to define American masculinity as ideally instinctual, impulsive, and primitive in contrast to an industrialized, bureaucratic, consumer-oriented, and sedentary civilization described as feminized.[75]

Feminization and overcivilization became the conflated antagonists to traditional masculinity aligned with a "masculine primitive" and defined in terms of physical strength, moral action, individualistic independence, and outdoors-centered interests.[76] A popular attraction, strongman/wrestler Eugen Sandow naturalized nakedness and its public display in personal appearances and as a protostar in front of Edison's new motion picture camera.[77] At the same time, boxers such as John L. Sullivan began to set a new standard for the public celebration of a well-developed male body in the spectacle of physical combat.[78] Such heroes, spectacularly muscular and athletically decisive, were not only revelatory of the *perfecting transformation* available to men through conditioning of the body but ultimately of a physical force that, at its most idealized, might be equated with morality defined as a vital process rather than as an abstract, inactive, and therefore "feminine" set of ideas.[79]

Taking the cult of the body into the realm of character building, boy reformers took for granted the logic of an assertive, vigorous masculinity's privileged place in their work. As Ernest Thompson Seton declared in 1910, "I do not know that I have met a boy that would not rather be John L. Sullivan than Darwin or Tolstoi. Therefore, I accept the fact and seek to keep in view an ideal that is physical."[80] Cult of the body ideals of physical development and an emphasis on the physical regeneration of America became the central focus of most character-building theories of masculine development. The physical demands of exercise were regarded as the ideal outlet for the healthy expression of masculine instincts. These instincts— the so-called driving force of masculinity (and "the race")—were in danger of being eradicated by overcivilization.

For boy reformers the new masculine ideal had to be possessed of a "physical conscience," or what YMCA founder Luther Gulick termed the "new sense of responsibility for things bodily."[81] As physical culture guru Barnarr MacFadden noted in *Manhood and Marriage*: "For building manhood . . . it is absolutely essential that you should make yourself physically as perfect as possible. In fact, there is nothing in the world that can take the place of muscular exercise for your purpose."[82] Character-builders believed that to achieve such an ideal, the modern boy, whether of the lower, middle, or upper class, needed to develop the strenuous, physical side of life within a positive, *masculine-dominated* environment. Exercise through sport and various forms of physical conditioning were believed to be crucial in transforming the boy into a well-developed man whose physical strength and kinetic energy confirmed both the individual's and the nation's manly character. In keeping with most boy reformers, Gulick regarded physical training as the key to creating moral vitality in boys, in part because "through the medium of athletics probably more boys can be reached by a moral leader than by any other means. The athlete is a hero of every boy."[83]

However, in forging the middle-class ideal of masculinity that character-builders promoted across the class spectrum, the brute physicality of working-class athlete-heroes such as Sullivan ("The Strongboy of Boston") had to be reconceptualized. Reformers' ideal of vigorous manhood had to be compatible with middle-class gentility. Thus, the era's cultish celebration of the male body in movement became a celebration of all-around perfection that began with the cult of the body's ideal of muscular physicality but did not end with it. For character-builders the physically developed male body in motion was not only a sign of physical perfection but the primary vehicle for the expression of character as a process.[84]

Although differing in philosophy and method, almost all boy workers advanced the view that ideal manliness was to be equated with vigorous, muscular physicality put in the service of a traditional goodness. Moral goodness was embodied in a transformed ("cultured") physicality that prepared the boy, and then the man, for positive action. In *A Manual of Boys' Clubs* William Forbush described the manly traits that were sought: "A mind that thinks naught unclean, a heart cheerful for every fate, a body supple and quick and strong, a will masterful but controlled, a soul reverent and watchful."[85] Such a well-rounded masculinity was promulgated by the Boy Scouts of America, but even more explicitly by the YMCA in its emphasis on muscular Christian manliness and in its self-described purpose: "The reclamation and uplift of the men of to-morrow—spirit, mind, and body."[86]

Character-builders preached that boys had to be virtuous without being feminine in a culture that believed women to be innately more moral then men.[87] Masculine conformity to codes of conventional morality had to be divorced from the passive and effeminate.[88] To counter the "feminizing of Christianity," masculinist authors like R. Warren Conant made Jesus Christ into the best model of the manly man. Conant asked in *The Virility of Christ*:

Was Christ less manly because he was free from [the Hebrew prophets'] grossness and moral blemish? A gentleman is not necessarily effeminate. There is altogether too much popular inclination to assume that goodness cannot be thoroughly manly. . . . Christ stands for the highest type of a strong, virile man, and there was nothing effeminate about him. . . . A leader of men must have force, especially physical force.[89]

The era's tendency toward hero-worship was extended by character-builders in their hope that boys' "instinctive hero-worship can be refined and elevated until it draws its nourishment from the highest hero—the Son of Man."[90]

The reconciliation between Christian goodness and the masculine primitive was especially evident around the time of World War I in the spectacularly rapid success of the Boy Scouts and the YMCA. Boy reformers lost no time, too, in theorizing the felt need for middle-class men to be physically active. Even as they had to be aggressively forceful in physicality, middle-class men were also charged to uphold a traditional, gentlemanly ideal of behavior. There is little doubt that during this era, adult anxieties regarding the ability of men to achieve the reconciliation of the primitive and the genteel were displaced onto boys and fueled the rapid creation of organizations for the reform of boy culture.

While the consolidation of male gender expectations around a balance of gentility and muscular vigor may not have infiltrated all of American society with equal success, it was especially evident in the mass media aimed at the middle class. Fairbanks's characters are exemplary of this consolidation, which Clyde Griffen has suggested had considerable effect on American masculinity. Griffen argues that turn-of-the-century unifying norms for middle-class masculinity resulted in "more rigidly circumscribed gender expectations" even though these expectations did not "define precisely all the boundaries between manly and unmanly behavior." They did create, he goes on to suggest, "a pervasive common ideal, one that had profound consequences for male socialization."[91] Of primary significance among these consequences was the closing off a certain plurality of masculine styles evident earlier in the nineteenth century.[92]

If the "common ideal" was evident in national ideals such as Roosevelt and Fairbanks, one victim of this process was an older model of adult Christian masculinity, the evangelically influenced "Christian gentleman."[93] This masculine style or personality increasingly was regarded as uncomfortably feminine, not merely different but deviant. Emergent gender-role pressures and trends like the cult of the body also worked to marginalize this mode of masculinity. Not only was a certain softness or fragility of the body becoming highly suspect, but behaviors that once were considered to be Christian and fraternal were increasingly regarded as effeminate and perverse.[94]

Nevertheless, in the transition to a new and narrower masculine ideal for American manhood, feminine traits were not completely rejected. Even the strongest advocate of the strenuous life, hyperrobust Teddy Roosevelt described his father as his masculine ideal in these terms: "My father really did combine the strength and courage and will and energy of the strongest man with the tenderness, cleanness, and purity of a woman."[95] In "What Men Like in Men," Rafford Pyke offers a similar notion of the qualities that the average man admired and, conversely, disliked. He notes:

> I suppose that every man who *is* a man would readily agree that he dislikes a "Sissy" . . . men dislike effeminacy. . . . Yet in the nature of men whom other men like best there is always to be traced a touch of something that is feminine. It is like a thread of silver woven in some useful fabric, gleaming amid the plain . . . imparting just a hint of beauty to the whole. This feminine quality in man gives fineness to the character. . . . Temperamentally it denotes gentleness, and the tenderness which is the perfect complement to strength.[96]

Such statements suggest that it was not easy to achieve the ideal merger of traditional moral values associated with feminine tenderness and altruism with the "masculine primitive" of rugged physicality and instinctual impulsivity. As we shall see, in many instances, even in Fairbanks's films, their coexistence in one person could be achieved only through extreme measures.

Savage Virtues and Higher Refinements

Aligned with popularized notions of Social Darwinism, most boy reform theories suggested that masculinity was founded on instinct; instinct was both the driving energy for the "race" and, ironically, the thing that ultimately needed to be suppressed in order for civilization to function. John Dewey expressed the dominant view: "All conduct springs ultimately and radically out of native instincts and impulses, and we must know what these instincts and impulses are . . . at each particular state of the child's development, in order to know what to appeal to and build upon."[97]

Boy culture reformers agreed that the instincts of boys from nine to fourteen were "savage." J. Adams Puffer's *The Boy and His Gang* offered the common character-building view on this issue: "The normal boy . . . is, therefore, essentially a savage, with the interests of a savage, the body of a savage, and to no small extent, the soul of one. He thinks and feels like a savage; he has the savage virtues and the savage vices; and the gang is his tribe."[98] Puffer's remarks follow the recapitulation theory of play advanced by G. Stanley Hall in his two-volume tome *Adolescence* (1905). Hall's work had immense impact on those concerned with male development in the 1900s. He believed that each boy repeated the "history of his own race-life from savagery unto civilization."[99] As Professor George Walter Fiske described it, "The whole process of child development like race development is a climb upward from savagery through barbarism to civilization."[100]

In this "climb upward," different classes had different requirements for character building as a transformational process with manhood as its goal. All needed supervised play and strenuous physical exercise, but the lower classes required greater degrees of modulation of instinct to attain moral vitality. The middle class needed encouragement in expressing instinctual behavior to correct physical softness and "squeamish" (i.e., feminine) sensibilities. In spite of such class differences, Hall, like many other reformers, believed that boys in general needed to be held back from maturity.[101] A vigorously energetic, instinct-driven (though asexual) boyhood needed to be prolonged in all boys.

From this primary assumption grew three guiding principles to character building: (1) promoting boys' "natural" interest in the outdoors, (2) finding appropriate play outlets for their impulsive, exuberant physicality, and (3) channeling their instinctive tendency to form gangs. These principles and their link to savage boy instincts are discussed by William McKeever in *Training the Boy*:

Boys . . . are especially fond of organizing in gangs with purposes that seem foreign to the teachings of the Sunday school. Such boys thirst instinctively for a free, wild life—to go out into the forest or mountains . . . and will expend a surprising amount of time and energy in an effort to see something killed outright or chopped to pieces alive. Now all this is nothing more than the cropping out of that savage animalism upon which the higher refinements of our best civilization are built, whether we realize the fact or not.[102]

To ensure building the "best civilization," boys' much-coveted instinctive behaviors of animal origin had to be modulated by morality and other qualities (such as sexual purity) stereotypically associated with the feminine. The result would be a perfectly balanced, vigorous manhood that combined the primitive and the genteel, the masculine and the feminine.

Fairbanks's *Double Trouble* (1915), one of his earliest films, explicitly foregrounds character-builders' theorization of masculine identity in relation to class, instinct, and morality. *Double Trouble* illustrates boy reformers' dichotomous view of the essential nature of maleness in the need to balance moral goodness with impulsive, overtly dangerous masculine instincts. The film places this duality within the same context of class difference that character-builders used to predict differences in the expression of boy instincts and behaviors. More specifically, *Double Trouble* illustrates how older models like that of the Christian gentleman had to give way to a balanced ideal of physically vigorous yet moral masculinity.

Considering the dominant discourse on masculine identity, it is not surprising that in *Double Trouble* Fairbanks essays a double role, of a literal dual personality. In different forms this same duality of identity would become a film convention that Fairbanks (and many other male stars of the period) returned to again and again, in the 1910s and into the 1920s. While in many of these films, as in *The Mark of Zorro* (1920), Fairbanks's character assumed two radically different styles of male identity to confuse his enemies and consciously further his heroic aims, in *Double Trouble* the character is subject to unconscious forces.

We are first introduced to the personality of Florian Amidon, the "perfect gentleman of Amityville" who is hit over the head in a train station mugging and awakens five years later. The intertitle informs us: "For five years after this unfortunate occurrence, Florian's life was a blank to him. When he came back to his senses he was in a Pullman, travelling to New York." Everyone on the Pullman knows Florian as Mr. Brassfield, a sport and criminally aggressive ward heeler. At this point in the film, Florian knows only that the checked suits which the porter assures him are his "spoke louder than words of his five years of forgotten existence. . . . What rash acts, even crimes, might he not have committed in clothes like these?"

Florian's concern about "rash acts" is the logical response for his type of man, for he is not only the "perfect gentleman of Amityville" but a perfect caricature of the Christian gentleman forged out of nineteenth-century evangelical Protestant values. Florian's life is centered around his role as president of the Sabbath Day Society. The implications would have been clear to an audience of 1915: Sunday schools and Christian organizations had "sissy associations." It was widely known that their failure to produce properly manly men had motivated the founding of the YMCA, with its aim of producing "red-blooded Christianity" through a rigorous program that physically stimulated the boy "to all-round development."[103] By the 1910s the movement to construct masculinity had self-consciously placed itself against traditional church-centered activities that now were tainted with effeminacy—so much so that it was reported that only 40 percent of Protestant churchgoers were male.[104] As one boy reformer noted, "To set [the boy] at Sunday School lessons under a woman teacher is a pedagogic

An appeal to boys' play instinct (Advertisement,
The Youth's Companion, June 15, 1916)

crime."[105] Sunday school teachers, stereotyped as females who were ignorant of boy development, were believed to promote a passive, feminine
faith. They did not understand why their sedentary, sentimental female-
dominated Sunday schools could not produce moral men from active,
"bad" boys. What was required was an appeal to boys' instincts through
play, which was believed to function as a recapitulation of primitive
mankind's work.

Once regarded as sufficient to build manly character, Sunday schools
and the guidance of parents were supplemented or even supplanted by
these ambitious new efforts that sought to radically alter the roles played
by family and society, work and leisure in shaping a moral, modern masculinity. These efforts led to the rise of reformers with a social vision of
organized play and the playground as the primary shapers of urban
(implicitly male) character. One progressive advocate of playground
reform suggested that new playground environments resulted in "more
ethics and good citizenship . . . in a single week than can be inculcated by
Sunday school teachers . . . in a decade."[106]

In *Double Trouble*, Florian is exemplary of the failure of Sunday
schools and traditional moral training to produce proper masculinity. A

sedentary bank clerk, Florian is mincing, wheezing, effeminate, with a greasy curl of hair carefully laced over each eye. In spite of his lack of masculinity, the young women of the parish flock to him. As the intertitles tell us: "The swish of a skirt would send his heart into a flutter of fear." His response is predictably timid, for Florian is a ladies' man who is a sissy. In one of the era's many descriptions of the type, Rafford Pyke explained: "He [the sissy] is polite and rather anxious to please. . . . He likes very much to be with ladies, and ladies like him—in a way. He is a most useful creature and absolutely harmless."[107] However, Florian's church is not sure he is harmless. The female parishioners' keen interest in Florian has motivated the church elders to vote him the fateful vacation from which he now awakens.

Ensconced at a posh hotel that knows him as Mr. Brassfield, Florian may be confused by the sporty clothes he wears, but he is even more confused by the hotel's outrageously swishy porter, who gets altogether too friendly. Pale, frizzy haired, and fat, the porter's mannerisms are much like Florian's, perhaps a trifle more feminine. Once in the hotel room, the porter's hands are all over Florian, and the former boldly sits down for a cozy tête-à-tête with the newly arrived guest.

Florian's mannerisms have led to a serious confusion: he has been assumed to be a sexual fellow traveler (so to speak) by the homosexual porter. Flustered, with his pinkie perched in his mouth, Florian first lightly kicks, then hysterically bats the porter (and the latter's hands) away. After he pushes the porter out the door, Florian is left alone in his hotel room to contemplate his "greatest shock to the mind," a love letter from a girl he cannot remember.

Ultimately, Florian seeks help from a church elder and family friend, Judge Blodgett (Richard Cummings), who secures the services of a hypnotist, Mme Le Claire (Olga Grey). Under hypnosis, Eugene Brassfield emerges from Florian's subconscious. For the last five years, Florian has been living as Brassfield, a working-class politician who blithely two-times the nice girl who loves him. Florian goes to investigate this girl, Elizabeth (Margery Wilson), and along the way discovers Daisy Scarlett (Gladys Brockwell), Brassfield's mistress. When the latter asks "Eugene" for a kiss, Florian walks away in his mincing fashion. Immediately, Daisy Scarlett imitates his high pinkie-extended, hands-intertwined-in-front-of-his-chest mannerisms.

Elizabeth, too, is miffed to distraction by Eugene's/Florian's newly evident effeminacy. When Florian starts twisting his fingers together, she

Coming out of a trance and into another male identity: Douglas Fairbanks, Olga Grey, and Richard Cummings in *Double Trouble* (1915)

slaps them down thinking that Eugene is making fun of her. After a dinner party, she chides him: "You should be ashamed, Eugene, the way you acted last night!" She imitates his mincing ways until Florian, now with Eugene's personality emergent, manfully lifts her onto the furniture to kiss her. "Now this is like my dear old Eugene!" Elizabeth coos (via an intertitle).

"Dear old Eugene" has obvious, manly charms. Like Florian, his character is a familiar stereotype. He represents a vital, lower-class masculinity described in character-building terms by one trade magazine review as "a wilder human being of primitive instincts long held in suppression."[108] For the remainder of the film, the Eugene and Florian personalities pop in and out as Brassfield campaigns for mayor with the help of his burly henchmen ("the violets," as they are called). Brassfield mixes his interest in "politics" (i.e., graft) with "chickens" (i.e., loose women), barroom brawls, and drunken preelection revelry.

Brassfield's is the vital masculinity boy reformers typically linked to urbanity. In such environs untouched by Progressive and boy reform, lower-class boys' instincts might not be sufficiently channeled toward morality. It was agreed that, especially in the cities, boys tended to short-circuit the proper prolongation of boyhood in the process of attaining a balanced, vigorous manhood. This could lead to a degeneration or perversion of boyish instincts. Urban life led inevitably to "temptation, prematurities, sedentary occupations, and passive stimuli just when an active, objective life is most needed."[109] Working-class city boys needed character-building organizations to curb cruelty and reign in the instinctive, impulsive, high-spirited gang behavior that was easily diverted into stealing, gambling, and early sex. Without the guidance of settlement houses, the progressive playground movement, and Boys' Clubs, this class's pent-up energy (derived from their natural, manly, savage instincts) would be perverted into the victimization of others.[110]

Such a pattern showed that cities were morally deadening and the citizens they produced, a danger to the nation's future. As some character-builders noted, the "highest type of citizenship" was on the wane and "antidemocratic tendencies have appeared in almost alarming degree in our social and political life."[111] Seton suggested more specifically that Americans had grown degenerate: "We know money grubbing, machine politics, degrading sports, cigarettes . . . false ideals, moral laxity and lessening church power, in a word 'City rot' has worked evil in the nation."[112]

The consequences of city rot are self-evident in *Double Trouble*'s characterization of Eugene Brassfield. To secure the election, Brassfield has a nefarious plan to frame a municipal whistle-blower. The plan puts the man in jail and almost destroys his family: his wife is going to commit suicide because of Brassfield's persecution, but Brassfield is transformed in the nick of time back into Florian, who begins to display new physical vigor, moral courage, and even romantic ardor. His personality is beginning to merge with Eugene's. The intertitles note:

> As Amidon he remembers nothing of the Brassfield life, but in time the two will gradually become merged . . . You must understand that a little of Brassfield stays on to harden the softness of Amidon; while the fineness of Amidon kills the evil of Brassfield.

Amidon rescues the beleaguered family, reconciles with Elizabeth, and assumes the mayorship as his own man instead of the political machine's.

In this resolution ensuring revitalized democracy as well as regenerated masculine character, *Double Trouble* humorously offers a fantasy resolution to the boy reformers' notions of perfectly balanced masculinity and its function in modern America. This new Florian Amidon is created from the merger of Brassfield's animal vitality and the old Florian's refined morality; thus, Florian's merged personality also achieves what the Boy Scouts worked so hard to establish: proof that there was no harm in savage, masculine instincts being given proper opportunity for expression if they were always under the control of higher Christian values.[113]

Obviously rooted in this same culturally dominant view of masculine identity is Booth Tarkington's classic characterization of Fairbanks the actor:

Fairbanks is a faun who has been to Sunday School. He has a pagan body which yields instantly to any heathen or gypsy impulse—as an impulse to balance a chair on its nose while hanging from the club chandelier by one of its knees—but he has a mind reliably furnished with a full set of morals and proprieties: he would be a sympathetic companion for anybody's aunt. I don't know his age; I think he hasn't any. Certainly he will never be older—unless quicksilver can get old.[114]

Tarkington's description of Fairbanks resonates with those of the Boy Scout, the era's most popular icon for the ideal yet average American boy.

Like the Scout ideal, Fairbanks embodied the ideal balance of chivalry with childish "tuft" impulses and animal spirits. Boys were expected to act impulsively and athletically in a harmlessly savage way. While such behavior fit into the necessary gang demands of boy life, boys were thought also to be capable of genteel propriety. Thus, the Boy Scout was trained to be courteous and respectful to his elders. His training to be a companion to aunts came primarily in the "good turn," which he was compelled by Scout Law to do every day; he also was told, by the same law, that he had to be helpful, courteous, and kind to all, "especially to women, children, old people, and the weak and helpless," even if it meant that his Scout chivalry led him to be ridiculed by boys who were not Scouts and did not understand the need for the good turn.[115]

Boy Scouts in this idealized mode were depicted in popular magazines, literature, and a number of films during the era.[116] Their presence in the latter was cinematically redundant since Fairbanks already had cultivated his own and his characters' resemblance to the Scout to a remarkable and remarkably popular degree. Although the argument could be made that none of his film characters of the 1910s stray far from the Scout persona, this resemblance is made particularly striking in *Knickerbocker Buckaroo* (1919). Kicked out of his Manhattan men's club for his practical jokes, Teddy Drake (Fairbanks) is off to the Great American Desert to do "something for somebody." Teddy has realized how selfish he has been in his existence and goes West to reform himself. In doing a good turn (i.e., helping an old lady while he is traveling), Teddy becomes enmeshed in a series of unexpected adventures involving Mexican bandits and a crooked sheriff.

The resemblance was also played on in *The Habit of Happiness* (1916), in which Sunny Wiggins (Fairbanks) is from a social-climbing family. They regard him as "worthless" since he doesn't want to emulate his father who, he says, wasted "a lifetime in acquiring a fortune." Instead, Sunny altruistically spends his time trying to cheer up men in bread lines. He brings flophouse residents home to the Wiggins mansion for baths and meals as he tries to pass along lots of his incredible optimism and also some of his father's money, "back to the poor devils who haven't any." While it would be foolish to regard the film as an argument for the redistribution of wealth, it would not be extreme to observe that Fairbanks's Sunny is the very embodiment of the maxim that the Scout "must never be a snob" because "The Scout is neither rich nor poor; he is simply a plain citizen boy, heir-apparent to independent, free-thinking, noble manhood."[117]

"Have you ever heard of a fish with the D.T.s?"

If Fairbanks achieved the literal embodiment of character building's most obvious middle-class ideals for boyhood, he offered too their most complex convergence in the mischievously playful, instinct-driven mode. Praised as being "almost as strenuous as Ex-President Teddy,"[118] Fairbanks was the movies' most vigorous embodiment of a realized ideal of American character as perpetual youthfulness and uninhibited, playful physicality. Carl Easton Williams, echoing other commentators, remarked that Fairbanks "embodies the spirit of refined comedy . . . with a dash that represents the spirit of American youth, and then some. . . . The things that he does, athletically and acrobatically, are not merely a matter of strength and speed, but of spirit."[119] The "spirit" that Fairbanks illustrated on film and offscreen was dependent on his ability to convey the attitude that manly physical pursuits were fun. He promoted an optimistic investment in physical culture, not as a grudging fulfillment of the mania for men to be in motion, but as play, which functioned as nothing less, noted one boy reformer, as "a royal road to health, happiness, and strength of character."[120] The actor's "extraordinary muscular development" was credited with enabling him "to put physical culture into the movies in the performance of some of the most spectacular athletic feats ever shown on the screen."[121] Commentators helped cement the impression that he was an athlete first and an actor second. One suggested he was an actor of "a different sort; in fact, scarcely an actor in that sense of the word. . . . [He] went thru life as though with some extra dynamic force behind him, doing everything so—biff! bang! All this, you must understand, is totally foreign to the soul of an actor."[122]

Photograph layouts in print media almost always depicted him playfully engaged in the midst of athletic motion: leaping, vaulting, heaving, lifting, running. Fairbanks-the-actor was presented as an all-around athlete who "swims well, is a crack boxer, a good polo player, a splendid wrestler, a skillful acrobat, a fast runner, and an absolutely fearless rider."[123]

Fairbanks's body, like those of his cult-of-the-body, celebrity predecessors, Sandow and Sullivan, was not celebrated as natural but as a creation demonstrating the transformative possibility of the male body. While other male stars of the time were also held up for scrutiny as strenuous "screen Apollos" engaged in daily exercise and the process of keeping physically fit,[124] Fairbanks distinguished himself in proving the potential for masculine perfection through the constructive process of physical culture conceived as play and fun rather than work.

Fairbanks presented himself on screen as the exemplar of how playful physicality was the key to a robust citizenhood. His characters sometimes go one step further to become character-building advocates who optimistically attempt to cure the ills of modern society through physical culture defined as play. Indeed, Fairbanks's most explicit representation of the central principles of physical culture as painless, playful character building is *Down to Earth* (1917), which was also known, appropriately, as *The Optimist*.[125]

In *Down to Earth* Fairbanks plays Billy Gaynor. Billy is "the boy," described by an intertitle as "lusty, and strong, and brave." He is first glimpsed as the hero of a football game. "Ethel Forsythe, the girl" (Eileen Percy), cheers his winning play, but she refuses his proposal of marriage. She is becoming overcivilized and overexcited through the influence of Charlie Riddle (Charles Gerrard). Gaunt, mustachioed, slick-haired, Charlie is "one of the things Ethel likes." He resembles one of those "black-coated, stiff-jointed, soft-muscled, paste-complexioned youth . . . [of the] Atlantic cities," derisively described by Oliver Wendell Holmes.[126] He parties with Ethel, "coddles" her, and leads her into an endless round of social trivia (teas, the opera, luncheons, manicures, shopping, and so on).

In the wake of ostentatious consumption, Ethel's enjoyment of genteel culture dissipates into degeneracy and sensation-seeking. While Billy enthusiastically scrambles up an icy mountain slope, Ethel moves downward into vice dens dominated by dancing and drink. As an intertitle notes, Ethel and Billy "go their separate ways—Bill trying to forget, and Ethel forgetting to try."

In similar fashion as Teddy Roosevelt went West in the wake of personal loss, "Bill seeks forgetfulness . . . month after month, from the top of the world to the Equator." Out on the western range, he gallops on horseback to the mailbox to receive news of Ethel's collapse, which has one positive aspect: it has occurred just in time to save her from marrying Charlie. Bill arrives at Dr. Jollyem's sanatorium to find the doctor catering to a coterie of hypochondriacs and victims of overcivilization, including his beloved Ethel.

In counterpoint to the male neurasthenia associated with overwork in the corporate world, Ethel is a victim of what was described by physical culture guru MacFadden as being "as bad as, or worse than, mental over-work": the "late hours and excitement" of "social dissipations."[127] Obviously (from his name), Dr. Jollyem is a medical quack; nevertheless he is in step with character-building theory when he tells Bill that Ethel "is in the condition of over half of our wealthy city-bred women. There's no cure for them, because they won't help cure themselves."

Even though nervous prostration and premature collapse are to be expected of modern urban living, Billy is not satisfied with Dr. Jollyem's MacFaddenesque prognosis for Ethel. He buys the sanatorium (for a mere $25,000!) and optimistically assumes the task of curing Ethel. On a yacht-ing trip, he purposefully strands all the sanatorium's patients on what he represents to them as a desert island. The epitome of the physical cultur-ist, Billy announces: "Some people are born healthy, others achieve health, but you're going to have health thrust upon you!" He proceeds to force "his" patients to exercise for their food.

As a character-builder, Billy's formula for health is perfectly aligned with character-building theories such as Luther Gulick's "gymnasium of citi-zenship." Gulick promoted the idea that health of mind and body could only be pursued through "the will to be cheerful." Without optimism, the pursuit of physical perfection was impossible. "The pessimist," Gulick declared, "has relatively poor circulation, digests food less well, is less mus-cular, and particularly has fewer motives in life than the optimist."[128] Billy is optimistic enough to think he can cure the sanatorium's resident drunk-ard as well as the recalcitrant Ethel.

In getting his patients onto the royal road to health, Billy's cure fulfills the era's idealized conception of outdoor exercise as instinctive play that would make children into adults and adults into children. In *Down to Earth* Billy teaches his patients how to climb trees, imitate birds, and crawl like animals. "Snakes are thin because they wriggle and crawl on the ground," he tells a portly woman who is then instructed to do the same for her breakfast. He admonishes the drunkard: "Did you ever hear of a fish with the D.T.s? Well, fish drink water–now that's your cue!" In the process, Billy's patients learn to enjoy the woods as if they were Boy Scouts following Seton's instructions in books such as *How to Play Indian* and *The Birch-bark Roll of the Woodcraft Indians*. In these tracts Seton preached "the absolute virtues of picturesque recreation in the woods."[129]

Seton's nostalgic obsession with the woods, woodlore, and woodcraft skills became a primary feature of character-builders' play-centered cure for the problems of American masculinity. With the distribution of millions of copies of his *Woodcraft Handbook*, the Boy Scouts practiced his notions of how to develop the ideal boy through sensible outdoor activities. Anticipating descriptions of Fairbanks as an all-around athlete, Seton declared the ideal American boy should have all the skills associated with rural boyhood or even frontier life. The boys of the past, could "ride, shoot, skate, run, swim; [they were] handy with tools . . . physically strong, self-reliant, resourceful," and "altogether the best material of which a nation could be made."[130]

Most boy reformers agreed with Seton that the current, imperiled generation of boys had to recapture those mythic qualities of masculine character that had been taken for granted as a natural part of vigorous boy culture of America's rural past. Those qualities were based on those "ancient virtues of savagery" that boys possessed instinctually but which had become the "vices of civilization."[131] They were skills easily acquired in the more savage past, but now they had to be taught by reformers to boys in much the same manner as Billy has to reeducate his patients.

The most socially radical of the Boy Scouts of America founders, Seton signed his letters with a paw print and was infamous for his refusal to bathe or trim his hair. More germane to his considerable influence on character builders in America, he believed a return to the principles of living in harmony with nature was an antidote to modern life. City life, in particular, was creating citizens who were "strained and broken by the grind of the over-busy world."[132] His description fits Ethel. She resists recovery but is forced to participate in woodcraft, including collecting bark and making baskets and bowls. Outdoor skills such as these were advocated by some reformers to build girls' character. However, these activities had to be chosen carefully to enhance "true feminine instincts" (i.e., domestic skills) and their ability to uphold "universal motherhood" in the fight against race suicide.[133]

Feminine recovery from degeneracy through woodcraft: Douglas Fairbanks and Eileen Percy in *Down to Earth* (1917)

The nostalgic primitivism theorized by Seton and integrated into Roosevelt's "strenuous life" became a primary tool for character building and an equally important part of Fairbanks's movie play. In this case, Billy's adult patients, female and male, engage in activities characteristic of summer camp or of youth organizations such as the Camp Fire Girls, Boy Scouts, and Girl Guides.[134] His charges learn the skills that correspond to *The Outlook*'s demand for the "primitive" experiences that would return privileged young people to the purpose of the "real camp":

a chance to get in close contact with the best that comes through a close acquaintance with the "primitive." . . . Give them no artificial amusements, but give them all the magnificent plays and games that can mean so much to boys and girls. . . . Let them make all kinds of things, from camp buildings to their own cots. . . . And you will build up the mental and moral stamina and resourcefulness that mean so much in counteracting the artificialities and necessary restrictions of city and school life.[135]

Billy's patients start camp fires and build shelters from poles and leaves. They also learn to play. Two months later, all, including Ethel, are happy and healthy.

As an important part of his public role as a physical culturist, Fairbanks successfully extended his persona as offered in films like *Down to Earth* as a character-building discourse through numerous pronouncements in general interest magazines; these included "How I Keep Running on 'High,'" "If I Were Bringing Up Your Children," and "Combining Play With Work." In the first article, Fairbanks offers Theodore Roosevelt as the model for staying young through "stunts" that defy "'dignity' . . . the accelerator of age." Echoing the activities depicted in *Down to Earth* (released the same year), he says: "Trees talk. To an old man they mean rest

Getting seriously into character building with a
series of books

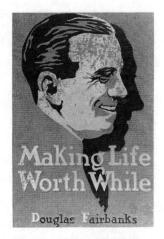

and shade, but every single tree in the woods shouts to a young fellow,
'You son of a gun, you can't get up me!' If they say that to you, you're
young. Climb!"[136]

Building on these pronouncements and using himself as his best advertisement for his expertise, Fairbanks got more seriously into the character-
building business with ghostwritten books aimed at boys and published in
a modest format to accommodate the pocketbooks of their youthful readers. These began with *Live and Let Live* (1917) and continued to include
*Initiative and Self-Reliance, Profiting by Experience, Laugh and Live,
Whistle and Hoe—Sing as We Go, Taking Stock of Ourselves* (1918), *Making
Life Worth While* (1918), and *Youth Points the Way* (1924), the last serialized in *Boy's Life*, a magazine published by the Boy Scouts of America.[137]

These books have been characterized as "innocent pronouncements on
clean living."[138] More accurately, what they really did was promote character-building principles and make them compatible with "New Style"
middle-class values that emphasized preparation for corporate careers and
family responsibility. Still, Fairbanks preached for strenuosity in terms that
echoed Roosevelt: "Resist everything that tends to make you soft and satisfied. . . . *Keep in motion* and do not accept the benefits of civilization too
easily. Work, fight, play for everything."[139] His books emphasized the
regenerative power of physical activity as touched upon in his star interviews and articles, and the convergence of physical regeneration with play.

Fairbanks echoes Roosevelt, Seton, and a host of other character-
builders in his explanation of why physical regeneration was necessary:

[Rome] was ruined by too much civilization. The sinews of the nation became
soft and flabby from too much contentment, too much ease and luxury, and
decay set in. I sometimes fear that we are facing a similar plight. . . . I see it [exer-

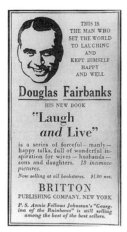

THIS IS
THE MAN WHO
SET THE WORLD
TO LAUGHING
AND
KEPT HIMSELF
HAPPY
AND WELL

Douglas Fairbanks

HIS NEW BOOK

"Laugh
and Live"

is a series of forceful — manly —
happy talks, full of wonderful inspiration for wives — husbands —
sons and daughters. *18 intimate
pictures.*
Now selling at all bookstores. $1.00 net.

BRITTON
PUBLISHING COMPANY, NEW YORK

*P. S. Annie Fellows Johnston's "Georg-
ina of the Rainbows" is still selling
among the best of the best sellers.*

Echoing the character-builders' call to be optimistic and cheerful in a manly way (Advertisement, *Photoplay*, c. 1917)

cise] as the great antidote for the softening and demoralizing effect of too much civilization.[140]

Rarely deviating from the principles of character building that underscored the Boy Scouts of America (which sometimes published his books), Fairbanks rearticulates, piecemeal, the Scout Law in its entirety. Almost every conventionalized element of character-building discourse was touched upon: Fairbanks's *Taking Stock of Ourselves* echoes the moral essence of character building. In it, he reaffirms physicality as the foundation to the whole personality: "A little energy would have saved the day, *a little 'pep'—and we laugh and live.* Laughter clings to good health as naturally as the needle clings to the magnet. It is the outward expression of an unburdened soul."[141]

Wedlock in Time (1918) is particularly attuned to giving confirmation to the middle-class goal of balancing physical vigor with the cultivation of gentility, which "pays dividends of the highest order, being, as it is a badge of character."[142] Gentility of behavior and a well-groomed appearance ensure that one may fraternize with men of quality, he suggests. While appropriate clothing can be purchased, good behavior must be practiced: "Acts of kindness are the outward manifestations of gentle breeding, a refinement of character in the highest sense of the word."[143] In true character-building fashion, he links social problems with deviations from the physical culturist construction of manliness: "All truly great men have been healthy—otherwise they would have fallen short of the mark. Prisons are filled with nervous, diseased creatures . . . [who] could have saved themselves if [they had] taken stock of themselves—*in time* . . ."[144]

Fairbanks declared of those adults who were not healthy: "What they need is play. . . . Get out into a field and throw stones. . . . Play! That dead stump over there is a bear. Zowie! See who can hit him! That's right, soak him one! *Kill him!!!*"[145] Often repeating his claim that he never used a double, fan magazines noted that Fairbanks insisted on doing his own stunts because they were, to him, "play"; in fact, they were dangerous feats often culled from his "play storehouse."[146] One fan magazine article even suggested that movie-making was so much like play to Fairbanks that perhaps he should pay the film industry for the privilege rather than vice versa.[147] Fairbanks declared: "Play, play, play . . . we are getting too serious, too methodical. Let us start a crusade for the glory of play."[148] Of course, in reality, the "crusade" had already started.

"Play: the elixir of life"[149]

Play was regarded as an issue of utmost seriousness to character-builders. As Thomas A. Russell suggested: "It is said that never before, at any time or in any country, was there a people so poverty-stricken for play . . . as those in the United States."[150] More than a decade before Fairbanks capitalized on it onscreen as well as off, social reformers and character-builders systematically promoted and conventionalized play in an age increasingly uncertain of masculinity's defining characteristics and virtues. Fears about the future of masculinity led to new theories about the regenerative role of physical activity and the importance of play as the instinct-driven "work" of boyhood and adolescence. Play was regarded as the instinctual work of childhood that recapitulated the work of primitive mankind. Parallel and convergent with the aims of character-builders were the attempts of progressive reformers to properly channel the "play instinct" among children, especially within the cities.

These "playground ideologists" believed that promoting morality in the service of the "great communal bonds of a Christian democracy" required new urban environments. The latter would allow for the careful cultivation—and monitoring—of children's play. John Lee, father of American playgrounds, suggested the moral force of such an enterprise: "Play is the intensest part of the life of a child and it is therefore in his play hours that his most abiding lessons are learned."[151] Playground reform emerged as an environmental strategy for eradicating urban vice of all types by positively influencing children. As one character-builder noted:

Children, when given a chance to play and to express the exuberance of youth in natural and wholesome sports and enterprises, are saved from the pitfalls dug in every community, deliberately by depraved men and women, and indirectly by neglect of the people to manage affairs properly.[152]

Through guided play, boys would be prepared for a manhood in which physical strenuosity now had to be artificially cultivated, organized, encouraged. Whether reformers invested in regimented games or wilderness wanderlust as the best form, play, it was agreed, would counter civilization's tendency to make boys (and men) into sedentary sissies.

Play for male adults was seen as part of the work of recapturing the vital characteristics of the national past, on an individual and collective basis. While its primary purpose was to help boys achieve proper manliness, character building also functioned to encourage those qualities of boyishness in grown men whose lives were transforming in response to threatening societal changes.[153] Underscoring character building was the attempt to develop the "man in the boy" but, at the same time, to preserve "the boy in the man." Although reformers considered play to be the work that guaranteed transformation into vigorous manhood, adult play and participation in helping boys play became evidence, paradoxically, of the boy instincts that determined manliness; ideally, a man should retain "plenty of the boy in him."

If much of middle-class reformers' emotional focus on boys was based on a nostalgic identification with them, the emphasis on liberating play in Fairbanks's films (rather than repressive middle-class realities) is illuminating. As important as his famous smile was in creating "Duggie" as a personality, it was his athleticism, accomplished with the "super-physical equipment" that was his body, that turned his romantic comedies of the 1910s into a world of play.[154] That his films were play rather than verisimilar reproductions of real life frequently was emphasized in the self-reflexive elements, including many of the title sequences or epilogues of his films. The films offer themselves not as real life but as fanciful concoctions set off by the actor's introduction of himself as their creator in his childlike pursuit of movie-making as play. In *Knickerbocker Buckaroo* he is seen in the titles literally cooking up the ingredients for his film. In the opening scene of *Manhattan Madness* Steve O'Dare (Fairbanks) leaps down from a cattle car at a railway yard and runs toward the camera. Posing for a close-up, he winks at the camera, then sets off for the heart of Manhattan to begin bragging about his adventures in Nevada. At the end of *Down to Earth* Billy and Ethel are sailing off in a boat as the other patients wave a collective good-bye. Suddenly, they begin to commiserate about their postnarrative status: "There's nothing to do but go and finish our nap—the story's over." Remarks like this throw into humorous relief the diegetic integrity of the film's story and foreground the constructed, fictional nature of the narrative.

A "Space-annihilating, Excitement-Hunting Thrill Hound" (Douglas Fairbanks in *His Majesty, the American*, 1919)

This same kind of foregrounding of make-believe occurs in the famous Loos-authored expository intertitles (enunciated from outside the story's space) that ironically comment on the events and characters.[155] Continued also in Fairbanks films of the 1910s not authored by Loos, expository intertitles function as ironic mega-commentary on the filmic narrative that sets the films apart as self-consciously fantastic, absurdly exaggerated play. In certain instances, this same effect is provided on a visual level, not only in exaggerated comic acting but also by the insertion of certain visual effects (such as an unusual masking of the screen).[156]

Beyond the frequent self-reflexive bracketing of their narratives as play, Fairbanks films of the 1910s evidence a nostalgia for perpetual early boyhood and character-building ideals of boy instinct that becomes the subject of both bemused detachment and idealization. Through a number of textual means they inscribe the middle-age Fairbanks as a figure of childish masculinity. The result is that he is figured as the cinematic embodiment of a reformist masculine ideal that may now seem curiously adolescent in consciousness. To establish the framework for the star's masquerade of childishness, Fairbanks's characters often appear without the repressive limitations of adult responsibilities, either familial or financial. In fact, their freedom is so extreme as to create a hermetically sealed world of play for the child's (the character's) lucid dream.

Asserting the physical prowess for a "big clean-up" (Douglas Fairbanks in *His Majesty, the American*)

For example, in *His Majesty, the American* (1919), Bill Brooks (Fairbanks) is described as "a Fire-eating, Speed-loving, Space-annihilating, Excitement-hunting Thrill Hound." Bill speeds through life chasing fire trucks and following his "police bell" so he can rescue women, children, and animals. To Bill's dismay, a reforming district attorney is cleaning up New York, "over, under, around and through." With New York ruined for adventure, Bill decides to sample Mexico's "brand of blood-curdling lawlessness." However, its "alluring promise of the wild and woolly" is cut short as Bill gets a tip that he will find his long-lost mother in Europe. As the intertitle notes, Bill "comes of a good family—but knows nothing about them." He has "pots of money—and doesn't know whence it comes." In Europe he runs through palaces, leaps onto balconies, chases villains from horseback, swings across rivers, and literally walks over a mob to effect "a big clean-up." He is reunited with his mother, wins the princess, and takes his rightful place as the democratic-minded Heir Apparent to the fictional Kingdom of Alaine.

Untouched by adult burdens, dilemmas, or fears, protagonists like Bill Brooks direct their energies to adventurous, dangerous journeys that confirm their vigorous, youthful manhood. Other Fairbanks protagonists are directed toward making themselves over from being gilded youth. In both cases, the adventures take place in "uncivilized" parts of the United States or in foreign lands. Films like *His Majesty, the American*, *The Americano*, and *The Lamb* offer narratives that foreground the protagonist's involvement in the politics of foreign lands as the hero of Big-Stick "democratic" interventionism. Nevertheless, the primary motivation for Fairbanks's protagonists and their excessive displays of childish energy is never very complicated or deeply inspired. Rarely is the hero motivated by adult convictions or commitments.[157] On the contrary, the impetus for the release of his boyish instincts is usually quite simple: for sheer fun, to follow a comely girl, or to find his (or others') parents.

If Fairbanks offered a pleasurable regression to acceptable remnants of a vigorous, old-fashioned boyhood, that regression was made compatible with a driven modernist ethos and the notion of the body as a machine, turbo-charged and built for the heightened, physically centered play activity that was the work of the man-to-be.[158] In character building, vigorous play became equated with a kind of industrial model of the dynamic process of becoming a man. In spite of the fact that this model, and Fairbanks's adherence to it, might be regarded as the essence of modernism, the character-builders' notion of body as machine was often made convergent with a nostalgic primitivism steeped in the values of antimodernism. Specifically, those values included the longing for intense, "authentic" experience, an escape from "the emotional constraints of bourgeois life," and faith in "simple and childlike rusticity."[159]

In this mythic reconciliation of the masculine past and future, the ideal American boy was often described by reformers in technological, industrialized terms, "a human engine of the high pressure type . . . [who] simply has to find an outlet for the suppressed energy within."[160] Fairbanks was constructed in publicity in similar terms; he went so far as to compare himself to an engine: "Long ago I found out that I was built like a flivver. I've got just two speeds. . . . A man who wants to know how old he is doesn't need a calendar; he needs to examine the engine."[161] Such pronouncements and many of his stunts (on and off screen) suggest a machine-age image of boyish masculinity in which the primitive and the technological merge.

In his films his suprahuman feats depend upon the body that functions as a modern energized machine. With techno-efficiency, "The Dynamic Dynamo" (aka "Mr. Electricity") can batter through walls or ceilings with his feet (*Wild and Woolly* and *Reggie Mixes In*), run through the countryside at breakneck speeds, or scale walls with such gravity-defying power so as to suggest the predictable pace of a geared machine. Reassuring his audience that the male body did not need to be replaced by machines but could become one, Fairbanks seemed possessed of a dynamic vitality that

"Yes, friends, it's Douglas Fairbanks. Let him perform!" (Douglas Fairbanks and Jewel Carmen in *American Aristocracy*)

acted as a countervailing force to staid traditionalism, or as one commentator suggested: "And no matter what he is doing, or where he is doing it, he is traveling like a ninety-horsepower, twenty-six-cylinder racing auto. Yes, friends, it's Douglas Fairbanks. Let him perform."[162]

Even when he is placed against the landscape of the nation's Western wilderness, Fairbanks was often depicted behind the wheel of a fast car, at the throttle of a railway locomotive, or hanging to an airplane (as in *The Lamb* or *Wild and Woolly*). When Fairbanks's adventures are played out against the backdrop of the romantic West, it is the West as upper-class tourist sight/site, the destination of monumentalism: the Grand Canyon, the Painted Desert, Canyon de Chelly, and the Hopi mesas. The "uncivilized," largely uninhabited frontier is made romantically congruent with technology, especially through the modern iconology of twentieth-century tourism. Such a paradoxical merger is explained in another context by Cecelia Tichi:

This enmeshment of images really signals a new worldview in the twentieth century. For the mix of American flora and fauna with pistons, gears, and engines indicates that the perceptual boundary between what is considered to be natural, and what technological, is disappearing. The world of the pastoral, the primitive, the edenic, the agrarian is fusing with that of machine technology.[163]

Character-builders shared in this enmeshment of apparently divergent iconographies. In fact, it was crucial to their attempt to forge a new masculinity, dynamically modern and transformative and yet naturally instinctive and nostalgically rooted in the small-town, agrarian values of America's past. Fairbanks's archetypal embodiment of this masculine merger of the nostalgic past and modernity is well illustrated in *A Modern Musketeer* (1917), in which Ned Thacker's (Fairbanks's) mother (Edythe Chapman) reads Dumas's *The Three Musketeers* while she is pregnant. Her doctor admonishes her: "You've been reading this sort of thing for six months—what do you expect your child to be like?" She expects him to be like D'Artagnan, but a cyclone hits the small Kansas town in which they live at the moment of her child's birth. As the intertitle notes, the result of "Cyclone plus D'Artagnan—Speed!!!!" Later, her husband blames her for their son's extreme antics even as Ned (Fairbanks) is glimpsed (in extreme long shot) scaling a church steeple with machine-like precision. Ned's mother boasts: "I'm glad. He will always be a boy."

Ned Thacker's mother serves as the model of how individual women, especially mothers, were encouraged to support the goals of boy reform. However, American women as a group were believed to be failing in this role and, indeed, they played a central role in the formation of character-builders' social anxieties. In fact, one of the primary fears that drove the institutionalization of boy culture into a national industry was the fear of feminization defined as the potentially emasculating influence of mothers. While it might be expected that mothers and fathers taught different ideals of manhood to their sons through different avenues of influence, most reformers believed that these forces were no longer appropriately balanced. Childishly savage and vigorous in their essence, boys (and their socialization into normative adult masculinity) were being imperiled by the overpresence of mothers and female teachers. "Petticoat rule," it was believed, had assumed dangerous ascendancy in their lives.[164]

Mothers, Mollycoddles, and Gilded Youth

> Does your mother know you're out?
> No, by thunder, no, by thunder!
> Does she know what you're about?
> No, by thunder, no, by thunder!
> —Anonymous children's rhyme, c. 1855[165]

By the 1910s the middle-class domestic realm was no longer thought to be ruled by unchallengeable patriarchs. This was the culmination of a perceived loss of male control over the domestic during the late Victorian years. As an 1895 article asserted, "Society is threatened with what has been designated a *matriarchate* or a return to the primitive state when the child was supposed to belong to the mother alone. . . . The decline of paternal authority is widespread, but nowhere has there been so great an abandonment of control as in America."[166] Conservative, character-building discourse regarded this decline as being the consequence of a specifically American phenomenon—"the rule of the mother."[167]

Reformers went so far as to suggest that middle-class domesticity was now under the control of women who had little if any understanding of those processes regarded as essential to the development of assertive, normative masculinity. In spite of the fact that there were actually more women in the workplace than ever before, the division of labor between the public workplace and the domestic, it was declared, "has been pushed to an extreme."[168] Women, it was feared, were taking control of the private sphere and ruining America's boys. With their fathers rarely at home or reluctant to interfere in the mother's domestic sphere, boys were being misraised by women who did not differentiate according to gender but treated the boy "as only a rougher and more troublesome sort of girl."[169] As well-meaning as mothers and women teachers might be, they were dangerous because they belonged "to the sex to which certain aspects of boy nature must be forever a closed book."[170]

The results of this situation were clear to boy reformers. J. Adams Puffer flatly stated: "If the boy stays at home too much, he is likely to become a sissy."[171] Too much "petticoat rule" was inevitably bad in its results because mothers tended to coddle their sons and retard their "self-reliance and . . . manliness."[172] Even worse, a mother might make "a decent and manly boy into a telltale and a coward."[173] Even if he avoided becoming a "goody-goody boy . . . too much like his sister,"[174] a middle-class boy was still in danger of being subjected to his mother's attempt to dress and groom him as if he were a girl. With his long curls and velvet outfits, Little Lord Fauntleroy became the archetypal fictional representative of normal boy instincts who becomes "an unwilling victim of mother tenderness."[175] Other boys rejected such victims of the new American matriarchy. Whether they were superficially (through clothing) or thoroughly (in behavior) sissified, these feminized boys were subjected to teasing and ostracization.

While character-builders linked women to a number of problems in the transformational process of making boys into men, women were blamed frequently for a specific type of failed adult masculinity: the "mollycoddle." The mollycoddle became the era's conventional adult figure of over-refined, feminized middle- and upper-class masculinity. The term—linked, perhaps, to the homosexual hangouts of eighteenth-century England known as "molly houses"[176]—was widely used to describe young men who had been sissified, coddled "like girls" by the women who raised them. As a result of such an upbringing, they were made overly civilized, morally passive, physically weak, and thoroughly effeminate. Character-building solutions were offered as the masculine antidote to these female-domi-nated domestic patterns of child rearing that were creating a permeable border between masculinity and femininity—the no man's land of the mol-lycoddle.

Fairbanks's first film, *The Lamb*, set the strategy for the literalness with which Fairbanks's immensely popular films of the 1910s would depict cur-rent social thinking on the problematic process of constructing masculin-ity, especially for the middle and upper classes. The film presented him in a screen role emblematic of boy reformers' post-Victorian discourse on imperiled American masculinity's relationship to mothers and overciviliza-tion. As the title character, Gerald ("The Lamb"), Fairbanks is offered in the role of an effete, upper-class Easterner, the perfect embodiment of the mollycoddle.

By the 1910s mollycoddles were familiar figures in plays, movies, liter-ature, and social commentary. Although they were thoroughly conven-tionalized and widely caricatured by the time Fairbanks came to film, they were also taken seriously and vigorously derided as a real—and danger-ous—social phenomenon. In 1914, echoing countless others, Michael Monahan told readers of *The Forum* that the United States was becoming a nation of mollycoddles:

In other words, we abandon our children in the crucial, formative years to weak-ness, hysteria, inferiority and incompetence (a few women of uncommon, that is to say, masculine, attributes do not change the rule). As a necessary result we are pro-ducing a generation of feminized men ("sissies" in the dialect of real boys) who will be fit only to escort women to poll or public office and to render such other puppy attentions as may be demanded by the Superior Sex![177]

The essence of everything character-builders scorned, mollycoddles were regarded by some boy reformers as beyond manly redemption. On behalf of the Sons of Daniel Boone, Daniel Carter Beard declared: "We want no Molly Coddles."[178]

However, most boy culture reformers seemed to assume that their efforts were aimed precisely at the boys who were in danger of becoming examples of this very type. Mollycoddles were regarded as an unfortunate and typical result of the feminization of middle- and upper-class domestic and educational environments. Unlike Ned Thacker's mother in *A Modern Musketeer*, most mothers were failing to grasp boy nature. They misunderstood the impulsive, almost fierce activity of a boyhood "devoid of passive states" and did not realize that the boy was actually a "wild creature . . . to be studied in the spirit of a naturalist."[179]

Where masculinity had once been contrasted with childishness, now a childish masculinity was contrasted with the feminine. In the late nineteenth century, a growing obsession with boys was marked strongly by an adult nostalgia for an idealized, "harum-scarum" boyhood of impulsive rebellion against domestic (i.e., feminine) authority and women's conventional morality.[180] By the 1900s, the so-called bad behavior of vigorous, mischievous boys was valorized as proof of healthy, specifically masculine "primitive instincts," or "boy instincts." Most reformers took these instincts to be the foundation of manly behavior. This valorization of instinct was, arguably, the single most important influence on the plethora of boys organizations that arose in the 1900s and 1910s. These organizations may have reflected the intensified felt need during the Progressive era of men to combat a whole range of "feminizations"—from the "rule of the mother" to women's increased presence in the public sphere to women's suffrage.

The unofficial Victorian "Cult of the Bad Boy" was elevated as a model to the point that, by 1917, one commentator wondered why there was "increasing intolerance" for a good boy "who helps his sister wash dishes instead of mixing green paint with her hair tonic."[181] One reason was obvious: by 1917 intolerance for the "goody-goody boy" had been given "scientific" validation and had become institutionalized. The cultish admiration for the bad boy who defied feminine domestic rule was extended and complicated in the 1900s and 1910s by developmental psychologists and reformers who believed that the bad boy's boyish, savage impulses had to be understood as natural and therefore properly channeled to save masculinity from mothers and women teachers who tended to repress boys' natural activities and kill the savage instincts that made them red-blooded, "embryotic" men.[182]

Promulgated by most boy reformers, these ideas were put into wildly successful practice by the British Boy Scouts, the Boy Scouts of America, and dozens of smaller organizations.[183] This view of boys' development in relation to women also contributed centrally to the era's semitolerant intolerance for the mollycoddle as a reformable species. Proper masculinity was not believed to be an immutable accident of birth, but an acquisition that could be encouraged or discouraged by familial, class, regional, and institutional influences. If trends of modern life were producing an overcivilized nation of mollycoddles (led by a mollycoddle President Wilson), then the nation had to be turned around by transforming one mollycoddle at a time into a vigorous, manly man.

After all, the term *mollycoddle* was attributed in its origin to the most famous former mollycoddle of them all, Theodore Roosevelt. As a youth, Roosevelt had been forced into semi-invalidism by various physical ailments including life-threatening asthma. In a story described in the 1910s as the most famous transition from childhood to adulthood in American history, Roosevelt had re-created himself from a sickly child of the upper class into a robust and roaringly egalitarian advocate for "the strenuous life" as an antidote to overcivilization. But even here, masculine influence was crucial: Teddy recounted in his autobiography that when he was twelve, his adored father challenged him to "make his body," but also to "take care of your morals first."[184]

Fairbanks was separated from other stars of the era by his perfect embodiment of transformative masculinity. Like T.R., his characters came to exemplify the process of becoming a manly man. Initiating this pattern, *The Lamb* plays on a whole host of established conventions concerning the development of masculinity exemplified by Roosevelt's story and theorized by boy reformers. Gerald's upper-class circumstances and class sensibility make him vulnerable to a failure of masculinity in the modern world. In *The Lamb*, Fairbanks's character, like Roosevelt, is a young member of America's social elite, a class recognized by most boy reformers as particularly vulnerable to a failure of masculinity. Upper- and middle-class boys were in much greater danger of "mollycodyism [*sic*]," of becoming sissies, than working-class boys or street urchins. These class differences were attributed to domestic (i.e., feminine) control. Lower-class urban and working-class boys had more opportunities to escape feminine influence when they took to the streets and to their gangs. But they might be in danger of delinquency because their boyish instincts and "splendid energy" had not been properly channeled away from the available bad-boy paths of mischievous pranks and lawlessness.

While the lower classes were thought to reveal the criminal potential of unbridled instinct-driven behaviors (as Fairbanks would portray imaginatively in the orientalist fantasy, *The Thief of Bagdad*, as well as *Double Trouble*), more privileged males were in danger because the moral order of femininity was too influential in their lives. Boys' sudden impulses and vital activity, the best evidence of the necessary savage instincts that created manly men, were being repressed at every opportunity by mothers and female teachers ignorant of male developmental processes.[185] It was believed that wealth and aristocratic privilege added an obstacle to the attainment of proper masculinity.

Advantageous circumstances could easily lead to physical coddling; the comforts of life provided the well-born boy were likely to make him fragile, soft, "gilded," like the passing epoch. During this period, one scholar has noted, "The men of Old Money were seen as passive and pretty, with soft, slender bodies, pettish temperaments, frivolous tastes, and squeamish sensibilities."[186] With little strenuosity demanded of them physically and even less need for self-reliance to get along in the world, such upper-class offspring were stereotypically regarded as illustrations of "the debilitating effects of a virtually inanimate life" on the male lineage of a monied class coddled by consumer comfort.[187] The dangerously passive, "feminine" elements of the upper class were believed to be extending into new middle-class lifestyles that embraced comfort and consumer goods, leisure and luxury. Thus, the rich were negative role models for an emerging middle-class identified with consumer culture.[188]

At the beginning of *The Lamb*, Gerald fits the typical mollycoddle stereotype of failed upper-class masculinity. He is passive and physically squeamish, but at least he shows promise. He is not feminized in the sense of being narrow-chested and slender-bodied, but he is physically inept, without a profession, and totally dominated by his mother. Through no fault of his own, Gerald has fallen prey to a classic mollycoddle-forming situation: not only has his effete, upper-class, Eastern upbringing made him vulnerable to a failure of masculinity but his upbringing has been left completely to his socialite mother by the circumstance of his father's death. As the introductory intertitle tells us: "This is the story of a Lovesick Lamb, whose Dad, an Old War Horse, had died. Clinching his Teeth in a Wall Street Bear, leaving The Lamb to gambol around on The Long Green."

Even though they might not be literally fatherless (as Gerald and many other Fairbanks heroes are), middle- and upper-class boys, it was believed, lived lives dangerously lacking in masculine influence. Economics and custom had reduced fathers to being minor influences in their sons' lives. No longer individual entrepreneurs, self-employed farmers, or skilled laborers working side by side with their apprentice-sons, fathers were separated from their boys by the exigencies of the new capitalism. They were "chained to business through the hours when their boys were free of the restraint of school, which is just the time when they most need wise guidance in finding a proper outlet for their accumulated energy and surcharged spirits."[189] As a result, character-builders believed, it was becoming more difficult for boys to identify with manliness.

In a comic representation of this, Gerald is allowed to gambol on his family green, but he is so physically awkward and repressed that he walks around in tiny, mincing, babylike steps. Like the archetypal mollycoddle of the middle and upper classes, Gerald has been shaped by the repressive watchfulness of women. His natural manly instincts for male companionship, physical exertion, and impulsive, playful risk-taking have been repressed. Exhibiting properly masculine instincts, Gerald attempts to tiptoe away from his society Mama's tea party, but he is too awkward to quietly navigate the stairs. He cannot even leap over a low hedge row unless he is lost in the throes of romantic bliss. When he does jump over, he looks back, unable to figure out how he managed to get to the other side. If he gets his hands dirty, he is at a loss as to what to do.

It is no wonder that Gerald's girl, Mary (Seena Owen), finds him wanting when she compares him to a burly visitor, a Westerner whom the intertitles dub: "The Cactus-Fed Goat" (Alfred Paget). In a moment of pique, Mary inspects Gerald's hands. She berates him for their shocking softness. Not long afterward, Gerald and his friends are at the beach. He sees a woman in the ocean in need of rescue. It is a situation typical of those for which Boy Scouts were trained to always "be prepared" through the acquisition of the skills of swimming and first aid. Gerald, however, is totally unprepared. Before he can do anything, the Westerner dives in for the rescue. Gerald collapses in a heap of self-loathing and fury. The intertitle notes the obvious: "The Lamb was Horrified that in the Crisis he had proved himself the Weakling."

Gerald has been unable to fulfill the Scout maxim that, for American popular culture in the 1910s, defined the ideal relationship between the male body and goodness: "Be Prepared in Body by making yourself strong and active and able to do the right thing at the right moment."[190] That American boys and men had to "Be Prepared" at all times to do the right thing was embraced by boy culture reformers as ideologically and politically necessary in a violent world. Character-builders on both sides of the Atlantic agreed that this situation was marked by deteriorating behavior in the leadership classes as well as by a newly emergent danger: the rise of non-Anglo-Saxon, "inferior" peoples.[191]

Goaded by his lack of preparedness for basic lifesaving and stung by his fiancée's earlier display of contempt, Gerald goes on a physical-training program. He has the desire to be something more than his Mama's repression and his untrained body allow him to be. To the horror of his watchful mother, he boxes and takes jujitsu lessons—two of Teddy Roosevelt's strenuous interests. These manly activities are signs that, however awkwardly, Gerald is discovering the cult of the body's decidedly unleisurely concept of leisure for middle-class men.

An emphasis on physical prowess in leisure sports and on the body as an instrument of action-oriented masculinity served as the middle-class means of regenerating and revalidating male identity in the face of the perceived feminization of American culture. Consumer luxury was not available to all, but it was believed that leisure time was. To avoid feminine softness and passivity, this leisure had to be transformed into the play of character building through physical exercise and demanding excursions, preferably into the woods or, better yet, in what was left of the Western wilderness. Gerald must leave his mother's domain. Gamboling on the green or even boxing in his bedroom is not enough to make a man of him.

Although Gerald starts the physical process of becoming a man, the graceful, athletic male body that was the primary icon of the cult of the body's validation of masculinity has yet to be achieved by the Lamb when he receives a telegram. He is invited to join the "Cactus-Fed Goat" and the vacation party of Mary's family in Arizona. As oblivious to the demands of geography as he has formerly been to those of proper masculinity, Gerald gets "all Dolled up in Alpine Togs," to follow Mary to the "Bad Lands." But the Great American Desert is not the Alps. Although he does not know it, the telegram has given Gerald the opportunity to make the era's classic journey of masculine regeneration.

Reformers generally believed that middle- and upper-class masculinity, especially, had to be returned to its more primitive, savage, instinctual origins through contact with the great out-of-doors. Gerald is like the "sissy boy" described by George Walter Fiske. Such a boy, who "failed to recapitulate the history of the race," needed merely "a good stiff dose of out-of-doors games."[192] Manly instincts were rooted in physicality, which was primarily served by physical exertion in an outdoor setting. The great outdoors was idealized as the natural habitat of boys and the best site for the development of manly self-reliance: it was where the moral strength of an adult individuality might be made compatible with a vision of communally minded, hardy male citizenship. Wilderness adventure best served the goal of the boy's having to learn to fend for himself, but also to help others.

Reformers and organizations such as the Boy Scouts of America put special emphasis on wilderness competence and the practical moral training to be derived from woodcraft, first aid, and survival skills. The landscape of the outdoor world required "training in resourcefulness and gumption which he [the city boy] can hardly get elsewhere. . . . The boy needs diamond and gymnasium and running track, but quite as much he needs mountain and lake and river and forests."[193] James Franklin Page suggested that it was "instinctive" for a youth to "get to the woods . . . whence his ancestors for ages untold procured a livelihood. . . . The tendency has been transmitted from them across the brief chasm of civilization to him."[194]

Masculine transformation was expected by reformers who advocated a regime of wilderness adventure. This was thought to be achievable even within the limited context of the new phenomenon of middle-class summer camps if, of course, the latter were primitive enough.[195] How was a taste of primitive hardship to be recaptured for adults? Many reformers implied that the best way to effect a recapitulation of "the history of the race" for those who were no longer children was through a literal return to the wilderness as an unsafe place. With the "official" closing of the frontier in the 1890s, the sense of a new era of uncertain promise motivated a search for the primitive as an antiurban sanctuary for the development of manliness. As Stewart Edward White declared in 1903: "The man in the woods matches himself against the forces of nature . . . [in] a measuring of strength, a proving of his essential pluck and resourcefulness and manhood, an assurance of man's highest potency, the ability to endure and to take care of himself."[196] Into the 1910s the wilderness continued to be regarded as the site for a unique validation of masculinity mythically compatible with traditional values linked to America's frontier experience.

Public fascination with forays into the wilderness as a place for forging manhood was made obvious through the media-driven adventures of Joseph Knowles. With plenty of press present to record the event, Knowles entered the woods of Maine in August 1913, buck naked, with neither matches nor knife. He came out in October in a bear skin to greet his mother and declare the need for all Americans, especially children, to "be toughened up." To prove his own toughening up, his attending physician declared him to have become the equal of strongman Eugen Sandow. Echoing character-builders and anticipating Fairbanks's extratextual pronouncements, Knowles explained his reasons for the self-described "stunt" in his best-selling book, *Alone in the Wilderness*: "I believed there was too much artificial life . . . in the cities. I found myself comparing our present mode of living with the wild rugged life of the great outdoors. Then, all of a sudden, I wondered if the man of the present day could leave all his luxury behind him and go back into the wilderness and live on what nature intended him to have."[197]

What was left of America's wilderness, especially in the West, was exalted in public discourse as the best place for the development of manhood. Even in its modern form, as tourist destination and temporary campground, it could be a place for rebuilding the values of the individual since it was through the wilderness that the original American values were believed to have been forged.[198] Thus, character-builders saw the West in terms of its originary appeal as the place of uncivilization that demanded the skills and qualities they regarded as an antidote to overcivilization or coddling.

As Roderick Nash has suggested, the "wilderness cult" enthusiastically promoted in the public discourse by urbane Easterners such as Roosevelt, artist-journalist Frederic Remington, and novelist Owen Wister was part of the multifaceted conceptualization of the Western wilderness as an upper-class tourist destination, a site of conservationist contemplation, as well as a site for manly adventure.[199] In this context, it is not surprising that in *The Lamb*, what is left of the frontier circa 1915 still is wild enough to provide Gerald with a regenerating encounter with wilderness adventure.

"Fleeced" and knocked senseless by stereotypical old-style Hollywood "Indians" selling curios, Gerald is left behind by the train and falls in amongst "Crooks from the East." He is then kidnapped by rebellious Yaqui Indians. However, by the end of the film, the innate strength of Gerald's pioneer stock and his own efforts have helped him overcome his beginnings as a laughable mollycoddle. Left helpless in the desert, Gerald learns to survive without fear, even if, as the intertitle tells us, he still keeps his "Regular Hours" as he gets up from the desert floor at noon.

Gerald discovers the roots of the "masculine primitive" on which to found a truly manly, uniquely American identity.[200] Left to his own devices, without money or companionship, he learns the resources of his own body. By the end of the film, he bounds across the Arizona landscape by horse, by car, and via his own athletic propulsion. Once incapable of resisting his society Mama's domestic control, he now wards off a band of Yaqui warriors with a Gatling gun. This transformation occurs because, as the intertitles inform us: "Blood will speak—though society drowns the conversation." Wounded, but triumphant, Gerald cannot quite manage to extricate his girl from danger, but at least they are alive and well when the U.S. cavalry arrives. In a vestige of childishly exuberant gentility, our hero enthusiastically bestows a thankful kiss on the cheek of the officer in charge.

In *The Lamb* the Western wilderness is still a free place. Character-builders believed man's natural primitive urges could find expression there, and Americans (if of the proper ethnic heritage) could go there to confirm and renew their instinctual, "racial" heritage.[201] While some social theorists believed that each individual recapitulated the frontier struggle in his own way, the issue of the frontier became central in the postfrontier effort to revalidate masculinity in physical terms.

This is the mythic, character-building West valorized by Roosevelt and painted by Remington. Although its dangers may be degraded (drunken Indians often serve as the foil in Fairbanks's films), the fantasy frontier still serves nicely as a testing ground for American manhood's physical and spiritual mettle. In this West, even a mollycoddle could attain a manhood in which natural primitive urges found expression because such experience recapitulated the past. A distinctively American masculine character was inescapably linked to the testing ground of the internal empire. However, in keeping with character-builders' view of a primitivism balanced with gentility, the West (or the wilderness) was not the place to become uncivilized but rather self-reliant, strong, and manly. If its way of life was obsolete, the West was not obsolete in its importance to the character of the nation, even if it were thought of as nothing more complex than a wide open space well-suited for a chase. As one commentator suggested, "The possession of no other qualities by a nation can atone for the lack of that vigorous manliness which the chase cultivates."[202]

This notion of the West fed off the belief that the strenuous life was a cure for the nation's character problems. It is this West, conceptualized by Easterners, that is the direct inspiration for a number of childish upper-class Fairbanksian heroes. Films like *Wild and Woolly*, *Manhattan Madness*, and *Knickerbocker Buckaroo* play on and with the legacy created by the convergence of character building and the wilderness cult in the attempt to standardize American masculine norms around a recovery of the masculine primitive.

"The wildest health and pleasure grounds"[203]

Not only was the contrived Rooseveltian solution of making a man in the "wilderness" compatible with the twentieth-century American worldview of a utopian merger of technology and the pastoral, it was compatible also with the dominant view of the American male's essential nature. In childhood and extended adolescence, this ideal man was still subject to savage impulses, to the instincts with which male children were born as little men-to-be.[204] Outdoor activities, even if accomplished while on primitive vacations, served as the surrogate frontier experience that many Americans felt was the nation's unique claim to forging manhood out of savage impulses and an all-male refuge from refinement.

A trip to the American West rather than the classic Grand Tour of Europe became part of a trend among urbane Easterners in the late nineteenth and early twentieth centuries. In the wake of threatening trends in immigration, America's private destiny was increasingly regarded as distinct from an Old World equated with effeminacy and overcivilization. Often quoted, George S. Evans "The Wilderness" in *Overland Monthly* (1904) still stands as a classic statement: "Dull business routine, the fierce passions of the market place, the perils of envious cities become but a memory. . . . And now you have become like your environment. . . . The wilderness will take hold of you. It will give you good red blood; it will turn you from a weakling into a man."[205]

Fairbanks's film narratives are played out against the backdrop of those sites most often associated with the extremes of masculine imperilment or redemption: the comfortable Eastern vacation haunts of the Old and nouveau riche and the regenerative respite of the Wild West. Fairbanks's films follow this pattern to suggest that the hero needs to find a radically different environment (native or foreign) to release his true heroic, manly, athletic self rather than finding an answer within an established urban (and therefore overcivilized and repressive) American setting. Thus, in *The Lamb* Gerald's salvation as a man results from his own desire to be a manly, prepared man as well as from his regenerative experience in the West.

In keeping with this solution, Fairbanks's heroes such as Gerald go from civilization, not into a pioneer confrontation with pure savagery, but into a tourist playground that requires a spontaneous interweaving of primitive skills with civilized gentility. Following in the famous footsteps of Roosevelt, Remington, and Owen Wister, Fairbanks's heroes are exaggerated, even obnoxious in their admiration for all things Western, but they are never unmanly. In *Manhattan Madness* (1916) the aptly named hero,

Tales of masculine daring and opprobriums for Eastern softness: Douglas Fairbanks in *Manhattan Madness* (1916)

Steve O'Dare (Fairbanks), returns to civilization after a regenerating encounter with the West. Steve regales his Manhattan men's club with tales of masculine daring and opprobriums for Eastern softness, also a habit of Frederic Remington's.[206] He starts arguments and declares: "New York is all wrong, superficial, un-American, overcrowded. I can't breathe—can't sleep—can't eat." In spite of his conviviality with his old college chums, his dismissal of the East is so irritating that his friends finally decide to teach him a lesson by enticing him into a fake adventure involving a foreign count and a damsel in distress. At the end of *Manhattan Madness*, O'Dare, whose excessive love of the West has made him the butt of his friends' elaborate hoax, turns the tables (and his guns) on them. He holds them hostage then employs his range hands to "cover him" while he elopes with the girl on his steed.

In *Wild and Woolly* (1917) the excesses of Fairbanks's character also provoke amused reactions that suggest the familiarity of the stereotype of the westernized Easterner. The film begins with a visual thumbnail sketch contrasting the Old West and the modern one, then shifts to the Manhattan mansion of a millionaire railroad tycoon. The tycoon's son, Jeff

A Boy Scout instead of a true buckaroo: Douglas Fairbanks in *Wild and Woolly* (1917)

Hillington (Fairbanks), has his own ideas of fun. He, like Roosevelt and Seton, has been stricken with "Western fever." His "fever" drives him, as the confined son of the privileged urban upper class, to emulate the more primitive life of cowboys, but he ends up looking more like a Boy Scout than a true buckaroo. In fact, the first shot of the boyish Jeff shows him sitting cross-legged in front of his tent in what might be taken to be an outdoors setting. Only when the camera pulls back is it fully revealed that Jeff has transformed his bedroom in his father's mansion into the indoor equivalent of a Boy Scout camp where he builds fires and hangs out in a teepee.

Jeff's homelife in Manhattan bears an uncanny resemblance to Puffer's description of how the instinct-driven boy with the "migratory impulse" compensates when in civilized confinement:

The son of a good home is usually made too comfortable, and unconsciously he feels the need of some more invigorating substitute for warm room and soft bed. When, therefore, nothing better offers itself, it often does a boy good to sleep out in his own back yard, with a dismantled revolver in his belt, and a lasso hung beside him on the clothes pole. He will probably not get much sleep, and he may catch cold; but the experience will be a powerful stimulus to his imagination, and at the same time will help, at small risk, to gratify a wholesome instinct.[207]

In spite of his confinement, Jeff also tries to hone other wilderness skills, including bronco riding, which he practices on sawhorse-mounted saddles as well as on the aging butler. To his dissatisfaction as a manly "boy" of normal boy instincts, Jeff knows the cowboy life only through repre-

The need for some more invigorating environment: Douglas Fairbanks in *Wild and Woolly*

sentations: through photographs, sculpture, and, of course, prints of Remington's paintings. He stares at one of the latter and imagines himself as the painting's fearless broncobuster. Like an overly imaginative film spectator, he identifies so strongly that he is able to literally insert himself into the painting, which becomes animated as if it were a movie with him in it. After riding the butler around the house, his emulation of cowboys continues in his wild rides on horseback through Central Park. These cause him to be dismissed as a "nut" by city dwellers. Even his feminine ideal is derived from western movies. We see him exit the movie theater and admire the display of the western serial's horseback-riding heroine: "That's the kind of mate I'm going to have!" he enthuses.

Jeff's frustrated father at last gives in, hoping that his son, "the Comanche Indian," will be cured of his Western fever by an encounter with the real thing. He sends him on a business assignment to Bitter Creek, Arizona, to attend to the matter of extending a rail line to a promising mine. The townspeople, forewarned of Jeff's fanatical love for the West of the 1880s, remake themselves and their town into a kind of western movie set to give the unsuspecting young man what he wants. However, currying the little capitalist's favor proves dangerous play. Like a boy of pure savage instincts, Jeff is ready to shoot at almost anyone. The town fathers covertly confiscate his live ammunition and send him off on long

Showing the value of boyish instincts as appropriately heroic: Douglas Fairbanks in *Wild and Woolly*

walks with Nell (Eileen Percy), the unsophisticated prairie flower who is really the city accountant's rather sophisticated daughter. But, of course, their plans go awry, a real crisis is instigated by a crooked Indian agent, and the situation demands Jeff's carefully cultivated frontier skills.

Typical Fairbanks vehicles from this era such as *Wild and Woolly* and *Manhattan Madness* are revelatory of the paradoxical fact that Fairbanks's films often self-reflexively kid the very movie (and character-building) ideal of masculinity that they ultimately endorse and that Fairbanks earnestly promulgated in the extratextual construction of his star personality. Certainly, the childishness of his characters was not lost on reviewers. The *New York Times* suggested in its review of *Wild and Woolly*: "The depiction of a young man still carried away with dime novel ideas must be over-looked. . . . Then it is redeemed by the farce developing into the real thing . . . the young easterner becomes a genuine hero."[208] One could argue that some of the most prominent men in America were carried away by dime novel ideas. *Wild and Woolly* pokes fun at the childish excesses of Rooseveltian primitivism and its privileged model of masculinity at the same time it endorses this model. Boyish instincts and appropriately heroic action were still required of men, at least within a fantastic West created by the film as well as by the citizens of Bitter Creek.

The excesses of Fairbanks's heroes appeared to have generated a dual-ity of response to the overly familiar stereotype of the Easterner, enamored with the West. His adventures, though recognized as absurd in the extreme, still spoke to the era's antimodernist yearning for intensified experience and masculine regeneration.[209] As *Variety*'s reviewer noted of the film:

You've got to laugh when the hero rides into the midst of a bunch of drunken Indians, swings the girl on the back of his horse and makes a getaway without being shot. . . . It is all so utterly absurd that you must laugh in spite of yourself. And then, having done so . . . [you] come to the realization that you "fell for it."[210]

That Fairbanks's image in its formative years participated in a degree of satirization of a much-lauded model of masculinity while at the same time he became an exemplar in the on- and off-screen attempt to sustain it speaks to the complexity of the construction and reception of the dominant model of masculinity during the earliest era of Hollywood's feature filmmaking.

While in *The Lamb* Gerald is a weakling who is toughened up through his isolating wilderness experience, Jeff has the spirit of the strenuous life. However, he has to enter the West to have it properly channeled. This follows the pattern established by people such as Roosevelt, Remington, and Owen Wister. In the East, all Jeff can do is ineffectually combat the urban/bureaucratic feminization of masculinity which he recognizes around him in the city, especially in the mollycoddled office clerk he casually tortures. The clerk bears all the stereotyped physical characteristics of the feminized male (thin, pale, bespectacled). Similarly, in *Manhattan Madness* Steve O'Dare offhandedly ridicules a similar type, an "insect" (thin, pinkie-ringed, monocled) who drinks a frozen cocktail unsuitable for a man (it is topped by an umbrella!).

In their treks West, Easterners like Jeff and Gerald, Roosevelt and Remington, went in search not of the roots of their European culture but for the regenerative roots of their masculine American-ness conceived in primitive terms. By way of contrast, it had long been suggested by American commentators that the Grand Tour of the idle rich would inevitably end in Europeanization and, therefore, feminization. Washington Irving had already suggested in 1835: "We send our youth abroad to grow luxurious and effeminate in Europe. . . . It appears to me that a previous tour of the prairies would be more likely to produce that . . . simplicity and self-dependence most in union with our political institutions."[211]

The contrast between these two destinations and their effect on masculinity is demonstrated in Fairbanks's *The Mollycoddle* (1920). Reiterating the era's conflation of civilization and femininity, *The Mollycoddle* defines its unlikely hero as "a man surrounded by supercivilization." The literal mother bemoaned in character-building discourse is replaced by a familiar substitute: Europe as the overcivilizing influence. The result is Richard Marshall V (Fairbanks), who has lost touch with the pioneer instincts of his ancestors, those American heroes of the past who were "leather-necked shaggutted buckaroos . . . such as Remington knew." "What forefathers!" the intertitles proclaim as the film shows his grandfather fighting off Indians.

Orphaned at age four in England, Marshall had an European upbringing that made him into a morning-coated, monocled mollycoddle. He is so effete and, therefore, un-American that he is mistaken for an Englishman by vacationing Americans in Monte Carlo. The group of youthful tourists made up of middle-class, melting-pot Americans (characters named Patrick O'Flannigan, Ole Olsen, and Samuel Levinski) are so shocked by the revelation of his nationality that they decide to lead Richard back to "the fold" of America: "That fellow is contrary to the Constitution of the United States. Something ought to be done about it!" So inspired, they serve as his boys' gang to help him regain a robust masculinity. Virginia Hale (Ruth Renick), a young woman touring with an older female chaperon, is sympathetic: "I like him. I think he has the makings of a man," she says to Mrs. Warren (Adele Farrington), who throws up her hands in disgust and flaps her wrists back down in imitation of him as she sputters: "Bah! That mollycoddle!"

The All-American gang's plans for their new friend are sidetracked when Richard is shanghaied by German spies. They wait to rescue him because they realize that "Work won't hurt him—it will help make a man of him." Richard emerges from the heat, the roll and the filth of the stokehole, "a different man," outfitted in the archetypal Fairbanksian (and Rooseveltian) tweeds. These have been provided by pooling the gang's extra clothing: "Suit by O'Flannigan—Cap by Olsen—Shoes by Levinski."

But the ship is still populated by German smugglers/spies, and Richard's amateur counterspying lands him in chains and then gets him tossed overboard. He is rescued again and is off to Arizona, the convenient destination of both smugglers and vacationers. It is also his birthplace, the site where generations of ancestral Richard Marshalls were "found in the vanguard of civilization—God-fearing, hell-bustin', fighting adventurers and two-fisted pioneers." On the rim of the Painted Desert, Richard Marshall V emerges from the Holbrook Mercantile Company in cowboy clothes, with his great-grandfather's medal for bravery pinned to his chest. An intertitle declares: "A western breeze, born on the snow-capped tips of the Apache range . . . swept straight to the heart of young Marshall—and the blood of his forefathers seemed to respond."

The film promotes the wilderness cult as a regenerative release of manliness linked to the genetic, race-specific compendium of qualities Roosevelt and Remington associated with Anglo-Saxon/American adventure. In Richard's regeneration of instinct through environment, he runs around disguised as a Hopi, rescues his friends from capture, leaps through roofs, and rolls down mountains. As Marshall slides down from a ridge on his belly in the process of rescuing his friends, an intertitle echoes character-building discourse: "Primitive cunning, born of instinct, now guides his every move." In the end Marshall rescues Virginia (who, it turns out, is really a U.S. government agent!), foils the spies, and even has time to check out the aches and pains he has acquired with his new physical ferocity. The film ends with Richard and Virginia sitting on a ledge in front of a beautiful sunset. With manly, cowboy ease, he shows her how to roll a cigarette with one hand, but his masculine prowess is counterpointed by the humorous visual effect of the innumerable bandages dotting his neck and face.

"I'm So Gosh Darn Tuft"[212]

Within an era of social insecurity and the desire of many for broad social reform, it is not surprising that the model for developing manliness displayed in *The Mollycoddle* and numerous other Fairbanks films was heavy with cultural nostalgia for a mythologized version of rural boys' upbringing in the nineteenth-century and for the past of the nation. No surprise, too, that many character-builders, to different degrees, clung to the values of all-male society and to primitive, savage boys' activities (hunting, warring, etc.) that foregrounded stamina and bodily strength.

Coming long after Roosevelt's generation began to call for the valorization of manliness revived by the strenuous life, Fairbanks's films often offered appealing fantasy versions of the transformative power of the West as the last romantic place in America. As a figurative "son of Roosevelt," Fairbanks acknowledged the farcical excesses in the familiar stereotype of the westernized Easterner. Nevertheless, the textual inscription of Fairbanks's vigorous childishness and athletic antics was perfectly convergent with the valorization of a regenerating "Wilderness cult." In spite of their satirical edge, Fairbanks's films inevitably reaffirm the value of the ideal, character-building masculine type: the genteel yet primitive manly man who emerges from a process of transformation. Also, through his extratextual pronouncements, Fairbanks reaffirmed character-building's manly nostalgia for wilderness adventure and the masculine primitive.[213] He also reaffirmed moral strength defined as preparedness for physical action. Echoing Roosevelt's diatribes against "slothful ease," "flabbiness," and "the unhealthy softening and relaxation of fibre that tends to accompany civilization,"[214] Fairbanks declared that the way civilization had been won was "by battling with the forces of nature. . . . The way to lose this civilization is by complacently enjoying it, by sitting in soft chairs and having things brought to us."[215]

But how does a movie star living in Hollywood battle "with the forces of nature?" Drawing from the discourse associated with character building, Fairbanks, the star, was publicly constructed as an ideal model of the modern man who cultivated wilderness adventure and the quality of wanderlust continually attributed by boy reformers to boy instinct.[216] The boy reform position is offered by J. Adams Puffer:

There is probably no more characteristic difference between boyhood and middle age than the strange *wanderlust* of youth. . . . The mere sight of the horizon is a challenge; and the boy longs to repeat the ancestral experience. . . . As the migratory impulse is far too deepseated and powerful to be altogether restrained, the only method is to indulge it under supervision and education.[217]

In a fan magazine interview of 1917, Fairbanks lays claim to boyishness by declaring that movies "satisfy my wanderlust. The element of adventure is always present. Location work takes you out in the desert and the mountains." He shudders at the thought of "stuffy theaters" and the stage's "routine, its artificiality and its unhealthy back-stage atmosphere."[218] In another article Fairbanks is presented as the essential, instinctual boy: "Three years ago, I got the *wanderlust* so bad that I couldn't stand it any longer, so I just 'beat it.' I took a steamer to Cuba and walked across the island. . . . Later, I walked all by myself across Yucatan." He returns to the United States to take a pack mule across the Great Divide to get "right close to nature" for "an experience that gives a man a mental and moral housecleaning."[219] In *Youth Points the Way* Fairbanks describes a western adventure "in which we almost froze to death," but declares of an experience any reasonable person might regard as extreme, "it was worth it, for we had lost our stale outlook on life and received a fresh point of view." He bemoans the effect of cities and declares in a phrase that echoes wilderness "nuts": "Give me wide spaces out west where you can breathe deep and think your own thoughts."[220] Like a Scout home from jamboree, he relates a more modest adventure, a hunting trip to California: "It's all fun, all adventure, all high spirits—a natural reaction and relief at breaking away from the cramping effect of the cities, of too much conventionality and too much civilization."[221] Even movie-making becomes a strenuous adventure which compels reviewers to wonder if "Doug" will exit the profession alive.[222]

Contrary to the ease with which Fairbanks's extratextual pronouncements suggest the availability of wilderness adventure to all, regardless of class, popular theories of masculine rejuvenation were at a relative loss on how to combat the "dull business routine" and "the perils of envious cities" and sustain old values of male individualism and self-assertion through a return to the wilderness.[223] In this respect Fairbanks aligns himself with Roosevelt, who, it was sometimes suggested, talked as if he thought every working man was within forty-eight hours of a wilderness or every businessman could afford to go on safari. But of course, in Fairbanks's films, his upper-class heroes usually can.[224]

In his films, as in his pronouncements, Fairbanks's boyish instincts are not bound by normal middle-class experience. To sustain the fantasy of male freedom and boyish wanderlust satisfied at a whim, his films avoid getting too close to middle-class anxieties and male frustrations linked to work and other class-specific motivating forces behind boy reformers' anxious quest to save American masculinity. With rare exceptions, Fairbanks's characters are never burdened by the exigencies of changing middle-class, adult life. Instead, his films of the 1910s most often centralize characters, like Gerald in *The Lamb*, Cassius Clay in *American Aristocracy*, and Sunny Wiggins in *The Habit of Happiness*, who are gilded youth, isolated by economics or class from the limiting middle-class economic realities and alienating work that provoked much masculine anxiety. Gerald is typical of the Fairbanks patrician protagonists who are from a moneyed background. No matter what is left of the family fortune, most Fairbanks heroes are idlers without direction or dilettantes with eccentric or inconsequential professions that increase their impression of childishness. In *American Aristocracy* Cassius Clay (Fairbanks) is a robust upper-class "bug-hunter" (i.e., entomologist). Tended by his valet, he camps out in a tent to follow the local butterflies until his interest shifts to a nouveau riche society girl who is frequenting a nearby resort hotel. Because his family "never went into trade," Cassius Clay is rejected as an "upstart" by the nouveau riche "aristocracy." Like a child who barely can manage to hold still to be groomed, Cassius is dressed as he suspends himself from the tent pole. He

A childish, upper-crust bug-hunter: Douglas Fairbanks as Cassius Clay in *American Aristocracy*

wraps his legs around his black valet whom he then kisses on the forehead and slaps on the back in childish appreciation.

Fairbanks emphasized boyish individual heroism in his films, his extra-textual publicity, and, especially, in his character-building books. But this validation of boyishly heroic masculinity was not that of a radical, prein-dustrialized masculine primitive centered solely on the body's physical instrumentality as driven by instinct and individualism. While he did retain characteristics of the old-style, physically based regenerative hero associated with the frontier ethos of individualism in the service of survival, he was also easily identified with the new organization man (an approach he used with notable success in his books). This modern man of business was genial and sociable, without the temperamental vagaries (of a T.R.), but possessed of constant, predictable energy, the eagerness and optimism that were required of modern corporatized Americans. Organizations like the Boy Scouts of America maintained a certain ambivalence in the relation-ship between individuality and community. So did Fairbanks, who pro-mulgated a small boy's notion of individual heroism in his films at the same time he preached, extratextually, a model of masculinity explicitly compat-ible with modern America's big-business values and middle-class cultural hegemony. This is in keeping with the era's dominant theories of male development. In their primitivist valorization of instinct and the mytholo-

gized rural freedom of the past, most character-building notions were ideologically antimodernist in spirit, but they generally sought to accommodate men to the status quo (i.e., the prevailing social system).[225]

In this context, there is some interest in the fact that the end of *Wild and
Woolly* offers Jeff a fantasy escape from the East, from work, and from his
father. The intertitles pose a dilemma to be solved: "For Nell likes The East.
Jeff likes the West. So where are the twain to meet?" The solution is a fabulous mansion with all the comforts set out on the range. Bewigged foot-
men open the doors for Jeff and Nell to greet the cowboys gathered to cel-
ebrate the couple's marriage with six-shooters and wild whoops. In creating a utopian reconciliation of East and West, primitive and sophisticated,
male and female, the film is characteristic of the many Fairbanks films that
leave their hero outside of restricting urban environs and middle-class adult
norms. It is as if the films do not trust that their heroes' boyish instincts can
continue to exist in modern American industrial society. Some Fairbanks
heroes of the 1910s end up as rulers of foreign lands, as in *His Majesty, the
American*. Finally, in the 1920s the star would beat a complete retreat to a
fictional past. As the new decade got off to a roaring start, recapturing the
romance of America's lost boyhood seemed to require more extreme measures than the reconciliation of modernity and "Western fever."

"When men were men"

Beginning with *The Mark of Zorro* (1920) and throughout the 1920s,
Fairbanks became identified with the historically based costume-adventure
movie otherwise known as swashbucklers and, to a lesser extent, with fantasy.[226] His shift to costume films was certainly not an unprecedented move
in Hollywood's generic field, and the profit-for-the-performers mechanism
of United Artists would provide the means through which Fairbanks would
shift from being a star of athletic, satirically minded comedies to the star of
epic-scaled costume productions. His were among the era's numerable costume epics, an extremely successful cycle of films now largely forgotten or
regarded as an "aberration."[227] In cost and opulence, Fairbanks's productions rivaled those of D. W. Griffith as well as those German costume productions making their way to the shores of America to impress audiences.[228]
Fairbanks's new films may have been noticeably "bigger," but what did this
shift mean to his depiction of masculinity?

Fairbanks had already taken a significant step in preparing his audience
for a change with his cameo appearance as D'Artagnan in 1917 in *A*

Masquerading as a gallant: "It's me!" (Douglas Fairbanks in *A Modern Musketeer*, 1917)

Modern Musketeer. The film begins with the question: "Do you remember D'Artagnan of France? Can you recall the thrills you got from the adventures of that famous swash-buckling gallant of three centuries ago?" In costume, Fairbanks comes galloping up on a horse. He dismounts, looks straight into the camera, smiles mischievously, and pulls impishly on his long, curled hair and the insouciant little mustache that would become his visual trademark of the 1920s. He winks at the camera and appears to mouth the words: "It's me!"

"It's me," indeed. In the 1920s the scale and settings of his films might have changed, but many of Fairbanks's lavishly produced star vehicles were drawn directly either from boy's literature or adventure romance. The former had become a recognized genre in the late nineteenth century; the latter included the work of writers (such as Robert Louis Stevenson and Alexandre Dumas) popular with boys and adolescents as well as the recycled, "authorless" stories identified as boys' favorites in the early 1900s, such as Robin Hood and the Arabian Nights.[229] It seems of little coincidence that Fairbanks assumes roles in the 1920s, such as Robin Hood, that were discussed by reformers as among the most appropriate, manly ideals for boys. More than one boy reformer thought of using Robin Hood as the chivalric centerpiece for his organization. Seton, recounting how he had looked for "an ideal figure" around which to center a boys' club, recalled, "I needed an ideal outdoor man who was heroic, clean, manly, brave, picturesque, master of woodcraft and scouting, and already well known. At first my thought turned to Robin Hood."[230] Just as Fairbanks's mustache was a dashing and exclusively adult addition to a face that, nev-

Revulsion in the face of effeminacy: Douglas Fairbanks and Marguerite De La Motte in *The Mark of Zorro* (1920)

ertheless, remained preternaturally boyish, Fairbanks's films of the 1920s have the ornate, aesthetic look of adult fare; at heart, however, they are still rooted in notions of regressive masculinity attached to childish adventure and the romance of legendary heroes. Their ideals of masculinity are still those of character-building discourse and boy's literature.

With *The Mark of Zorro* (1920) as the prototype, Fairbanks's costume films often present the star in a vehicle that continues to exploit the figure of the mollycoddle. Anticipating action-hero comics of the 1930s like *Superman*, Fairbanks's character pretends to be a sissy boy or effeminized male.[231] In *The Mark of Zorro* he is Don Diego Vega, who physically resembles Florian in *Double Trouble*. In his masculinity Don Diego is marked as deviant by his indolence, his prissy manners, and his interest in fabrics, clothes, and parlor games. Although his family wants him to marry Lolita (Marguerite De La Motte), his sexual disinterest in her is matched only by her revulsion in the face of his overwhelming effeminacy. However, Don Diego has assumed such an unmanly guise for political purposes. To liberate the local peasants from oppressive rulers, he must mask

The romance of virile, manly masculinity: Douglas Fairbanks and Marguerite De La Motte in *The Mark of Zorro*

his true manly self given expression as "Zorro," who is vigorously heroic and romantically virile.

The Mark of Zorro broke attendance records in New York City. Some suggested it was not because it was a completely different entry in Fairbanks's repertoire but because it cleverly exploited what Fairbanks had always done. One reviewer noted: "The new Fairbanks picture, by the way, is typical of his recent work. Its story is negligible but it has a series of the most amazing stunts. . . . Despite the fact that it is a 'costume play' . . . it is strictly up to date."[232] Another remarked on the film's savvy combination of difference and sameness: "Many exhibitors throughout the country say that this is unquestionably Fairbanks's greatest attraction because it is full of real activities and typical Fairbanks stunts, and a riot of fun and thrills, something entirely different from anything Doug has ever done before, jammed full of the thrills that 'Doug' is made of, with the thrills running neck and neck even before the terrific climax making it entertainment extra-ordinary."[233]

When not pretending to be a "puny youth,"[234] Fairbanks's otherwise vigorous heroes of the 1920s (such as Zorro—and Don Q, son of Zorro) spend their time liberating individual women or entire nations (or both) from villains. The childishness of his heroes was asserted aggressively in the 1910s. While that quality is somewhat compromised in the 1920s by Fairbanks's more mature physicality, it was still inscribed textually in the protagonist's familial relationships. In the 1910s, a Fairbanks hero was likely to be fatherless or in rebellion against his father's lifestyle. His protagonists often struggled to become men through an assertion of primitive boyishness or through their proving that masculine heroism could be useful in the modern world. In the 1920s, Fairbanks would still be playing sons in films like *The Mark of Zorro, Don Q, Son of Zorro* (1925), and *The Black Pirate* (1926). However, these sons/heroes often operate within a revenge mode. At times, they use masquerades of mollycoddlism to prove their manhood to their fathers, whether the latter are alive, dead, or surrogate. As a consequence, these films retain a character-building emphasis on the transformative possibilities of masculine identity, especially within the context of a need for paternal approval.[235] Thus, it is logical that, at the end of *Robin Hood*, after he has saved the kingdom, Robin (Fairbanks) lays his head against the manly chest of King Richard in what would appear to be as emotionally a fulsome moment as when Robin takes Maid Marian in a conjugal embrace.

Certainly, there are complex cultural, box-office, and personal reasons for Fairbanks's shift to these kind of films, but the shift should not be attributed simply to a decline in the popularity of comic-romantic films, especially those with western settings. It should be remembered that, in many respects, Tom Mix continued to succeed in the twenties in acrobatic adventure films that were very much in the vein of Fairbanks's light-hearted, romantic-comic westerns of the 1910s. Perhaps Fairbanks's contemporary roles of the wartime and immediate postwar years no longer held any interest for the artistically ambitious star.

In any case, the masquerade of the costume film allowed him to provide the same basic generic formula of stunts, comedy, and romance that he had used in the 1910s, but this time within an epic, prestige picture format— which one disgruntled small-town exhibitor, responding to *The Black Pirate*, called "artistic junk."[236] Such a strategy of presentation may have been a more effective vehicle for giving the bourgeois the "mental holiday" that Jackson Lears has suggested was provided in the early twentieth century through fantasy, the fairy-tale vogue, and historical romances.[237] He argues that such imaginative vehicles, aimed at both children and adults, were evidence of the "exaltation of childhood merged with the cult of the strenuous life."[238] In light of this, Fairbanks's costume films may have been more effective, at least for a postwar audience, in providing a narrative escape from the self-conscious construction of masculinity and gender relations in contemporary settings. Thus, while his films of the 1920s still constitute a patriarchal proving ground for normative masculinity in the character-building mode, the star's retreat into a fictional past secured a place where his protagonists could continue their heroics without confronting those adult prerogatives and impurities made synonymous with the Roaring Twenties. It is appropriate then, that the introduction to Fairbanks's *The Three Musketeers* (1921) asserts that the film's return to France of old will take the viewer to a time: "When life was life, and men were men."

In spite of these changes, Fairbanks's onscreen masquerades in the 1920s continued to give voice to masculine nostalgia for a world of childish play where heroic adventure and chivalrous innocence would never feel the pressure of being merely "a playful prelude to the careful business of life."[239] Although, on their surface, his costume films of the 1920s might seem divorced from contemporary issues, they still managed to speak, albeit more covertly, to issues of masculine identity at the center of character-building discourse. That identity was (as the next chapter will also detail) intensely reactive to intensifying cultural dilemmas stemming from the contrary demands of modernism and antimodernism, urbanization and agrarian ideals, women's changing social roles and the desire for traditional gender arrangements.

As his costume films such as *Robin Hood* (1922), *The Thief of Bagdad* (1924), and *The Black Pirate* (1926) grew more spectacular, more opulent, and more artistically sophisticated, Fairbanks was still constructing these films as reform-minded art appropriate for children. Advertisements for *Robin Hood* described the film as "Real literature of the screen–sponsored by a man with a high ideal."[240] As if he were the Teddy Roosevelt of filmland, he presented himself as a moral leader of an industry in danger of succumbing to capitalistic greed. He was quoted as defying exhibitors who wanted him to make four and five pictures a year so that "we can all clean up"; instead, he aspired to leading the industry by giving "the best I can. . . . Why go on giving the public the same old pictures simply because there is a name to capitalize upon and a trademark which has been established?"[241] Although his films might look like other costume films, reviewers were quick to praise them for those qualities dear to the hearts of boy reformers. Fairbanks's films were said to be "clean in the best sense of the word . . . virile romance [that makes] wholesome things a thousand times more interesting to youth and age than the type of work which his influence has done so much to supplant."[242]

It is within this framework that even the most apparently escapist of the star's 1920s films such as *The Thief of Bagdad* continued to perpetuate character-building ideals of masculine regeneration as they foregrounded antimodernist, chivalric ideals adopted by much of the masculinist reform movement. *The Thief of Bagdad*'s story line offers a variation on the familiar Rooseveltian/Fairbanksian transformation of a mollycoddle into a man. What requires transformation within this context is not the overly civilized male who must reawaken his manly instincts by building up his physique and getting up his nerve for challenging experience, but rather the boyish criminal, the juvenile delinquent, whose strong, manly instincts have instead led him into crime. The film tells the story of Ahmed (Fairbanks), whose carefree life of crime is interrupted by his glimpse of a princess (Julanne Johnston). At first, he plans on drugging and kidnapping her in fulfillment of his motto: "What I want—I take."

When three exotic princes from the East arrive to court the princess, Ahmed masquerades as yet another princely suitor. The princess falls in love with Ahmed at first sight as he confidently approaches the palace on horseback. Visually, he is the most manly of her suitors. While the Prince of the Indies is compromised by his inactivity and passivity, the Mongol Prince, whose first appearance elicits gasps of fear from the princess, hides his cadaverous face behind an ever-fluttering, feminizing fan. The rotund, babyish Prince of Persia is even portrayed by a short, corpulent actress (Matilde Comont). On meeting the princess, Ahmed becomes too ashamed to carry out his plan. He has a spiritual conversion sparked by her utter chasteness. As he tells her, "When I held you in my arms, the very world did change. The evil in me died."

After being expelled from the palace as an imposter, Ahmed turns to a holy man who tells him that his nobler aspirations will be rewarded if he learns that "Happiness must be earned," a motto seen written across the night sky in the film's opening. Ahmed sets out on a perilous journey to procure the rarest treasure that will win him the princess's hand in marriage. After numerous thrilling adventures, he returns to Bagdad, where he thwarts the nefarious plot of the Prince of the Mongols (So-Jin), who plans to take over the city and kill the Caliph of Bagdad (Brandon Hurst).

In the end Ahmed, the thief and beggar, is accepted as true royalty because of his brave deeds. He and the princess ride away on a flying carpet. He has learned the truth in the maxim reiterated yet again as the final intertitle shows a holy man addressing a small boy under the open night sky: "Happiness must be earned."

Ahmed is governed by the natural, lawless, savage instincts of childhood. He is like those city boys who character-builders feared would grow up unsupervised by men and would, therefore, never achieve a true manliness that wedded physical perfection with spirituality defined through action. *The Thief of Bagdad* uses its hero to suggest a spiritual transformation into manhood that adheres to the principles of character-builders' search for moral meaning through validating and revitalizing physical experience. Fairbanks articulates this viewpoint in a statement attributed to him in the souvenir program for the film's Liberty Theatre debut:

"It [the film] is a tribute to the fineness that I believe underlies the workaday philosophy of men; a recognition of the inner forces that belie the sordidness of life. . . . The brave deeds, the longing for better things, the striving for finer thoughts, the mental pictures of obstacles overcome and successes won are nearer to our real selves than our daily grind of earthly struggle."[243]

In keeping with his aesthetic experiments of the 1920s, Fairbanks in *The Thief of Bagdad* exploits the sensuous textures of the Orient often evoked in German costume films such as *The Loves of Pharaoh* and *One Arabian Night*. Through costume design and other elements of mise-en-scène, Fairbanks's film imitates the look of the Ballets Russes' scenic design and the star imitates, in his highly stylized physical movement, the modernist ballet techniques associated with Serge Diaghilev's controversial ballets.[244]

Naked from the waist up, darkly bronzed and perfectly muscled, Fairbanks was certainly an exotic physical spectacle as Ahmed; his appearance may seem to owe its origins to the success of Valentino's example of male physicality, but this was not the first time Fairbanks had appeared sensuously stripped-down.[245] Perhaps in response to his exotic looks and balletlike movement, a reviewer, while praising the film's visual artistry, wondered how *The Thief of Bagdad* would be received by Fairbanks's fans. He suggested, "There are intervals when he is not the Fairbanks as we have come to recognize him," and concluded: "In all likelihood most of them [his fans] would prefer him in such a role as he portrayed in *The Mark of Zorro*. . . . Will [*The Thief of Bagdad*] be a financial success? We offer no predictions."[246]

However, at least one film observer saw beneath the veil of exoticism in *The Thief of Bagdad* to find a more familiar Doug. Poet/film critic Vachel

Character-building transformation in the midst of orientalist opulence: Douglas Fairbanks in *The Thief of Bagdad* (1924)

Lindsay extravagantly praised "the greatest movie so far in movie history" as a revelation of the lost dream world of childhood. He thought it allowed "every child now grown old" to reexperience the thrills of the Arabian Nights. However, Lindsay was skeptical that all the nation's citizens could appreciate either the Arabian Nights tales or Fairbanks's film:

When people tell me they do not like it [*The Thief of Bagdad*], I say: "Did you ever read the Arabian Nights?" They answer "No." . . . The kind of unfortunate steerage passengers, now in good clothes, that never read the Arabian Nights at eight years old, will continue to despise *The Thief of Bagdad* . . . and despise all the arts. People that merely "paint China" are better Americans.[247]

Although other critics might be fooled by the film's exotic visual style , Lindsay is not. He articulates its obvious link to the romantic adventure favored by boys even as he rearticulates the xenophobic values of Americanism made explicit in the work of many character-builders.

Characteristically merging Fairbanks's offscreen self with his current role, a publicity article published a few months following the release of the film also reasserted the star's link to boy culture and character-building associations. In it the star claims that his childhood was one of mischievous adventure-seeking that would have landed him "within the clutches of Ben Lindsey's Juvenile Court" except for the fact that "Lindsey hadn't started that court yet."[248] As if to downplay the film's stylistic experimentation and reinforce the appeal of *The Thief of Bagdad* as a conventional character-building tale, Fairbanks went so far as to declare the film to be "the story of every man's inner self."[249] In the maturation of the "bad boy" of Bagdad, moral and masculine certainty—even the certainty of the American work ethic—are rearticulated out of the potential disorder of oriental fantasy dominated by sensual scenic opulence and the virtuosic display of the male body. The all-important therapeutic values of morally directed male energy and exuberant activity are reasserted in narrative terms that signal the overwhelming need to reinscribe filmic masculinity in culturally comfortable, sexually unambiguous terms. As we shall see in the next chapter, such defensive strategies for reasserting masculine norms suggest growing tensions in Hollywood's representation of an ideal of masculinity centered around the efficacy—and exhibitionism—of the male body.

Conclusion: "I wish I were a boy again"

As a movement that emerged over the course of a number of years, character-builders' post-Victorian preoccupation with the lives of boys may appear as nothing more than a socially systematized intensification of a long-standing Victorian obsession with boys. In many respects, the boy reformers' nostalgic ideals can be attributed to the movement's origins in late Victorian culture and middle-class anxiety about the meaning of masculinity in a newly industrialized, increasingly urbanized world. That combination of nostalgia and anxiety that took hold in the post-Civil War years was expressed in such late Victorian popular entertainments as James Barrie's *Peter Pan*, and F. Anstey's popular novel *Vice Versa*, in which a stuffy stockbroker magically changes place with his schoolboy son after he utters the phrase "I wish I were a boy again."[250]

In his films, without literally becoming a child, Douglas Fairbanks seemed to effect such a magical change, a change that many American men in routine-driven, sedentary, bureaucratized jobs yearned for. He affirmed the release of childishness reasserted in the "instinctual" male activities of hunting, fighting, and seeking adventure in the wilds. He also reaffirmed the high value of character building, not only as a way of raising children but as a validation of the masculinity of the men who vicariously participated in childhood through their supervision and reshaping of boy culture.

Although the public's fascination with Fairbanks's validation of a masculine ideal was unusual in being so long-lived and intense, it was neither an isolated nor a unique phenomenon. It was, in fact, a predictable result of the era's self-conscious focus on male identity in relation to a changing society. Fairbanks did not represent a child's fantasy of adventurous adulthood, but an adult veneration of childhood. On and off screen, Fairbanks shared in character-builders' promotion of what has been described as "a small boy's view of masculinity suited to a period of life when boys . . . reinforce each other's fears of seeming weak."[251] Charles K. Taylor suggested of the star's appeal to men and boys:

"The Black Pirate" appeals to the adolescent that is in every healthy adult. . . . Every healthy man dreams at times of descending on Wall Street and routing the bulls and bears, or performing some other feat that he knows is equally impossible. This, no doubt, is a reason why men as well as boys find a thrill in seeing Douglas Fairbanks make the impossible come true.[252]

Fairbanks's stardom offered confirmation of the childish type of man as the ideal symbolic merging of a dynamic masculinity associated with modernity and an anachronistic male individualism associated with the "primitive" American past and cultural nostalgia.

In the broadest sense, then, Fairbanks can be seen as serving as an appealing mediator between America's nineteenth-century past and its twentieth-century future, between the body and the machine, wilderness and urbanization, intensified social control and a nostalgic desire for a mythically free, childlike past. In the process, the onerous psychic and physical demands of masculinity could be held in abeyance by a hero who embodied qualities of intensity, vitality, and instinctual liberation which seemed, to many, to be more and more difficult to acquire and retain amongst the complacency, compromise, and consumeristic comfort of modern bourgeois life.[253]

While Fairbanks's films of the 1920s like *The Thief of Bagdad* extend and complicate the obsessionary cultural preoccupation with the formation of male subjectivity evidenced in his films of the 1915–1919 period, their muting of the contemporary cultural context for that preoccupation parallels a similar shift in public discourse. As the next two chapters will detail, even as Fairbanks asserted an increasingly defensive ideal of normative masculine subjectivity, there was a growing shift to a cultural preoccupation with apparent changes in female sexual and social identity and their effect on masculinity. While masculine ideals advanced by many of the "boy problem" or "boy culture" reformers still held hegemonic sway over interpretations of American masculinity in the 1920s, overt emphasis on regenerative masculine activity gave way to a focus on American women's

The grown-up schoolboy: no longer sufficient to control women? (Douglas Fairbanks and Jewel Carmen in *American Atistocracy*)

changing sexual subjectivity and its imperilment of male identity through the creation of deviant, "woman-made" masculinities.

These changes suggest the timeliness of the retreat of Fairbanks's childish masculine ideal into a fictional past in the 1920s. If Fairbanks's cheerful star image was actually revelatory of anxiety regarding masculine identity as a process inseparable from gender relations, it seems appropriate that his films, operating as escape valves for masculinity, began, in the 1920s, to retreat more and more into a fictional and fantastic past as an intensification of certain social trends threatened stable (i.e., traditional) gender relations. Questions were beginning to be raised about the childish man's ability to meet contemporary demands of women's disturbing sociosexual evolution. In fact, some conservative commentators thought that the Fairbanks ideal of masculinity, "the grown-up schoolboy type" who "believes in chivalry," was no longer sufficient to handle the country's women, who were "totally out of hand," power-mongering, and therefore, nothing less than "male women."[254] Notably, the masculine type Fairbanks represented was being dismissed as merely more evidence of the modern woman's influence: "He is a man who knows nothing about women, but he is usually athletic, breezy and fond of games—i.e., he is harmless. The fact that he now stands as the pattern of the 'manly' man reveals the influence of the female standpoint in our modern communities."[255]

The feminization of culture, the devitalizing effect of modern labor, and the urban environs of the cities had done their work. Childish men were no longer trusted to stave off cultural disaster. Women's values had perverted masculinity so that even the character-builders' most manly man was no match for the modern age.

It could be argued too that Fairbanks's films of the late 1920s (such as *The Gaucho*, 1928) also begin to register a greater anxiety in relation to masculinity and youthfulness. In *The Gaucho*, Fairbanks begins the film looking like Valentino and acting like a carefree bandit, but as the film progresses the initial image of sexy, youthful exoticism is undercut. "El Gaucho" enters into an oddly asexual relationship with a spirited mountain girl (Lupe Velez), and events paint a dark picture of the price of sin. Although Fairbanks still swaggers and grins (and even drinks a toast to his own shadow as if he were Peter Pan), he is world-weary and cynical. At one point El Gaucho callously tells a leper that he should go kill himself. He proclaims his own godlessness, but when he himself is struck down with leprosy, he begs the Girl of the Shrine (Geraine Greear), whom he drunkenly planned to seduce (or rape), to teach him how to pray. His desperate prayers bring him a vision of "Our Lady of the Shrine" (Mary Pickford as the Madonna) and a cure. Although the film affirms the possibilities of masculine redemption, Fairbanks's protagonist is no longer a mere juvenile delinquent, as in *The Thief of Bagdad*, but a selfish and surprisingly cruel adult.

The apparent contradiction between Fairbanks's preternatural childishness and his true age (and status as a filmmaker) also began to elicit unfavorable commentary aimed at the star himself. The contrast between Fairbanks's prodigious power in the Hollywood film industry and his cultivation of an easygoing, affably juvenile presence was rarely deconstructed or held up to examination in the late 1910s. However, in 1926 *Photoplay* suggested that exhibitors who made too much money from Doug's pictures were quickly stripped of their excess profits by the actor, who was a ruthless businessman even when he "begins to look childlike and prattle about business."[256] Also suggesting a troubling gap between the actor-producer and his childish image, a fan magazine article of 1928 remarked that Doug "never tired of creating the impression of being the athlete," and that in "staging" interviews, Doug was into mere "overtime acting": "By the time you are around to the first question Doug, in all likelihood, will be chinning himself on the chandelier, or playing leap-frog with the furniture."[257] While such unflattering treatment of star personalities in the scandal-saturated Hollywood of the late 1920s was not unusual, it was unprecedented in reference to Fairbanks. Perhaps it reflected a growing disillusionment with his middle-age embodiment of the juvenile, especially in his offscreen persona.

Under such growing extratextual, textual, and cultural pressures, Fairbanks's last silent film, *The Iron Mask* (1929), offers a fitting conclusion to a career that was effectively at its end. Contrary to Booth Tarkington's famous characterization of the actor as a "faun who had been to Sunday School," Fairbanks and his favorite character were no longer "quicksilver." In *The Iron Mask* the ever-youthful D'Artagnan is no longer so. His hair is flecked with gray, his chin sags; his figure is fit but decidedly middle-aged. At the film's conclusion, D'Artagnan falls in defense of the king. Nevertheless, the hunger for perpetual boyhood need not die even when Fairbanks heroes must. Drawing his last breath, D'Artagnan looks up to a vision of his three fallen comrades who boyishly beckon from the heavens: "Come on! There is greater adventure beyond!" He joins them in a heavenly romp. Childhood may have remained "the paradise of the race," but Hollywood could no longer sustain this paradise for men— except in dreams of a homosocial heaven.[258]

Two

"Impassioned Vitality": John Barrymore and America's Matinee Girls

> Any actor who can make love on the stage in a way to make women sit up becomes at once that darling of fortune, the matinee hero, before whom even managers cringe and pay, for women crowd the theaters to see the counterfeit of the romantic lovemaking that they never see in real life.[1] —Elizabeth Gilmer,
> "The Art of Wooing," *Cosmopolitan* (1905)

> Young girls still love romance but they do not find it in the legitimate theatre.[2] —Julia Dean, "What Women Like Best in the Plays of Today," *Green Book* (1914)

In November 1922 *Motion Picture Magazine* featured a poem, "The Movie Fan." "She may live in Pinochle, Wisconsin," the poem, declared, "but she holds the whip on Hollywood."[3] Two cartoons accompany the poem. One shows a female moviegoer weeping as she gazes at the screen. This spectacle of feminine suffering is counterpointed by another cartoon showing the aftermath of women's excessive—and apparently aggressive—attachment to Hollywood cinema: a woman stands with a hammer in one hand and a newspaper in the other. The sculpted bust of her favorite male film star lies shattered on the floor. Echoing the kind of coverage that greeted revelations regarding early movie idol Francis X. Bushman, the newspaper's headline reads: FLOYD PHILMSTAR HAS WIFE AND CHILDREN.[4]

The poem and accompanying cartoons crystallize an impression of female spectatorship that has been perpetuated by much of contemporary feminist film theory. Women's attachment to the cinema is regarded frequently as an emotional overinvestment—too personal, too intense,

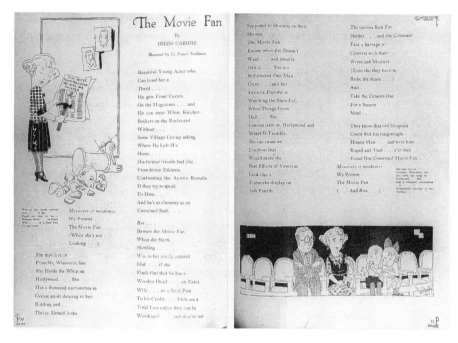

Female fans' aggressive attachment to male stars (*Motion Picture Magazine*, November 1922)

inevitably attached to suffering if not checked. Mary Anne Doane has suggested that female spectators' "nonfetishistic gaze maintains a dangerous intimacy with the image" not shared by male viewers.[5] Doane regards women's desire for the cinema as impossible to gratify, a "desire to desire" that remains misplaced onto shadowy cinematic signifiers.[6] Stars, exemplifying such signifiers, could be expected to become primary objects of women's "excessive collusion with the cinematic imaginary."[7]

The poem "The Movie Fan" and its cartoons may be interpreted as supporting such a notion of female spectatorship, but they also allude more securely to a historical phenomenon: the rise of male movie stars, especially those "matinee idols" whose careers were perceived as depending upon female fans. Chapter 1 traced how character-builders from the 1880s through the 1920s, even in the process of formulating norms for manhood, were keenly aware of deviant forms of masculinity believed to be shaped by women. In the context of character-building discourse, mothers, school teachers, and Sunday school teachers were thought to be the initial culprits in misshaping masculinity by turning boys into sissies or mollycoddles through their increasing control of American homes and schools. But as the previous chapter noted, these women were not the only females thought to threaten masculinity. By the 1920s women were being blamed for promoting a "womanly ideal of man" that made even the "grown-up schoolboy" type of man (such as Fairbanks) inadequate because he could not control the many American women who had been led astray by feminism.[8]

The transgressive implications of this "womanly ideal of man" in destabilizing historical norms of masculine identity will be examined in this and the next chapter. These two chapters highlight the role of the female spectator/consumer in a perceived crisis in masculinity in the early twentieth century. Character-building discourse of the time targeted the influence of mothers and female teachers, but social discourse of the time also reflects the belief that women *as consumers* were altering masculinity. In their wholesale consumption of popular representations of men, women were thought to be the force behind the creation of fictional ideals of masculinity that, in turn, negatively influenced real-life men. For example, Anthony Ludovici was typical in suggesting that this occurred because "the bulk of modern readers . . . are women. This fact [is] too well known to editors and publishers." As a result, a "womanly ideal of man" was becoming the "beau-ideal of Anglo-Saxon society"; this fictional model, made to fit women's desires, was part of the process by which women were, he claimed, endangering normal gender relations and "the survival of humanity."[9]

This discussion of a threatened masculinity in relation to women's desires must be understood within the emergence of consumer culture in the United States, which as one scholar has observed, "*required* women to play a more active part in public life."[10] Women's consumerism had to meet the demands of industrial mass production. By the 1920s public discourse posited them as the primary participants in America's new consumer culture. Advertising worked to secure their desire for a wide range of the country's mass-produced offerings—among them fashion and cosmetics, technologically innovative household goods (such as electric clothes washers) and automobiles.[11] More problematic than their consumption of these kinds of goods was women's emergence as the primary figure in the consumption of cultural forms of masculinity.

Within this context, "The Movie Fan" serves reliably as a historical indicator of women's public preeminence as Hollywood's most "rabid" consumers of male stars in the 1920s. The disgruntled spectator in the poem who "holds the whip on Hollywood" also suggests the considerable force that American women, as consumers, were believed to exercise over the

Hollywood film industry in the 1920s. Box-office records of the post-World War I period are untrustworthy and serious studies of the gender-differentiation of the audience virtually nonexistent.[12] Nevertheless, during the decade of the 1920s, the female portion of the American film audience was estimated by exhibitors' trade journals, fan magazines, and numerous casual observers as being between 75 and 83 percent.[13] A 1928 article from *Exhibitors Herald/Moving Picture World* asserted that "it has become an established fact that women fans constitute the major percentage of patronage or at least cast the final vote in determining the majority patronage."[14]

Industry commentary advancing the notion of a female box-office majority in the twenties may be tainted by Hollywood's desire to solicit women as consumers of both film and film-related tie-ins, i.e., consumer products. Certainly, women may not have constituted the majority at the movies in the 1920s.[15] Nevertheless, there is no doubt that female fans, especially middle-class fans, were a coveted audience. They were believed to go frequently, to control the film-going habits of their family, and to have the money to spend on tie-ins and industry-related items, including fan magazines. In response, *Exhibitors Herald* warned its readers in 1925: "DON'T FORGET HER! In every exploitation campaign, it would be financial suicide to leave the women folk out of consideration. They are the ones who go to the movies the most, and they are the ones that give the youngsters the pennies needed to attend your matinees."[16] Such assertions cannot be confirmed as having a factual basis, but producers, distributors, and exhibitors were all vocal in their sensitivity to female audience members as a particularly influential segment of the post-World War I movie-going public.

It is no wonder that women became the focus of a cultural debate that included discussion of film's role in a perceived destabilization of American masculinity. As this chapter and the next will detail, this debate appeared to be reaching a climax in the 1920s as women were accused of destroying traditional sexual and domestic relations and of creating a new type of man, the "woman-made man." Lorine Pruette described this type for readers of *The Nation* in 1927: "If it is true that man once shaped woman to be the creature of his desires and needs, then it is true that woman is now remodeling man. . . . The world is fast becoming woman-made."[17] Beatrice Hinkle suggested in 1925 that middle-class women's desires were leaving American men perplexed: "The men have been pathetic in their bewilderment at the turn of affairs. How many times I have heard husbands and fathers say, 'What is the matter with my wife (or my daughter)? . . . Why is she so restless?'"[18]

This chapter will trace the influence of America's "restless" women on cinematic masculinity in the 1920s by retracing the same time period (1880s–1920s) discussed in chapter 1. As that chapter noted, during these years character-builders anxiously attempted to fight what they perceived to be a multifaceted feminization of culture—and its influence on masculinity. While the previous chapter offered a broadly based examination of the phenomenon, this chapter will shift focus to show how the American theater played a crucial, formative role in the contentious discussion surrounding the notion of a masculine type constructed by and for women's desires in the 1920s.

The theater became one of the middle-class entertainments most successfully (albeit controversially) engaged in catering to the interests and tastes of both the "transitional" woman of the late nineteenth century and the "New Woman" associated with the 1910s and 1920s.[19] In exploring the historical roots of feminine fandom in American popular culture and its influence on male representation, we should not be surprised to discover that an assertive, cultish, and libidinally charged female spectatorship that has been associated almost exclusively with the Valentino cult was neither so new nor so unusual as had once been thought.[20] In fact, by the time Valentino became the most (in)famous construction of screen masculinity for women in the 1920s, womanly ideals of masculinity were already being inscribed in a theater overtly linked in social discourse to the "pernicious" feminization of American culture.

Thus, the theater became an important arena for challenging hegemonic norms by presenting a sexually ambiguous, transgressive vision of objectified masculinity that wreaked havoc with rigid gender dichotomies and with the conventional ideals of the cult of the body so well represented by Douglas Fairbanks. This vision of transformative *yet* transgressive masculinity on the post-Victorian stage was constructed in relation to a demandingly expressive feminine desire. That desire was publicly registered in a long-standing consumer-linked feature of late Victorian middle-class culture: the notorious matinee girl.

In film studies, the lack of acknowledgment of these theatrical antecedents has led to lingering gaps in our knowledge about the construction of screen masculinity in the post-World War I years as well as in our understanding of Hollywood's aim at women during this time. In the recent revival of interest in Hollywood stars and their relationship to gender-defined spectators, there has been an almost exclusive feminist focus on Rudolph Valentino's stardom as the exemplar of how masculinity was constructed by Hollywood for its female viewers during the post-World War I period.[21]

However, what should not be overlooked is that Valentino's phenomenal popularity among women may have been unprecedented in its scope, but not in type. If, as Richard Koszarski has suggested, Valentino was "king of the exotic costume romance," then his movie kingdom was an inherited one.[22] Commentators of the era, while acknowledging the force of his star power, regarded him as a successor, albeit an uncomfortably foreign one, to a string of other screen idols. These actors often had been stage idols or were, like Valentino, presented on screen and off in ways largely consistent with the conventional theatrical idioms surrounding those male stars who had romantically ruled the stage.[23]

Thus, this chapter will argue that the screen's structuring of male sexuality in the 1920s for a cultish female film audience involved a complex, transformative adaptation of existing cultural discourses on the male body dating from the nineteenth century. Some of these were aimed at women in ways that changed as they incorporated newly emergent discourses on women's sexuality and its effect on gender relations in the Jazz Age.

In spite of these changes, and just as Valentino was emerging as a screen idol, "The Movie Fan" registered what, in 1922, was already a clichèd view of female fans and their volatile emotional attachment to male stars. That emotional attachment was provided with a prototype in the matinee girl and the theatrical object of her affection, that "adored creature," the male matinee idol.[24]

"Barrymore . . . the only, irresistible, brilliant, and idolized!"

As the prime case study and focus of my exploration of the theatrical influence on Hollywood's objectification of masculinity for female spectators in the 1920s, I am using one of the most successful of these "adored creatures"—John ("Jack") Barrymore. In the discursive web of ongoing cultural debates centering on masculinity and female desire, the exhibition of Barrymore and his body is doubly revealing since he became a screen star in the 1920s after a decade and a half career in the legitimate theater. By the early 1920s, Barrymore was dubbed the country's "great tragedian," but previously he had been known as "one of the most popular, if not the most popular, matinee idol of the stage to-day."[25] He had distinguished himself among those male actors whose careers depended heavily, if not exclusively, on the devotion of their predominantly female audiences.

John Barrymore (c. 1910): "One of the handsomest men on the American stage" (*Photo:* Culver Service; Courtesy of the Museum of the City of New York, 50.178.241; Gift of Mr. and Mrs. Spencer Bergen)

Son of the archetypal matinee-idol-gone-mad, Maurice Barrymore, and nephew of the debonair John Drew, the "amusing matinee idol," John Barrymore took to the stage in 1903. Five short years later, *Vanity Fair* declared him to be "an irresistibly fascinating matinee idol."[26] His matinee idol following and his status as "one of the handsomest men on the American stage" were much discussed in the press.[27] This phase of his stage career was dominated by musical comedy. No doubt, because of his family's theatrical preeminence, critics praised Barrymore at the same time that they begged him to do something more challenging.[28] Already a gender bias in his audience appeal was apparent. In *A Stubborn Cinderella* (opening in Chicago in 1908), he sang and danced, wore period costumes and a corkscrew-curled wig. He also earned effusive accolades: "The only, irresistible, brilliant, and idolized Barrymore!" cooed female critic and irrepressible Barrymore fan, Amy Leslie.[29]

Musical comedy vehicles were often regarded as the refuge of male audiences (who wanted to ogle chorus girls), but the appeal of Barrymore to women was played up in publicity. In 1910 he married socialite Katherine Corri Harris. She was promptly thrown off the social register for marrying a man who had already been linked to numerous women, often scandalously. America's other women, however, were assumed to be green with envy. All over the country, in newspapers large and small, it was reported that Lloyd's of London was forced to pay Cohan and Harris, the managers of Barrymore's current (nonmusical) hit play, *The Fortune Hunter*, $50,000 because, fortuitously, they had "insured their matinee idol against depreciation on account of matrimony."[30]

In keeping with other matinee idols of this transitional period in the theater, Barrymore survived and prospered through the development of

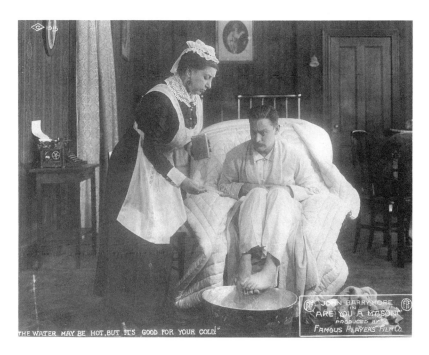

Needing to be transformed into proper manhood: John Barrymore in *Are You a Mason?* (1915) (*Photo:* Famous Players Film Co.; Courtesy of the Museum of the City of New York, 34.79.392; Gift of Gilbert J. Holden)

new skills. He moved on to more sophisticated comedies such as *The Affairs of Anatol* (1912) and then to serious drama. By 1919 Alexander Woollcott commented on his "precipitous" rise to fame and dubbed him as no less than the "legitimate successor to Richard Mansfield."[31]

Following the lead of many other stage actors, Barrymore began to flirt with occasional filmmaking in the mid-1910s. In 1913 newspapers reported: "And now fascinating, captivating, aggravating John Barrymore has deserted the 'legit,' at least for the time being, for the 'movies.'"[32] During the next few years, Barrymore was quietly shuttling between his Broadway triumphs and knockabout comedies such as *Are you a Mason?* (1915) and *The Dictator* (1915), in which he was usually featured as a refined hero of gentle manners and upper-class beauty who needed to be transformed from "mollycoddlism" into manhood.

By 1920 Barrymore had made thirteen films of uneven quality and limited production value. The most important of these was *Raffles* (1917), a film version of a stage vehicle associated with Kyrle Bellew, beloved matinee idol of an earlier generation. *Raffles* marked a significant departure in Barrymore's film repertoire in that it attempted to exploit the actor's current on- and offstage persona: suave, self-consciously handsome, a "blade" with a Wildean insouciance and cameo-perfect profile.[33] While continuing to make pictures, Barrymore returned to the stage in serious efforts: *Peter Ibbetson* (1917), *Redemption* (1918), and *The Jest* (1919). *Redemption*, adapted from Tolstoy, was somber enough fare to "have frightened away many of Barrymore's old admirers," but *Peter Ibbetson* and *The Jest* broke Broadway box-office records to position—and then even more forcefully reposition—the actor as American theater's preeminent matinee idol.[34]

As his career became established, John Barrymore represented ideals of masculinity aimed at a theater audience regarded by contemporary American commentators as increasingly and distressingly dominated by women. In response to *The Jest*, one commentator suggested: "It is the women who make or break a play. *See any manager.* And the women have made John Barrymore into the most popular after-dinner actor on our stage today."[35] By the late 1910s Barrymore's performances were eliciting a discourse of female fan behavior that not only prefigured the Valentino cult in its intensity of expression but soon had the distinction of cutting across the demarcation lines of film versus theater. As another critic noted:

I heard two women at a performance of *Redemption* exclaiming in rapture over Mr. Barrymore's good looks. I did not hear them say a word about the play. They were Barrymore "sharks," for they proved that he was not wearing his hair the same way in *Redemption* as he was in a motion picture that they had just seen him in. And they had liked him *even better* in the motion picture, which was, by the way, a cheap picturization of an asinine farce yclept, *Here Comes the Bride* . . . John Barrymore, the only living matinee idol now in captivity.[36]

Photoplay was soon asking why John Barrymore had "never tried anything but the thin stuff of films."[37]

The Movies and the Matinee Idol: "Women's New Plaything"

By the time he moved beyond the "thin stuff of film" with a first-class Hollywood vehicle, *Dr. Jekyll and Mr. Hyde* (Paramount/Artcraft, 1920), Barrymore was regarded as one of the last true matinee idols of the stage. By 1915 the perception that such matinee idols were passé had considerable currency. In 1914 author-actor Leo Ditrichstein explained to readers of *The Green Book* "Why the Matinee Idol Was Shattered." He suggested that "the adored creature" was "buried and unmourned" as "realism's easy victim." Modern playwrights, he claimed, had abandoned their dubious duty of writing for the beautiful male idol, and the popularity of cheap movie-going had sealed his fate: "The crowds coming to the theatre district have almost ceased to be. . . . The matinee idol is no more and he could not be brought to life."[38]

However, Ditrichstein's assessment was not quite true on two counts. True, theater attendance in general and touring company attendance in particular were markedly down.[39] It was true too that the most revered generation of idols was thinned by old age and retirements, but Barrymore's successes in the late 1910s demonstrated that the matinee idol as a type was decidedly not dead. More generally, however, the matinee idol was being co-opted by the movies, as "male stars by the dozen deserted to the surer profits of the film-drama."[40] Those who now vied for movie box-office receipts included the venerable Robert Mantell, Lou Tellegen, William Faversham, Arnold Daly, James K. Hackett, Robert Edeson, De Wolf Hopper, Robert Warrick, Douglas Fairbanks, and John Barrymore.[41]

The shift of the matinee idol to film was concurrent with the broader shift of legitimate stage actors from the theater to screen. Charles W. Collins, writing in *Green Book* in 1914, declared that the motion pictures were now "women's new plaything"; those who had once frequented the theater were flocking to the movies, standing in line with all classes of people and "awaiting a chance to view a matinee idol of the 'movies'" such as King Baggott, who, ironically, was engaged in filming stage plays that had been matinee idol fare.[42] The emergence of the feature film as direct competition with the legitimate stage meant that by the 1920s the long-established feminine interest in stage matinee idols had been supplanted by movie fans with their new or retreaded matinee idols of the screen.[43]

As a matinee idol for women, Barrymore defied these movie-oriented trends with the biggest hit of his career, *The Jest*, opening in April, 1919. In early 1920 *Variety* noted that *The Jest* closed with "the greatest box office record for dramatic or non-musical shows in American theatrical history"; Barrymore's premature departure some weeks before had sealed the play's fate as a star vehicle: after he left, attendance plummeted from 19,000 to 6,000 weekly.[44] Reaching the critical heights of his stage success in *Richard III* and *Hamlet* in the 1920–1922 seasons, Barrymore simultaneously became a "cinema artist"[45] in Hollywood costume films such as

Matinee idol charms transferred to film: John
Barrymore as Beau Brummel (1924)

The Lotus Eater (1921), *Sherlock Holmes* (1922), and *Beau Brummel* (1924).[46] In these films, his matinee idol charms were not obscured but regularly shown to good effect.

When he finally left the stage to become a Warner Brothers star in 1925, Barrymore was promoted as "the greatest living actor" in tribute to his recent Shakespearian triumphs on Broadway; but as a measure of the studio's financial respect for Barrymore's specific ability to attract women's box-office power, Warner's entrusted the feature film debut of its sound-on-disk process to a Barrymore star vehicle, *Don Juan* (1926). The film, written by frequent Barrymore scenarist, Bess Meredyth, recycled a role that matinee idol Richard Mansfield had played on the stage to longtime success. It was immediately perceived as addressing women. *Variety* noted: "As a box office winner *Don Juan* is sure fire—it aims directly at the women for pulling power and that takes in everything."[47] Another reviewer suggested that the "dramatic romance" would "merit the attention of the fan crowd."[48]

Within the discursive web of cultural debates centering on masculinity and female desire in the 1920s, Hollywood's display of masculinity for the "fan crowd" at that time cannot be separated from the precedents established in the theatrical articulation of a post-Victorian masculinity for American women consumers. And that masculinity was often articulated within the framework of costume dramas. As the previous chapter suggests, costume dramas did not exclusively target a female audience. Nevertheless, many textual accommodations were made to female specta-

Aiming "directly at the women": *Don Juan* (1926)

tors even in action-oriented swashbucklers of the 1920s. These can be found in Douglas Fairbanks's "boy literature"-based films (such as *The Black Pirate* or *Robin Hood*) as well as in the western comedy-adventure films of Tom Mix that were thought to appeal strongly to youthful or a "wishing-to-be-youthful" male audience. Plot lines imitating juvenile literature often were augmented to give more than a passing nod to adult romance. This means, oddly enough, that a film such as Tom Mix's *The Great K&A Train Robbery* (1926) may seem uncannily similar in narrative structure and tongue-in-cheek tone to a production of the same year assumed to be primarily female-aimed, such as Valentino's *The Son of the Sheik*.[49] In these films, romantic love, presented in ways associated with women's interest in objectifying men, existed side by side with the paradigmatic structures of male-centered adventure fiction: hair-raising escapes, breathless chases, coincidence aplenty, and ample narrative space for childish (i.e., male) physical daring.

Other costume films inscribe female structures into an established male fictional order and are less equivocal in tone and more assertively feminine in their spectatorial aim. These films seem clearly in line with what Elizabeth M. Gilmer, in a theatrical context, referred to as plays full of "romantic episodes"; their narratives foreground courtship and theatricalize the "art of wooing."[50] Evoking "music and moonlight and thrills,"[51] these star vehicles emphasize romantic rather than action thrills and revolve around the erotic attraction created by one of the many matinee idols who specialized in make-believe lovemaking.

In the 1920s movies in this vein frequently were distinguished in reviews as "romantic melodramas" or "romantic dramas." Constructed according to familiar theatrical terms of address and set in freely imagined historical landscapes or improbable exotic locales were costume films such as *The Night of Love*, *The Cossacks*, *The Beloved Rogue*, *The Sheik*, *The Arab*, *Tempest*, *Monsieur Beaucaire*, *When a Man Loves*, *A Sainted Devil*, *Scaramouche*, and *Don Juan*. These might appear to be little more than historical curiosities, inexplicable remnants of an earlier Victorian sensibility, and part of a last, postwar gasp of antimodernism. But their appeal was considerable—and familiar. Many costume films were "presold" star vehicles, adaptations or shameless plagiarisms of the quarter century repertoire of popular theatrical male matinee idols including E. H. Sothern's *Villon*, Richard Mansfield's *Don Juan* and *Beau Brummell*, Lewis Waller's *Monsieur Beaucaire*, James K. Hackett's *Prisoner of Zenda*, Kyrle Bellew's *A Gentleman of France*, and Otis Skinner's *Blood and Sand*.

Thus, although 1920s Hollywood acknowledged women's changing sexual subjectivity, its discourse on masculinity and the male body was adapted from other cultural arenas—including the theater—to offer a presold formula of (presumably) heterosexual fantasy. As a result, its construction of matinee idols was dependent on already established strategies for commodifying male stars. This is in keeping with other trends. The conventions of the theater, especially the high-class, respectable theater, were quickly incorporated into film in the mid-1910s, as the latter embraced the feature as the standard film form.[52] Yet this theatrical inheritance has been virtually ignored in accounts of film's representation of masculinity in the 1920s, nor has it figured in any attempt to account for film's appeal to women in the post–World War I years. To "set the stage" for my discussion of Barrymore in film, in the next section we shall discover just what feminization meant to the American theater—and to its creation of the matinee idol as a woman-made man.

"Oh, Hideous Phrase!—The Matinee Girl"

In the years 1900–1918 the feminization of the American theater was much-debated and discussed in the popular press. This debate centered on what was often identified as the most obvious element in this feminization. There was a huge increase in theater attendance by women, both chaperoned and, especially during the daytime, unchaperoned. By 1918 *The Nation*, echoing prominent theater managers like Augustin Daly and Charles Frohman, even suggested that there was a "preponderance of women in the audiences of to-day."[53] Whether or not this was uniformly the case, especially beyond large urban centers, or even true at all, is certainly debatable. However, as with Hollywood cinema of the 1920s, such perceptions of female audience power may be more pertinent than an elusive empirical truth.

Women began to attend the American theater in significant numbers in the 1850s; by the mid-1860s they had made the afternoon performances their own.[54] Coincidentally emerging in the late 1870s, when character-builders were beginning to warn of the specter of cultural feminization, "matinee girls" flourished well into the next century, in spite of frequent denunciations. In 1901 *Century* magazine published a typical assessment of this phenomenon, regarded as peculiarly American: "A subspecies of the genus parlor boarder existing among us, and among us alone, no other nation disputing our claim to this possession, is—oh, hideous phrase!—the matinee girl, a type one shade less attractive than the tramp."[55] An audience of matinee girls, suggested Edward Bok, editor of the *Ladies' Home Journal*, could be described as "an army of young girls" often numbering in the "hundreds."[56] Eliot Gregory described them more vividly as "throngs of idle minxes . . . trooping [on the streets], opera glass in hand."[57]

Like the movie fan after her, the matinee girl was condemned as being both too independent and too obsessed.[58] This gives a somewhat different picture of theatergoing than that offered by Lary May in his analysis of popular culture and early cinema, *Screening Out the Past*. May gives the impression that movies were a momentous revolution of mass culture, in large measure because the Victorian theatrical experience was respectably hidebound in every sense: the formality of class and gender distinctions in the audience being matched by the propriety of stage vehicles.[59] However, the feminization of the American theater and, more specifically, the phenomenon of the matinee girl, suggest we should reconsider such a generalizing view. We should also consider the implications that these linked

The matinee girls: "Throngs of idle minxes"
(*Century* magazine, November 1901)

theatrical phenomena hold for the representation of Hollywood masculinity in relation to female fans in the 1920s.

To target such an active female audience is in contradistinction to how late nineteenth- and early twentieth-century "womanhood" in America has often been discussed in film studies. Late Victorian femininity has been discussed frequently as a rather uncomplicated extension of the early Victorian "cult of true womanhood" rather than dynamically fluctuating, formed and re-formed by competing discourses, both progressive and traditional.[60] Instead of acknowledging the dynamic quality to cultural construction of gender and the importance of compromise or transitional models, the cultural construction of femininity is treated as if it were easily distinguishable into neatly separate and periodized modes.

This is especially true in references to the Victorian woman, defined traditionally as a sacrificing mother or passively chaste maiden confined almost exclusively, it is often assumed, to the domestic sphere. In actuality, American womanhood—in both its experiential reality and in its ideal—was constantly in transition during the years between the turn of the century and World War I, and women's access to the public sphere (including the cinema) varied considerably in relation to age, class, environs, and ethnicity.[61] These were the years in which women appeared to flood into white-collar work; they not only became salesgirls and office clerks but took on nontraditional roles such as that of newspaper reporter.[62] The structures of American society remained patriarchal and gender-divided, but they were not impervious to change. As Jackson Lears asserts:

The twentieth century's "revolution in manners and morals" . . . was not an overnight result of post-World War I disillusionment but the outcome of gradual, almost imperceptible fits and starts of cultural change stretching back into the late nineteenth century . . . a culmination of half-conscious wishes and aspirations among the respectable bourgeoisie.[63]

The theater, and later, the movies, were places where those "half-conscious wishes and aspirations" seemed particularly evident, especially when it came to women and what they wanted from men.

Although the matinee girl came under particularly heavy fire at the turn of the century, her theatrical fascination with the male matinee idol and her shockingly inappropriate (i.e., unfeminine) pursuit of him could be traced back almost a quarter of a century when the first actor to be labeled a matinee idol, English import Harry Montague, stirred spectatorial passion in late Victorian bosoms. Handsomely urbane, Montague had been featured in sentimental Boucicault melodramas and romantic light comedies that prompted women to pack his performances. Sometimes they crawled upon the stage during his plays and, in less assertive moments, as producer William Brady recalled, they "collect[ed] at the stage doors every day to watch Harry come and get out of his carriage."[64] It was reported that he had been forced to hire a bodyguard to deal with his female fans.[65]

Montague's sudden death, at the age of thirty-five in 1878, was marked by reactions, albeit on a smaller scale, that anticipate those greeting Valentino's unexpected demise in 1926. At the memorial service in the San Francisco hotel where Montague expired, female and male cast members, in turn, threw themselves on their costar's flower-covered casket in front of the crowd of hundreds that had gathered all day.[66] In New York a newspaper report suggested that his death "has created a greater sensation in theatrical circles than any event in recent occurrence, and has even had the rare effect of saddening the entire community."[67] Some two thousand mourners attended the service there, a turnout attributed to Montague's unusually "friendly terms with his audience" and to his "gentle, generous, unassuming" character.[68]

Certainly these incidents do not compare to the widespread public response to Valentino's lying in state. The *New York Times* characterized it as "rioting . . . without precedent in New York," as a melee broke out in a crowd of at least thirty thousand, "in large part, women and girls" who had stood in line for hours to get a glimpse of Valentino's body.[69] It is of interest, nevertheless, that the atmosphere created by the "thousands [that] desire and made the effort to attend" Montague's funeral, like the public demonstration that greeted Valentino's lying in state, seemed strangely transformed by what the *New York Sun* characterized as "the eagerness with which most people avail themselves of an opportunity to see public characters in their everyday cuise [*sic*]."[70] No doubt there were many Montague mourners who had never seen the actor on the boards. Out of these, there were probably many to whom the actor's professional life (or death) mattered little in forging the spectatorial value of an event (his funeral) that conveniently brought together a bevy of celebrities. Of Valentino's curious "mourners," the *New York Times* would suggest a similar emotional impurity of purpose: "Hardly one looked even sorrowful, much less reverent."[71]

Montague's stardom demonstrated that in life, as in death, appreciation of the matinee idol might extend beyond the matinee girl, but it was she, with her sometimes unpredictable behavior, who sustained him. When English actor Kyrle Bellew took to the American stage in 1885, he too was pursued by matinee girls. It was said "[they stood] by the hundreds outside the stage door in the rain, in the snow, in the mud, in defiance of chaperones and guardians, just to say 'I saw Belloo [*sic*]! My, but he's handsome—just as handsome off as on!' "[72] Many proceeded to follow him on his walks, build bureau-drawer shrines to him, and organize Kyrle Bellew fan clubs.[73] Bellew publicly resisted the association with women fans: "I am not a matinee idol, I never was a matinee idol, and I won't be a matinee idol."[74] In spite of his protestations, he was still portrayed in the press as an overgroomed fop with a ridiculously exotic autobiography invented, it seemed, to appeal to gullible American women. That appeal extended to the two intrepid souls whose fandom led them to stow away on the vessel that took him away from America's shores in 1888.[75]

Women were being "carried away" by the appearance of "mashers" like Bellew. It did not matter what plays provided the excuse for presenting "these leaders in unreal romanticism."[76] By the turn of the century, the theatrical tastes of the matinee girls were maligned as frequently as their "idle" public freedom. They were blamed for lightweight theatrical fare and for the plethora of romantic love stories that demanded happy endings. Yet, in contradictory fashion, they were also regarded as the source for new, immoral trends. Bok, usually sympathetic to American women's desire for increased freedom, thought these young women distressingly daring in their theatergoing; they flocked to plays that "thousands of mature men of healthy taste absolutely refuse to witness." Not properly controlled by their parents, these young middle-class women were having their minds "soiled" by daring problem plays ("dirt and mire") that dealt

"Just to say, 'I saw Belloo!'" (Kyrle Bellew, c. 1903, in *Munsey's* magazine)

with topics like birth control, adultery, and the oppressiveness of conventional marriage.[77]

A growing number of plays during the years 1900–1918 seemed aimed not just at a middle-class female audience, but at a distinctly youthful female audience. In any case, most commentators agreed, dramas rose and fell on their appeal to women.[78] While the perceived results of women's theatrical interests might occasionally be applauded in women's magazines, the phenomenon was more generally condemned.

In one of a number of hysterical attacks on the feminization of the theater, the unnamed author of "The American Girl's Damaging Influence on the Drama" (1907) declared that men were being driven to cheap and coarse musical comedies for "gutteral satisfaction" by the diet of "dramatic saccharin" forced on them by women's tastes; the theater was racked by "insipidity" because too many plays were aimed to "appeal chiefly to the limited intelligence of immature girlhood."[79] The matinee girls, generously defined by another author to include "indolent women" of any age, were labeled as nothing less than "the most pernicious tendency of the American playhouse."[80]

Women's increased participation in theater audiences was implicated in the transformation of the stage into a forum for stars rather than for drama. The stage was dominated by "the glamour of personality."[81] American theater audiences had been denounced for their star-centered theatrical interests before (in particular, in the 1820s).[82] In 1870 one actress observed that "I have no hesitation in saying that the Americans care much more for the actors than for the merits of the play itself. This predilection is constantly accompanied by a regard less to a perfect ensemble than to the excellence of the 'star' of the evening."[83]

Perhaps because of their numbers and their apparent enthusiasm for "omnivorous theatergoing" as an "emotional safety valve,"[84] women were regarded as the primary starmakers. They were also implicated in this trend because of their theatrical interests, widely regarded as shockingly superficial. Women were accused of being after vicarious thrills; some of these thrills were provided by their viewing of glamorous actresses in gorgeous clothes and stylish coiffures.[85] They got other vicarious thrills through their consumption of romantically charged stage vehicles in which handsome male matinee idols demonstrated lovemaking unparalleled (at least offstage) in its persuasiveness.

While women old and young were implicated in every fault of the post-Victorian theater, the annoyingly active, sometimes shockingly aggressive behavior exhibited by youthful matinee girls was regarded as particularly distressful in relation to these male matinee idols.[86] In 1919 former matinee idol Charles Cherry romanticized the matinee girls from his past as "discreet," "timid," and "impersonal," but most others did not regard their deportment as so refined—or benign.[87] In 1903 *The Theatre* noted: "The matinee girl who makes herself conspicuous is to be seen at all the theaters. . . . Usually she is in bunches . . . and invariably she is noisy. All through the play one hears such snatches of conversation as: 'Isn't he just darling; I think he's the most handsome man I ever saw.'"[88] Another commentator remarked:

An actor of my acquaintance, most unromantically in love with his wife, tells me that his theatrical life is made weary by girls of this category, who write to him, send him flowers, stand in groups at the stage entrance, or, eluding the janitor's vigilance, appear at his dressing-room door, in quest of autographs and compliments.[89]

This kind of censorious commentary seemed inevitable: the matinee girl's behavior in the public sphere was a perversely exhibitionist reversal of the Victorian norms of male sexual initiative and female acquiescence in the private sphere of sexual negotiation.

In light of this reversal, the matinee idol might evoke sympathy as the object of the matinee girls' more shameless pursuits. Barrymore's second wife, Michael Strange (aka Blanche Thomas), recalled how one female fan would order a duplicate of the costume worn by Barrymore's current leading lady and "whenever her feelings got the better of her . . . appear in the public lobby of his hotel, confronting him as he dove for the lift, with extravagant gestures of worship and abandon."[90] Like Bellew, Barrymore was stalked by an admirer who claimed he had proposed marriage to her.[91] Such incidents might encourage a sympathetic identification with matinee idols as besieged men but, as woman-made idols, they were more generally regarded by the press with ambivalence, if not marked disdain. One newspaper ran a satirical piece that described Barrymore as turning down offers of matrimony between courses of breakfast; it mockingly implored: "Girls, in the name of humanity . . . do stop besetting him."[92]

Matinee idols were often depicted as narcissistically and commercially complicit in sustaining the matinee girls' interest. Bellew was criticized for insisting "on every prerogative of his starship" and was accused of hogging center stage so much in *Raffles* (1903) that the production became nothing more than "an exhibition of petty vanity unworthy of a grown-up male human being."[93] Even the most ruggedly virile *beau sabreur* like Lewis Waller was not immune to ambiguously phrased descriptions that suggested the illusory nature of his matinee idol appeal and the insufficiency of his manhood.

Waller, an Englishman whose roles included Monsieur Beaucaire and Shakespeare's Prince Hal, was criticized in a typical article in *The Theatre* entitled: " 'Shakespeare Well Acted Pays,' Says Lewis Waller." Unlike a Fairbanks whose work was depicted in extratextual materials as an outlet for healthy masculine instincts, Waller is characterized as being interested primarily in profit. (This anticipates the later discourse surrounding Valentino, for the idol, it is said, likes to speak "not infrequently" of money.[94]) More damning still, Waller's fans are warned to "shun him in the morning hours" because "morning light is cruelly uncompromising." He is best seen in the "soft glow" afforded by theater lights; the idol should be glimpsed when the "spell of the fictitious romance is still upon him when he has not 'let down' from the exalted state into which he got himself with his satin coat, his lace frills and his powdered wig."[95] This assessment of Waller is in keeping with *Green Book*'s suggestion in 1915 that matinee idols whose "good looks have departed" might be subject to a humiliating, unmanly fate. With their beauty compromised by age, they would have to marry for security. A faded male idol (whose interests no doubt still revolved around monetary gain) was likely to become the "lapdog" of a rich wife.[96]

Endowed by much of extratextual discourse with the worst qualities of women, the matinee idol was regarded as a product of the same feminization of culture that fueled male anxieties. As chapter 1 suggested, those anxieties were crystallized in the figure of the mollycoddle. While the stage idol might be praised for his accomplishments, his masculinity was held in suspicious contempt. The "male professional beauties," as they were sometimes called, were said to be particularly vulnerable to career reversals when, like Bellew, their offstage behavior did not fit their onstage image of "daring, courage and dash."[97]

Barrymore, like Bellew and other matinee idols, often was depicted as foppishly feminized in his attractiveness. Newspaper accounts were quick to suggest that "the slim petulant one" was sensitive to accusations of unmanliness.[98] One article noted that Barrymore was "one of those actors who prides himself upon his masculinity," while another claimed in a tongue-in-cheek account that, although he did not spend time being strenuous in the woods, Barrymore "desires that all shall know him for a hero in embryo. . . . He wishes hotly to deny that heroism goes with muscle and the ability to subsist on canned salmon, slat bacon and Scotch musci [*sic*]."[99]

Such extratextual discourse was a predictable consequence of the stereotype of the matinee idol's suspect masculinity. However, Barrymore's roles may also have become a factor in how he was characterized. In the first part of his career, he was consistently cast as a juvenile lead who was elegant, refined, and often a weakling. His Nathaniel Duncan in *The Fortune Hunter* (1909) was described as a "decorative but indolent youth . . . neatly fitted to young Mr. Barrymore's graceful person."[100] In 1911 Barrymore played a character who masqueraded as a mollycoddle in the comedy farce, *Uncle Sam*. In the play, Robert Hudson (Barrymore) "pretends to a superabundance of effeminacy" to disgust his uncle, a robust miner who wants to haul his nephew back to Nevada and end his self-indulgent attraction to German beer gardens.[101] However, many of his characters were young men who were not pretending to be mollycoddles, but were obviously sissified. His title character in *The Affairs of Anatol* (1912) was described as "a young butterfly of Vienna."[102]

Although, as Douglas Fairbanks so often showed, some mollycoddles could be easily recuperated into normative masculinity, the underlying problematic—of masculinity having to be forcefully constructed from an inappropriate effeminacy—was not so easy to solve. The specter of a man exhibiting feminine qualities suggested not only class-endowed foppishness but, as my analysis of Fairbanks's *Double Trouble* suggested in chapter 1, became more and more explicitly troublesome during this era in its link to homosexuality. What if mollycoddles were not fixed by the belated acquisition of manliness? What if women preferred them to "real" men?

No wonder that the effeminacy that could be eradicated in the protagonist within the course of the play often lingered around the image of the matinee idol offstage. Barrymore's suave comic portrayal in *The Affairs of Anatol* was greeted by critical kudos, but also fell subject to ridicule. Arnold Daly, a popular vaudevillian, declared Barrymore's continental seducer to be "intermediately sexed" and then "sissed it" (the role) in his act at the Palace Theatre.[103] The matinee idol was reported to be "on the hunt for Daly with blood in his eye."[104] About the same time, the actor was the subject of sarcastic headlines. "Jack Barrymore Manages to Lick Someone at Last," declared the *New York Review* on the report that the actor had gotten into a brawl with a Los Angeles barber over a haircut.[105] Later, it was reported that Barrymore had encountered another barber who had come forth with a startling revelation: the actor was not man enough to grow his own mustache. An article sarcastically asked: "That prototype, that exemplary moustache of the age, attempted by many but achieved by few, that idol at whose shrine the stenographers, telephone operators, parlor maids and debutantes of the country have worshipped, that fetich [*sic*]—false?"[106] The barber had said "yes," and the article's author proceeds to bemoan spectatorial standards that allow "plays that had no interest *anywhere* [to] ride in on the top wave of popular success because the feminine portions of the audience were 'just crazy about the male star.'"[107]

Unlike a Fairbanks, who would be characterized, even as a stage star, as "the very best type of clean-limbed, well-bred American young man, wholesome, self-reliant, and ingratiating,"[108] matinee idols like Barrymore were woman-made objects who were not likely to be transformed into men by action, either on or off the boards. No matter how they proclaimed their manhood, they remained ambiguously gendered, passive objects of women's interest. That interest, it was believed, had allowed women to assume unprecedented control of the American theater at the same time that their influence was making inroads into other social arenas.

"A Lucky Actor"?

Once women's presence in the theater was regarded as a refining influence, but now women theatergoers were considered a threat even to the illusory male idols whom they worshiped and whose careers they sustained. By the turn of the century, matinee girls were widely condemned for their disturbing public role in following after stars. That participation appeared in two major forms. They sometimes became an official group like the band of "gallery girls" who, adoring the obviously adorable Lewis Waller, called themselves the "KOW" or "Keen Order of Wallerites."[109] Or they might be united only by their gender and their common object of adoration in sustaining the career of one of their favorites, such as premiere matinee idol Richard Mansfield. Commenting on a late Mansfield performance (1901) in the Booth Tarkington/Evelyn Greenleaf play, *Beaucaire* (a role Waller and Valentino would repeat), James Metcalfe declared:

His Baron Chevrial made many a roué think what a ridiculous creature a roué might become. As Prince Karl and Monsieur he brought stars to the eyes of many a matinee girl of a past generation. Those matinee girls, who are now mothers of matinee girls, are still his stanch [*sic*] admirers, and their daughters have followed in their mothers' footsteps. It is a lucky actor who can command a clientele of roués, matinee girls and their mothers . . .[110]

Each matinee idol might have a specialty, but—like Mansfield—they knew the formulas that appealed to their female audiences. They also adapted to new trends, so that the stereotypical description of matinee idols as inactive, "good looking tailor's model[s] with cleft chins and hand-kerchiefs tucked into their cuffs" belied the type's real versatility.[111] However, that versatility was often held in check by the demands of a public that preferred their idol in best-loved characterizations. A following could contribute in limiting the actor's acceptance in anything but a very narrow range of roles, a fate attributed in its most extreme example to James O'Neill, who portrayed Edmond Dantes in a reputed five thousand performances of *Monte Cristo*.[112]

At its worst, a following could become "a veritable Frankenstein monster, sneering at all worthy ambition and laying waste with vapid laughter and maudlin chatter the whole field of [a star's] . . . endeavor."[113] Thus, star loyalty was a double-edged sword, described in terms that evoke an odd combination of fascination mingled with an element of consumerist, judgmental distance. One critic suggested that "cold-blooded and distinctly audible first-night comments . . . suggest the talk of a slave or cattle market."[114] This kind of "cold-blooded" objectification of actors, male as well as female, was not exclusive to the matinee girl, but as usual she was blamed for the worst excesses of this peculiar kind of star worship.[115] No wonder she was regarded widely as brutal, callous, insensitive, and without "an old-fashioned piece of anatomy called heart."[116]

The matinee girls' behavior was particularly ripe for male ridicule in the press. In spite of the growing number of actresses in romantic roles, widespread public discussion did not take note of the existence of any parallel collective phenomenon in men's mass theatrical spectatorship in the late nineteenth century.[117] Whether or not men pursued actresses in such numbers requires further research. A more obvious reason for the ridicule of the matinee girls was that they (unlike any possible male counterparts) had symbolic significance in relation to American middle-class social and sexual norms. As a result, commentary—and, no doubt, the general public— seamlessly lumped their actions together with "athletic girlhood" and with the indulgent release of young women from traditional domestic duties. Taken together, these actions formed prima facie evidence that the United States had become a "society where the young girl rules supreme."[118] The road to ruin for the American theater—and American men—seemed paved with theater tickets.

"Vivid Enough to Found a Religion"

While a Victorian phenomenon in its origins, the rise of the matinee girl became part of a growing, intense public debate centered on gendered social and sexual identity. The matinee idol was an acknowledged stimulant on the imagination of the matinee girls. Although the latter's excesses in the pursuit of their idols were widely denounced, they were never explicitly named as sexual in intent. In 1916 Anna Steese Richardson acknowledged that "a generation back," the matinee idol had been regarded as a "creature whose influence for evil filled the maternal heart with dread."[119] Even in this rather candid commentary, the matinee idol might be condemned for luring "stagestruck" girls to careers in front of the footlights, but it was not openly suggested that he could be the bait that might lure his fans into the moral twilight of illicit sex.[120] Charles Cherry defensively claimed that "those who worshipped [the matinee idol] did so in perfect safety. . . . They knew that he could never make the mistake of offending their best instincts of good manners and good morals."[121]

   In contrast to such accounts, the daughter of matinee idol Richard Bennett noted of her father's relationship to his fans:

Overbearing and puritanical about the women in his own family, he exercised no such restriction for others. . . . His matinees were mobbed by flushed, agreeable ladies who fairly quivered in his presence. I must admit, he was often extremely charitable in rewarding their attentions, individually, and the demand was never more than he could supply.[122]

Michael Strange recounted that she was warned by an elderly actress that actors who came under the influence of the matinee girls' persuasive combination of worshiping, writing, and waiting often "surrendered to the

impassioned vitality of their hunters"; they would then ensconce their pur-
suers as the head of "a second illegitimate family nearer the theatre than
their regular home."[123]

The erotic possibilities that might emerge from the matinee girl's pursuit and the actor's sexual availability were never acknowledged in public
forums, even though the social implications of the matinee girls' defiance
of public codes of proper feminine behavior were subject to vociferously
negative public injunctions. However, the sexual implications of their
behavior evoked an even stronger response: erasure, repression, and recuperation. As various historians have pointed out, many middle-class late
Victorians privately acknowledged women's sexual needs and interests but
keenly felt cultural contradictions made it almost impossible to attribute
assertive sexuality to middle-class Victorian womanhood.[124]

Private heterosexual passion might be cherished by individuals at the
turn of the century, but the public reshaping of views of female sexuality
took time. In the late nineteenth century, a discursive context was created
that both permitted the acknowledgment of the mutual pleasure in sexual
relations between middle-class men and women and yet also smoothed
over the Victorian bourgeois culture's long-held ambivalence toward the
sanctioning of feminine erotic desire. This discursive legitimation was
accomplished in large part through an emphasis on sexuality (married, of
course) as a spiritualized passion that "vivifies [the couple's] affection for
each other, as nothing else in the world can."[125]

Sexual intimacy was acknowledged as having a crucial function in middle-class marriage, the latter viewed progressively as having as its primary
goal the creation of "a bond between two people who sought a transcendent sense of well-being through their relationship."[126] As a result, good
(marital) sex was compared to fusion, spiritual bliss, the perfect union of
opposites, and religious ritual. These terms—suggesting the triumph of
higher religious values over mere carnal pleasure—provided the basis of
conventional nineteenth-century idioms used in popular forms of romantic discourse at the turn of the century. These same terms exerted a powerful influence on public discourse's approach to heterosexuality during
the transitional years of the 1910s and 1920s.

As the next chapter will detail, during these years women's sexual pleasure was granted legitimacy within the context of an emergent modernist
ethos associated with Jazz Age values. However, from the 1880s through
the 1920s there was also a widespread anxiety in the matter of gender relations and an emergent antimodernist discourse linked to retrenchment and
recuperation in gender roles. If, for a variety of reasons, late Victorian dis-

Unsublimated erotic appeal couched in romantic rhetoric: John Barrymore and Mary Astor in *Beau Brummel*

courses were anxious to inscribe sexuality in terms of spiritual idealism, they were especially eager to bring women's sexual objectification of men into this same category of understanding. Visual iconography and romantic rhetoric invoking transcendent spirituality were embraced in theatrical discourse that sought to normalize the matinee idol's often unsublimated erotic appeal to women at a time of changing gender norms. They also may have been used to negotiate the hero's lack of normative (i.e., strenuous) masculine attributes that sometimes, as in Barrymore's case, resulted in characters who were sexually ambiguous "sissies."

Stephen Kern has suggested that "Victorian artists allowed female desire to burn hottest when far away or long ago."[127] Taking a lesson from such an approach, post-Victorian theater and Hollywood films of the 1920s could more overtly appeal to female spectators' libidinal passions when the male object of idolatry was allied to an exotic or historically distant rendering of erotic thrills. The historical displacement of female sexuality to costume plays and films would not be out of the ordinary because, as chapter 1 suggested, historical and fantastic settings were enthusiastically employed by American men during this time. They helped to fulfill what Jackson Lears labels their nostalgic search for intensely felt, "'authentic' alternatives to the apparent unreality of modern existence."[128] Referencing late Victorian British writers of romantic adventure enjoyed by boys, such as H. Rider Haggard, Joseph Bristow suggests that while these authors were especially enthusiastic about works such as *The Arabian Nights*, they scorned romance for women as "'false,' 'idealistic,' and predictable."[129] However, these settings and stories of masculinist adventure were easily co-opted by women, who, as chapter 1 noted, were often accused of dominating the fiction market. By the end of the 1920s there seems to be a convergence of the narrative formulas and settings found in Fairbanks's, Barrymore's, and Valentino's films. This may be the result of the hegemonic (male) model reasserting its control over the woman-made one, but it also has other implications. In the theater and film, medieval (chivalric), high Anglo-Victorian, or orientalist settings served an additional function for female viewers: emphasizing pastness could elide criticism that such products, marketed primarily for the consumption of female spectators, were attempting to elicit women's modern sexual feelings. Indeed, the contemporary move toward a deregulation of female sexuality was rarely beyond the reach of controversy in the 1910s and 1920s. As the next chapter will detail, discussions of female sexuality were constantly being associated with social issues that evoked masculine anxiety if not hysteria: white slavery, miscegenation, birth control, flapperism, the social dance phenomenon, and childless companionate marriage.

Antiquated settings and the Victorian-influenced rhetoric of romantic idealism worked to prevent such vehicles for female (and potentially homoerotic male) fantasy from becoming too disturbingly sexual. The historical distanciation also may have prevented their audience from linking these narratives of passion to contemporary debates about female sexuality and the realignment of gender roles and expectations. Women's longing for a full expression of sexual desire might be acknowledged within these texts, but the latter's antimodernist codes also allowed women to placate the strong pressures brought to bear for them to be loyal to respectable bourgeoisie morality. Such wish-fulfilling texts might allow women a fantasy release while they still (paradoxically) satisfied the regulatory demands of that morality. Sexual passion was made sentimental and ideal. As we shall see with Barrymore, in this form sexual desire was an integral part of many of the costume dramas and historical romances aimed at women. Through such means, the matinee idol could become an erotically charged presence in the ecstatic atmosphere so valued by matinee girls.

This erotic element in the vehicles and stars aimed at female theater fans did not escape attention. In the late 1910s some commentators were coming close to naming the previously unnameable in the matinee girl phenomenon. They were alluding to the sexual motivation underscoring the interests of a new generation of matinee girls whose behaviors were not noticeably different from those of their mothers. In a 1917 article a drama critic coyly suggested that Barrymore's "'spiritual beauty'" and "'aesthetic charm,'" emphasized by his faithful fans as the source of their "rapture" over his looks, made them oblivious to the real moral lesson of his current play, *Justice*.[130]

Sexuality represented as "transcendence" and "spirituality" was part of the romantic idiom emphasized in Barrymore's stage vehicles. The most blatant example of this is *Peter Ibbetson*, in which the title character carries on a lifelong love affair solely through a psychic or spiritual meeting of the minds with his childhood beloved, Mimsey, grown up into Mary, the Duchess of Towers (Constance Collier). Peter is a youthful idealist who revisits the country estate of his deceased parents. There, he has a vision of his childhood and of his lost love, Mimsey, whom he then encounters, albeit unrecognized, as an adult. After a time, she recognizes the wistful, kind young man as her beloved childhood soul mate, "Gogo." In response to this, at the end of the first act, Peter embraces Mary's bouquet of flowers to the accompaniment of Schubert's "Serenade." The moment he presses them to his lips was described by Alexander Woollcott as recapturing "a romantic charm almost vanished from our stage."[131]

Peter, it turns out, was raised by Colonel Ibbetson (Lionel Barrymore), a harsh uncle whose name and English ways he has been forced to assume. In the third act, the evil Colonel Ibbetson maliciously suggests to their mutual host that Peter's mother was his mistress and Peter may be his natural child. Knowing this to be a lie, Peter quarrels with his uncle and kills him. The shy, frail Peter is sentenced to death, but his punishment is commuted to life in prison. He and Mimsey begin to "dream true," to share dreams and engage in a "spirit romance."[132] As Woollcott sympathetically described the play: "[In] it unfolds the romance of two kindred spirits who . . . developed the power to meet in their dreams, so that for many years they spent the magic hours of the night in a transcendent union that glorified their lives and cheated utterly the stone walls which made no prison for Peter Ibbetson."[133] Another commentator suggested that, even though the play was adapted from George du Maurier's first novel, serialized in 1890, it was archetypal matinee girl fare:

[The] play . . . if it had been written nowadays, would certainly have convicted its author . . . of having written [it] to stimulate the lachrymal effusions of the shopgirl, a play about which she might telephone her girl friend, at which she might eat bon bons, and powder her nose again in the street.[134]

Woollcott, who confessed to being "inordinately fond of *Peter Ibbetson*," admitted that the play was sentimental fare; he admitted too that its excesses might bring an audience to laughter as easily as to tears.[135]

In its romantic excess the play's revision of the novel's original, prison-bound final scene was particularly troublesome to critics. The new ending suggests the kind of woman-centered, infantilized masculinity that character-builders were keen on reforming. Peter follows Mimsey in death. He meets both her and his mother ("My little son!" she cries) under the apple trees in a heavenly version of his family's old estate. More than one critic dismissed this maudlin finale for its resemblance to Little Eva's ascent into glory in *Uncle Tom's Cabin*, and a disgruntled critic further characterized the entire play as being "utterly submerged" in a "scum of saccharinity."[136] There were positive reviews that tended to focus on the acting. One praised Barrymore for the "notable spirituality in his performance," and another described the play as "a most unusual story of an ideal love . . . the essence of spirituality is wrought out in an atmosphere of poetic sentiment."[137]

Barrymore's second wife seemed to echo general female reaction when she said the play allowed Barrymore to become "the radiant lyrical approximation of Romance."[138] Both the play and Barrymore's performance as the tender (if fragile and ultimately powerless) title character evoked strong responses from women. One female reviewer noted: "As the elusive, pink-wigged Peter he carries you with him. You . . . believe him, I know I did, and my senses—all five of them—did a little swimming."[139] Barrymore's appearance in the touring production of *Peter Ibbetson* was said to have prompted sighs from women all over the nation. A New York woman announced that she had seen the play forty-five times;[140] another was rushed from the theater to the hospital because of "an unaccountable weeping hysteria."[141] *Variety* called the play "the biggest theatrical draw on tour"; this followed its breaking of box-office house records at the Republic Theatre in New York.[142]

Barrymore's costar, Constance Collier, declared the play to be a watershed event that would ensure the return of sexual idealism to the theater. "I am sure that we shall never see any more sex plays on the stage," she remarked to an interviewer.[143] In keeping with the play's spiritual rendition of romance, Amy Leslie declared Barrymore to be "vivid enough to found a religion."[144] Soon after, Charlotte Fairchild photographed Barrymore as St. Francis of Assisi.[145] This last example points to how the appeal to women through matinee idols emphasized an idealized iconographic rhetoric. That rhetoric often focused on the aesthetic and spiritual value of the charismatic male body or face.

A "totemistic aura" is how Nina Auerbach characterizes such a phenomenon in reference to women. Such an aura, she notes, was regularly attributed to parts of the body, especially women's hands, in late nineteenth-century art and literature.[146] Emulating this discourse on the female anatomy in its mystical and spiritual expressiveness, *Woman's Home Companion* offered a drawing of Barrymore's hand in 1919 and noted: "John Barrymore's hand is lean and powerful in structure, able and productive, with limitless potentialities along the lines of all artistic expression, a truly constructive hand."[147] More predictably, the actor's famous profile was reproduced in line drawings, cameo silhouette, and soft-focus, painterly photographs.

Peter's Ibbetson's soul-elevating fusion with the beloved Mimsey was a blissful communication through the imagination. In this respect it perfectly represented a Victorian intensity of sexual feeling expressed through a spiritually infused aura. Peter is delivered to a classic late Victorian reunion, oedipalized and oceanic, with Mimsey and his beloved mother. Through such strategies, ardent love could be fulfilled delicately, without the need for entwining bodies in the here and now. But even if physical desire was effectively displaced in *Peter Ibbetson*'s Victorian-originated narrative, the suggestion of it was not—nor could it be—eliminated from the performance of the male matinee idol.

Why did this strategy appeal to an audience of "New Women" thought to be on the cusp of a sexual revolution? Rather than substitute for the erotic male body, the rhetoric of spirituality and redemptive transformation contextualized the visual presentation of the star-object to erotically enhance the matinee idol's fascinating, often sexually ambiguous allure. As suggested, Barrymore's "knife-blade profile" was widely admired, and Michael Strange characterized her husband's performance in *Peter Ibbetson* as "a poetry of head and throat."[148] However, the play did not neglect to offer ample display of the thirty-six-year-old actor's unusually youthful figure. Form-fitting costumes emphasized his elegant, slim physicality in languid poses of love and suffering.

Barrymore's performance as Peter traded on the sexual allure of a physically androgynous, psychologically feminized male. Although Peter is boyish, he is more of a mollycoddle than a Fairbanksian man-to-be. The effeminate mollycoddle type, as the previous chapter suggested, was usually reserved for public censor by that vigorous army of advocates for the strenuous life. The type was succinctly characterized by a vociferous opponent of the feminization of culture, William James, in a description that could serve specifically for Peter Ibbetson: "There is no more contemptible type of human character than that of the nervous sentimentalist and dreamer, who

"A poetry of the head and throat"—and body: John
Barrymore as Peter Ibbetson (c. 1917) (Courtesy of
the Museum of the City of New York, 50.178.250;
Gift of Mr. and Mrs. Spencer Bergen)

spends his life in a weltering sea of sensibility and emotion, but who never
does a concrete manly deed."[149] The play does provide its romantic dreamer
with one "concrete manly deed"—the killing of the cruelly paternalistic,
hypermasculine male. Nevertheless, it also provocatively suggests qualities
that may help explain the range of strong reactions that Barrymore and his
matinee idol vehicles sometimes elicited—from men as well as women.

Peter Ibbetson, the beautiful, sad young man, seemed to have had
tremendous appeal to male critics in spite of their lambasting of the play's
sentimental, matinee girl aspects. Certainly, as the previous chapter noted,
the era's ideal of masculinity did not exclude gentleness or gentlemanli-
ness, or even an admission of the need for a little touch of the feminine in
a well-balanced man. At the same time, there was demonstrable fear of the
masculine antiself personified by the adolescent sissy or boyishly immature
mollycoddle.[150]

As demonstrated in many of Fairbanks's films, the mollycoddle might
be brought safely into proper masculinity through transformation.
However, as the previous chapter showed, the precariousness of such a
transformation seems to have elicited much anxiety during the period. A
process-driven construction of masculinity emphasizing the acquisition of
manliness admits inherently the existence of other modes of masculinity
negatively linked to femininity, passivity, and even worse possibilities.

Peter Ibbetson's youthful gender ambiguity and implicit rejection of
polarized gender dichotomies suggest not only the effeminate, supple,

unformed youth waiting to be transformed into proper heterosexual masculinity but also the homosexual—defined most often during the era as the feminine personality in a male body.[151] Such a reading is consistent with what Eve Kosofsky Sedgwick has identified as the "turn-of-the-century male homo/heterosexual definitional panic" that revolved around the representation of the "desired male body" in sentimental, anachronistic figuration. Such representations, ironically, served to underscore the existence of homosexual desire as a "near-irresistible impulse barely transcended if transcended at all."[152]

Male critics were uncannily uniform in their praise for Barrymore and in their ability to recuperate the sad young man he played into a classification of normative masculinity. Critic Marsden Hartley described the ethereal character in rhetoric that suggests what Sedgwick refers to as the "paranoid-associated homophobic alibi, 'I do not *love* him: I *am* him.'"[153]

A tall frail young man . . . blanched with wonder and with awe at the perplexity of life, seeking a solution . . . as only the dream and the visionary can, lost from first to last, seemingly unloved in the ways boys think they want to be loved; that is, the shy longing boy, afraid of all things, and mostly of himself, in the period just this side of sex revelation.[154]

In keeping with this pattern, Julian Johnson enthusiastically (if incoherently) praised Barrymore's portrayal as a revelation of "the unlit red fires of an unfired manhood."[155]

More than occasionally there is an unpersuasive quality to many of these self-identified descriptions of the adult Peter as a child emerging from latency, as a boy who has yet to be formed into proper masculinity. Boyishness and spirituality become the watchwords of obsessive redundancy.[156] Although the character's lack of action and physical strenuosity would seem to disqualify him from fulfilling cult-of-the-body standards of manhood, Barrymore's *performance* was reconfigured by male critics to meet these standards: "Barrymore was electric in his virile, dominant revelation of this vital individual."[157]

To women, Barrymore's Peter seemed both vital and virile enough to warrant their interest. Although generalization might be difficult within the context of 1918, and an era of cultural transformation, *Peter Ibbetson* does suggest that the dimensions of romance as a woman's form counts on the female's enjoyment of a collapse of gender polarities. For women, visual satisfaction focuses on a beautiful, feminized male. The consoling narrative of *Peter Ibbetson* that made a man more like a woman both emotionally and physically might also serve to calm fears about masculine difference in an era in which aggressive, strenuous masculinity was the stereotyped dominant ideal. If Barrymore's abilities in the "art of wooing" met women's expectations of the requirements for courtship, his character's sensitivity, gentle devotion to his mother, and patience also suggest female-derived ideals of behavior that, if shared by men, would promise a more egalitarian domestic relationship after marriage. Barrymore, not unexpectedly, registered his own, defensive masculine repudiation of the dreamy, love-obsessed Peter as "a marshmallow in a blond wig."[158]

"Tickle-my-chin, what are you, cock or hen?"

In spite of his disdain for Ibbetson, in 1919 Barrymore essayed the role of yet another soft, suffering male, Giannetto Malespini. Giannetto is an adolescent Renaissance painter who uses his wits rather than physical prowess to avenge himself against his enemies in the hoary stage melodrama *The Jest*. Critical reaction to Peter Ibbetson showed how an apparent woman-made type of man, soft and feminized, might be recuperated into hegemonic ideals of masculinity, especially when his one assertion of violence is a murder in defense of his mother's name. Barrymore's role in *The Jest* was even more remarkably explicit (and less recuperable) in its representation of an androgynous male as the object of the audience's desire.

The play exploited Barrymore's ability to be both intensely phallic and intensely feminine, a strategy reminiscent of Nijinsky's dance appearances in the Ballets Russes a few short years before. With *The Jest* the sexualized display of the beautiful male matinee idol generated a barely veiled erotic charge for theater audiences—female and male. Barrymore's entrance in *The Jest* was legendary for its effect on its audiences. A medieval banquet is in progress. Suddenly there is a knock at the door. From the rear of the stage, huge gates open to reveal Giannetto (Barrymore). A dwarfish man is at his feet and a dagger is tucked in his doublet, but there was a more crucial element thought to figure in making this a memorable moment for theatergoers. Michael Strange recalled that the Renaissance tights her husband wore "left no faint fragment of his anatomy to the imagination."[159] With signs of virility veiled but still visibly displayed, Barrymore's entrance was regularly greeted by the sighs and gasps of his audience.[160]

Even as it seemed to play directly on the erotically polymorphous possibilities of spectatorship for both men and women, *The Jest* suggested a heightened gender awareness in its narrative. As the play unfolds, the central protagonist's gender ambiguity makes him the object of homoerotically charged teasing by a pair of oaffish brothers. Burns Mantle, writing in the *Chicago Tribune*, described the foppish, cowardly Giannetto as "a suffering lad. . . . They have cuffed him and beaten him and taunted him upon his womanish ways."[161] Giannetto recounts how he met the brothers Chiaramentesi, Neri (played by Lionel Barrymore) and Gabriello. Six years before, as a twelve-year-old, he had observed them wrestling. He paused to admire their strength and beauty. They stop. Neri cries out to him: "Hi, tickle-my-chin, what are you, cock or hen?" Giannetto recalls that he started to cry, and "from that day to this, we never met, but that they fell upon me with their fangs and claws." He admits to being too cowardly to resist. He cries himself to sleep, night after night, until he meets Ginevra, the daughter of a fishmonger. They are to marry, but the Chiaramantesi brothers pay her father and carry her away. She is installed in their castle as Neri's willing mistress. After the brothers attempt to kill Giannetto by throwing him, bound in a sack, into the river, he devises a plan to destroy them both. Giannetto's revenge succeeds in making Neri appear to be insane. He then lures Neri into accidentally killing his own brother. Neri goes mad for real.

In spite of a plot and dialogue that some dismissed as suited for antiquated melodrama, the play drew raves. Dorothy Parker told readers of *Vanity Fair* that they should see the play even "if you have to raid the baby's Thrift Stamps to buy the tickets."[162] Much of the praise went to the brothers Barrymore, and particularly to John's performance:

> He was a splendid and exotic sight in *The Jest*. His long, slim shanks were encased in mineral green, and he moved through the gore and passion of the play with the grace of a young sapling—a green flame against the shadow of the bully. . . . Much of that same slim, febrile quality has come into all roles he has played since—even into his Hamlet.[163]

In the *New York Times* John Corbin declared that "John Barrymore has never been more strikingly, mordantly beautiful."[164] H. I. Brock suggested that, with *The Jest*, Barrymore succeeded in appealing to more than matinee girls: "He won the admiration of others, less emotional and, perhaps, more discriminating."[165] But other reactions indicate that what the matinee girls admired in Barrymore did not go unnoticed by others. Several observers noted that some playgoers claimed to be so shocked by the production's frank language and sadistic, last-act revenge that they were compelled to leave before the final curtain came down. Michael Strange speculated that people found the play shocking because it hit "the bull's eye of epileptic sensuosity."[166] Strange continues: "After this portrayal, men, women and children left Jack in no doubt as to their intentions if only they

Heightened gender awareness in a hoary stage melodrama: Maude Hanaford,
Lionel Barrymore, John Barrymore, and Arthur Forrest in *The Jest* (1919)
(Courtesy of the Museum of the City of New York)

could get hold of him. For he had looked as arresting as Lucifer, in his
dynamic beauty, and bravura evil, and seemed emotionally to project a
startling degree of promise."[167]

Barrymore's performance proved that the male bodily image, normalized in its public display via the cult of the body and stars like Fairbanks,
no longer could escape attention in another potential, more threatening
(or liberating) theatrical function: as an object of a sexual gaze available to
both women and men. That gaze, focusing so determinedly on the seemingly youthful, bisexually beautiful male, threatened to make explicit the
homoerotic potential of the male body, so vigorously defended against by
cult of the body advocates.

Reactions to *The Jest* may imply that the American stage in the late
1910s tolerated, if not perpetuated, a discourse on male beauty with connotations of gender anxiety, sexual ambiguity, and social marginalization
(as well as other interesting elements) linked to women's desires and their
consumption (and implied creation) of a deviant, effeminate masculinity.

These subversive connotations were difficult to contain fully, even under the rubric of normative transformative masculinity. The latter barely tolerated the feminized male as a formative precursor to true manliness, but as response to *Peter Ibbetson* demonstrates, one way to defuse such a masculinity's subversive potential was to place it under a familiar category of understanding.

In keeping with such a pattern, *The Nation*'s reviewer compared the play to a story of a diver who breathes air from an ancient pirate ship and is transformed from a "mild-mannered youth" into a "swaggering swashbuckler."[168] Even though Giannetto's cunning revenge against his tormentors never changed his physical demeanor as "an effeminate youth," Woollcott made the play sound like a Fairbanks film and linked the revenge plot to boy culture: "Every young boy who has ever indulged himself inexpensively in a daydream that devised torture and deposition for some tyrant in his little world . . . knows what a clean, complete, and purging satisfaction, *The Jest* can afford."[169]

Giannetto's superficial adherence to character-building ideals of masculine transformation might have been provided by the revenge motif incorporated into the play, but there was something more than mere boyish youthfulness to Barrymore's Giannetto. On the European stage, the character always had been played by women, including Sarah Bernhardt. Barrymore's own understudy was "Miss Gilda Versi," and the actor's interpretation of the role was said to have suggested more than a measure of effeminacy.[170]

Photographs of Barrymore in costume from the play confirm this. These photographs, published in theater and movie magazines, follow the already established tradition of matinee idol portraits in composition and in their soft-focus style. One photograph shows him standing clothed in tights, doublet, and cape. His hand rests languidly on his hip, his legs and buttocks are given prominent, "profile" display. He looks over his shoulder and directly into the camera in a manner duplicating conventional feminine poses. In another version of the portrait, he looks down soulfully. In *The Jest* the "startling degree of [sexual] promise" suggested by Barrymore seemed dependent on his performative androgyny. By the end of the 1910s, *Peter Ibbetson* and *The Jest* cultivated a rather remarkable degree of sexual ambiguity in the representation of their matinee idol star.

Barrymore's embodiment of a blending of the masculine and feminine as an erotic ideal—and threat—did not stop when he stepped off the stage: it also circulated in attendant star discourses. One critic divided his face

"Tickle-my-chin, what are you, cock or hen?" (John Barrymore in *The Jest*)
(*Photo:* Culver Service; Courtesy of the Museum of the City of New York,
50.178.253; Gift of Mr. and Mrs. Spencer Bergen)

into its masculine and feminine elements, nose and forehead as masculine,
chin and mouth as feminine.[171] Some well-publicized elements of
Barrymore's personal life also suggested a modern sliding of gender norms
generally regarded by conservatives as "noxious" and "emasculating."[172]
The actor's second marriage to poetess/playwright/heiress Michael
Strange seemed to exemplify the disturbing consequences of a man made
by the New Woman who endeavored to usurp masculine style and privileges.[173] In a blurring of traditional gender difference, they made public
appearances in matching suits and fedoras. In much the same fashion as
Valentino would later be rebuked for succumbing in unmanly manner to
his second wife's artistic aspirations, Barrymore, it was suggested, unwisely
let his suffragist wife become the arbiter of his career when he produced
and starred in her play, *Clair de Lune*. As a lithesome, be-tighted medieval
mountebank, Barrymore was, it was noted, visually arresting as usual.
Although Barrymore drew praise for his performance and the play's opening nights were packed with the curious, the star's female following could

(or would) not save what critics lambasted as his wife's "murky pathological poetry."[174]

Transforming the "dainty altruist"

In 1927 one fan magazine reader recalled how, as adolescents, she and two
girlfriends had nursed "the most persistent crush" on John Barrymore the
stage actor. In typical matinee girl fashion, they wrote poems to him and
spent many nights watching for his exit from the stage door after performances of *The Jest*.[175] Although almost a decade had passed since *The Jest*
had broken records on Broadway for a nonmusical, Barrymore was still a
star, but exclusive to the movies. Nevertheless, his movie stardom, like that
of many other male film stars of the 1920s, owed much to the conventions
of representing masculinity established on stage in the 1910s. Those conventions attached to romantic stage vehicles not only exerted a fascination
over female fans but continued to complicate and even undercut dominant
ideals of masculinity.

Hollywood in the 1920s quickly learned the value of adapting and
exploiting a model of theatrical masculinity with proven, presold appeal to
women. Matinee idol masculinity and the romantic costume dramas that
constituted its privileged theatrical vehicle were often declared passé by the
1910s, but such vehicles would meet with great success in many varied
guises in Hollywood in the 1920s. However, as observed in chapter 1 with
the Ballets Russes' impact on Fairbanks's *The Thief of Bagdad*, Hollywood
was skilled at incorporating the most controversial influences while, at the
same time, incisively removing their most radical implications. It follows
that Hollywood would co-opt a potentially transgressive, woman-made
model of masculinity from the theater and work to tame its most threatening aspects.

Barrymore's theatrical stardom in the late 1910s problematized the
notion of a character-building, Fairbanksian transformation into proper,
strenuous masculinity while it cultivated sexual ambiguity and cross-gen-
dered erotic appeal. As the 1920s came to a close, Barrymore's film vehicles would mute those qualities. In spite of such ideological accommoda-
tion for its mass audience, Barrymore's film vehicles in the 1920s, like
Valentino's, still manage to suggest that hegemonic models of American
manhood could be destabilized, even in something as convergent with
character-building ideals as the historical romance and costume swashbuckler.

An "unsoiled and rather dainty altruist" (John Barrymore as the good doctor in *Dr. Jekyll and Mr. Hyde*, 1920)

Within this context, the formula of Barrymore's romance films of the 1920s—including *Beau Brummel, The Beloved Rogue, When a Man Loves, Sea Beast, Tempest,* and *Don Juan*—uses the materiality of the male body as an all-important yet paradoxical vehicle. It both proclaims the "natural" attraction of sexual difference and yet disavows that difference. Some of these films and their attendant promotional materials employ strategies for presenting that body that are consistent with Barrymore's plays from the late 1910s. However, the resemblances between Barrymore's theatrical presentations and his filmic presentation would be most evident in two of his earliest vehicles of the 1920s, *Dr. Jekyll and Mr. Hyde* and *Beau Brummel.*

In *Dr. Jekyll and Mr. Hyde* (1920), Barrymore's first major film success, the actor's visual representation as a matinee idol followed him intact to the silver screen. In fact, one critic noted, with some amusement, that "his entrance—tight-trousered, withdrawn, highbred, pale—is an almost exact reproduction of Peter Ibbetson's stage entrance."[176] There was no doubt, too, that the feminization of the heroes in *The Jest* and *Peter Ibbetson* was also

Transforming erotic tensions between men into matinee idol fare: John Barrymore and Martha Mansfield in *Dr. Jekyll and Mr. Hyde*

evident in Barrymore's screen portrayal of Dr. Jekyll, who was described by the same Boston critic as an "unsoiled and rather dainty altruist."[177]

In similar fashion, as Barrymore's matinee idol predecessor Richard Mansfield had done, Barrymore offered Dr. Jekyll as a much younger and more attractive protagonist than Robert Louis Stevenson's original bachelor hero. One critic noted that this "younger, more beautiful Dr. Jekyll . . . is made a bit too self-consciously goody-goody . . . but at least, so far as the actor's impersonation of the character goes, he is interesting and human, as well as beautiful."[178] From a certain perspective, Barrymore's beautification of the character is ironic because of its potential to draw the erotic gaze of male spectators. Sedgwick suggests that Stevenson's novel, as a late Victorian "bachelor" narrative, evidences "erotic tensions between men" and functions as a cautionary tale against same-sex desire, which the narrative displaces onto drug addiction.[179]

Perhaps deflecting such tensions as well as being in keeping with Barrymore's stage persona as a lover, the film adds a love interest for Dr. Jekyll in the character of Millicent Carewe (Martha Mansfield), and scenes of drawing-room lovemaking emphasize the hero's lovely profile and figure rather than the heroine's. The film even provides an object of heterosexual lust for the repulsively simian Dr. Hyde; he acquires a lower-class "victim of his depravity," the exotic music hall dancer, Miss Gina (Nita Naldi).[180]

What transpires in Barrymore's *Dr. Jekyll and Mr. Hyde* is, on one level, a reversal of the expected transformation of the matinee idol hero. Early in

Mr. Hyde (John Barrymore): a eugenicist's nightmare of manhood in *Dr. Jekyll and Mr. Hyde* (with Brandon Hurst)

the film, Sir George Carewe (Brandon Hurst), an old debaucher, declares of the youthful doctor: "No man could be as he looks." Instead of going from indolent, self-indulgent youth to romantic hero, Dr. Jekyll, an "idealist and philanthropist," is tempted into an uncontrolled release of passion, albeit distinctly heterosexual passion. He is tempted into this by Carewe, who suggests to Jekyll: "The only way to get rid of a temptation is to yield to it."

Carewe takes Dr. Jekyll to a London music hall where they see Gina dance. Jekyll's attraction to her gives the young doctor "a sense of his baser nature." Thus, he is led to experiment in separating "the two natures of man" into different bodies. Under the influence of the drug that he brews up in his lab, Jekyll creates his other, more primitive self, Mr. Hyde. Jekyll's other self is a eugenicist's nightmare of man, a humpback who walks with a crippled hop and whose misshapen head extends up into a grotesque, balding point. Inevitably, his experiments lead Dr. Jekyll into uncontrollable physical alterations and spiritual disintegration. As Hyde, he throttles Carewe. Eventually he attacks Millicent, but gains control of himself just long enough to administer a suicidal dose of poison.

Looked at from the perspective of character building, the film offers a caricature of boy reformers' notions of masculine transformation in relation to instinct and civilization. Dr. Jekyll's transformation into Mr. Hyde is a grotesque exaggeration of the desired transformation of the overcivilized sissy boy too busy with being good to be interested in more manly pursuits, including the pursuit of women. Jekyll, the sissy, is transformed into Hyde, who suggests an extreme embodiment of some of the qualities of the primitive, instinctual man thought to be natural but also to constitute a danger if unchecked, especially in lower-class, urban men.

On a visual level, the film plays on the wild contrast between Jekyll's attractive form and Hyde's extravagant physical repugnance. Jekyll's face is captured in some dozen soft-focus, backlit close-ups, primarily of Barrymore in profile. The visual style also emphasizes his body in unobstructed full shots that set him apart from other actors and the settings. The negative transformative of the male body ends in the final physical and spiritual release of Dr. Jekyll from the dead Hyde. Conveniently meeting the expectations of matinee idol fare, there is a return to Jekyll's noble profile and fragile, languid body stretched over a chair. Jekyll's/Barrymore's fetishized profile (head, throat and upper torso) is then offered up, via the magic of lap dissolve, for one last view. This image, as well as those of Dr. Jekyll's drug-induced throes on his laboratory floor, certainly harken back to stage convention, but they also serve to crystallize, in visual terms, the process of masculine transformation that character-builders made the centerpiece of their notion of natural, normal masculinity.[181]

Changes in Barrymore's filmic presentation of masculinity occur over the course of the 1920s that seem to make his image (like that of Valentino's) converge with some of the conventions of robust Fairbanksian masculinity. Although his heroes, as in *The Beloved Rogue* (1927), may become more physically playful and Fairbanksian in their daring stunts, Barrymore maintains certain differences in presentation that mark him as woman-made. In this respect, *Dr. Jekyll and Mr. Hyde* is prototypical of Barrymore's films of the 1920s in important ways.

"Too Polished to Be Natural"

Barrymore's films throughout the decade are aware of the value of eroticizing the male body for a female audience, but they accomplish this through means which complicate our notions of what it means to represent a man as an erotic object.[182] Steven Neale argues that in the homosocial patriarchy, "Only women can function as the object of an explicitly erotic gaze"; males who are sexually displayed are "feminized with the same conventions that govern the eroticization of women."[183] The eroticized presentation of Barrymore that I have discussed in reference to his stage vehicles of the late 1910s and the construction of his erotic allure in

John Barrymore—the soft-focus boy in
Beau Brummel

his films of the early 1920s seem more aesthetically, culturally, and histor-ically complex than Neale's briefly stated formula allows.[184]

Perhaps because of the actor's age, in Barrymore's films, even more than in Valentino's, the softness of the hero is literal as well as figurative as shimmering soft-focus cinematography transforms the hero into what one fan magazine writer dubbed "the soft focus boy[s]."[185] The matinee idol's visual idealization creates an illlusion of youthfulness that parallels the con-ventions of feminine eroticization and helps ensure his romantic appeal to an audience of young women. As in *Dr. Jekyll and Mr. Hyde*, the display of the male, especially of his face, is mediated by soft-focus photography that offers up the woman-made male star to the female spectator in sustained moments of static, two-dimensionality—the visual terms of address usually associated with the erotically charged representation of women for male film spectators.

However, those scenes suggesting such a description complicate Neale's notion of the screen "feminization" of the male. Although they are femi-nized by body language, Barrymore's characters often make stereotypically masculine attempts at dominating others, emotionally, physically, or sexu-ally. This is well illustrated by a scene in *Beau Brummel* in which Brummel (Barrymore) tries to reconcile with Lady Margery (Mary Astor), who loved him but was forced to marry someone else. She comes to his apart-ment in disguise as the Duchess with whom he is supposed to rendezvous. She wants to warn him of his enemies at court and the danger that his sex-ual behavior poses to his standing there.

In this scene, Barrymore demonstrates the presentation of his body in ways that not only secure his visual centrality as the star of the film but also suggest a complicated use of the male body as erotic object that relates to

Polished performative masculinity—seductive and effeminate, but still pursuing stereotypical masculine goals: John Barrymore in *Beau Brummel*

his stage work. Brummel sits besides Lady Margery to tell her that he still loves her, in spite of his many affairs. He tries to physically persuade Margery into rekindling their relationship by creating an empathetic attachment to her with the line of his body, the angle of his face as he looks up, submissively, imploringly, into hers. This same configuration of techniques was suggested on stage by Barrymore's Peter Ibbetson as the character's means of creating romantic intimacy with his beloved. However, in *Beau Brummel* these techniques are revealed to be something else—a masculine performance.

Brummel's apparently sincere search for romantic intimacy depends upon the very same techniques he uses performatively to achieve stereotypically masculine goals: sex or money. Like a matinee idol, Brummel has cultivated his techniques of persuasion and performs them indiscriminately on men as well as women. Brummel will cadge money out of a stereotypical poodle-under-the-arm homosexual with some of the same techniques of romantic persuasion he uses on Lady Margery and his many female conquests.

It is typical of romantic film melodramas of the 1920s that when the hero's physical perfection and beguiling demeanor are presented as having little purpose except the seduction of women, he must be rejected by the heroine. Like many heroes of twenties' costume films, many of Barrymore's characters, including Brummel and Don Juan, resemble matinee idols whose bevies of sexually eager female fans want to experience the romantic thrills that polished lovemaking provides. While the hero's sexual experience is posited as being part of his considerable appeal, Barrymore's films tend to suggest that he must be transformed to redeem himself from a sexuality seen as relationally empty and repetitive.[186] He must seek spiritual redemption in monogamous sexual grace. However, Brummel has engaged in performative masculinity so long that the polished physical and verbal rhetoric of all his insincere seductions is the only resource he has left for expressing his real desire. Lady Margery recognizes how Brummel's practiced seductiveness has corrupted him and rejects him.[187] The order of "feminine" love cannot be constructed from the moral disorder of "masculine" sexual desire. In Brummel's failure to speak true love, physically or verbally, the film signals the hero's inability to be transformed romantically and spiritually. The result is his inevitable downfall, which will be inscribed most vividly on his body. By the end of the film, Beau will be a decrepit old man who uncannily resembles Mr. Hyde in Barrymore's earlier production.

Suffering for Love (and Sensuality)

Throughout his film career in the 1920s, publicity and advertising assumed that even though the actor was known as "the prince of profiles," female film audiences, like the matinee girls, were interested in more than Barrymore's famous nose. *Screen Secrets* alludes to this as late as 1928: "How could a story about this Don Juan be complete without at least one picture showing the famous Barrymore figure?"[188] While Barrymore's cinematic incarnation in numerous costume dramas of the 1920s seemed to offer some very modern gratifications for female audiences who appreciated his figure, movie exhibitors reconfirmed the film industry's perception that the male body was what attracted women audiences. Even in the heartland of America (i.e., Ann Arbor, Michigan), advertisements for Barrymore's *Tempest*, like those for Valentino's *Monsieur Beaucaire*, featured Barrymore in a pose from the film in which he is stripped naked to the waist.

The cult of the body muscularity and stalwart poses featured in advertisements for these two stars associated with transgressive, woman-made masculinity may suggest Hollywood's desire in the late 1920s to minimize their difference from robust masculine norms as the debate concerning women's influence on masculinity intensified. It is increasingly evident in the mid- and late 1920s that Barrymore's films present his body in ways that become more consistent with a normative standard of cult of the body masculinity—muscular, athletic, stalwart. The charismatic male body as an exemplar of the values of the masculine primitive is used to turn aside the potential for the perverse that characterized the actor's more androgynous, indolent, and decadent protagonists of his stage career. Barrymore becomes less languid, less morally and sexually ambiguous. In this respect, he is brought into a more normative order of masculinity represented in costume films by Fairbanks.

This leads us to conclude that Barrymore's cinematic incarnation as an idol was not static in its presentation of his body, but adapted to trends in the 1920s that wedded cult-of-the-body physicality with matinee idol values. On one level, these changes many have served as a defensive maneuver to tone down some of the actor's pangender sexual magnetism and the homoeroticized responses associated with him as a male theatrical idol. In many of Barrymore's films a style of presentation reminiscent of his stage plays would be emulated, but these references do not necessarily suggest the exact same kind of sexual ambiguity Barrymore cultivated in *Peter Ibbetson* and *The Jest*. For example, one of Barrymore's costumes featured in *Don Juan* is virtually an identical copy of his costume from *The Jest*, but the rampant effeminacy of Giannetto is modified through Barrymore's more masculine gestures and poses and through a narrative that gives ample opportunity for robust swashbuckling swordplay. In answer to Neri's question asked in *The Jest*, there is now no doubt that our matinee idol hero is a cock and not a hen. This stands in contrast to how Barrymore's body is erotically implicated in his stage work and, especially, in the early costume films, where it is often supple, willowy, pliant, indeed often imploringly "feminine," even "dainty," in attitude.

In films like *The Sea Beast* (1926), *Don Juan* (1926), *When A Man Loves* (1927), and *Tempest* (1928), there is an effort made also to make Barrymore's character a more active figure, comfortable in the company of men. In many of these films, as in Fairbanks's *The Thief of Bagdad*, masculinity is achieved in part by comparison.[189] Everyone else is more effeminate by comparison unless they most obviously personify (like Neri in *The*

No doubt now who is the cock:
John Barrymore in *Don Juan* (1926)

Jest), an oppressive, phallic masculinity. Although they keep company with men, these movie heroes (with the notable exception of Beau Brummel) cannot be conceived to be seducers of men (on screen or in the film audience) because their bodies, while an erotic lure to the spectator, are not established as a lure to other males in the narrative. For safety's sake (in sexual terms), their pals in stereotypical male pursuits (drinking, "whoring," and so on) are grotesque: Villon's (Barrymore's) fat and lean compatriots in *The Beloved Rogue* (Mack Swain and Slim Summerville) are rivaled by Ivan Markov's (Barrymore's) beloved Bubba (Louis Wolheim) in *Tempest*. In spite of these changes, Barrymore's films continued to offer an acknowledgment of the erotic lure of the male body, not only through privileged camera perspective but by setting the hero apart through costume, placement in the frame, and lighting. The male body invites the erotic look.

This contrasts with Steven Neale's claim that most Hollywood films anticipate their ideal spectator as male and so must leave the cinematic male body "unmarked as [an object] of erotic display" to stifle the homoerotic possibilities of men looking at men."[190] Such a cinema would refuse to grant little or any acknowledgment that the represented male bodies are on display for this ideal spectator's gaze. As a result, "mutilation and sadism," says Neale, become the "marks of repression" through which "the male body may be disqualified as an object of erotic contemplation and desire."[191]

While Neale argues that ritualized sadistic violence against the male

The male body inviting the erotic look: John Barrymore and Mary Astor in *Don Juan*

body functions to repress eroticism for the male spectators of Hollywood film, Miriam Hansen has argued that Valentino's films use violence against the hero to evoke eroticism for their female audiences.[192] As I suggested earlier, Barrymore's body serves primarily as the visual vehicle through which romantic "feminine" love is constructed from the moral disorder of "masculine" sexual desire. Under the imperative of such a love, ritualized scenes of violence against the male body serve a higher purpose than just the spectator's sexual arousal: they serve as reaffirmation, as proof—in suffering—of a "lasting form of love."[193] Even the rhetoric of extrafilmic publicity pushed the angle of male suffering in a manner to remove it from conventional stalwart heroism. The original program for the premiere of Barrymore's *When a Man Loves* described the end of the film, an adaptation of *Manon Lescaut*:[194] "While the battle rages on the swaying deck, Fabien bears Manon to the boat . . . 'All for me, Fabien,' Manon sighs. 'For me you have suffered, suffered.' He draws her to him with ineffable tenderness. 'What matters suffering, Manon, when a man loves.'" The program goes on to describe the "Greatest Lover of the Screen" in ways that continue to evoke the critical discourse surrounding Barrymore as a

Constructing feminine love from ineffable tenderness: John Barrymore and Dolores Costello in *When a Man Loves* (1927).

romantic star of the stage and, in particular, his role as Peter Ibbetson: "What a *Fabien* is John Barrymore! So piercingly tender is his love, so breathless with passion and regret, so tragic in its implications, so aching with the transports and tortures of love. *Fabien*, the slim, comely, brooding, unworldly youth . . . Spiritual, luminous *Fabien*!"

Although the erotic male occupies, in some respects, a stereotypically feminine role in love and in suffering, his feminization is qualified through *actions* aimed at protecting or avenging the heroine. Nevertheless, the hero must reassure the audience of his willingness to sacrifice in traditional feminine terms. Suffering serves yet another function in making the hero woman-made. If, as Bataille suggests, "suffering alone reveals the total significance of the beloved object,"[195] then female worth is also confirmed through male suffering. Finally, suffering substitutes for the sex act. Sexuality becomes equated with the swoon, the moment of shared sensation in keeling over in the spiritual bliss of pleasure and anguish. Such romantic moments are illustrated again and again in Barrymore's films.

In *Beloved Rogue* the king's ward, Charlotte, is held hostage in a tower. François Villon is brought out for torture in a moment that visually recalls Barrymore's theatrical entrance in *The Jest*. From a door in the back of the set, he enters a stagelike torture chamber. In this lingering shot, he steps into a full-figure pose that serves little purpose other than to offer a satisfying view of his glistening, seminude body. He is then whipped (in medium shot) and his body is cruelly lowered over a fire. Afterward, he is

Allowing spectators to sexually scrutinize the idol's body: John Barrymore in *The Beloved Rogue* (1927) (Courtesy of the Wisconsin Center for Film and Theater Research, Film Archive)

thrown into a wooden cage to be hauled up the side of the tower. When Villon awakens into consciousness, his cage is opposite a tower cell. From its window, Charlotte calls to him. They slowly extend their hands toward one another, but at the very moment they are about to touch, Villon collapses once more into unconsciousness. Charlotte then proceeds to faint.

This convergence of violence and the unveiled male body may have served a heretofore unacknowledged purpose within an era in which traditional standards of feminine behavior and women's expression of sexuality were at odds. The hero's unveiling in *The Beloved Rogue*, his flaying and frying, is coded as decent since it is for love. Writhing under the blows proves that it is violence that is indecent rather than the spectacle of the hero's glistening, naked body and, most important, rather than the woman spectator who has paid to gaze in fascination at that body. Hence, what we have here is not a straightforward, simple, "sadistic" pleasure, but a detached masquerade of looking in which the hero's punishment removes the taboo from the female look as she contemplates the erotic male object constructed for her visual consumption. With ample precedent in traditional Christian iconography, the taboo of suffering and the taboo of the unclothed body cancel each other out. The hero's punishment does not necessarily foster identification with him or demand an enjoyment of his pain. By imitating the familiar structures of aggression against the male body, the film permits women spectators a cover for quietly violating the taboo against sexually scrutinizing and objectifying the body of the male matinee idol.

Stripped by circumstance for the inevitable erotic encounter: John Barrymore and Camilla Horn in *Tempest* (1928)

Violence may have been used in such vehicles to mask the taboo status of the spectator's own sensual visual pleasure that also proved so frightening (and compelling) to historical audiences viewing *The Jest*.[196] Thus, Neale's claim about Hollywood film's repression of male erotic looking through violence may be correct in reference to very specific historical (and generic) examples, but it could also be argued that such violence may not curb erotic looking at all—for anyone (male or female). In the historical context of the 1920s, it may have functioned as a conventional filmic strategy that served to remove the taboo of sexual exhibition from the eroticized male body.

Moments of violence in these films may also help purge the matinee idols of an exhibitionist self-awareness of their status as woman-made stars. Indulging in a heightened awareness of his own desirability would serve to feminize the star and throw him into one of the categories of disreputable men, such as those tango pirates discussed in the next chapter, who lived off their looks and catered to feminine sexual indulgence. To keep from becoming one of these species of woman-made men, moments of the hero's most extreme sexual exhibition for the female spectator must be disavowed through the hateful gaze of his enemies or normalized through the presence of other, inevitably less attractive men in a similar state of indecency, as in *Tempest*, when the communal river bath of men and horses for Ivan Markov's (Barrymore's) regiment permits him to be stripped down by circumstance for the inevitable erotic encounter with the heroine.

Transformation and Utopian Masculinity

In spite of these strategies, the films often encourage a conflation between Barrymore's characters and the matinee idol as a figure. This is best illustrated by *The Beloved Rogue*, in which Barrymore plays the French poet François Villon. François's interests are wine, women, and poetry. Although he spends most of his time carousing with his vagabond buddies, Villon discovers that he has a female fan when, in throwing food (and brandy) to the masses, he is accidentally catapulted into the apartment of the king's ward Charlotte (Marceline Day). As if already trained in the Kyrle Bellew school of matinee girl devotion, she is worshiping at an altar adorned by a crucifix. Gripped in Charlotte's hand is not a Bible, but a volume of poetry—Villon's poetry. He tells her: "You have an odd taste in prayer books." She is elated that her unexpected visitor claims to know Villon, whose poetry she adores. But Charlotte is visibly disappointed when she later discovers that this dirty and disheveled man is her "adored creature."

Charlotte and Villon are, in the tradition of melodrama, a most improbable couple, but the presence of Barrymore in the role of the medieval matinee idol who cannot measure up to his fan's expectations means that the film audience and Charlotte need only wait for the transformation of Villon's body and the revelation of his true spirituality (and sexual fidelity). The signal of change comes when Villon tells Charlotte, "You have swept my heart clean." Although, as the next chapter will demonstrate, these crucial transformations of masculinity can be discussed in other terms, their inheritance from Victorian and post-Victorian theatrical conventions is obvious. Villon whispers in Charlotte's ear: "Every man has two souls—one for the world and one for the woman he loves."

Villon is apprehended by King Louis's men for breaking the terms of his exile from Paris, but his execution is delayed. The quick-thinking beggar-poet tells the superstitious King Louis (Conrad Veidt) that their lives are linked: when Villon dies, the king's death will shortly follow. Louis takes him into protective custody. The result is that Villon next appears to be trans-

Comically catapulted into the room of a medieval "matinee girl"
(John Barrymore and Marceline Day in *The Beloved Rogue*)

formed physically into a conventional groomed and be-tighted courtier. He is now a physically appropriate partner for Charlotte, whom he woos in a scene that is played out in a formal garden evoking many a stage set for *Romeo and Juliet*. But in a typical pattern (noted above for *Beau Brummel* and including Valentino's *Monsieur Beaucaire*) the heroine rejects him.

This momentary failure of male transformation foregrounds the fantasy appeal of love as a spiritual transmutation for the male. Love for the heroine must be the impetus for the hero's rejection of sexuality without emotional commitment. It also, contradictorily, registers the appeal of the hero's association with rebelliousness and social marginality. Even within these apparently antimodernist narratives, the hero must rescue the heroine from social and sexual conventionality in a pattern that surely must have resonated with the lives of "transitional" and "new" women searching for escape from restrictive gender norms.

In *The Beloved Rogue* and other Barrymore films, the appeal of the hero as a social and sexual rebel is inscribed typically as a class difference. Thus, the opening title of *Tempest* announces itself as "The storm tossed romance

The fan's odd taste in prayer books: John Barrymore and Marceline Day in
The Beloved Rogue

of a poor dragoon and a princess." As in *The Beloved Rogue*, recuperable class difference displaces what were, in the 1920s, perhaps perceived as the more unsolvable dilemmas of gender difference. Difference takes a social, hierarchical form that reverses normative sexual ideology—prince and beggar girl (Cinderella) are replaced by princess and beggar boy, a formula of great popularity in costume dramas of all types in the 1920s. Rather than becoming the sign of the class elevation of the poor female, marriage marks the woman's acceptance of a beautiful male who is socially marginal. The woman rejects the conventional, safe life and chooses the physically attractive, socially inappropriate male whose fascination is primarily sexual rather than social or economic. Thus, at the end of *The Beloved Rogue*, Charlotte stands dressed in lower-class male clothing, ready to join her roguish husband in his life as the poet of beggars and thieves.

As simple as this romance formula may appear, Barrymore's romantic melodramas of the 1920s use this strategy to create a complex relationship between the female viewer and heroine through the inscription of the gaze that echoes theatrical strategies of the 1910s. It is complicated, however,

Villon as a conventionally groomed and be-tighted courtier: John Barrymore and Marceline Day in *The Beloved Rogue*

through the inscription of peculiarly cinematic means (exchange of gazes) that call attention to the process. The heroine serves as the moral anchor of traditional feminine sexual purity (as she tends to do throughout the Jazz Age, even in flapper films), but she is not precluded from exhibiting a sexual interest in the hero not unlike that presumed of an anticipated female spectator. When the heroine appraises the male body, the act does not always mark the presence of a vamp. The good girl is also allowed a desirous look, but with qualifications. For example, in *Tempest* the heroine, Princess Tamara (Camilla Horn), gives the poor hero, Sergeant Ivan Markov (Barrymore), the once-over when she sees him standing before the military review board in his quest for an officer's commission. She stares at him, but when he looks back she stops looking, and what started as a playful interchange leads to a potentially tragic misunderstanding, one not shared by the audience. The princess, unaware that, in an earlier moment, Markov had almost swooned into unconsciousness at the sight

A revolution reveals his compassionate and noble nature: John Barrymore and Camilla Horn in *Tempest*

of her, thinks that the sergeant is merely lustful. The audience, armed with the privileged sight of Barrymore virtually fainting from bliss after his first glimpse of Tamara, knows Markov is in love. Consequently, the audience is prepared to wait patiently for the unification of the couple, which will necessitate the Bolshevik revolution to level the class differences between them and reveal to her his compassionate and noble nature.

The spectator can revel in the superiority of her reading of patriarchal masculinity over that of the heroine since she sees the full range of compassion, kindness, and tenderness present in the hero's basic nature long before the heroine. She can also stand once removed from the hero to adjudicate the kind of masculine transformation which she regards as important. His is not a character-building transformation into robust manhood, but one that promises that he will become the ideal lover who combines heterosexual satisfaction with an ability to nurture the heroine in a feminine, even maternal way. Thus, it is the hero's emotional transformation that satisfies the central fantasy of a utopian reconciliation between masculinity and femininity.[197] We can speculate that these romances might, at some level, have articulated elements that spoke to women's hope in the 1920s to reconcile patriarchal norms of femininity and masculinity into one impossible mate—a feminized man constructed to satisfy womanly ideals of masculinity.

However, according to Janice Radway, revelation of the hero's hidden feminine sensibility means that modern ideal romances avoid addressing the cultural construction of masculinity: the desired transformation of the hero is actually an already accomplished fact from the beginning.[198]

An unusual ability to retain a caring, playful intimacy with a woman: Villon (John Barrymore) and his mother (Lucy Beaumont) in *The Beloved Rogue*

In keeping with her observation, Barrymore's *The Beloved Rogue* and Valentino's *Blood and Sand* share a noteworthy and similar strategy for inscribing the hero's feminine nurturing capabilities: the heroine's first gaze of attraction coincides with the appearance of the hero's mother. Hansen reads this moment in *Blood and Sand* as one that serves to sanction Carmen (Lila Lee) as the "legitimate companion" for Valentino.[199] But the audience's gaze at mother and son is followed by a close-up of the heroine's face. The camera reasserts the trajectory of her gaze at the loving mother-son couple. This exchange of looks strongly figures in the process of sanctioning Juan (Valentino) to the audience as an appropriate partner for Carmen while it marks her as aligned with the anticipated (female) spectator.

In *The Beloved Rogue* a similar pattern occurs with added, humorous play on the improbability of the romantic couple and the mother's expectations for her roguish son. In their escape from the Duke of Burgundy's soldiers, Villon and Charlotte slide down a snowy embankment into his mother's apartment. Up until this moment, Villon has seemed puckish and childishly asexual, in spite of his reputation. He promises he will not peek up Charlotte's skirts as she slides down the embankment into his arms. Mother (Lucy Beaumont) and son greet each other with elation. He kisses her all over her face and rocks her back and forth in his arms. A reverse close-up shows a smiling Charlotte as she watches them. As in *Peter Ibbetson*, the loving interaction of the hero and his mother affirms his unusual ability to retain a caring, nonsexual intimacy with a woman and shows that he has not completely rejected his expressive, "feminine" side.

If women-made men such as these suggest the desire for a masculinity more on the order of stereotypical femininity, they do not completely feminize the hero. Emphasizing his association with adventure, with excitement, and playful masquerades of identity, Barrymore's later costume films such as *The Beloved Rogue* and *Don Juan* echo Fairbanks and may have provided female (as well as male) viewers with a figure of exuberant activity and freedom who was more in keeping with normative, character-building standards of masculinity. In spite of this, they remain transgressive in serving as important articulations of the social and sexual discontent of their historical female audiences. One reviewer saw screen romance as having a new didactic function within the twenties' changing social climate:

The girls get a great kick out of the heavy love stuff. They come out of these pictures with their male escorts and an "I wonder if he's learned anything?" expression. They claim the screen's the closest they can get to it. But pity the modern lover. He's so tired from holding up a raccoon coat he can't compete.[200]

Providing a secure setting for indulging in a fantasy of mutual romance and sexual interest, matinee idol fare, with its mythologized settings and socially marginalized heroes, signals a rejection of a middle-class lifestyle— or at least a patriarchal stereotype of what the conventional modern lover offers. By doing so, these films may have registered a measure of feminine discontent with the normative model of American courtship and marriage in the early twentieth century.

We must not forget, however, that they still worked to calm women's anxieties about masculinity. Perhaps they satisfied a utopian wish for a man who breaks down gender dichotomies in ways that speak specifically to female needs and concerns. But in their structuring of a fantasy reconciliation of femininity and masculinity, these films neither redress the inequality of male-female relations in the 1920s nor do they question the heterosexual presumption for women. In this respect, they are entirely consistent with other culturally transmitted messages to women in an era obsessed with masculinity in relation to the social and sexual empowerment of

"Kidding the girls" about love?

women. This should not be surprising since, as noted earlier, many costume films of the 1920s and their precursors in theatrical romance drama shared in the cultural retrenchment of antimodernist values. As chapter 1 suggested, they also indicate the displacement of a variety of cultural and gender-based dilemmas into a less-threatening fictional, historically flavored setting. Also, the escapist textual regime of the films might make imitation difficult outside the text, and the woman-made masculine ideal promoted by the films was vociferously rejected by American men. Perhaps a sense of that is evidenced in the numerous letters of protest from men who told fan magazines that the film industry should "quit kidding the girls" about love.[201]

As a domain of representation inseparable from coextensive cultural forms addressed to women, Barrymore's films would not be read in a representational vacuum but be interpreted as one of a number of fictions, of constructed cultural fantasies which fed off important antecedents outside of film. Building on these intertexts and their histories, these films allowed women to adjudicate screen masculinity and its ability to reconcile with feminine values. However, as reaction to the matinee girls suggests, women's influence on cultural constructions of masculinity was controversial. By the 1920s it was under intense and intensely critical scrutiny.

While fans' investment in the theater's and then film's "cult of personality" was subject to ongoing criticism, public diatribes against women's consumption of male matinee idols appeared to reach their zenith in the 1920s. If "The Movie Fan" suggests the real and metaphoric violence attributed to female spectators, male reactions to star images of masculinity aimed at female fans were sometimes equally violent if not more so. In the next chapter we will consider such responses to the most famous and exotic form of woman-made masculinity of Hollywood in the 1920s. We will also explore women's restless desires in relation to this star, regarded by some as the greatest—and by others as the most disturbing—matinee idol phenomenon of them all: Rudolph Valentino.

Three

"Optic Intoxication": Rudolph Valentino and Dance Madness

Let Youth have its fling—but not where it will be soiled and despoiled.
. . . Waltzing has given way to the tango. . . . The Matinee Girl, with
her soda and caramels, her romantic "smile" on the leading man,
whose photograph she hides in her bureau drawer, and to whom, in a
fit of ecstatic admiration, she indites poetic epistles, is being metamorphosed into—what?[1]   —Ethel Watts Mumford,
  "Where Is Your Daughter This Afternoon?" *Harper's Weekly* (1914)

"I wonder where dancers come from," commented the girl.
"Gutter," said the man sententiously. "You can see 'em any day in
Cherry Street bobbin' up and down to the hand-organs."
"But the men? You never see the boys dancing."
"The men? Oh, Lord!" He expressed disgust.[2]   —Louise Closser
        Hale, "At the Back of the Cabaret," *McClure's* (1914)

After his appearances in *The Four Horsemen of the Apocalypse* (1921) and
The Sheik (1921) combined to make Rudolph Valentino into a household
name, the star was promoted to women as the "ideal lover," the "continental hero," "the polished foreigner," and "the modern Don Juan."
Famous Players-Lasky/Paramount quickly realized that Valentino appealed
almost exclusively to women audiences, a fact commented on again and
again in reviews of his films.[3] Women's apparent enthusiasm for their new
film idol was accompanied by the studio's carefully orchestrated strategy of
stirring up interest in the star by stirring up controversy. One newspaper
article (based on a publicity release) following the debut of *The Sheik* issued
an explicit warning: "Don't read this if you don't like a controversy."[4]

To many observers of the 1920s, the stardom of and controversy surrounding Rudolph Valentino was not just the result of studio hype. It was
created because the Italian-born star was the greatest evidenciary support

of women's challenge to traditional sexual relations and American ideals of masculinity. Barrymore's oft-cited suggestion of effeminacy attached to his status as a matinee idol and in his characterizations may have compromised his masculinity to many—including the actor himself.[5] However, Valentino's emergence as a woman-made man was an even more serious matter. The implications were debated on a nationwide scale as the star became the most infamous example of screen masculinity aimed at women.

To large numbers of Americans, Valentino's emergence as an idol seemed to be the result of women's perverse search for a new model of masculinity with an erotic promise that made him much more dangerous than the physically passive mollycoddle or effeminate sissy boy. Normative manliness appeared beyond the reach of a newly emergent type of man in the 1910s and 1920s who was believed to vividly demonstrate the dreaded possibilities of woman-made masculinity, a phenomenon discussed and denounced in antifeminist tracts, general interest magazines, and popular novels. In 1914 Michael Monahan warned readers of *The Forum* that, as a result of "too much womanism," America's "tradition of great men" was lost; taking its place was "an epicene type [of man] which unites the weakness of both sexes, a sort of man-woman."[6]

While this type was sometimes simply labeled a mollycoddle, he was taking on decidedly more dangerous qualities than mere mollycoddles of the past. This new type of man was believed to be dominating fiction even as he was finding real-life counterparts in the world of dance. By the mid-1910s American women had gone "dance mad" and were consorting with "lounge lizards," "cake eaters," "boy flappers," "tango pirates," and "flapperoosters" who, for money, mindless pleasure, or the lack of anything better to do, indulged dangerous feminine desires—on the dance floor and off.[7]

This stereotype of transgressive masculinity was already well established—and much decried—by the time Valentino came to stardom. In 1919 *Photoplay* ran an article praising actor Montague Love by comparing him to the "epicene" male types, described in terms that anticipate descriptions of Valentino: "These are the male ingenues, the civilian wearers of wrist watches, the cigarstand Romeos, the disporters of pink silk handkerchiefs in a corner coyly protruding from the breast pocket, the smokers of perfumed cigarettes, and nine out of ten of them are 'dancing just simply divinely.'"[8] While there were many variations on this stereotype of sexualized and greedy masculinity, at his most dangerous he was darkly foreign, an immigrant who was ready to make his way in the New World by living off women and their restless desires.

This foreign type was considered to be especially cunning in his exploitation of women's "dance madness." Tango pirates of suspect lower-class, often immigrant backgrounds were believed to be using their access to middle-class women at afternoon tango teas to begin relationships that elevated them up the class ladder. They were attaching themselves to indiscriminate women (young and mature, unmarried and married) who chose these parasites for their good looks and smooth lovemaking.[9] These qualities could be cultivated in a leisure-time that normal American men either did not possess or used to make themselves better men through the strenuous life.

Such immigrants inevitably defied normative standards of robust, ebulliently childish American masculinity. After all, as Dan Beard declared, turning a boy into a real man was a transformation rooted in utter Americanness: "We play American games and learn to emulate our great American forebearers in lofty aims and in character."[10] In the context of character-building notions of a perfected American manliness linked to a Protestant, Anglo-Saxon past, immigrants on the order of Rudolph Valentino were viewed as beyond the realm of character-building, no matter how muscular they might become. In an era in which eugenics and notions of racial purity came to the foreground in American social discourse, these men of suspicious foreign origin were thought to be an insidious threat to the nation. Their ability to sexually entice America's women meant that the latter were weakening in their will to fulfill their primary charge: keeping the nation's blood pure.[11]

As this chapter will show, the controversy surrounding Valentino's stardom was part of a broader public debate that centered on the stereotype of the degenerate man who was "dancing just simply divinely" and, it was agreed, seducing American womanhood into rejecting (either in fantasy or reality) the sincere, stalwart American man. As a former paid dancing partner to café society matrons, Valentino was easily dismissed as one of the "menial and sensual" immigrants who made their living by exploiting women's desire for the morally and sexually dubious pleasures that surrounded nightclub and tango tea dancing.[12] His commodification as a dancer threw him into the category of "male butterflies," the ultimate in woman-made masculinity described by one novelist as "that species of male vulgarly known as 'cake-eaters' and 'lounge-lizards,' . . . young men of extremely good looks . . . [who are adopted by women] for amusement much as kings in olden times attached jesters to their persons."[13]

The debate over Valentino, much like the one surrounding social dancing that emerged in the 1910s, centralized issues of ethnicity, masculinity, and female sexuality. In keeping with discussions of dance, it was depicted in the press as assuming a rather strict gender division of loyalty. During his five short years of stardom (1921–1926), Valentino's great number of women fans were counterpointed in their devotion by his well-documented rejection by American men. In 1924 Adela Rogers St. Johns explained: "The men of America have resented Rudolph's popularity. . . . They resent it because they believe he appeals to the worst side of women, because they claim his is the same attraction for women that a vampire has for men."[14] Valentino's vampish sexual desirability, combined with the knowledge that he had lived off women in his past career, fed into the popular assumption that he was, and continued to be, a lounge lizard who pursued the distinctly unmasculine goal of living off the millions of female fans who turned America's movie palaces into "Valentino traps."[15] In terms of popular discourse, he was a "pink powder puff" a "wop," and, in the opinion of the *Chicago Tribune*, the most influential instructor in Hollywood's effeminate "national school of masculinity."[16]

The female cult surrounding Valentino's "ambiguous and deviant identity" has been read as a radical subversion of traditional American gender ideals and a signifier of women's sudden libidinal rebellion against societal strictures.[17] Certainly he appeared to violate twentieth-century codes of American masculinity rooted in a Rooseveltian virility cult, but, as chapter 2 suggested, so did other male stars of the time, including John Barrymore. Nevertheless, Valentino's popularity as a "Latin Lover" was most obviously deviant in going against the grain of the virulent xenophobia directed during the 1920s at immigrants from southern and eastern Europe. Such xenophobia has led Sumiko Higashi to ask: "Was it coincidental that Valentino achieved stardom as a Latin lover during the same years that Italian anarchists Sacco and Vanzetti were unjustly tried and executed?" She concludes that "such questions require a more detailed probing of history than has been provided by previous scholarly work on Valentino."[18]

But what aspects of history should we probe to understand the relationship between Valentino and the historical moment in which he achieved fame? As contradictory as Valentino's stardom may seem, it was the logical result of trends already apparent in film, the theater, and (as this chapter will argue) dance. Here I will explore how dance figures as an important dimension of Valentino's controversial masculinity and its appeal to women. I will argue that Valentino's dance background was a significant factor in shaping his textual and extratextual construction (and reception) as a male matinee idol for women, and that dance conventions figured heavily in his representation of a transgressive masculinity that seemed beyond cultural recuperation. Thus, I am suggesting that the paradoxical rise to fame of Rudolph Valentino can only be understood by reference to the codification of masculinity preexistent in dance, in both its high and low cultural manifestations. Nevertheless, dance has been all but ignored in attempts to delineate the source and meaning of Valentino's enormous popularity with female audiences or to account for the problematic status of his masculinity within American culture of the 1920s.

"A Synonym for Vice"

Dance critic Sigmund Spaeth once noted that "the decade between 1910 and 1920 can be identified primarily as the period in which America went dance mad."[19] The American cultural scene was transformed by a virtually unprecedented interest in dance. Dance madness was characterized by the popularity of new, social dance forms perceived as indecent. At the same time, art dance brought a decadent sensuality to the American concert stage, to vaudeville, and to hundreds of local halls across the country as dancers like Ruth St. Denis and Roshanara performed interpretive ethnic dances that invariably linked orientalism and eroticism in capitalizing on a long-standing American fascination with the East and Eastern dancing.

As a consequence, by the time Diaghilev's Ballets Russes arrived in the United States in 1916, Americans were already familiar with dance's capacity to disturb sexual and ethnic conventions. In true American entrepreneurial spirit, Gertrude Hoffman's Les Saisons de Ballet Russes had not only proceeded to rip off the Diaghilev-Fokine *Schéhérazade* as early as 1911, but she also co-opted Diaghilev's *Cleopâtre* and Strauss's opera *Salome*. The latter had an aborted debut at the Metropolitan Opera House, killed by censorship, but Hoffman's dance version persisted nicely, with one critic remarking: "It grovels, it rolls in horrible sensuality. . . . Can we endure this indecent physical display?"[20] How indeed? Dance was developing an astonishing physicality; nationwide it was regarded as "slightly dangerous," or as one critic called it, an "optic intoxication" that was "awakening all our latent and barbaric sensibilities."[21]

Elizabeth Kendall notes that dance's shocking displays of the body possessed "a special appeal for women—perhaps because of their very unrestraint."[22] After the turn of the century, women filled concert halls to view matinee dance performances. They enthusiastically responded to the demonstrations of physical freedom offered to them by female dancers who, in embracing modern, often exotically flavored idioms of dance, appeared bare-legged and barefooted, sometimes in defiance of censors. Because dance was so closely associated with a heightened awareness of the body, its fascination for women was noted with varying degrees of alarm. In 1920 one female commentator pointedly criticized Americans for being "below par in appreciation of dancing": "We are still prudes. . . . The minute a dancer appears there is a tightening of the muscle and a closing of the mind, as prone as we are to be ashamed of the body. We are still shocked by bare feet."[23]

Ballets Russes danseur Adolph Bolm noted that actors had been superseded by dancers as the primary class of social outcasts; they were exhibited for entertainment but otherwise shunned: "Today the dancer is looked upon in much the same Puritan scorn and aloofness."[24] Actress Ellen Terry seemed to offer confirmation of this new pecking order among theater-bound performers when she suggested that "the word 'ballet' [was] a sort of synonym for vice" because "it provides an opportunity for women to attract admirers—not of their dancing but of their physical charm."[25]

The social barriers created by such notions did not stop veritable hordes of girls and young women from entering dance schools, which sprang up all over the country in the 1910s. The preeminent schools (including Denishawn, the Kosloff School, and the Noyes School) attempted to imbue themselves with respectability through an emphasis on the sheer multiplicity of dance's moral and physical benefits to young womanhood; in response, Frederick Lewis Allen poked fun at them in a *Vanity Fair* article of 1915, as "schools of rhythm, hygiene, physical culture and correlated arts prancing among the sand dunes."[26]

Women were so dominant in American dance that it was suggested that the participation of more men "would help relieve the dance of the curse of femininity and cure us of the false idea that dancing is female and frippery."[27] Nevertheless, when male dancers did appear, they often were derided. Credited with resituating the male dancer at the center of ballet, Vaslav Nijinsky provoked special antagonism among the nation's male critics, who dismissed him for his "lack of virility" and "unprepossessing effeminacy."[28]

Critics ran hot and cold when it came to Nijinsky and were especially hostile toward his "effeminate" performances in *Narcisse* and *Le Spectre de la Rose*. One snidely remarked that the "impersonation of Narcisse seemed to be congenial to Mr. Nijinsky, who robed it in feminine graces,"[29] and it

Nijinsky as the Golden Slave: provoking special antagonism for his lack of masculinity (Courtesy of the New York Public Library for the Performing Arts, Dance Collection; Astor, Lenox, and Tilden Foundations)

followed that Nijinsky's appeal to women seemed a mystery to many commentators: a *New York Journal* reporter asked: "What is it . . . that exercises such an extraordinary fascination? His charms appear to lie entirely in his figure. His face can hardly be an attraction, unless there are some women who love ugliness." Uncannily anticipating the discourse on Valentino, the racial nature of this particular attack becomes apparent when the reporter goes on to remark that Nijinsky "has the high cheek bones, the broad flat nose and the thick lips of the Mongolian race."[30] Occasionally, other danseurs were praised if, by comparison with Nijinsky, they managed, like Mikhail Mordkin, to appear "more virile and quite as much at home in the air."[31] But to mention any male dancer meant that the issue of masculinity required discussion, for Nijinsky's "effeminate quality," remarked upon in numerous reviews, was regarded by many Americans as "almost inseparable from the male Ballet dancer."[32]

The debate on dance and masculinity elicited by Nijinsky and his performances was just one of the controversies provoked by the Ballets Russes, those "last orientalists" who were also, says Peter Wollen, the "first modernists."[33] The American public was already familiar with modern dance's reliance on orientalist fantasy, but the Diaghilev company was particularly adept at commercially exploiting its transgression of gender and sexual norms.[34] The Ballets Russes' national tour seemed to prove that the appeal of art dance was inseparable from the appeal of controversy. Publicity anticipated and then surrounded the company's shocking depictions of everything from orgiastic racial miscegenation in *Schéhérazade* to

Nijinsky's choreographic interpretation of masturbation for *L'Après-midi d'un Faune*.[35]

In spite of art dance's controversial inscriptions of the human body and sexual desire, aesthetic motivation (and European inspiration) often provided an adequate excuse for the shock of the new. As a result, the most unrelenting condemnations of dance were frequently directed beyond the proscenium arch, at American social dancing, which was fostering a startling casual intimacy between men and women.[36] The new social dances enthusiastically taken up by middle-class women in chic urban cabarets and tango palaces were regarded as indecent in their movements, immoral in their influence, and shocking in their "American and South American negroid origin."[37] A *New York Sun* commentator declared: "Far from being 'new,' these dances are a reversion to the grossest practices of savage man" and "are based on the primitive motive of orgies enjoyed by the aboriginal inhabitants of every uncivilized land."[38]

The "grotesque" movements of these "primitive" dances brought women into unprecedented physical contact with their partners. Especially at afternoon tango teas, these men were not likely to be their husbands since the latter would still be at the office—earning a living. Thus, objectionable dances like the tango, turkey trot, and grizzly bear were denounced by one Catholic clergyman as being "as much a violation of the seventh commandment as adultery."[39] The influence of these dances on young, unmarried people was equally destructive. Another commentator suggested that the dances were "well named *animal* dances, arousing as they do little else," and degrading the "moral texture of thousands of boys and girls."[40]

The Destinies of Dance and Film

The titillating aspects of dance did not stop its influence. In fact, the American cinema was primed for its influence of the dance-mad teens. Even though it sometimes has been assumed that dance was not important to American film until the 1930s, the heyday of the sound musical, in those fleeting years between the advent of feature films and the coming of sound (1915–1927) the movies embraced both social and high art forms of terpsichore. Dance found a secure place in American film as the latter became increasingly sophisticated in narrative form, in production values, and in its exploitation of popular cultural trends that might attract a more high-toned, middle-class audience.

The destinies of American film and dance, especially concert dance, were marked by a multifaceted, complex convergence. Both were preoccupied with finding new ways for the body to move, with developing an expressive vocabulary beyond verbal language, and with creating visual spectacle accompanied by music. Dance and silent film had, from the very debut of the latter, shared the spectacle of the human body in movement; film quickly added live music as a conventionalized element of its appeal. Film's silent mime, like that of dance, moved to music, not only in its presentational mode but also in its creation, as on-the-set musicians frequently provided music for actors to emote by. As a result, dance's expressive pantomime seemed to have a natural affinity with silent film acting.

Moreover, it was apparent that Hollywood had a keen textual and extra-textual interest in dance as it existed in a broad variety of venues.[41] Elizabeth Kendall claims that during these years, Hollywood was willing to exploit theatrical dance because some film directors, like many dancers and choreographers, conceived of dance as "distilled action, pure motion," and as a result, "Movies made dance a presence, a mood, rather than a choreographic art with rules."[42] But if dance's formal choreographic presence in film often seemed limited, its influence was still abundantly demonstrable, especially in the movie industry's enthusiasm for the visual styles associated with dance, for dance-inspired costumes, poses, and decor, and for the themes and personalities of dance.

Dance's influence on film textuality was also evident by the late 1910s: many films included scenes featuring contemporary or historical social dances such as the tango and Castle Walk, the waltz and minuet. Directors such as D. W. Griffith used dancers as actors (notably Carol Dempster), encouraged Delsarte-based, dancelike pantomime, and, more obviously, incorporated dance scenes into some of their films.[43] Joining a long list of dancers who had appeared on film (including Loie Fuller and Annabella), European ballet dancers such as Anna Pavlova and Theodore Kosloff went a step further to enter the domain of Hollywood as actors and choreographers, costume and set designers.[44] By the end of the decade, café society dancers Irene Castle, Mae Murray—and Rudolph Valentino—became movie stars.

The Melting Pot Sizzles

The rise of social dance culture in the United States between 1910 and 1920 took place within a broader ideological framework marked by women's growing economic and sexual emancipation. In 1914 William Marion Reedy declared that "Sex O'Clock" had struck in America and was creating "a wave of sex hysteria and sex discussion." This phenomenon was not a problem to be solved with patrol wagons, police raids, or "slumming expeditions by legislative committees of investigation," he declared, because the cause was not to be found in the lower classes: "If society is going to hell by way of the tango and the turkey trot and the cabaret show, who started it in that direction?" Why, "'the best people' . . . [who] have made the cabaret show and demanded that it be ever more and more highly spiced."[45] Very prominent among the best people were the "parasite women, the indulged women, the women who do not think" but who allowed themselves to be swept up in fads like social dancing.[46]

To many observers, like Reedy, American women's challenge to traditional sexual roles and male domestic authority in the 1910s was exemplified by the popularity of nightclub dancing and tango teas. The latter, in particular, were regarded as evidence of how American gender relations were changing. During the 1910s large numbers of American women were perceived as departing from long-standing gendered norms in courtship behaviors, in the dynamics of marriage and motherhood, in their expression of economic independence, and in their search for public pleasure. These changes were thought to be spiraling out of control, and a new morality, whether practiced by feminist design or careless consent, was taking hold. Women's active search for public (and private) pleasure was becoming so extreme as to erase any disavowing claim to their traditional middle-class ideal role as spiritual and maternal guardian of the domestic sphere. The advent of reliable birth control, the childless "companionate" model of marriage, and a new sexual consciousness linked to Freudianism all contributed to the legitimation of women's sexual demands.

As chapter 2 suggested, American women were not new participants in the public sphere of entertainment, but during the 1910s they were perceived as actively searching for pleasures that now had more frightening connotations. Nightclubs were drawing female patrons of all ages to negatively influence, it was said, their dress, cosmetics, language, and humor.[47] Women went to see and be seen, to dance and watch dancing. In the 1910s dancers like Maurice Mouvet, Vernon and Irene Castle, Mr. and Mrs. Douglas Crane, Mae Murray and Clifton Webb, Joan Sawyer and Carlo Sebastian, Bonnie Glass and Rudolph Valentino appeared in nightclubs that catered to both men and women. However, in nightclub ballroom dance exhibitions, the sexually transgressive aspects of popular dance, as well as its all-too-obvious violations of class and ethnic norms, might still be controlled. One demonstration of how that regulation could be achieved occurred with the tango.

Maurice Mouvet: a dangerous, dancing "gigolo"
sketched for *Current Opinion*, October 1913

DANCING THE ARGENTINE TANGO

Credited with bringing both the tango and the *apache* dance to the United States, cabaret dancer Maurice Mouvet ("Maurice") consciously exploited the sensual, lower-class origins of these dances. Establishing a precedent for other dance teams, Mouvet also exploited the apparent ethnic contrast between himself as a dark "foreigner" (he was really from Brooklyn) and some of his female partners, particularly blonde Madeleine d'Arville.[48] In anticipation of Valentino, the dangerous "Latin gigolo" aspect of Mouvet's appeal was inseparable from his association with "primitive" dances (like the tango and *apache* dance) that played out ritualized extremes of sexual domination and submission. In keeping with this pattern, Mouvet was regarded as a "tiger" for women to "both desire and fear,"[49] an exoticized caricature of the dominance/submission agenda of patriarchal heterosexuality later exploited with even greater success in Valentino's career.

Ted Shawn cynically noted that Americans' extreme self-consciousness and their fear of being different contributed to the toning down of dances like the tango.[50] Public discourse usually cited moral concerns behind the demand that suggestive and barbaric dances be cleaned up. In any case, the era's most popular dancing team, British-born Vernon Castle and his fashion-setting, American wife, Irene, happily obliged. The controversy surrounding the new social dances was so extreme that pictures of the couple doing their dance routines in *Ladies' Home Journal* in 1914 unleashed an avalanche of protest.[51] However, the Castles were able to turn public opinion around. They smoothed out the shocking sensuality of new steps and

Two "tigers" for women to desire: Maurice Mouvet and Rudolph Valentino with unidentified woman (perhaps dancer Joan Sawyer) on the set of *Blood and Sand*, c. 1922

promoted dance as "a beautiful, useful and healthful art which every one should practice."[52] They managed to de-eroticize even the tango with their trademark air of unruffled elegance and lighthearted charm (as well as revised movements). Irene commented in their autobiography: "If Vernon had ever looked into my eyes with smoldering passion during the tango, we should have both burst out laughing."[53]

Less amenable to moral safeguards than professional cabaret dancing and accordingly regarded with disdain by social commentators were the afternoon "tango teas" in which women rented male escorts to take them through the new steps. Ethel Watts Mumford suggested that the atmosphere of the teas was "heavy with unleashed passions," yet the parents of

The Castles' tango: unruffled elegance and lighthearted charm instead of smoldering passion (Courtesy of the New York Public Library for the Performing Arts, Dance Collection; Astor, Lenox, and Tilden Foundations)

the young women who frequented the teas "do not dream that the miasma of the evil night has risen . . . and trespassed upon the safe and protected hours." These girls were exploiting their "daylight privileges" without a chaperon. Sneaking off to the four-to-seven teas, they were "learning the insidious habit of the early cocktail" and dancing "cheek by jowl with professionals whose repute is not even doubtful."[54] At night, America's young women were convincing their irresponsible, youthful escorts to take them to nightclubs. Exposed to a "Dance of Death" at cabarets and afternoon tango teas, these "foolish virgins" were being morally unhinged—permanently—through the influence of dance and alcohol.[55]

While *Harper's Weekly* reassured its readers that dance was not a "sex stimulant" in an alcohol-free environment, young, middle-class women seemed to be purposeful in their pursuit of such stimulation.[56] Countless editorials, short stories, and articles condemned the *dansants* as a dangerous violation of sexual, ethnic, and class norms: middle-class American women were participating in the "careless forming of undesirable acquaintances, the breaking down of barriers of necessary caution" that could lead only to "recklessness of demeanor and action, corruption and moral laxity."[57] If, as Irene Castle declared, "dancing is the language of the body,"[58] then the women who frequented tango teas were learning to speak in a foreign dialect.

Dance was making the American melting pot sizzle. The paid dance partners at tango teas—the so-called tango pirates and lounge lizards—were stereotyped as immigrant, lower-class Italians and Jews who, it was presumed, had acquired a sufficient veneer of clothes and manners to allow them to cater to American women's new preoccupation with the pleasure of dance.[59] William Inglis described them as "flitting languidly here and there, various tall, slim, languid-eyed, hollow-cheeked fellows of anywhere from twenty-five to forty years . . . [who gave] the inescapable suggestion of life spent unwholesomely withindoors [*sic*], of late hours, and sleep by day."[60] Inglis went on to observe: "There was something so clutchingly familiar in the manners of the girls' partners—most of the partners, that is—that one could not help feeling that he was intruding on a scene that should have no witness."[61]

With their primal scene atmosphere and reversal of the expected gender alignment of sexual commodification, the tango teas offered shocking confirmation of how women were breaking with traditional standards of middle-class feminine behavior. From another perspective on this same situation, tango teas epitomized a perversion of the standards by which modern women were supposed to judge manhood. In 1920 Knight Dunlap's *Personal Beauty and Racial Betterment* observed that men were traditionally chosen by their ability to provide, but now economic resources were more likely to be the result of "social accident, rather than of personal quality and efficiency." Consequently, women were cautioned to ignore wealth and regard male beauty as a "sign of fitness for parenthood." Yet what might be taken as an endorsement of the values of the tango teas was not. Women had to judge beauty according to a standard of "highest value," which, Dunlap concluded, was the exclusive domain of a narrowly defined "white race."[62]

By 1922 feminist Charlotte Perkins Gilman conjured up readers' memories of infamous true-life cases (like that of Eugenia Kelly) and echoed eugenics-oriented commentaries such as Dunlap's. She bemoaned young women's mistaking of "social decadence" for progress. They were ignoring "their racial authority, their power to rebuild humanity by a discriminating motherhood" and, thus, their opportunity to "cleanse the human race of its worst inheritance by a discriminating refusal of unfit fathers." Operating contrary to the best interests of the nation, young women's primary concern, she noted, "seems to be chiefly in mastering birth-control and acquiring 'experience.'"[63] The danger to America's biological future was clear: the nation's dancing, pleasure-mad women were leading the country into "race suicide."

The notion of race suicide was an obsession during the 1910s and 1920s. During these years the United States was in the midst of a nativist movement that had been building since the mid-1890s. Even as the number of immigrants ranged upward toward 650,000 per year in the early 1900s, a radical shift in their nationality had occurred—with the majority of immigration no longer from northwestern Europe, Germany, Scandinavia, and Great Britain. The immigration debate began to take on the tone of a racial argument as politicians, influenced by nativists, turned their concerns toward southern and eastern Europe.[64] The assimilation of these new immigrants was regarded as a threat rather than a solution: it would lead to a mongrelization of the Nordic/Anglo-Saxon "race" in the United States.[65]

The concepts of nationality and race were conflated and these distinguishable outsiders—Jews, Italians, eastern Europeans—were easily recognized outsiders who were susceptible to having their whiteness questioned. Congressman Thomas Abercrombie of Alabama voiced a sentiment no doubt secretly shared by many Americans when he declared: "The color of thousands of them differs materially from that of the Anglo-Saxon."[66] These new "colored" immigrants were not regarded as appropriate material for quick assimilation through education. The rise of the eugenics movement into a secular religion gave a certain scientific credibility to claims of nativists such as Lothrop Stoddard, who declared the offspring of mixed nationalities to be "a walking chaos so consumed by his jarring heredities that he is quite worthless."[67] A successful political consensus was created to close the door legislatively to immigration by these suspect groups whom reputable scientists dismissed as degenerate breeding stock.

Men's fascination with the racial or ethnic Other (à la Theda Bara) continued to be tolerated even in a climate of intolerance, but the perceived freedom and sensuality of the "New Woman" did not allow that tolerance to be extended to the "weaker" sex. Movies such as *The Birth of a Nation* could be read as among the number of stern warnings against race-mixing that suggested that women should perceive the new immigrants in the same racist terms that surrounded African-Americans. In particular, dancing women were condemned for ignoring the potential for personal and national disaster in their contact with the dark and degenerate new immigrants who populated the *dansants*. Under the influence of alcohol, primitive dances, and the flattering attention of good-looking men of dubious origin, these women, it was agreed, were putting the nation's racial purity at risk. They were shattering the sexual double standard, with desultory effects.

While women were swooning in the embraces of tango pirates, their "husbands and sons [were] slaving away in downtown offices." But even these dutiful husbands and sons were not immune from the debilitating influence of dance as a social phenomenon: it was believed that women's "pleasure would ultimately force respectable men to ape the manners of these menial and sensual men to hold their own women . . . and this process would leave them lost and adrift, incapable of success."[68] One editorial remarked ironically that young men should stop worrying about studying law or business: "Why slave in an office or behind a counter when one may dance with the wives of tired businessmen or their youthful daughters and get from $30 to $100 a week for doing it?"[69] Dance, women's pleasure, and the future of American male identity, if not the future of the country, were united in popular discourse even as Rudolph Valentino, film star, would be grafted onto this same controversy.

Transformations of the Picturesque

> The world was dancing. . . . Paris had succumbed to the mad rhythm
> of the Argentine tango.
> —Intertitle, *The Four Horsemen of the Apocalypse* (1921)

After playing the villainous foreign gigolo in a handful of films, Valentino's first leading role came with his casting in *The Four Horsemen of the Apocalypse* (1921), an epic family melodrama that became the biggest box-office hit of the 1920s. As a former paid dancing companion and cabaret exhibition dancer, Valentino's successful film entry into stardom suggests a compromise formula typical of Hollywood's approach in the 1920s to controversial issues, especially those involving women.[70] While *Four Horsemen* capitalizes on the socially transgressive sexual implications of dance, it balances this with elements that suggest an alignment with ideological imperatives that might guarantee the film's success.

The notion that such an epic production necessitated the casting of ethnic actors like Valentino to insure its authenticity was implied by promotion and quickly picked up by reviewers. A *New York World* review noted that "the characters [are] used primarily to give color to the picture— South American natives, Spanish, French, and German specimens—are all strikingly individualized."[71] Another reviewer remarked of Valentino:

A picturesque figure drawn from type: Rudolph Valentino in *The Four Horsemen of the Apocalypse* (1921)

"Here is a particularly well chosen player for type. Especially so since the part calls for an adept dancer of the Argentine tango, for Valentino was a dancer before he was a movie actor."[72] Chosen "for type," Valentino was cast as Julio Desnoyers, a character described as a "romantic South-American hero" and a "picturesque figure."[73] The film exploited the exoticism of non-Anglo ethnicity as well as the audience's familiarity with deviant forms of dancing masculinity, including the male butterfly and the tango tea gigolo. However, it also works to make Valentino's deviant mas-

Taught to be a young libertine: Julio (Rudolph Valentino), with his grandfather Madariaga (Pomeroy Cannon) in *The Four Horsemen of the Apocalypse*

culine type acceptable to a wide audience within a xenophobic and nativist culture.

Before he is ever shown on camera, Julio is described as the spoiled heir to an Argentine ranching family. But he is not to blame, for, as the intertitles tell us: "What chance had Julio Desnoyers to be other than a youthful libertine?" His "wild ways" are encouraged by his indulgent grandfather, Madariaga. At his grandfather's death, Julio moves with his parents to Paris, where he becomes an artist whose only visible talents are collecting female models and dancing. He relies on the latter, his "boyhood pastime," to secure the funds he needs "to satisfy his extravagant tastes": he teaches aging dowagers how to tango.

The film was a complex family-centered narrative with spectacular special effects and extraordinary production values, but many of its advertisements were focused on what was assumed to be its primary box-office attraction: "You cannot have known how the tango can be danced until you have seen: *The Four Horsemen of the Apocalypse*," proclaimed one, while another declared: "It is a dance for the hot countries, a dance of tropic passion! At first seductively slow then abruptly changing to steps of lighting quickness and lithe grace."[74] Not surprisingly, Valentino's first appearance in the film occurs in a stunning dance scene that speaks to the era's fascination with (and fear of) dance as a stimulus on the sexual imaginations of American women.[75]

Dressed in a fantasy version of a gaucho's outfit, Valentino/Julio appears in close-up, puffing on a cigarette as he stares at a woman in a Buenos Aires dance hall. The foreign setting and costuming are important because they serve to momentarily naturalize and normalize Julio's masculinity by distancing it from the potential feminizing traits (sartorial excess, love of pleasure, avoidance of work, consumption) that were associated with the tango pirate in the United States. Julio cannot be accused of being a tango pirate at this point in the narrative since he is a native son whose ability to dominate women finds a thoroughly masculine outlet in "el tango."

The disreputable low origins of the tango as a dance of Argentine pimps and prostitutes are reasserted through the setting and in the heavily made-up female with whom Julio dances. Displaying a barely constrained "primitive" sexuality, Valentino proceeds to whip the woman's dance partner into submission, then slides her across the dance floor in the sensuous maneuvers of the tango. The woman is far from beautiful, the saloon is obviously working-class: but in spite of this—or rather *because* of this—the effect is devastating: Julio's beauty and sexual appeal are inscribed in the tango's ritualized grace and blatant machismo. Julio is the master of the woman's body in the tango's controversial "hot hip contact,"[76] but just as important, he is master of his own. Valentino's body becomes the authoritative instrument through which his character's exotic menace is combined with the erotic potential of a dancer's refined physical expressivity.

The combination of refinement with the dangerous or "barbaric" was a staple element in Mouvet's cabaret dancing as well as in Diaghilev's Ballets Russes. As a concept, it was already being exploited in Hollywood miscegenation dramas of the late 1910s, especially those starring Sessue Hayakawa. In such films the oriental male's despotism was played against his overrefinement to help produce, in the words of one ad, the "delectable romance so inseparably associated with Oriental subjects of the higher class."[77] However, in *Four Horsemen of the Apocalypse* the barbaric and the refined find expression through dance, a form linked in popular discourse of the time to women's pleasure and, as Judith Lynne Hanna

Hot hip contact in "el Tango" (Rudolph Valentino in *The Four Horsemen of the Apocalypse*)

asserts, a mode of communication that may play to women's superior sensitivity to nonverbal communication.[78]

The next appearance of dance in *Four Horsemen* occurs in connection with Julio's calculating, self-interested seduction of Marguerite Laurier (Alice Terry), an attractive young woman married to one of his father's friends. The beginning of their affair is set against the backdrop of a decadent Parisian tango palace where dance-mad dowagers and their male escorts share space with lesbians in drag. In this debauched atmosphere, Julio displays the suave duplicity associated with the lascivious pan-European seducer, a stereotyped role that Valentino earlier had essayed in films like *Eyes of Youth* (1919). Julio invites Marguerite to his studio. There, after a number of her visits, he appears as usual: polite, charming, attentive, accommodating. His pet capuchin monkey (a prop affected also by Vernon Castle) amuses his guest. With teacup perched in hand, Julio makes a rather effeminate figure as he sits on a low settee, his pressed knees together at an angle. He appears to be listening intently to Marguerite's

A Parisian tango palace in *The Four Horsemen of the Apocalypse*

conversational pleasantries. But, in a matter of seconds, Julio is on his feet. He ignores Marguerite's protests and employs a blend of physical force and verbal persuasion to initiate sexual intimacy.

Such conventionally villainous behavior was associated with the mercurial sexuality of the European. Personified in film by Erich von Stroheim, such a man was believed to masquerade his essential bestial nature behind a carefully cultivated facade of continental manners. As a result, to attain normative masculinity Julio must atone for his sexual transgression. Like Barrymore's heroes, he must be redeemed through suffering and the realization of true love, but here, Julio's transgression requires the ultimate sacrifice. Julio and Marguerite's affair is discovered, and they are forced to part. With the advent of the Great War and the loss of Marguerite, Julio realizes a purer love for her, but also a greater responsibility. He dies on a muddy battlefield in France, but effects a ghostly return to encourage Marguerite to fulfill her duty to her now blind husband. Julio's family mourns his loss. To them it is an overwhelming tragedy, but one that can be counted only among the millions.

Julio—charming, attentive, seductive: Rudolph Valentino and Alice Terry in
The Four Horsemen of the Apocalypse

This movement from Julio's apparent misogyny and brutality displayed
at the beginning of the film to love and self-sacrifice is not indicative simply of an "oscillation of his persona between sadistic and masochistic positions," as Miriam Hansen has claimed of Valentino's films.[79] The process
seems more complexly nuanced. *Four Horsemen of the Apocalypse* foregrounds a *transformation* of masculinity that more closely resembles
Janice Radway's description of the construction of the hero in the modern
romance novel as referenced in chapter 2 in relation to Barrymore's
heroes. This should not be surprising since the literary phenomenon of the
romance novel for women, Carol Thurston suggests, may have had its prototype in Edith M. Hull's sensational novel, *The Sheik*, made into
Valentino's most influential film in 1921.[80] Neither should this seem
unusual, in light of the era's obsession with the transformative potential of
masculinity as discussed in the previous chapters. However, as chapter 2
noted, there are different possibilities for transformation, some foregrounding character-building values that produce stalwart manliness, and

others (as in many of Barrymore's films) focusing on a transformation that produces an ideal, utopian lover.

Radway argues that, in the Harlequin romances, the male object of desire must undergo "the imaginative transformation of masculinity to conform to female standards." Initially possessed of a "terrorizing effect," he must be revealed to be other than he originally seems since the narrative must prove that male behavior (and, therefore, heterosexual romance) "need not be seen as contradictory to female fulfillment."[81] This is accomplished by introducing a feature of "softness" that tempers the hero's hard masculinity in the beginning, and then, by showing that the hero has the "quite unusual ability to express his devotion gently and with concern for his heroine's pleasure."[82]

In *The Four Horsemen of the Apocalypse* the hero's "terrorizing effect" is inscribed in the opening tango scene, but it should be remembered that misogyny and sadomasochism were highly conventionalized elements in the tango and the *apache* dance promulgated by familiar ethnic dancers like Maurice Mouvet. Thus, the tango can be seen as metaphorically representing the essential reality of patriarchal relations through its dramatic exaggeration of masculine domination and female submission. Its conventions permit the female spectator to enjoyably experience a ritual confrontation with male brutality. Within the suspended time and space of the dance performance, sexual violence is carefully controlled, just as it is in the romance novel so that a reconciliation with masculinity can occur.[83]

As a consequence of this process, the female spectator of *Four Horsemen* did not necessarily participate in a simple masochistic fantasy reproducing the dance partner's submission to the dark, mysterious, brutal man. She may savor the tango as a *"safe* display"[84] of dangerously eroticized heterosexual relations because she can rely on the conventionalized patriarchal dynamics of dance to displace responsibility for her own arousal onto the powerful male dancer. The actualities of casting and presentation offer the spectator the imaginative space to enjoy being superior—in class, ethnicity, and/or physical beauty—to the woman in Valentino's arms.

Her presumed superiority also allows the spectator to reinterpret the hero's misogynistic male behavior in a sympathetic light that prepares the way for the reconciliation of masculinity with feminine ideals. For example, when Julio returns to his table with his dance partner, his grandfather suddenly collapses to the floor. Julio roughly discards the woman on his lap when she (thinking, perhaps, that the old man is drunk) laughs at him. However, the female spectator may regard Julio's rejection of the inadequate (i.e., slovenly, lower-class, insensitive) woman as appropriate. Ironically, what the film accomplishes at this misogynistic moment is the revelation of Julio's "feminine" side in his tender concern for his grandfather who, in actuality, is dying.

In romantic terms, this revelation is quite significant. It will be extended to Julio's boyish interaction with his mother, whom he unashamedly kisses and caresses on a number of occasions. The emotional and physical closeness of mother and son demonstrated in *Four Horsemen* is duplicated to great effect in Valentino's 1922 vehicle, *Blood and Sand.* A similar revelation of tenderness figures importantly in *Monsieur Beaucaire* (1924) in a moment in which the Duke of Chartres (Valentino) suddenly comforts a black child. The child, a servant to the court, has broken a delicate fan and, expecting punishment, starts to cry. When the fan is discovered, the Duke announces that he accidently broke the fan. The princess Henrietta (Bebe Daniels), who heretofore has dismissed the Duke as a worthless womanizer, has observed his interaction with the child. As a result, she is pleasantly surprised by the revelation that he may be a man of feeling and compassion. A similar strategy is evident in vehicles of other matinee idols of the era, including, as the previous chapter noted, those of John Barrymore. This strategy resonates with Radway's claim that Harlequin narratives of masculine transformation reassure the female reader that the patriarchal system is really benign as they fulfill her deeper need to symbolically recover, through heterosexuality, a mother's love that promises that the heroine will have all her needs passively satisfied.[85]

The early demonstration of Julio's tenderness in the context of familial love in *Four Horsemen* serves to suggest the hero's capacity for such "maternal" nurturing in which tenderness is not merely a prelude to a sexual encounter focused on satisfying *his* desires. That capacity for tender nurturance will ultimately find romantic confirmation in Julio's transformed relationship with Marguerite: he becomes a war hero who reverently kisses the hem of her nurse's veil. This same quality of tenderness would be emphasized in other Valentino vehicles. An advertisement for *The Eagle* (1925) declared its hero to be "as soft as a woman when the heart rules."[86]

In *Four Horsemen of the Apocalypse* dance also provides a nuanced physical revelation suggesting that the beautiful but misogynist man possesses a latent capacity to be another kind of lover, one who combines strength and tenderness. In dance, the hero's authoritative masculinity promises sexual excitement, but women spectators, like romance readers, may see

Tender familial love (Rudolph Valentino and
Rose Rosanova) in *Blood and Sand* (1922).
(A boy's best friend is his mother!)

something else in his refined grace. They may see, in Radway's words, that
he is also "a man who is capable of the same attentive observation and intu-
itive 'understanding' that they believe women regularly accord to men."[87]
It is of no little interest that an interview with Valentino for *Dance Lover's
Magazine* stresses some of these very same qualities in dance: "Would-be
tangoers," Valentino is quoted as saying, "should remember that the good
dancer gives his exclusive attention to his partner."[88] By projecting feminine qualities on the overvalued erotic object, the reader/viewer is reassured that her fantasy lover's sensitivity will preclude his transgression of
the boundaries of her desire. This strategy within the context of dance
anticipates Valentino's declaration to Yasmin (Vilma Banky) in *The Son of
the Sheik* ("A love such as mine can do no harm") and participates in a
wish-fulfilling denial of patriarchal realities.

Subsequent to the release of *Four Horsemen of the Apocalypse*, magazine
articles often catered to the fantasy of dancing with the star. In "When
Valentino Taught Me to Dance," author Mary Winship gives a first-person
account that suggests Valentino's transformation from hard masculinity to
a softer ideal attuned to feminine needs. She begins, "Naturally, I was
scared to death. Who wouldn't be?" and progresses to this description:
"His arm supported me like a brace. I swung myself back, closed my eyes,
breathed in the music and—followed. I couldn't have been so proud if I'd
swum the English channel. . . . The music stopped. Rudolph gallantly
applauded. He's really awfully sweet."[89] Like author Winship, female read-
ers/spectators may have been sensitive to the promise of dance as a trans-

Tender reverence for womanhood: Rudolph Valentino and Alice Terry in *The Four Horsemen of the Apocalypse*

formative experience in which they, as well as the hero, might readily participate.[90] Radway argues that a fictional transformation of masculinity played out in such terms particularly appeals to women unsure of their equality,[91] a situation surely applicable to many American women in the 1920s.

However, it is another type of masculine transformation that probably helped to solidify a wide audience for *The Four Horsemen of the Apocalypse*. Promotion capitalized on the more traditional, character-building spectacle of Julio's transformation from male butterfly into sacrificing war hero. One advertisement described the situation that requires a transformation: "Their [the lovers'] butterfly mentalities do not even respond at first to the sudden shock of war that breaks about them"; another declared: "And when he did enlist it was from a greater force than merely being lonely without his boulevard companions. It was the first time in his life anything but pleasure had actuated him."[92] Of course, men who danced instead of

Julio transformed into a hero: Rudolph Valentino in
The Four Horsemen of the Apocalypse

worked for a living were regarded as prime candidates for a little war service, and Julio's attainment of proper manhood certainly would have provided a measure of wish fulfillment for a broad segment of the American
public: Americans had regarded the Great War as a moral crusade that, in
the words of the *Washington Post*, could turn any "slacking, dissipated,
impudent lout" into a man.[93]

Julio would not be the only Valentino character to require such an ideologically normative transformation. This very same approach to masculinity would be continued in publicity for another Valentino film,
released the following year, *Moran of the Lady Letty* (1922), a seafaring
adventure advertised as the story of "a soft society dandy whom love made
a man."[94] In this so-called "Love Story with a Viking Heroine," Ramon
Laredo (Valentino) is a rich young sportsman who appears to be a "softy"
but needs only to be shanghaied off to sea to prove (à la Douglas
Fairbanks's characters) that he is actually an appropriate, manly partner to
a robust female sailor, Moran.[95]

Nevertheless, such variations on the culturally familiar transformation
of a mollycoddle into a man would not become a regular feature of
Valentino vehicles, perhaps because his characters, as post-mollycoddle
butterflies and lounge lizards, were regarded as more difficult if not impossible to transform into true American manliness. This absence may
account, in part, for the difficulty of those films after *Four Horsemen* to
define Valentino's image of masculinity as socially acceptable (to men) as
well as sexually persuasive (to women). Even when Valentino assumed the
dual personality masquerade of heroic man of daring action and molly-

coddle as put into vogue by Fairbanks's *The Mark of Zorro*, the distance between the normative and insufficient modes of masculinity collapses.

For example, in *The Eagle* Lieutenant Dubrovsky (Valentino) assumes the guise of a mild-mannered French tutor, Monsieur Blanc, and that of an avenging, Zorro-like character, "The Black Eagle." However, by the end of the film, in the guise of Monsieur Blanc, he has made love to the heroine, and it is this less robust personality that seems truer to his real self. Dubrovsky abandons his plans to kill the local landowner, Kyrilla (James Marcus), who stole his family's estate and caused his father's death. Defying Fairbanksian plot machinations and the film's own narrative trajectory, the greedy Kyrilla is left unpunished because he is the heroine's father. Dubrovsky decides that "sometimes a girl is sweeter than revenge." While this affirms the woman-centered values of matinee idol romance, it defies the oedipal, revenge motif of boys' action adventure and its confirmation of man-made, character-building ideals of masculinity.

"Who Said Lounge Lizard?"[96]

In the wake of his appearance in *The Four Horsemen of the Apocalypse*, Valentino's extratextual persona was constructed squarely within terms already applied to "divinely" dancing men, and his career as a dancer was simultaneously disavowed and exploited in fan magazines and film promotion. In particular, the early star exploitation of Valentino as yet another "young and pretty" romantic movie idol revolved around the film industry's manipulation of predictable negative reaction against the star as a woman-made dance commodity of dubious foreign origin.

As early as 1922 *Motion Picture Magazine* published an article, "The Perfect Lover," that described Valentino in terms that both catered to the fascination with the tango pirate and simultaneously attempted to defuse Valentino's (and the pirate's) transgression of American gender norms. Author Willis Goldbeck describes the actor as "suave, enigmatic, with a glistening courtesy alien and disarming." Immediately after this description befitting a gigolo, he advises the reader to "first of all dismiss the idea of the sleek and the insidious. There is nothing repellent, nothing unmasculine about Valentino. Merely a heavy exoticism, compelling, fascinating, perhaps a little disturbing."[97] Although Goldbeck plays with negating the idea that he has raised (of "the sleek and the insidious"), he goes on to hint of another characteristic often attributed to the foreign tango pirate when he notes of the young star: "His manner is always one of repression, repression—volcanic repression, one thinks nervously."[98] Valentino's continental facade hides what some might have interpreted as exciting sexual promise, but others regarded as dangerous foreign bestiality.

Valentino was not the first ethnic, romantic male star, nor was he the first male vamp, but his darkly handsome good looks and his dance background meant that he could not receive the same treatment as other notable ethnic male stars. In the late 1910s Antonio ("Tony") Moreno was promoted in terms that attempted to lessen the potentially disturbing sexual implications of his Hispanic ethnic origins to "white" Americans, and by the mid-1920s he was thoroughly Anglicized onscreen in leading-man roles like that of Cyrus Waltham, New York department store heir, in Clara Bow's *It* (1927). In publicity photos accompanying a 1919 fan magazine article, Moreno wears a paisley sarong and sports a pirate earring. His head is covered by a bandana. One bare, muscular arm is menacingly flexed, his fist is clenched, and his eyes are cast sideways as if observing some unknown assailant. Thus the potential femininity of his costume (the latter unexplained) is lessened by his aggressively masculine stare and muscle flexing—the latter a strategy taken up with a vengeance by Valentino in publicity. Moreno's exoticism is also mediated by another photo in which he grins widely for the camera as he perches in his Sunday suit. He fondles a derby and looks ready to confirm his status as the right type of Americanized male ingenue. "Tony," declares the article's author, possesses "the air of the proud small boy. . . . He is distinctly, refreshingly ingenuous." To conform to the family discourse of fan magazines, the article recounts how Tony's mother planned that her son would become a "great priest." Also squelching any suggestion that Moreno might not be the right kind of ethnic, it is noted that he has "a healthy viewpoint" which includes his "healthy distaste for New York or any sort of night life, cabaret life, etc."[99] In contrast to the "healthy" assimilability of Moreno, not only had his stint as a paid dancing partner marked Valentino as a beautiful but parasitic lounge lizard, but his elevation to professional cabaret dancer had done little to make his masculinity less suspect since the professional dancer was regarded as being "heavily involved in sensual expression, combining the traits of expressiveness, absence of work, love of luxury, and fascination with women."[100]

In the same year, a Paramount-produced fan magazine reveals a direct (if heavy-handed) approach to the problematic implications of Valentino's former profession. Noting that "most screen stars [are] capable of taking up other professions," *Screenland* recites the work-centered accomplishments of other Paramount male stars, then defensively declares: "Rudolph

Valentino could make a good living as a dancer, though he doesn't like it as a profession, but his real qualifications, aside from his skill as an actor, is [*sic*] landscape gardening."[101] In 1924 a letter to a newspaper summed up a view of the star that obviously continued to have currency: "And as for Rudolph Valentino, I doubt whether he could earn a living outside of a motion picture studio or a dance hall."[102]

Rather than redeeming his humble immigrant beginnings in America, the well-known facts of Valentino's multifaceted connection to dance, in combination with the cicumstances of his rise to stardom, merely confirmed his status as a woman-made man. He was woman-made as a professional dancer since he partnered already-established female dancers: Bonnie Glass, and then Mouvet-trained Joan Sawyer.[103] His first wife, Jean Acker, publicly despaired of her efforts to make a man of him during their divorce proceedings and recounted, damningly, how she had been forced to support him: "I gave him money, underwear and clothes."[104] It was reported that he had been brought to film fame by a woman, screenwriter June Mathis, who was later described by fan magazines as "A Maker of Young Men." After her discovery of Valentino, it was claimed, Mathis was besieged by other "young Valentinos [who] constantly obtrude themselves into her home, over the very bodies of her servitors, imploring to be 'made' . . . [and regarding her] 'with conscientiously amorous eyes.'"[105] According to racial stereotype, these stories reconfirmed Valentino's place of public preeminence among dark, desperate, dancing young men with ambition—and good looks.

In spite of publicity pronouncements that attempted to detach Valentino from his association with dance and, therefore, with the foreign tango pirate, that connection was inevitably exacerbated by interviews and fan magazine articles in which Valentino's concern for women's pleasure as well as his ethnicity were emphasized. In an early article for *Photoplay*, "Woman and Love," Valentino (or, more likely, a studio ghostwriter) comments on American sexual relations and speculates on the reasons why the star is disliked by American men. Echoing conservative commentary, Valentino calls American women "too restless"; he then makes statements that capitalize on his characterization of the "masterful" Sheik, Ahmed Ben Hussain, even though Valentino's Sheik was considered by most reviewers as only marginally masterful, a "Continental gentleman" in comparison with his literary counterpart:[106]

I do not blame the women for all this. I blame the American man. He cannot hold a woman, dominate and rule her. Naturally things have come to a pretty pass. He is impossible as a lover. He cares nothing for pleasing a woman. He is not master in his own house. . . . He expects to feed a woman on the husks left from business and gold and money, and satisfy her! . . .

In his blindness therefore, he despises the young European who comes here. He laughs at him, makes fun of him, calls him insulting names. Why? Because this man, versed and trained in all that goes to make everything from the lightest philandering to the deepest amour, exquisite and entertaining and delicate, this man—what do you say—shows him up? Yes.[107]

Exploiting the conservative idea that America's restless women really wanted a "masterful man" to rule them, the article also recirculates the stereotype attached to the tango pirate as the "Continental gentlemen" best known (and least liked) by American men.

This kind of exploitation of the star as a controversial figure was successful, but Valentino's attacks on American men as being obsessed with business and bad lovers to boot were bound to fan the flames of negative male response. Such a publicity strategy exploited Valentino's foreignness in negative terms in much the same way as Universal promoted Erich von Stroheim as "the man you love to hate." But while the strategy for selling Valentino, like that for von Stroheim, appears as the conscious manipulation of predictable xenophobic reaction against a foreign commodity, the publicity discourses surrounding Valentino seemed unable to contain that reaction. Was it because Valentino's prototype, the tango pirate, seemed both more familiar and of more immediate danger than von Stroheim's Hunnish "cross between a crown prince and a weasel"?[108] Was it inadvertent, a result of the inability to control discourses emanating from the star system? Or was it based on Hollywood's ideological and aesthetic discomfort with Valentino combined with the country's discomfort with the immense scale of his transgressive popularity?

Hollywood's familiar strategy of attempting to give Valentino the sheen of European aristocracy failed. The facts of his immigrant life in the United States—as dishwasher, bus boy, gardener, and dancer-for-hire—quickly became common knowledge. One admiring fan noted:

One of the papers commented quite nastily on the fact that they had discovered that Mr. Valentino does not spring from a high-class Italian family, and that at one time he worked as a dishwasher, bus-boy and several other things. I say the lower his origin, the more menial his past work, then the greater glory he deserves, for rising to the heights he now occupies.[109]

The revelation of Valentino's background linked him also to those dark immigrants who wanted to hide what was believed to be their most dan-

Fan magazines stir the flames of controversy about Valentino's masculinity

gerous characteristic: their racial/genetic inferiority. Through their false claims to aristocratic lineage, foreigners like Valentino, it was thought, tried to mask that inferiority while they attempted to appeal to the vanity and naïveté of American women[110]

Valentino's good looks were subject to a debate that put into play racial terms familiar in the discourse surrounding both social and concert dance. The racial nature of earlier attacks on Nijinsky was echoed by Adela Rogers St. Johns, who told *Photoplay* readers in 1924 that Valentino, "with his small eyes, his flat nose and large mouth, fails to measure up to the standards of male beauty usually accepted in this country."[111] Even if her opinion was not shared by millions of women, Valentino's good looks did not allow him to escape the stigma of his ethnic origins. Nor did it satisfy all female fans; the attitude of one *Photoplay* reader was simply stated: "Rudy looks wicked to me maybe because he is not an American."[112] Another responded to Valentino in familiar terms by suggesting that "charm, poise, magnetism, and, above all, good breeding are deciding factors. . . . Beauty is secondary to these."[113] Racial ideology, then, may be a factor in the frequent tragic or bittersweet endings of Valentino's films that prevent romantic coupling.[114]

Race suicide discourse of the time dwelt on a fearful future world scenario resulting from those American women who chose racially inferior foreigners to be the fathers of their children. Within the context of America's racialist discourse, race was the determining factor in class, and no amount of beauty, money, aristocratic trappings, or movie fame could change racial character. It was feared that American women, duped by immigrants—especially those, like tango pirates, who achieved a masquerade of good breeding—would bear offspring who would inherit the ancestry of their dark foreign fathers, an ancestry that was considered to be tainted.

A broad range of popular discourse revealed American xenophobia and the projection of sexual and racial anxieties onto women. One popular novel, *Possible Husbands* (1926), offered a cautionary tale of an American woman married to a European "aristocrat." The novel's heroine, Pauline, tries to stop her sister from repeating her own mistake. She was duped into marriage by a Bulgarian with a "title" because he appeared "graceful, soft-spoken . . . spectacular, witty, suave—and most entertaining to women." But her husband's gigolo charms (which recall descriptions of Valentino) ultimately cannot hide his genetic makeup. Pauline finally reveals her horrible secret: "'The poor fools couldn't stand bearing children,' she sobbed, 'who are cripples at birth because the husband's ancestry is rotten through and through for generations.'" To confirm her words, her young son limps into the room on his crutch.[115] American women were told that foreign sexual entanglements would not only cause them to bear "cripples" but a subrace. As a result, they would be responsible for a situation with far-reaching political as well as genetic implications: they would have created the equivalent of an invasion of American soil by a foreign power. In addition to "mongrelizing" the dominant Nordic/Anglo-Saxon "race," they would be responsible for subverting the nation's democratic values.[116]

By the mid-1920s America's susceptibility to such a foreign invasion through sexual penetration seemed to many to be confirmed on numerous fronts: by tango teas, by movie-star marriages like Gloria Swanson's and Mae Murray's to European "princelets,"[117] and by Valentino's popularity as American women's ideal fantasy lover. Even as fan magazines appeared to acquiesce to women's perceived desire for an exotic model of masculinity, they often also worked to undercut Valentino, as if in response to a need to bring their own discussion of the star into alignment with ideological imperatives at odds with his studio and more important than he.

Instead of unequivocally endorsing him as a profitable film commodity, *Photoplay* attempted to demystify Valentino as the center of women's personal fantasy scenarios. Adela Rogers St. Johns noted that he might represent "the lure of the flesh" to women in his screen image, but in real life he was an "ordinary young man with atrocious taste in clothes, whose attributes render him devoid of physical charm." His leading ladies, she told readers, got absolutely no thrill in playing love scenes with him.[118] Similarly, Herbert Howe warned readers not to "confuse the man with his stellar shade": "He . . . is the pilgrim boy as far as trifling with hearts is concerned."[119] Such discussions implied that just as Valentino's aristocratic heritage was fake, so were his credentials as a lover.

In varying degrees, Valentino's films would also reflect this same ideological undercurrent. In *Cobra* (1925), one of Valentino's rare modern dress films, Valentino is an aristocratic Italian who attempts to escape his heritage of philandering. "I try to behave, but it doesn't run in the family. Women and trouble, trouble and women," he moans with mock sorrow. To escape the angry father of a jilted lover, he befriends a naive American businessman, Jack Dorning (Casson Ferguson), and accepts the latter's offer to return with him to the United States to join his antiques business. Once ashore in New York, Rodrigo Torriani (Valentino) adopts the Puritan work ethic, Americanizes his name to "Rod," and develops a crush on the company's demure blonde secretary, Mary Drake (Gertrude Olmstead). Rodrigo is amazed that Jack can treat girls like Mary "like pals." His own sexy European ways quickly get out of control, even in America. Women ogle him in restaurants and on the street. Ex-lovers blow him kisses from passing cars. Although he is secretly in love with Mary, she doubts his ability to be faithful to one woman. Rodrigo is led into temptation with Jack's new wife, the darkly vampish, modernly materialistic Elise (Nita Naldi). After a single passionate kiss, he agrees to rendezvous with Elise at a hotel. Because of his friendship with her husband, however, he finally rejects her advances and leaves. She calls another man to complete the love tryst and meets a convenient death in a hotel fire. Valentino then sacrifices Mary, his "first pure love," to preserve that rarer treasure, friendship between men. Leaving Jack in the arms of his devoted secretary, a crestfallen Rodrigo returns to Italy to fulfill the film's opening intertitle: "There are times when friendship becomes the most important thing in a man's life—even more than love itself."

Cobra seems to suggest the irredeemability of a European heritage tainted, at the very least, by promiscuity. Rodrigo's forefathers are implicated in a flashback depicting a courtier (Valentino) beset by women. Even Rodrigo's own compulsive flirtations mark him as an inappropriate marriage partner for an average American girl (like Mary). Europe and America are irreconcilable: Valentino must go home to Italy. Thus, the film conforms to racialist discourse just as it conforms to sexist discourse, especially in its depiction of the predatory modern woman. With respect to the latter, *Cobra* anticipates Edward Sapir's warning in 1929 that America was "still suffering from the aftermath of the feminine revolt"; it could not abandon the Puritan codes because Americans needed "an irrational fidelity in love." Sapir declared: "It would be nothing short of a cultural disaster if America as a whole surrendered to continental European feeling and practice."[120]

One fan magazine letter reacted to criticism of Valentino as a foreigner by reminding other readers that "we are speaking of actors and their acting and not of intermarriage with them."[121] Nevertheless, it seemed that the fear that America's dancing women might intermarry with darker, decadent "races" was strongly shaping the response to Valentino as the archetypal representative of those new immigrants from southern and eastern Europe who were the "slag in the melting pot" of America.[122] The "American idol" could not be made American enough.

Refiguring the "Cult of the Body"

It has been claimed that Valentino "inaugurated an explicitly sexual discourse on male beauty" and destabilized "standards of masculinity with connotations of sexual ambiguity, social marginality and ethnic/racial otherness."[123] However, by the time Valentino brought a dancer's grace and exotic sensuality to film, not only had the tango pirate accomplished all these things but concert dance was imbricated in these same already-existing trends. In fact, the latter's iconography literally set the stage for the filmic representation of Valentino's exotic model of masculinity.

Influenced by European ballet tastes, dance in the United States was offering a startling transformation of gender norms through androgynous inscriptions of the male body and reversals of sexual role-playing, often mediated through an iconography of the Orient that reversed the long-standing male fascination with the culturally taboo (i.e., darker) woman and that conflated a wide range of foreignness—Mediterranean, Middle

Eastern, Russian, and Asian. Confirmed by the success of Diaghilev's Ballets Russes, high art dance narratives, like tango tea dances, were often semiotically loaded with ritualized violence within a libidinal economy of excess. As Peter Wollen notes, the Ballets Russes (and the company's many American imitators and precursors that Wollen overlooks), not only unsettled gender norms but helped solidify a cultural fantasy revolving around the Orient as the locus of decadent passion often characterized by a gender inversion of sexual power. In ballets like *Thamar*, *Cleopâtre*, and *Schéhérazade*, it is the phallicized woman who is desiring and the feminized male who is desired and sexually objectified.[124]

In their decadent regendering of desire, the Ballets Russes' oriental dance-dramas exploited the sexually ambiguous quality of Leon Bakst's costume designs, designs that influenced women's fashions for a number of years. While his ballet designs often emphasized the display of a voluptuous female body, they androgynized, if not outright feminized, youthful male dancers. See-through gauze pantaloons, iridescent halter-tops, colorful turbans, robes of intense color juxtapositions with oversize patterns were given shape in sensuously textured materials that frankly displayed the male body as a decorative object rather than as a functional subject. The combination of Bakst's designs with Michel Fokine's choreography helped the Ballets Russes visually redefine "the image of the body, especially, but not exclusively, the female body."[125] Dance's retextualization of the body through the fantastic iconography and moral disorder of an imaginary Orient allowed the male body to speak in terms that many associated with the feminine: androgynous grace, gestural nuance, physical energy expended in the service of submission, and a polymorphously suggestive exhibitionism.

By offering up an eroticized, androgynous, and often orientalized male body, dance—especially that evoking the androgynous exoticism of the Ballets Russes—appeared to be threatening an athletic, physically based American masculinity.[126] Dancing men were particularly dangerous because they seemed to suggest that the admirably fit male body in motion was not enough to guarantee a proper masculine character. One dance critic astutely noted: "While we try to assure ourselves in this country that dancing is as masculine as boxing and the dancers the physical peer of the fighter, we don't honestly believe it."[127] American character, masculine in its essence, was believed to be shaped fundamentally through action defined as bodily movement. While the muscular male body in movement, especially in movement across the American landscape, seemed to ward off

Collapsing the differences between the sexes: orientalist dance as the ultra-natural and the ultra-artificial (a dance study of Anna Pavlova and Hubert Stowitts) (*Shadowland*, c. 1921)

Pavlowa
Returns

the enfeebling influence of women in an overcivilized world, dance was associated with the immoral chaos of "Eurasia" and a perceived feminization of American culture. The Ballets Russes, Denishawn (Ted Shawn, Ruth St. Denis, and their students), and other dancers on the stage and in vaudeville, including Mouvet, exploited orientalism as a meeting of the "'ultra-natural' (wild, untamed, passionate, chaotic, animal) and 'ultra-artificial' (fantastic, androgynous, bejewelled, decorative, decadent)."[128]

Ostensibly, the domineering behavior of the Sheik and an emphasis on Valentino's muscular physicality might have supported circulating views on manliness rooted in a cult of the body, but American men regarded Valentino as a foreign beauty rather than as an athlete. He was a decadent dancing specimen, who, like the "flapperooster," confirmed the increasing effeminacy of men and the masculinity of women. Prominent male dancers like Nijinsky, Ted Shawn, and, later, Valentino undercut the foundation of the cult of the body since they were obviously muscular and athletic yet, at the same time, they were regarded as effeminate if not "queer."[129]

In spite of the popularity of dance, especially in an oriental mode, Americans were mistrustful at best, scornful more typically, of danseurs foreign or homegrown. "Apollo-like" Ted Shawn, the most self-consciously American and "virile" of concert dancers, stirred up controversy about the relationship between dance and masculinity in virtually every venue in which he appeared. In an ironically toned article (characteristic, too, of commentary on Valentino), a Los Angeles paper remarked: "Mr. Shawn has been rather disgusted at certain critics who appear to regard a man who dances as necessarily effeminate. Such foolishness! He is merely

Ted Shawn: obviously muscular and athletic, yet queer (Courtesy of the New York Public Library for the Performing Arts, Dance Collection; Astor, Lenox, and Tilden Foundations)

a well-balanced and splendidly formed man."[130] In one of his numerous defenses of the male dancer's masculinity, Shawn declared: "There is a great difference between having some of the feminine qualities and in being effeminate."[131] But that distinction was lost on most American men, at least in reference to dancers in general and to Valentino in particular.

The role of dance in determining Valentino's popularity was most forcefully illustrated when Valentino walked out on his contract with Famous Players-Lasky in late 1922. He and second wife Natacha Rambova, a trained ballet dancer, embarked on a highly successful dance exhibition tour under the sponsorship of Mineralava beauty clay. The tour no doubt was partly responsible for Valentino's being named the fourth most popular *dancer* in the United States in a poll taken in 1924.[132] If the tour increased dance lovers' appreciation of Valentino, by way of contrast the star's endorsement of Mineralava, a cosmetic beauty clay, in connection with that tour obviously accomplished little in modifying opinion regarding the actor's offensive masculinity; neither did newspaper reports of his relationship to Natacha, who had first come to Hollywood with Theodore Kosloff's ballet company. His marriage to Natacha (aka Winifred Shaughnessy), dancer and designer, fit the gigolo stereotype: she was the Utah-born stepdaughter of Richard Hudnut, a millionaire cosmetics manufacturer.[133] Ironically, it would not be her possible inheritance but her influence over her husband that became the final confirmation that

Sexual fascination inseparable from his connection with dance: Rudolph
Valentino in a dance scene from *Monsieur Beaucaire* (1924)

Valentino was hopelessly woman-made. It was widely reported that she
made unreasonable attempts to control all aspects of his film productions,
including his leading ladies. She was blamed when his films did not please
(especially *Monsieur Beaucaire*), for his sartorial habits (his notorious slave
bracelets), and his artistic pronouncements (Paramount as a purveyor of
trash). One newspaper article of 1924 reported that Natacha wielded "a
mighty hand over the head of Rudy."[134]

In spite of negative reactions against Valentino and his woman-made
violation of a functional, work-centered American masculinity, the star's
films and their extratextual promotion assumed that his fascination for
female audiences was inseparable from his association with dance. His films
continued to feature a dance scene (*Blood and Sand, A Sainted Devil,
Monsieur Beaucaire, The Eagle*) or scenes that incorporate dancelike movements and rhythms.

An example of the latter particularly worthy of discussion within the
context of concert dance is the "rape" scene in *The Son of the Sheik* (1926),

Dancelike movement and repose: Rudolph Valentino and Vilma Banky in *The Son of the Sheik* (1926)

the sequel to *The Sheik*. At this point in the film's narrative, Ahmed (Valentino) believes that the beautiful street dancer Yasmin (Vilma Banky) has betrayed his love, an act resulting in his being brutally beaten by the gang of ruffians with whom she and her father travel. He kidnaps her. First cowed by his anger, she takes courage from her innocence. She becomes defiant. She tries to escape, but he throws her to the ground in stylized *apache* dance fashion. Yasmin gets up to defend herself. They stand face to face as she repeatedly declares that she hates him. Suddenly, he grabs and kisses her. She resists and runs away. With a measured pace, he very slowly stalks her into the bedroom as she retreats. He wordlessly holds his arms out to encircle her as he moves toward her. The scene ends with a fadeout as Ahmed continues to advance on Yasmin.

This scene appears as a highly stylized balletic interpretation of rape. Because of the quality of movement displayed, the scene could hardly be read as being a realistic depiction of sexual assault. Through dancelike movement and repose (sometimes Valentino rests in an arabesque position), the scene may make violence acceptable to the film's female audience by controlling and containing the vicious and brutal aspects of male behavior that women might find objectionable or offensive. As Radway

Direct imitations of dance rituals and poses: Monsieur Blanc (Rudolph
Valentino) and Mascha (Vilma Banky) meet in *The Eagle* (1925)

explains of Harlequin's readers, "Violence is acceptable to them only if it
is described sparingly, if it is controlled carefully, or if it is *clearly* traceable
to the passion or jealousy of the hero."[135] Yasmin, like the romance novel
heroines Radway describes, "is misunderstood by the hero, mistreated and
manhandled as a consequence of his misreading."[136] But reconciliation
between Yasmin and Ahmed can ultimately take place to the satisfaction of
the female spectator, in large part, because the conventions of dance have
permitted a "*safe* display" of the dangers of masculine domination.

   Valentino's dancelike movement, with its ritualistic and refined embodiment of male sexuality, suggests a semiotics of physicality virtually synonymous in the 1920s with notions of dance as a traditionally feminized
mode of expression. These expressive codes of dance are employed in
almost all his films. Only the most badly directed, such as *Cobra* (1925),
seem unaware of the importance of his body as a vehicle for addressing his
female audience and, as a result, obscure Valentino's figure with a heavy
reliance on medium or medium close-up shots, editing that breaks up the

flow of his movement, and props that block our view of him.[137] Remarkable in the extreme is the deliberateness of Valentino's movement, a deliberateness of pacing unmatched by any other male star of the era. If Valentino moves with dancelike precision, refinement, and grace, it is often in direct imitation of the rituals associated with dance (the opening bow), in dance-driven repose, or in modified dance steps—as in, especially, the courtship scenes with Mascha (Vilma Banky) in *The Eagle*.

As the "rape" scene of *The Son of the Sheik* suggests, what sets Valentino's films apart at their most sexually persuasive is not a unique enunciative pattern, nor is it his "feminization" through soft focus, but the narrative as a vehicle for masculine transformation into a utopian feminine ideal, and the role played in this transformation by the dancer's body in suggesting a nuanced range of erotically charged moods, from a languid, passive sexuality (as in *Blood and Sand* when his mother and wife discover him with his dominatrix lover) to a tensely authoritative, domineering one (as in *The Son of the Sheik* or moments in *The Eagle*). While he was much imitated, the dancelike movement and repose that characterized his onscreen presence constituted a talent that his many screen copycats, both ethnic and otherwise, could not duplicate.

In ways related to how modern dance and the Ballets Russes helped redefine the male body within a specific aesthetic context, Valentino helped, at least temporarily, to visually redefine the cinematic image of the male body. This occurred through his onscreen, dance-inspired move-ment, but also through his textual and extratextual costuming. Although his early publicity photos duplicated the starch-shirted attire of Anglo matinee idols such as Wallace Reid and Anglicized ethnics like Antonio Moreno, Valentino's publicity photos increasingly displayed him in ethnic costumes from his films and/or showed him assuming costumes (or lack of them) and poses similar to those employed in portrait studies of inter-pretive and ballet dancers. Most ethnic stars like Moreno had been sub-jected to a strategic visual assimilation into normative ethnic and mascu-line patterns, but Valentino's costumes and dance poses perpetuated the aura of concert dance's violation of ethnic, sexual, and gender norms.

His costumes for *The Young Rajah* (1922), designed by Natacha Rambova, resembled those assumed by male dancers in the decorative mode including Arthur Corey and the Marchon brothers, who performed orien-tal fare everywhere from vaudeville to society balls like Chicago's Pageant of the East. Designer Adrian's Cossack costumes for *The Eagle* (1925) bore an uncanny resemblance to those for Diaghilev's ballet *Thamar*. In addition,

Perpetuating the aura of concert dance's gender, ethnic, and sexual ambiguities: Rudolph Valentino in Rambova-designed costuming for *The Young Rajah* (1922)

Valentino was frequently photographed by Nickolas Muray, whose soft-focus pictorial or painterly style appeared in studies for many American danseurs, including Pavlova's former partner Hubert Stowitts.

Thus, in ways that were already conventionalized in dance, Valentino altered codes used to construct male spectacle in his films and also in the film industry's supporting discourses of fan magazines and advertising. The problematic link between dance representations and Valentino's woman-made masculinity was crystallized in an infamous photograph by Helen MacGregor published in the fan magazine *Shadowland* in 1923.[138] In this publicity still, Valentino appears costumed as Nijinsky for his role in *L'Après-midi d'un Faune*. While Nijinsky was shown wearing tights and a leotard in his faun pictures, Valentino is almost nude. His faun spots are painted on, with the presence of a G-string to preserve his modesty.

Although she was not yet married to Valentino, Natacha was thought to be the guiding hand behind Valentino's emulation of the male dancer most criticized in the United States for his effeminacy. Alexander Walker claims that the couple was so hard-pressed to explain the photograph that they were forced to pretend that it was a costume test for a film about fauns.[139] Soon after Valentino's death, Adela Rogers St. Johns character-ized Natacha as "dominating, artistic, fascinating" and noted that the cou-ple's "stormy matrimonial voyage . . . is generally conceded to have greatly injured Rudy's career."[140]

Conjuring up male anxiety within an area of changing gender relations, Valentino, like *Schéhérazade*'s "Golden Slave," seemed to represent the racial/ethnic misplacement of female desire, but the star also stood for the many American males of the late 1910s and 1920s who perceived themselves as being in danger of being desired and dominated rather than desiring and dominating.

"A Ladies' Man Who is a Regular Guy"

In similar fashion, as the tango's ethnically and sexually titillating effects were first tolerated within American social dance then tamed, Hollywood initially exploited Valentino's decadent differences then reversed itself during the last two years of his career and worked toward a desperate reconciliation of his Otherness with masculine American norms. The reasons for this change can be traced to Hollywood's investment in numerous Valentino imitators and in disturbing rumors that the star's box office appeal among women was slipping. In 1926 *Photoplay*'s Herbert Howe declared, "The Valentino storm has blown over, leaving Rudy to paddle his bark by main strength of histrionic ability."[141]

Textually, the push toward reconciling Valentino with masculine ideological norms becomes apparent in Valentino's last three films. *Cobra* is obvious in this attempt but opened in December 1925 to poor reviews and disappointing returns. Borrowing heavily from a proven Fairbanksian formula for film success, *The Eagle* followed. Demonstrating unusually high production values, *The Eagle* also attempts to mold Valentino into a more athletic Fairbanks-style Slavic hero whose first act is to ride to the rescue of a runaway coach. In contrast to *Cobra*, the film has a light, tongue-in-cheek humor characteristic of the "Lubitsch touch," due, no doubt, to the scenario-writing of frequent Lubitsch collaborator Hans Kraly. As noted earlier, the film's emphasis on action and the hero's motivation of familial revenge give way to Valentino's transformation from masquerading hero to effete French tutor and sensitive lover.

The Eagle also comments on Valentino's matinee idol status through its hero, Dubrovsky. He, like Rodrigo in *Cobra*, must cope with the unwelcome romantic attentions of women. In this case, he draws the attention of a sexually aggressive woman who happens to be his czarina. Catherine the Great (Louise Dresser), swoons over Dubrovsky's charms. She prepares the ritual dinner that initiates young lieutenants into the sexual fast-track for generaldom. But Catherine's sexual designs are foiled by Dubrovsky's own scampish ability to evade her: "I volunteered for war duty only," he grouses after stomping out of her private quarters.

Scampishly evading women's sexual interest: Dubrovsky (Rudolph Valentino) and his czarina (Louise Dresser) in *The Eagle*

Valentino's last film, *The Son of the Sheik* (1926), released posthumously, returns to the same orientalist setting and the dynamics of kidnapping as *The Sheik*. However it, like *The Eagle*, is structured more on the order of a Fairbanks film and includes the typical Fairbanks father-son matrix typified by *Don Q, Son of Zorro*. With its exaggerated swordfights, gallery of grotesque villains, and display of the star as both stern father and robust son, the film attempts to recuperate Valentino into normative cult-of-the-body, character-building masculinity in ways similar to Fairbanks' later films. The *New York Times* reviewer noted, in fact, that the film's emphasis on revenge left little time for the matinee idol's expected screen forays into leisurely lovemaking.[142]

The relative lack of screen passion in Valentino's *The Son of the Sheik* is ironic since, by 1926, the representation of the romantic hero as ethnic erotic object had become a vogue. After recruiting ethnic actors during Valentino's standoff with Paramount, Hollywood discovered the most acceptable Latin Lover: actors who were thought to be from sturdy Anglo-Saxon stock were recruited to play swarthy, passionate foreigners, albeit within the framework of romanticized, Old World settings in films like *The Night of Love* (Ronald Colman), *The Cossacks* (John Gilbert), *The Thief of Bagdad* and *The Gaucho* (Douglas Fairbanks) and *The White Black Sheep* (Richard Barthelmess). Such stars could temporarily satisfy female desire for erotic exoticism without threatening either American men or the nation's Nordic/Anglo-Saxon purity. *Photoplay* promoted Ronald Colman in a 1924 article entitled "A Ladies' Man Who Is a Regular Guy: Ronald Colman Is a Favorite of Both Sexes." Real men, articles like this implied, would never be content to be matinee idols, but wanted to be directors, gentleman farmers, or really good actors.[143] Such stars could, like Colman in *The Night of Love*, masquerade as a vengeful gypsy chief who, in sheik-like fashion, kidnaps a princess, but they also could satisfy the need to channel women into ethnically, racially, and nationally normative models of heterosexual fantasy in a nativist culture.

Even as Anglo-American stars were capitalizing on the ethnic trends popularized by Valentino, the assignment of pejorative feminine and racist traits to Valentino intensified. One typical attack in the *New York World* described a Valentino press conference in which the star's managers told the press that men were swarming around the star because he was "magnetizing" them with his masculinity. Was Valentino aggressively seeking a male audience, as the article implies? A confirmation of this might be found in the textual shift of his last movies to a more Fairbanksian format, but the reporter suggests that the star's shift to seeking male fans is absurd: "In spite of press agents he will probably go until his death a lady's man, smiling that slow white smile, his sooty eyes watching effects."[144] The idea that this dancing foreigner, wearing slave bracelets given to him by his domineering wife, might (like a woman) watch whether he was arousing his fans, was too much to take. Dick Dorgan's classic Valentino diatribe, "Song of Hate," seemed much too mild to express the current level of feeling. It was no longer sufficient to say the obvious, that "all men hate Valentino."[145]

Not long after these reports, in early 1926, Valentino was interviewed for *Collier's*. In the interview dance is portrayed as the last resort of an immigrant's honest attempts to make a living. The star recounts falling back on his dance talents *after* he has pursued all other alternatives: "polishing brass, sweeping out stores, anything." He is quoted as saying of his film career: "I wanted to make a lot of money, and so I let them play me up as a lounge lizard, a soft, handsome devil whose only aim in life was to sit around and be admired by women. . . . And all the time I was a farmer at heart, and I still am."[146]

Only those dancers who appeared to consider dance as purely a business enterprise could hope to be regarded as "regular fellows"; yet the difficulty of any dancer in achieving a nontransgressive masculinity is illustrated by the fact that slurs were even leveled at Vernon Castle, the darling of café society until he went off to World War I to train pilots. A Detroit newspaper editorial, printed after the dancer's war-related death in 1918, bears uncanny resemblance in tone to the *Chicago Tribune*'s infamous "Pink Powder Puff" attack[147] directed at Valentino shortly before his death eight years later:

Masculinity redeemed by death in *The Four Horsemen of the Apocalypse*

Here was a guy who combed his hair back flat an' then polish' it. He hung around tea tables and wore soft shoes. Th' dames with kale used to pay him so much per second for lettin' 'em tred on his toes while a bunch o' crazy niggers beat a lot o' dishpans. . . . A guy that makes a business of it—you know, it's sort o' queer, ain't it, now . . . All I gotta say is—we was all wrong. . . . My hat's off to Vernon Castle.[148]

Another newspaper eulogized the dancer as "the butterfly who became an eagle."[149] Like Julio in *The Four Horsemen of the Apocalypse*, Vernon's masculinity could be redeemed by death: Valentino would not be so lucky.

Where Good Dancers Go

In October 1926 *The Dance* satirically declared that Hollywood was the heaven of opportunity "where good dancers go when they die."[150] Valentino's sudden death of peritonitis five weeks before the magazine's appearance demonstrated a deep if no doubt unintended irony in that statement. Death would not end the debate over Valentino's symbolic place within the perceived crisis in American sexual and gender relations.

In spite of his American citizenship, his contradictory status as erotic outsider would be emphasized even in his death notices. Headlines in the *New York Times* proclaimed: "Valentino Passes with No Kin at Side; Throngs in Street."[151] Newspaper coverage reflected a distinctly unsympathetic bias toward the star. The *Times* reported at length on the fact that his hometown of Castellaneta, Italy, was "indifferent" to his death.[152] In another article it noted, "Flew Floral Offerings," then disavowed the significance of the lack.[153] Coverage acknowledged tributes that poured in from Hollywood to assert for one last time that Valentino was "one of the cleanest and finest stars in the motion picture world."[154] Nevertheless, the *New York Times* felt compelled to undercut such testimony with a report that the Vatican had remarked on the need for *two* priests at Valentino's bedside: "It [the Vatican organ] regards his popularity, with a crowd of young girls crazy about him, as a sign of the decadence of the time."[155]

Valentino, like dance, had become symbolic of tumultuous changes believed to be taking place in the system governing American sexual relations. If concert and social dance confronted post-Victorian America with a "confused realm of beauty and moral uncertainty,"[156] Valentino had confronted the country with other uncertainties as well. While some of these gender-based uncertainties converged with those offered by other matinee idols, such as John Barrymore, Valentino presented a higher order of problematics that circulated around the convergence of female fantasy with the dangerous, transformative possibilities of dance and with the highly restrictive norms for constructing ethnic masculinity in a frankly xenophobic nation. Valentino, "The American Idol," generated a discourse in which he could not escape condemnation as an indolent foreign male whose beauty and grace in motion constituted a mask behind which he was thought to hide the genetic corruption attributed to all such immigrants. Fears linked to genetic inheritance were not isolated in the Valentino phenomenon. Fueled by nativism and the eugenics movement, they were, as the next chapter will show, played upon in other star vehicles far removed from matinee idol fare aimed at women.

Even as Valentino embodied anxieties to some, he represented a promise to others. Just as the Ballets Russes had been poised between old and new aesthetic orders, Valentino had been culturally poised between a traditional order of masculinity and a utopian feminine ideal, between an enticing sensual excess ascribed to the Old World and the functional ideal of the New. Ultimately, the aesthetic implications of American efficiency, productivity, and economy brought formal changes to the arts in America,

The ironies of being an American idol

including film and dance.[157] But the wholesale textualization of the body as a kinetic machine would have to wait, for at least a moment, as Hollywood offered women the "optic intoxication" of Rudolph Valentino and generated a fantastic vision of the reconciliation of masculinity and femininity through a privileging of the dancer's body as a site of expressive knowledge and sensual understanding.

Sideshow Oedipus: Lon Chaney and Film's Freak Possibilities

Aside from such unusual attractions as the famous three-legged man, and the Siamese twin combinations, freaks are what you make them. Take any peculiar looking person . . . play up that peculiarity and add a good spiel and you have a great attraction. . . . It is both amazing and astonishing to see how many freak possibilities there are all about us. . . . One begins to wonder if the whole world isn't one vast sideshow.[1]   —George Brinton Beal,
                                            Through the Back Door of the Circus

The proposed banishment of "freaks" from one of the circuses has been the occasion of much genial comment. Regret has been expressed for their departure, as if they had really been old friends. To some it may have seemed that, having no immemorial pantomime, this nation had made the circus "annex" provide a substitute. . . . Yet . . . [the freaks] were doomed from the day when the public began to realize what they really were. . . . There is, in fact, sound reason behind every one of the efforts to get rid of the morbid and unwholesome in our life.[2]   —"Amusement at the Abnormal," *The Nation* (1908)

In the 1920s the freak show was in its heyday. An entertainment tradition of long-standing popularity in both rural and urban America, it was assumed to appeal to a broad spectrum of people seeking cheap amusement. As a result, freak shows were everywhere. They were part of the circus sideshows, state fairs, circuit vaudeville, Wild West shows, and the "ten in one" tents of the burgeoning carnival business. They had also formed the basis of a venerable institution, the dime museum—on the decline because it could no longer keep up with competition from the numerous other venues for freak exhibition.[3]

In spite of its role as a cultural phenomenon for over half a century, the

The freak show comes to the movies (*The Unholy Three*, 1930 version)

freak show's heyday would soon be over. In the 1920s jurisdictions and municipalities began to restrict the freak show as disgusting and grotesque, as inappropriate and even pornographic.[4] New social pressures would drive the freak show to more marginal, mobile, and obscure venues that would lead to the sideshow pit's demise in midcentury. Nevertheless, in the 1920s the freak show continued to enjoy a perhaps unexpected but equally successful arena—the movies. There the freak show found its most potent and powerful filmic representation in a decade's worth of films of one of the most consistently popular box-office attractions of the 1920s—Lon Chaney. Although he was literally on the sideshow platform in only a handful of his films, he was, as this chapter will show, perhaps no less than America's greatest freak exhibit of the twentieth century.

This may appear to make Chaney a singular personality when it comes to male stars of the 1920s. Chaney's freakish stardom seems to run contrary to the more obvious trends in screen masculinity discussed in previous chapters. However, as often as Chaney's stardom may radically counterpoint these models, it also reveals some unexpected convergences. If a

Lon Chaney, America's greatest freak exhibit: publicity still for *The Unknown* (1927)

star like Douglas Fairbanks was the vital screen exemplar of a blissful, boyish ideal of American masculine perfection, Chaney embodied a startling rejection of those character-building, cult-of-the-body norms. In an understatement, one fan magazine article calls Chaney the star "who made homeliness pay."[5] Chaney's variations on the grotesque male body create a radical contrast with the beautiful male body foregrounded for the audience's specular consumption of Barrymore, Valentino, and, albeit in less explicitly sexual ways, of Fairbanks. By depicting estranged, often bitter men with grotesque bodies and faces, Chaney represents a radical negation of the Fairbanksian ideal. By the end of the 1920s, the star came to occupy a position of symbolic opposition to Fairbanks's representation of the era's high ideals for normative American masculinity in all its possible moral, physical, and spiritual permutations of active, optimistic perfection.

Thus, Chaney's stardom suggests a markedly different response to the same profound anxiety surrounding the cultural construction of masculinity that has been discussed in earlier chapters. Chaney's extraordinary, grotesque physicality came to represent a masculine difference that turned him into a suffering object, both on screen and off. Onscreen, Chaney starred in films whose plots were often lurid meditations on the disabled or pain-racked male body. Offscreen, Chaney's much-discussed lack of a unique star personality was ultimately subsumed under the weight of his onscreen persona as a strange, stigmatized, and suffering man. These strategies pose a radical challenge to the era's normative notions of masculinity, and their challenge, on a fundamental level, exceeds that of transgressive, woman-made models offered by Valentino and Barrymore. However, there is a specific cultural framework for Chaney's almost unbe-

The beautiful male body for specular consumption: Rudolph Valentino in
Monsieur Beaucaire (1924)

lievably excessive male masochism that provides at least one link to the
other stars we have considered.

As noted in chapter 3, John Barrymore was associated with a romantic
suffering motivated, in his plays and films, by the need to prove masculine
sincerity in love and to offer an excuse for the "violent" revelation of his
body to his female audiences.[6] In a way, Chaney's characters extend this
overdetermined phenomenon, which may also have functioned as part of
an antimodernist "fascination with suffering."[7] Jackson Lears suggests that
this fascination was a trend among men of the era who reacted to modernism by seeking out pain to sharpen their "otherwise dull existence."[8]
Such a fascination, at its mildest, might be expressed by a Fairbanks
through the cult of strenuosity in the star's courting of danger and
response to tests of courage and strength. At its most self-abasing and disturbing, we find it in the films of Lon Chaney.

Named by exhibitors as the most popular male star of 1928 and 1929,[9]
Chaney's most obvious connection to the freak show is through the ten
films he made with director Tod Browning, a former sideshow talker. In

Lon Chaney as Alonzo attempts to pass as an armless knife thrower in *The Unknown* (with Nick De Ruiz, seated)

some of their films together, including *The Unknown* (1927), *The Unholy Three* (1925 version), and *West of Zanzibar* (1928), Chaney actually plays sideshow or circus performers.[10] For example, in *The Unknown* he plays "Alonzo," a criminal with freakish double thumbs who binds his arms so that he can pass as an armless knife thrower in the circus. However, the connection between Chaney's film career in the 1920s and the tradition of the freak show's construction of its human-centered spectacle is more pervasive than these handful of films and roles might indicate. Not only does it influence the full range of his roles in the 1920s but, as we shall see, the offscreen presentation of Chaney's star image was amazingly convergent with the freak show.

Remarkably, this fascinating cultural connection between the movies and a significant facet of early twentieth-century popular culture has not been discussed, perhaps because Chaney's popularity has escaped the attention of almost all considerations of Hollywood of the post-World War I period. The films he made with Browning have garnered a cult reputation, but this has not resulted in any sustained analysis beyond the occa-

The box-office bonanza of a human-centered "freak" spectacle: Lon Chaney as Alonzo in *The Unknown*

sional review of a film revival. His best-known films remain *The Hunchback of Notre Dame* (1923) and *The Phantom of the Opera* (1925). While these epic-scaled films provide the actor's most famous creation of horrific makeup, the numerous other films from his seventeen-year movie career are almost totally neglected by contemporary scholars.[11] Instead, Chaney is remembered chiefly by the epithet used for the title of a 1956 fictional film biography on his life: "The Man of a Thousand Faces."

The suggestion of unlimited versatility in this epithet is ironic, for it bypasses the relentless return of "The Star Sinister"[12] to a very narrow range of roles during the height of his stardom. There is irony too in the fact that, in spite of his famed use of makeup and disguise, Chaney was not a star whose face became the exclusive centerpiece of performance. Following freak show tradition, his expressive body was as important as his face in creating roles that came to be characterized as his "experiments in self-torture."[13]

Man-Made "Monsters"

Chaney's historical and scholarly neglect is understandable. The actor specialized in roles in the 1920s that seem so strange as to make accounting for them difficult by any theoretical, historical, or critical standard.

"The Frog" pretending to be paralyzed: Lon Chaney and Betty Compson in *The Miracle Man* (1919)

Contrary to the popular assumption that he was the star of horror movies, Chaney's films in the 1920s were usually straight melodramas that were classified by reviewers as "suspense shockers," "thrillers," "mysteries," or "mystery-melodramas." In many of these Chaney played characters who, through melodramatic misfortune (birth or circumstance), were disabled or disfigured. Even more interesting, he often played characters, as in *The Unknown* and *Flesh and Blood* (1922), who for one reason or another choose to fake debilitating conditions of form and physique. This was a pattern established early in his star career and followed with startling consistency in spite of working with different directors and moving from Universal to MGM in 1924.

In 1919 Chaney came to stardom as a supporting player featured as "The Frog" in *The Miracle Man*. In the film he appears as a con artist who pretends to be paralyzed. By 1925 the silent version of *The Unholy Three* would be viewed as an aberration in the actor's career. *Variety* noted: "He isn't all hunched up, he isn't legless, he isn't this, that, or the other thing

"He isn't all hunched up, he isn't legless, he isn't this, that, or the other in deformities" (Lon Chaney as Echo in *The Unholy Three*, 1930 version)

in deformities."[14] In the Browning-directed box-office hit, which the star chose to remake in 1930 as his first sound picture, Chaney portrays a sideshow ventriloquist, Professor Echo. Tired of sideshow life, Echo enlists a midget and a strongman into a criminal gang to find better "grift" in the outside world. They become "the unholy three." In both screen versions, Echo masquerades as a little old lady who runs a pet shop that specializes in talking birds. As part of the cover for their robbery scheme, his midget companion, Tweedledee (Harry Earles), masquerades as a baby.

In spite of these freakish complications, *Variety*'s reviewer of the 1925 version thought that the actor was "great" as "just plain Lon Chaney," so great, that he was sure that Chaney would no longer play deformed characters; he was confident that "from now on it's going to be another story." But it was not "another story." In the following year, Chaney portrayed a Cockney crook ("The Blackbird") who creates a completely different persona to escape the police. When necessary, he becomes his imaginary brother, The Bishop, a disabled urban missionary beloved by all for his saintly ways and work. In a pattern repeated by many of Chaney's films, *The Black Bird* (1926) moved one reviewer to suggest that the actor was again "satisfying his penchant for portraying a twisted and crippled character."[15] A trade magazine reviewer remarked of the Browning-directed film: "They're still playing up the fact that Lon Chaney can make himself more hideous and misshapen than anybody in pictures."[16] Considering such reactions, it is not surprising that by the late twenties Chaney was frequently defending his choice of roles. In 1927 he was quoted as saying: "It is not morbidity that made me turn to the type of role with which I have become identified. . . . I play unusual characters not for the sake of apply-

A fake granny and a fake baby make sure their fellow grifter knows the score: Lon Chaney, Harry Earles, and Lila Lee in *The Unholy Three* (1930 version)

ing grotesque make-up but always to advance the drama of a startling plot. . . . Grotesqueries as such do not attract me."[17]

Although Chaney may have disavowed an attraction to "grotesqueries," his career became the object of cultish admiration among several generations of male fans who seemed to be quite willing to confirm their own attraction to the grotesque. In August 1958 Chaney was enthroned among the horror icons of Hollywood through a legendary fan magazine aimed at adolescent males and boys called *Famous Monsters of Filmland*.[18] Men have figured almost exclusively as the authors of numerous picture books and biographies of Chaney.[19] These patterns of interest would seem to follow the gender-related trends of viewing established in the 1920s when both studio promotion (such as pressbooks), reviewers, and exhibitor reports seemed to agree that Chaney's stardom was supported, by and large, by the spectatorship of men and boys.

Chaney's star vehicles consistently drew a large following of men even though, as one reviewer succinctly remarked in 1925, "One does not expect much fun in a film featuring Lon Chaney."[20] Reviewers warned women and children off Chaney's films. In spite of its link to classic literature, *The Hunchback of Notre Dame* was thought to be too shocking and grotesque fare for many moviegoers. *Variety* dismissed *Hunchback* as a "two-hour nightmare. It's murderous, hideous and repulsive. . . . [It] is misery all the time, nothing but misery, tiresome, loathsome misery that doesn't make you feel any the better for it."[21] More generous in its review, the *New York Times* thought that Chaney had thrown "his whole soul into making Quasimodo as repugnant as anything human," and predicted that the film "will appeal to all those . . . who don't mind a grotesque figure and a grim atmosphere."[22] In 1927 a trade magazine's advice to exhibitors on marketing *The Unknown* hints at the disturbing tone and tenor of many of Chaney's films—and why they were often regarded as unwholesome fare:

Play up as Chaney's weirdest character study to date. Exploitation Angles: Use plenty of stills of [featured player] Joan Crawford. Drawing Power: Star will pack the house. Not for the children. Theme: Melodrama of circus—with freak avoiding arrest by posing as Armless Wonder. He plots diabolical vengeance but is frustrated.[23]

The capsule exhibition review only hints at the bizarre quality of a film in which the protagonist poses as an Armless Wonder to evade police but also to satisfy his girlfriend Estrellita (Crawford), who has a phobia about having a man's arms around her. To guarantee her love, Alonzo goes to a quack and has his arms amputated. When he returns to the sideshow, Estrellita has overcome her phobia and is in the arms of her new boyfriend, the strongman Malabar (Norman Kerry). To avenge himself, Alonzo rigs Malabar's act so that the strongman's arms will be torn from his body.

Such films as *The Unknown* contributed to the general agreement in the trade press that Chaney's films were "not for the children," and exhibitors frequently claimed that Chaney's films were disliked by women. In *Moving Picture World*'s column, "Straight from the Shoulder Reports," exhibitors reported on their own experience handling Chaney's releases. *The Phantom of the Opera*, one exhibitor thought, was a "dandy" film for sophisticated city audiences, but "It is too gruesome; women will stay away."[24] *The Black Bird* was described as "liked by most of the men and boys. . . . A few women said it was a good picture."[25] *The Road to Mandalay* (1926), characterized by one reviewer as being based on "Oriental monstrosities,"[26] featured Chaney as "Singapore Joe," a monstrously scarred character with one white, blind eye, a daughter he does not know, and a penchant for brutal revenge. The film's audience was described in one exhibitor's report: "Had mostly men to see this show; women are afraid of him since the *Phantom of the Opera*."[27] Also reporting on *The Road to Mandalay*, another exhibitor noted: "Pleased the men and a few of the women. Chaney is 'some' character actor, but his characterizations are too hideous."[28]. The very next year, *The Unknown* prompted an exhibitor to write: "Played this to a large Saturday night house. Chaney is slipping here . . . a little too realistic. When the women folk start to tell you they don't like him, better let him alone."[29]

No doubt in response to such reports, studio promotion materials often armed exhibitors with various ways to pull female audience members into Chaney's films even as they targeted their ongoing appeal to men—on which Chaney thrived. In a pattern also evidenced in promotion materials for *The Big City* (1928) and Chaney's 1930 remake of *The Unholy Three*, the pressbook for *Mr. Wu* (1927) noted: "Lon Chaney is a popular favorite with most of your men patrons. . . . In order to assure yourself of the same amount of feminine interest it would be advisable to incorporate some special and unusual style element of appeal."[30] Tie-ins featuring fashions worn by the films' female leads were presented as a means of securing an elusive "feminine interest" in Chaney's films. Such a strategy recalls the attempts by some sideshows, including that of the Sells-Floto Circus, to sell freak show attractions as an amusement for all. The main advertising banner to Sells-Floto's "complete congress of strange people, novel and unique performance" included prominent text that reassured potential patrons that the show was "For Ladies" as well as for gentlemen and children.[31]

Why was Chaney so popular with men? There are many possible explanations but, considered within the framework of the freak show, Chaney's stardom resonates with the revelation of a mystery. The freak show, as Leslie Fiedler suggests, has a metaphorical connection to a sexual secret; its appeal, he argues, is linked to the pornographic, to the unveiling of a human mystery. Fiedler suggests the freak show's ambivalent fascination resides in

the sense of watching, unwilling, but enthralled, the exposed obscenity of the self or the other. And only "freaks," therefore, seems a dirty enough word to render the child's sense before the morphodite or Dog-faced Boy of seeing the final forbidden mystery: an experience repeated in adolescence, when the cooch dancer removes her G-string.[32]

The mystery that Chaney's stardom exploited was the revelation of what may have been the equivalent of "the final forbidden mystery" in an age that glorified men's physical perfection and unflappable "bully" optimism.

Grotesque, yet capable of suffering for love: Lon Chaney and Mary Philbin in *The Phantom of the Opera* (1925)

Chaney's roles offered a revelation of the "exposed obscenity of the self"—as Other—as masculinity allowed to be failed and freakish. The masculine self exposed in Chaney's films was in the freak show mold of the Other constructed in contradictory terms: stigmatized and yet aggrandized, grotesque and yet still romantically capable of suffering for love. This male suffering is totally unlike that of a Barrymore hero. Chaney's characters demonstrate love as a veritable pathology of emotions, a sickness that can never be cured, but remains unrequited until death.

Although, in retrospect, Chaney has been associated with monsters, his monstrosities of masculinity are almost never attributed to the supernatural, but to nature, to the tragic results of human disaster, or to his characters' assumption of masquerades of mutilation and self-stigmatization. In the eighteenth century, French tetralogists, in classifying those who were anatomically anomalous, were careful to separate those who were born "monstrosities" from the "*mutiles*" (i.e., the blind, the paralyzed, hunchbacks, harelips, amputees, and victims of disasters). The latter's bodies, changed by misfortune, seem to prove that anatomy is destiny when social curiosity transforms them into everyday spectacles of mundane "monstrosity."[33]

Chaney's depiction of the body-monstrous may be read as a symptomatic instance of the anxiety surrounding masculinity and the male body during this postwar period of American culture. A theory of historical trauma might relate Chaney's grotesque construction of a deviant and deformed masculinity to the era's postwar anxieties in relation to the war and its horrific demonstration of the vulnerability of the male body.[34]

An improbable couple—the disheveled magician and his beautiful wife: Lon Chaney and Jane Daly in *West of Zanzibar* (1928)

However, Chaney's films, like the freak show, may have provided a rather more complicated and nuanced function. They both may have provided an outlet for a more broadly based "antimodern fascination with suffering" among men that predated the war.[35]

Jackson Lears suggests that this desire for suffering and self-sacrifice was expressive of a yearning for authenticity in an age in which comfort had produced masculine anxiety and a perceived dissassociation from the experience of real life.[36] Character-building and the cult of strenuosity articulate one possible expression these yearnings. However, the romantic posturing in Chaney's films suggests a validation of suffering masculinity with even richer suggestiveness. In his melodramatic films, especially his later vehicles with Browning, violence is present in the form of a quest for terrible revenge against those he believes have made him the defiled, suffering object who cannot be loved, who cannot be integrated into the fabric of the family and society.

The Browning-directed *West of Zanzibar* (1928) is typical of Chaney's films in this regard. The film opens at a music hall performance. The first intertitle, "Ashes to Ashes! Dust to Dust!" is combined with a sinister opening: a black coffin stands upright. A man starts to take off the lid. The scene is a music hall where Phroso (Chaney), a comically disheveled magician, performs with his beautiful, beloved wife (Jane Daly). However, Phroso soon discovers that his wife is planning to run away to Africa with Crane (Lionel Barrymore). When Crane confronts Phroso with the news, they struggle. Phroso is sent tumbling over the edge of a high railing. He falls, his body is shattered.

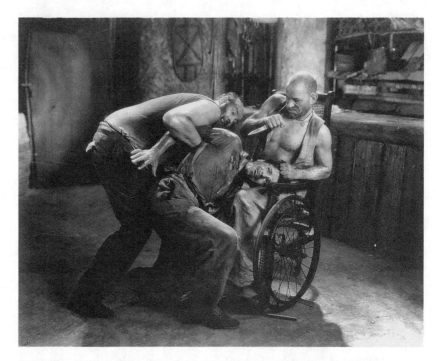

"Dead Legs" (Lon Chaney) as the unspeakably cruel dictator over his own corner of Africa (*West of Zanzibar*), with Tiny Roscoe Ward and Warner Baxter

In the next scene, Phroso is seen on a wheeled platform, propelling himself with hand rollers into a church. There, as he crawls across the floor, he sees his wife—dead—and a baby. Phroso swears revenge: "For all the suffering he brought her . . . he's going to pay! He and his brat will pay!" Flashforward eighteen years and Phroso has become "Dead Legs," unspeakably cruel dictator over his own corner of Africa. Still plotting revenge, he steals ivory from a local trader—Crane. With implacable cruelty, Dead Legs has had the baby girl he found so long ago raised in a brothel. He sends for her. Holding her captive, Dead Legs turns Maizie (Mary Nolan) into a drunkard. He then lures Crane so that he can bring Maizie before her father. At the moment of revelation, Crane starts to laugh uncontrollably. He reveals that the girl is really Dead Legs's daughter. The horror is compounded because Dead Legs has put into motion a scheme that will condemn Maizie to die. On his previous command, Crane is killed. According to native tradition, "That means the girl goes with him!" as Doc (Warner Baxter) exclaims. Dead Legs must save her. "My baby! My own little girl!" he whispers. He does his coffin trick once again. When the natives come for her, he places Maizie in the coffin, as he placed his wife so long ago, then completes his trick and replaces her with a skeleton. Maizie and Doc escape while the natives burn Dead Legs on their ceremonial funeral pyre: "Ashes to Ashes! Dust to Dust."

In typical Chaney narratives such as *West of Zanzibar*, masculine retribution and redemption through suffering are emphasized so that the star's characters emerge as human monsters. They are portrayed as monstrous not only because of their physicality but because of their madness. From Erik in *Phantom of the Opera* to Dead Legs in *West of Zanzibar*, it is a madness that arises from their perversion of emotion and their insatiable desire to revenge themselves against a cruel world. Nevertheless, as in both these films, the character's mad, obsessionary behavior often gives way to pathetic vulnerability and tender emotion. Incapable of being loved, the protagonist embraces suffering to redeem himself and save his impossible love object.

In this respect, many of Chaney's films create a perverse vision of the family as the site of patriarchal monstrosity, but also of redemption. In sacrifice, the moral superiority of the patriarch (Chaney) is proven, but he cannot escape the necessity of his expulsion as the polluted object. While he plays literal fathers in many of his films, such as *Flesh and Blood*, *Mr. Wu*, *The Road to Mandalay*, and *West of Zanzibar*, in many other films, including *He Who Gets Slapped*, *Laugh, Clown, Laugh*, *Mockery*, *The Hunchback of Notre Dame*, and *The Unholy Three*, he portrays a man who by virtue of age or appearance is an inappropriate, inadequate match for the woman he loves. That woman is consistently defined by the plot in Chaney's films as someone's daughter—a daughter in need of protection and nurturance (especially in *Hunchback* and *He Who Gets Slapped*). In film after film, Chaney becomes the substitute father and would-be lover whose disappointment in desire seems inevitable, even before the appearance of a youthful and handsome rival suitor.

Thus, these narratives of male loss suggest the impossibility of Chaney's characters attaining what David Rodowick, commenting on melodrama, calls the "active sexual identity in which patriarchal power can be confirmed and reproduced."[37] Instead of a patriarchal sexual identity, his characters only can achieve a redemptive, masochistically romantic transformation through their thwarted desire. In *The Hunchback of Notre Dame* Quasimodo is transformed from the kidnapper of Esmeralda (Patsy Ruth Miller) to her rescuer. When he swoops her away from her public execution to safety, he carefully places her on a bed in one of the cells of the cathedral. He kneels by her in reverential ecstasy and, through pantomime, allays her fears when she awakens and startles in fright at his hideous countenance. In the final scenes of the film, Quasimodo sacrifices himself to save her from the archdeacon's lecherous brother, Jehan (Brandon Hurst). Mortally wounded, he sees the handsome Phoebus (Norman Kerry) embrace Esmeralda. As if he were a father giving away a bride, Quasimodo nods assent to this coupling before he dies. A similar transformation of the protagonist occurs in *Mockery* (1927), in which the peasant Sergei (Chaney) cannot comprehend that the heroine cannot accept him as a lover. He becomes, in the words of the film's pressbook, "a dangerous beast, and then, when loyalty and love touch this strange metamorphosed character, into a bulwark of a besieged [female] aristocrat." Sergei, of course, makes the "supreme" sacrifice to save his beloved.

Through an ironic turn of events in romantic or domestic entanglements, Chaney's characters inevitably emerge as willing victims, the masochistic centerpiece around whom the films' combination of sentimentality and brutality revolves.[38] Chaney's protagonists/freaks often endure failure, humiliation, sexual defeat, and even physical maiming in the beginning of the film and then move through the wreckage of their lives satisfying aggressive and revengeful goals until they commit themselves to an act of symbolic self-immolation (literally in *West of Zanzibar*). Because these films imply a family discourse that must be set right by the patriarch's sacrifice, Chaney may destroy his enemies, but only in his own sacrifice can (feminine) purity and innocence be sustained. The moral order of the patriarchy is restored after it is revealed as being deeply perverse. Thus, in *West of Zanzibar*, Dead Legs's complete moral degeneracy is shown in the fact that his search for revenge makes him perfectly willing to let Maizie be raised in a brothel even though she is his wife's daughter. Until she is revealed to be his own daughter, he sees her merely as a tool for revenge. Never does he *feel* empathy for her. No wonder the film withholds her recognition of him as her father. Maizie thinks his sudden change of heart must be another trap. Doc, who loves her, reassures her that "he can't do what he plans to do and still hate." Barely recovered from seeing Dead Legs as her mortal enemy, she can only say in a laughable moment of understatement: "Gee, but you're a strange man."

Within these bizarre family melodramas of patriarchal revenge and redemption, the influence of the freak show requires consideration as it relates to Chaney's depiction of masochistic male exhibitionism. Chaney's

Sentimentality and brutality to ensure a sacrificial transformation (Advertisement for *Mockery*, c. 1927)

films suggest a representation of masculinity marked with the stigma of Otherness. That Otherness is not necessarily imposed solely from the outside, from society's stigmatization of difference. It also is defined as a masochistic self-defilement that marks Chaney's masculinity as profoundly different within an era that might have been fascinated with pain but nevertheless still preferred to glorify the perfect male body in the midst of daring action.

In this context, Chaney's justification for his portrayal in *The Unknown* (1927) seems to inadvertently raise more questions than it answers:

There are many freak make-ups that I might evolve, but I would not wear them unless to some definite purpose. In *The Unknown*, I contrived to make myself look like an armless man, not simply to shock and horrify you but merely to bring to the screen a dramatic story of an armless man, or rather one who pretended to be so.[39]

Certainly, such explanations raise questions about the appeal of an actor who, in film after film, appeared as characters who were armless, legless, or horribly mutilated, or who simulated the impaired male body as a masquerade, a convenient disguise until they themselves became mutilated or disabled for real. While this situation occurs at its most extreme in *The Unknown*, it is also found in *The Black Bird*, where Chaney, as the title character, hurries to twist his body into his disguise as his disabled missionary brother. He falls onto the floor, breaks his back, and dies in disguise, as the good, "crippled" brother, mourned by all.

With vehicles like this, no wonder Pauline Kael finds Chaney's "fabulous popularity" so strange as to suggest that "one might be moved to speculate on the peculiar tastes of the mass audiences of the twenties."[40] Such a critical reaction is not new. It merely echoes reviewers and commentators of the 1920s who responded to Chaney's films and performances with ambivalence. Kael's comments also echo many of those who have tried to locate the appeal of the freak show. Remarking on the dime museum's fascination, historian Alvin Harlow's attitude toward the display of freaks anticipates Kael's feeling toward Chaney and his audience: "Why anyone should want to look at a mere obscene lump of fat weighing five or six hundred pounds is beyond the comprehension of a balanced mind, as is also the morbid desire to see deformities, monstrosities, and mutilations, human and animal; but it is so."[41] Even reviewers who admired Chaney's performances used words like "grotesque," "morbid," "lurid," "unhealthy," and "sordid" to characterize his films. These were the same adjectives that had already been applied time and time again to the freak show.

Contradiction and the Construction of Curiosities

To understand Chaney's relationship to the established conventions and presentational styles of the freak show, it is first necessary to understand the cultural and performative framework created by the sideshow as a primary place for the exhibition of "human curiosities" in the first quarter of the twentieth century. At the center of the freak show as a spectacle of difference were the "freaks," human beings who had become visual commodities. As Robert Bogdan has suggested, many of these people were self-defined as entertainers or "showmen" in a process that served to define their differences but also constructed a specific, conventionalized discourse around it.[42]

The marketable status of freaks was secured in a process that assumed that their appearance and/or their specialized skills could draw a crowd. Sideshow marketing depended on visual enticement but also upon a "good spiel." Outside the typical sideshow tent, the talker's spiel aroused curiosity and interest in the mystery of the freaks. Except for a performer who might share the bally platform to stir up interest (and painted banners that might suggest the appearance of individual performers), all were hidden from view until tickets were sold and the money collected. Once revealed, the freak attractions characteristically offered a spectacle of difference that was expected to disturb, shock, or mystify.

Because successful freakdom was so dependent on this process of construction, anyone could become a freak if properly handled. Unusual acquired skills or rare physical attributes could be subjected to a promotional process in which tall people might be turned into giants, the diminutive into the world's tiniest man or woman. Similarly, an African-American from New Jersey named William Henry Johnson could become "Zip, the What Is It?" The latter's top-knotted "pinhead," gibberish, and ape-man suit made him "the dean of freaks" for over sixty years (1859–1926).[43]

As fantastic as it may seem, there were many freaks who were even more obviously "made" than Zip. These were the otherwise apparently "normal" people who chose a life marked by the freak show's stigma of difference.[44] They were the curiosities who had cultivated peculiar skills such as sword swallowing, fire-eating, contorting their bodies or snake-charming, or had subjected themselves to processes—such as tattooing—that would set them apart from the norm. However, the origins of all freaks depended upon the promotional strategy that put forward elaborate and often unbelievable fictional explanations for the mystery of their being. Thus, in the 1920s two albino African-Americans would be offered to the public as envoys from Mars. Fantastic accounts of origin seemed especially important in the promotion of those freaks who were of limited mental capacity, such as Maximo and Bartola, microcephalic siblings who, as "The Last of the Ancient Aztecs," elicited a great deal of popular and scientific interest in the 1880s. If fictionalized origins and explanations were imperative to the profitable commodification of all human curiosities, they were especially so for the so-called gaffed freaks.

Gaffed freaks were totally constructed; the physical condition or appearance that provided the basis of their act was fabricated. They included faked cojoined twins and the famous two-headed man, Pasqual Pinon, who was exhibited by Sells-Floto Circus from 1917 to 1920 with astonishing commercial success.[45] However, the most consistently popular of gaffed freaks were the "half-man, half-woman" exhibits whose sexual division was vertical. Half-and-halfs were often saved for the "blowoff," when the most intriguing freak presentations—which might even include nudity—would be shown. Freak show customers quickly learned that the most dramatic attraction, demanding an extra payment, was characteristically set aside for the blowoff.

Freaks were the raw material for a spectacle defined by specific strategies and processes, and those who paid to see freaks were part of the carefully designed encounter between the "normal" (sucker or rube) and the freak (showman). The encounter with the freak did not necessarily end with the latter's appearance on the platform in "the act." Formal photographic portraits were sold. In the nineteenth century they took the form of "cabinet cards" and, in the twentieth, postcards. These were often inscribed by the human curiosity to be kept by purchasers as mementos. Varying in format over the years, "true life-story" brochures would also be hawked.

Typical of the twentieth-century freak show brochure was "Facts Concerning Johnny Eck: The Only Living Half Boy" (circa 1920). While the cover of the three-page brochure calls the legless teenager "Nature's Greatest Mistake," it also features him in an attractive formal portrait. One page is devoted to "Questions and Answers" such as "Does he enjoy life?" and "Was he born this way?" The remaining two pages serve to recount why "his accomplishments today are unlimited." It is noted that he is an "Artist, Designer, Model Builder, Acrobat, Trapeze Performer, Tight Wire Walker, Gymnast, Juggler, Dancer, Punch and Judy Entertainer, Magician, Humorist, Cartoonist, Musician, and Motion Picture Actor." Beside these skills, Eck is touted as being well educated, well traveled, and well read.[46]

Eck's brochure demonstrates an "aggrandized mode" of presentation, one of several strategies of freak construction that Robert Bogdan identifies as historically dominant in the traditional exhibition practice of freak shows.[47] Varying from the low to the high, this mode of aggrandizing stressed the normality of the subject or even, in certain ways, his/her superiority to the norm. It stressed social elevation, exemplified by P. T. Barnum's promotion of "General" Tom Thumb, and unusual accomplishments emphasized in published accounts of Millie Christine, a cojoined set of twins. The latter, promoted as the "Two-headed Lady" and "Eighth Wonder of the World" in promotion handouts, visited Queen Victoria at Buckingham Palace in 1884; there, she entertained the monarch with her/their melodious singing voices.[48]

These examples suggest that the presentation of freaks exaggerated the contradictions that Erving Goffman has suggested are typical patterns put into play to define a stigmatized social identity. Such an identity is inevitably convergent with historically and culturally determined stereotypes. Within a specific social context, a stigmatized person is defined as possessing "defiling" or "deeply discredited" attributes.[49] These attributes then become "stigma symbols." In contrast, Goffman identifies "prestige symbols" as creating a claim on "prestige, honor, or desirable class position . . . that might not otherwise be presented or, if otherwise presented, then not automatically granted." Prestige symbols, as conventionalized social signs, can lessen the effect of "stigma symbols" by drawing away attention from the "debasing identity." Also operative in the process of managing the stigmatized freak's "spoiled social identity" are what

Goffman calls "disidentifiers," signs of fissure in the flow of coherent social information. These signs (often at the level of behavior or costume) serve to throw doubt on the individual's social identity. They disidentify the person from the primary stereotype used to define the individual as part of a stigmatized social group.[50]

Adapting Goffman's ideas regarding the construction of identity in relation to stigma, it might be argued that the freak show's complex and contradictory formulation of the social identity of freaks fits into the pattern of how stigmatized subjectivity is more broadly defined. The freak show created a predictable social archetype around the person perceived to be deviant and defiled. In light of Goffman's useful notions, it is interesting that both Eck's and Christine's accomplishments allot special emphasis to the role of these prestige symbols in relation to the value and versatility of the freaks (i.e., stigmatized individuals) as performers/entertainers rather than in relation to their private lives, which remained a mystery unless they could be exploited directly, as was the case in the marriage of "Percilla the Monkey-Girl" and "Emmitt the Alligator Boy" who together became a more profitable draw: "The World's Strangest Married Couple."[51]

Freaks constituted a socially constructed phenomenon in which there was a creation of a self to be displayed for specular consumption. Insiders often suggested that most freaks regarded their public construction as just that, the display of a theatrical persona. It could be argued that, in this respect, there was no fundamental difference between real freaks and gaffed freaks. Both depended upon constructing a particular mode of promotion and display to secure their status as marketable spectacles. Nevertheless, visible differences were inevitably categorized at the same time that they were exaggerated.

Although anyone might be made into a freak, freak shows were synonymous with the display of people with visible differences, especially those who showed unusual physical anomalies. Claude Lecouteux has offered categories that seem to be applicable to the freak show's creation of standard exhibition archetypes in this regard: "Separated from the natural order of things and creatures, monstrosity assumes several forms: enlargement or diminution of existing beings, absence or excess of certain organs, hybridization by the attribution of a single subject of members belonging to different species than its own."[52] Predictable freak show curiosities included cojoined ("Siamese") twins, microcephalics (pinheads), those who were born without or who had lost arms or legs (Armless or Legless Wonders). They also included the morbidly obese (Fat

Ladies and Men), the diminutive (midgets), as well as persons whose bodies were hosts to underdeveloped, parasitic twins (double-bodied enigmas). Finally, there were those freaks with pathological skin conditions (reptile men and elephant women), and extreme growths of tumors or hair (bearded ladies). Many freaks of these types, such as "human torsos" and cojoined or "Siamese" twins, were physically disabled or anomalous in extreme ways that put them at the mercy of managers or family who exhibited them for profit and sometimes treated them as chattel.[53] Thus, the promotional aggrandizement of their performing abilities was often in contrast to an oppressive reality.

Even for people with anomalous physicalities, the aggrandizing mode usually incorporated a family discourse not unlike that stressed in the star-centered extratextual discourse of movie fan magazines. As in the fan magazine, this discourse was a predictable part of the presentational identity of those performers who were depicted as Anglo-American. Thus, Eck's brochure mentions and shows his "perfectly normal" twin in a dress suit. Other brochures typically showed the subject freak with parents, or with a spouse and, often, with children, usually "normal." In the picture presentations of the family, the freak was often depicted in a formally posed portrait common to the period. For example, Myrtle Corbin, the double-bodied lady from Cleburne, Texas, would be shown in the late 1910s as a middle-class housewife with husband and daughter. Smiling, her family stands beside her in Sunday-best clothes. However, the difference between Myrtle and other Texas matrons is clear. In her seated pose, her skirts are lifted above her knees so that both pairs of her legs can be prominently displayed. As Myrtle Corbin's portrait demonstrates, constructing freaks depended upon a discourse that may have sought to normalize its subjects but also, in contradictory fashion, sought to foreground or exaggerate the distinguishing peculiarity that was thought to make them objects of repulsion, of social stigma, and of fascination.

Exoticism in the Service of Topicality

As often as the freak show depended upon the spectacle of physical difference in its constructions of aggrandized freaks, it also cultivated cultural exoticism in its many variations on the "exotic mode" of presentation that exploited the display value of a heightened cultural exoticism. Thus, no matter what their real country of origin, those who had the potential to have an exotic (i.e., non-Anglo-Saxon) appearance might be turned into

Circassian snakecharmers, Wild Men of Borneo, "Fiji Cannibals," or "The Last of the Ancient Aztecs" in response to an already evident fascination-with cultural events and controversies, from the political turmoil in Borneo to the scientific claims arising from eugenics.

Freak exhibitions in this mode depended upon the audience's preexistent desire for the exotic. The spiel for exotic attractions traded on long-standing notions of the existence of other, often monstrous races of men living in remote areas of the earth.[54] Many freaks aroused curiosity because their strange appearance was manipulated to fit the audience's topical concerns. Hence, exoticism increasingly came to be defined in the late nineteenth century not only as cultural difference but also as genetic or hereditary difference. For example, in the late nineteenth and early twentieth centuries much was made of freaks from non-Caucasian races as illustrations of Darwin's theories, particularly the popular notion of "de-evolution." The idea of a missing link in the genetic chain of man's descent from ape became the basis for many freak presentations including Krao, a hypertichosistic female from Thailand, whose excessive hair led her to be billed as "Darwin's Missing Link."[55]

At the turn of the century, older theories of freak origin were replaced by new framing discourses.[56] As the previous chapter noted, in the 1910s and 1920s Americans of widely varying political stripe were strongly influenced by "hereditarian attitudes" that asserted that racial improvement and superiority depended on carefully controlling the genetic pool. In the United States, many educators, scientists, and politicians were keen on using eugenics theory to explain and prevent the appearance of feeblemindedness, criminality, and even poverty.[57] Some believed that Africans and Asians were "fossilized" at a lower stage of human evolution.[58] In contrast, the "native" American type, believed to be of Nordic stock, was exalted. The president of the National Institute of Immigration declared in 1906: "It is not vain glory when we say that we have bred more than sixty millions of the finest people the world has ever seen. . . . Therefore any race that we admit to our body social is certain to be more or less inferior."[59]

If "better minds in sounder bodies" was the goal of eugenics, then the freak show of the 1920s was a negative epiphany illustrating eugenicists' deepest fears.[60] Spurred by changes in attitude encouraged by medical science and eugenics theories, the display of human beings ("living curiosities") was no longer regarded as part of natural history, as suitable for exhibition in "museums" as in carnivals. Unusual physical and mental traits once thought to be acquired by maternal trauma during pregnancy or because of the preconceptual environment were given new explanations rooted in theories of genetic origin and evolution.

In the early twentieth century, freaks could be read as exemplars of frightening biological imperfection within an era of Americanism that, as previous chapters have suggested, glorified physical perfection as proof of moral, spiritual, and finally, racial superiority. Freaks were stigmatized in new ways that made them not only odd and uncanny but beings whose very existence reverberated with current biological determinism and racist political fears centered on deteriorating races. No wonder that exoticized freaks associated with "genetic throwbacks" and "de-evolution" were usually depicted as being of foreign origin. When Americans of apparent Anglo stock like Myrtle Corbin were depicted in family portraits, their sturdy, normal children were perhaps the greatest prestige symbol of all in the freak show process of aggrandizement.[61]

The "Carnival of the Cinema"

Considering the obvious star-centered nature of the freak show, it is to be expected that in the stardom of Lon Chaney, the freak show retained this essential quality. That the freak show should make an inroad into Hollywood film should not be unexpected too, if one considers it as one of the many established mass entertainment forms from which turn-of-the-century filmmakers drew performers and techniques of presentation. In the earliest days of American cinema, Edison's camera captured freakish attractions: from female impersonators ("The Old Maid in the Parlor"), to an elephant being electrocuted, to Fatima, the belly dancer. Also brought to Edison's New Jersey studio, "The Black Maria," were Annie Oakley, Eugen Sandow, and other respectable, nonfreak specialty attractions that were cheek by jowl in some of the same broad venues as the freak show (such as the Wild West show and the circus).

In this respect, spectators may have been primed to recognize "primitive" cinema's connection to the freak show. The most obvious connection is evident in the movie's earliest style of representation, in a style of cinematic enunciation that Tom Gunning has called "the cinema of attractions." Gunning suggests that this is a cinema based on "its ability to *show* something. . . . [It] is an exhibitionist cinema." He characterizes this early cinema as one that "displays its visibility," and is willing to rupture a self-enclosed fictional world for a chance to solicit the attention of the spectator."[62] Gunning suggests that "this earlier carnival of the cinema" was influenced by nonnarrative forms, including the fair, circus, and sideshow.[63]

Although the "cinema of attractions" involved specific techniques (such as addressing the camera) which are not necessarily featured in Chaney's films, his films frequently still manage to suggest the lingering influence of these earlier amusements (the fair, circus, sideshow, and early cinema) that were involved in "exhibitionist confrontation rather than diegetic absorption."[64] In one respect, the unusual emphasis on Chaney's makeup technique and on the manipulation of his body into unexpected and even shocking shapes would encourage a cinema of exhibitionist display. Additionally, the often-noted weakness or outright incoherence of the plots of many of his films (especially those with Browning) might also encourage us to examine the apparent influence of the freak show as a star-centered form of exhibitionist spectacle. In fact, as I will show, Chaney's films have amazing moments and sequences of such display centered on their star-as-freak exhibition.

The most famous example of this in Chaney's work is the unveiling of Erik's (Chaney's) face in *The Phantom of the Opera*. Motivated by curiosity, his captive opera singer protégée, Christine (Mary Philbin), removes his mask. One might expect that a conventional Hollywood inscription of this action would reveal Christine's reaction to her unmasking of him and then, in a reverse shot, the visage that has precipitated her horror (or vice versa). Instead, the film treats Erik's unmasking as a moment of exhibitionist spectacle for the audience that preempts Christine's reaction. Christine tiptoes undetected up to Erik as he plays the pipe organ. The camera reverses to show his face and body as she moves behind him and snatches off the mask. The camera stays put to fully exhibit Erik's cadaverous face to the audience first before he turns to confront Christine with his self-proclaimed "cursed ugliness." Likewise, many of Chaney's other films—including *The Shock*, *West of Zanzibar*, *Hunchback of Notre Dame*, *He Who Gets Slapped*, *The Black Bird*, and *The Penalty*—seem to create situations in which the camera's "eye" occupies the place of the freak show spectator fascinated with the spectacle of Chaney's masquerade of disability and deviance, stigmatization and aggrandizement. Thus, his films may reaffirm the influence of an early amusement attraction possessed of the power of an exhibitionism revolving around attraction and revulsion. It is this power that the freak show—and Chaney's films—cultivated in all its ambivalence.

"Are you a contortionist?"

After a knockabout career in regional theater, Chaney started in Hollywood in 1912 as a bit player at Universal. In some seventy-five films in five years, he increasingly foregrounded his ability to change his appearance through the application of makeup and distortions of his body that made him the equivalent of a "gaffed freak." As noted earlier, Chaney's breakthrough role to stardom came with *The Miracle Man* (now lost except for partial scenes), one of the biggest critical and popular hits of 1919. In the film, Chaney played a featured role as "The Frog," who contorts himself into appearing as a paralyzed "cripple" to further a gang's scheme. The gang plans to exploit a blind faith healer by using "The Frog" to rise up before him and thus confirm his healing ability. However, the faith healer has real powers. A young boy is cured, and "The Frog" is brought to moral and spiritual redemption.

After playing this gaffed freak, Chaney was catapulted into stardom as a character actor whose spectacle of grotesque difference was defined extratextually, as well as textually, in ways strategic also to the freak show. At the most obvious level, several of the earliest fan magazine articles on the actor claimed that his role in *The Miracle Man* was scheduled to be filled by a contortionist, but the man was fired because he could not act.[65] At least two interviews with the actor center around the question of whether he was also a contortionist because, as author Herbert Howe asserts, "That's the question everyone wanted to ask [The Frog] after seeing *The Miracle Man*."[66] Chaney's answer to this question was always a resounding "No," but this use of his body evoked a comparison that would continue to be reasserted in publicity for subsequent films.[67] In similar fashion as the contradictory discourse of the freak show sought to normalize and aggrandize the freak while calling maximum attention to his/her grotesque and/or exotic difference, extratextual discourse sought to normalize Chaney's freakish physicality through several strategies. Some were temporary, used early in his career; others became incorporated into the dominant mode of constructing Chaney's offscreen self as a star.

Early star articles sought to explain Chaney's ability to obtain the grotesque, freak-show effects necessary for the role of "The Frog" in ways that would emphasize his actorly professionalism, his shared humanity with his audience, and his utterly banal normality. Fan magazine discourse about new film personalities typically conflated onscreen character and narrative with the actor's yet-to-be-fully-formulated offscreen persona. Echoing the plot of *The Miracle Man*, several fan magazines asserted that his depiction of the grotesque was achieved through faith. Chaney was quoted as explaining how he achieved the effect of a "groveling, deformed paralytic":

> "I just had faith that I could do it—some way. Then, like a flash, I remembered a dance I did years ago in musical shows. It ended with a sort of whirl and twist of the legs. I threw myself on the floor, twisted my legs and hands, rolled my eyes back into my head, a fluid make-up streaming like matter from the eyes, and I squirmed over the floor toward the camera. 'Ugh!' exclaimed Mr. Tucker [the director]. 'That's horrible. We can never show the public a close-up of that face!'"[68]

In the ensuing years the public would, of course, see a number of grotesque close-ups of Chaney's face. Much was made in extratextual discourse of him as "the man who can put on the most gruesome make-ups in pictures."[69]

Nevertheless, in keeping with *The Miracle Man*, his films frequently foregound his physicality as being of primary exhibitionist interest. This is illustrated in an interesting way in *Flesh and Blood* (1922), advertised as a "Heart-Gripping Photoplay of Cruel Revenge and Ultimate Reparation." In this film Chaney plays the equivalent of a gaffed freak. His character, David Webster, spends fifteen years in prison for a crime he did not commit. On his escape, he effects a "disguise" as a cripple who must use crutches. He meets his grown daughter, who is called "the Angel Lady" for her work in a slum mission. While he frequents the mission to be near her, he also seeks out the man who was responsible for his unjust imprisonment. However, his plans for revenge are given up when he discovers that his daughter is in love with the son of his sworn enemy. In the film's final, amazing scene, Webster limps up on his crutches to the gates of the prison where he had been held for fifteen years. The guards tell him to move along. Only when he drops the crutches and straightens his back and legs do they recognize him as the man they have guarded for years. The film asks us to believe that the disguise of his physical disfigurement has been so masterfully effective that the prison guards do not recognize his face. Ironically, this otherwise incredulous moment is believable as a negative inscription of cult-of-the-body values. Here, it is not male physical perfection that tells the truth about masculine identity, but the ability to masterfully manipulate the body into the appearance (and disappearance) of disability.

While freaks might be regarded as entrepreneurs or stars in their own world because of their value as commodities, the public emphasis on their accomplishments took place in a process of aggrandizement set into play

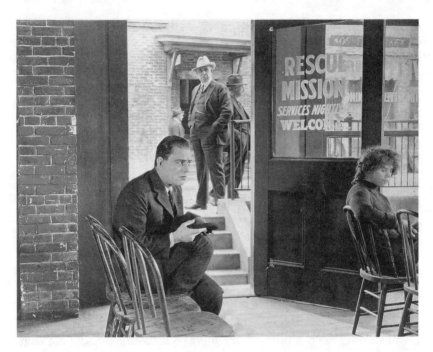

David Webster (Lon Chaney) masquerading as a "cripple" in *Flesh and Blood* (1922)

by "prestige symbols" that served to normalize and humanize them. In this respect, the cards and brochures they sold were presented in the aftermath of the shock that their spectacle of difference was presumed to deliver to the audience. Aggrandizement through prestige symbols also served, in some measure, to counter the stigmatizing view that freaks were passive victims of an exploitative system of exhibition. Although display procedures varied, freak performance and discourse (including brochures, photographs, and spiel) carefully constructed the exhibit to be everything but an object of pity or sympathy.

While society at large often regarded stigmatized people as the victims of circumstance, the freak show assumed that asking for pity was a certain turnoff for audiences.[70] Engaging audience sympathy might lead to an emotional response that was at odds with an entertainment centered around the satisfaction of curiosity through the exhibitionist display of a human commodity. Instead, exhibitions sought, in varying circumstances, to arouse in curious onlookers awe, wonderment, sexual fascination, repugnance, and occasionally horror, but all within the confines of a look made safe by a quality of voyeuristic detachment.

Chaney's films often constructed him in a manner that alternatively aggrandized and stigmatized his freak-associated physicality. Visual emphasis and narrative action oscillated between revealing the extreme, pathetic difficulty of his movements (as in *The Shock* and *Flesh and Blood*) and aggrandizing his characters as remarkably agile and capable of extraordinary physical feats, as in *The Penalty* and *The Hunchback of Notre Dame*. An example of emphasis on the former occurs in *The Shock* (1923), in which Chaney plays Wilse Dilling.

Dilling, a mysterious "dope-peddler, safe-cracker, gun-man" is part of a Chinatown gang in San Francisco led by the ruthless Queen Anne (Christine Mayo). Dilling hobbles around on crutches because of an unexplained condition that has rendered a foot twisted, his legs virtually useless. Queen Anne sends him out of "the cesspool of poppyland" to a small town where, under the influence of sunshine and friendly neighbors, he falls in love with Gertrude (Virginia Valli), the daughter of the banker he is supposed to frame. As he says, she "paused to pity," but became his teacher "and first real friend." "Most people haven't much use for cripples," he tells her, but she counters his pessimism with optimistic sayings from the Bible and a book called *Right Thoughts*. At one of their soirees on her lawn, he is shown approaching her in his wheelchair. After a reverse of camera position to reveal her, the camera returns to Chaney as he rises out of the wheelchair to mount his crutches. Then, the camera moves from a medium shot (on her) to a long shot trained on him to capture the full effect. The camera remains fixed as, on crutches, Dillling haltingly moves from extreme foreground right to the back of the scene to a lawn chair on the left. The camera lingers over Dilling's walk for an inordinate amount of time that suggests an exhibitionist approach to Chaney's performance specialty. However, this carefully constructed visual emphasis on the character's physical condition is combined with other scenes that suggest the utter horror of disability. When Gertrude is disabled in an explosion, Wilse hysterically exclaims: "God . . . Doctor! Not like me!"

Such moments suggest that in their cultivation of pity as a response to the distorted male body, Chaney's films reflected the increasingly influential medical view of the freak show. Chaney's construction as a pitiable object in many of his films can be accounted for in how medical science and eugenics theory were changing society's view of freaks. Thus, Chaney's films operate on a somewhat more complicated level of affect

Heavy-handed attempts to elicit pity
(Advertisement for *Mockery*, c. 1927)

than the sideshow presentation of freaks that sought to exclude this influence. Extratextual discourse, both in fan magazines and in promotional materials, also worked to extend his films' often heavy-handed attempt to elicit pity or sympathy for his characters and their conditions.

In the 1920s, under the influence of eugenics, "scientific physicians" sought to give freaks' unusual physical appearance very precise explanation as they began to promulgate a view of freak performers as pitiable victims of pathology.[71] Even though freak modes of presentation might not seek pity, the medical emphasis on freaks as case histories encouraged people to see them as inferior and suffering. Freaks were discussed in public discourse as diseased, sick with conditions medical science now considered to be "merely pathological."[72]

As a result of this medical discourse, around the time that Chaney came to stardom, the act of viewing human oddities was being altered in the public consciousness. An article in *The Nation* suggested that once circus patrons realized that "the human pincushion, the elastic-skinned man, the blue man, the dog-faced boy, and their ilk are all victims of rare diseases [like] other sufferers, who are unwilling to exhibit their afflictions [but] are under treatment by physicians, these, too, lose most of their fascination."[73] A physician-authored article of the same time (1908) suggested a similar view:

Most of these humble and unfortunate individuals whose sole means of livelihood is the exhibition of their physical infirmities to a gaping and unsympathetic crowd, are pathological rarities worthy of more serious study than they usually receive.

. . . In most civilized countries there are now enacted laws forbidding the public exhibition of monsters and revolting deformities. A more refined and a more humane popular taste now frowns upon such exhibitions.[74]

Under the influence of the medical establishment, freaks were stigmatized as case studies, victims of their physical conditions, as well as potential victims of an exploitative display. In spite of the establishment of the conventions of freak show presentation in the nineteenth century, the cultural connotations of the freak show underwent a marked changed in the early twentieth century as medicine worked to undermine the mystery of freakdom and to label freaks as exploited and pathological.

Within this context, *The Hunchback of Notre Dame* is characteristic of how Chaney's films inscribed him in ways that were presumed to elicit revulsion and pity in a formula of melodramatic excitation and exaggeration that extended and changed the freak show's construction of subjectivity. The difference also relates—significantly, I believe—to the family discourse created by Chaney's film narratives. The family in the 1920s was regarded as in transition, with the father's traditional role made problematic by the assertions of domestic control by wives (as discussed in chapter 1) and the behavior of rebellious young moderns seeking fun outside the home.

Chaney's films accord him a symbolic role as the suffering male whose actions are tinged with paternalism and whose desire is judged to be incongruous with his monstrous physicality.[75] Rarely is his freakish difference "healed" so he can enjoy the fulfillment of desire. The exception is in *The Shock*, where, after saving Gertrude from disability, from Queen Anne, *and* from the San Francisco earthquake, Dilling has an operation that allows him to walk up to Gertrude and embrace her as his future wife. More often, Chaney's character dies or, as noted earlier, he must leave the young woman he loves—a woman inevitably defined by the film as his own daughter or someone else's. Thus, Chaney's films create an oedipalized field of desire that complicates the freak show family discourse. The latter used promotional depictions of the performers' normal families as prestige symbols to recuperate their socially stigmatized difference. In Chaney's case, only his extreme sacrifice for the family—and his expulsion from it—can guarantee that recuperation.

Chaney's family discourse of romantic sacrifice occurs with startling dramatic results in *He Who Gets Slapped* (1924), one of Chaney's most profitable films. Directed by Victor Seastrom, the film tells the story of the clown "He," who was once Paul Beaumont, a dedicated scientist. One day

Mistaking a declaration of love for part of a masochistic act: Norma Shearer and Lon Chaney in *He Who Gets Slapped* (1924)

his mentor, Baron Regnard (Marc MacDermott) claims Beaumont's life's work and his wife. Beaumont becomes a clown whose masochistic act (in which a mob of clowns ritualistically bind, gag, and slap him) symbolically reenacts his humiliation before the Academy of Sciences when the Baron presented Beaumont's ideas as his own. Protesting the plagiarism, Beaumont is ridiculed as a nobody, laughed at, then hauled away.

In his new identity as "He," Beaumont is the star of a fabulously successful circus act that is a masochistic reenactment of his traumatic past. "He" appears to be half mad. When he is in the ring, he looks out over the laughing crowd and sees the scientists who ridiculed him. His one link to normality is a young bareback rider, Consuelo (Norma Shearer). "He" loves her from afar until her corrupt father, Count Mancini (Tully Marshall), connives to marry Consuelo off to the Baron Regnard. "He" reads her fortune and warns her: "Look! You are doomed, Consuelo—it is written there. Your father will sell you to that beast—there is only one who can save you." "He" reverently kisses her dress. Then, he finally declares his love for her: "I love you—I worship you!" Consuelo mistakes his declaration as part of his masochistic act: she slaps his face. "He" recoils and demures that, of course, he is "never serious." To save Consuelo "He" confronts her father: "To sell your daughter! No true father could do that!" The film affirms Chaney's typical, oedipally tinged role as the sacrificial ideal father/impossible lover. "He" releases a lion on the Baron and Count Mancini and returns to the ring for his act. Fatally wounded by the Baron's sword, he collapses and dies in Consuelo's arms as he utters his last words: "You see, I am happy, I am smiling. A fool is always smiling." Only in death, can "He," like many of Chaney's other characters, such as Dead Legs in *West of Zanzibar* and Tito the clown in *Laugh, Clown, Laugh* (1928), become aggrandized morally through their sacrifice for "family."

However, many of Chaney's films also aggrandize their characters' amazing acrobatics or "freak" skills. *The Hunchback of Notre Dame* gives extended attention in the beginning of the film to Quasimodo's agile cavorting over the walls of Notre Dame Cathedral and his defiant "performance" for the Paris crowd. Such scenes suggest the kind of aggrandizement of freak physicality typified in the Eck promotional brochure and sustained in Chaney films with mesmerizing but unsympathetic protagonists—as in *The Penalty* and, later, *West of Zanzibar.*

Yet, as might be expected of the time, *Hunchback* also makes Quasimodo a victim of his pathology through its emphasis on his social stigmatization and his emotional isolation. Intertitles offer an objective, even protomedical perspective: "Deaf—half blind—shut off from his fellow men by his deformities . . . to the townspeople he was an inhuman freak, a monstrous joke of Nature." Because of this tendency to medicalize the freak as a victim of pathology, the supreme moment of Quasimodo's exhibition (the equivalent of the blowoff) occurs when he is flogged in the city square for attempting to kidnap a gypsy girl, Esmeralda (Patsy Ruth Miller), at the behest of his cruel master. Quasimodo's clothes are stripped off him to the waist. He seems surprised, as if his physical disabilities prevent him from quite knowing what is going on. A dwarf turns over the hourglass to mark the punishment. Quasimodo's tongue darts in and out of his head like a lizard's, but his humanity is pathetically confirmed as the first lash hits his back, and he cries out. His pain is met only by jeers and catcalls until Esmeralda takes pity and brings him water to drink. She tenderly lifts his shirt over his back and shoulders.

Many other Chaney films deal more complexly with the interplay between the older realm of freak exhibition and the newer mode of med-

"A fool is always smiling." "He" dies in Consuelo's arms: John Gilbert, Norma Shearer, and Lon Chaney in *He Who Gets Slapped*

icalizing the freakish victim of pathology. At the level of visual presentation, they operate primarily through an acrobatic and physically aggrandized mode of freak presentation as demonstrated by the Johnny Eck brochure. Of these films, *The Penalty* (1920), was one of Chaney's most successful early star vehicles. It came within striking distance of breaking attendance records at several major theaters.[76] It also established the precedent for Chaney's regular portrayal of characters whose reactions to being disabled, or to the experience of other forms of loss and stigmatization, set into motion a plot centered around revenge and redemption.

In *The Penalty* Chaney starred as "Blizzard," a piano-playing criminal mastermind who seeks to revenge himself against Dr. Ferris (Charles Clary). Years before, in his youthful incompetence, the doctor had unnecessarily cut off the legs of a child as a cure for a blow to the head. This child was Blizzard. Grown to adulthood and now leader of an underworld empire, Blizzard readies himself to take over San Francisco with an army

A sadistic criminal mastermind: Blizzard (Lon Chaney) in *The Penalty* (1920)

of "disgruntled foreign laborers" who will take up rifles and overwhelm the city's law and financial centers. To recognize each other, these foreign agents will wear the straw hats made in a secret sweat shop where Blizzard has employed dozens of women. Sadistically keeping them in line, Blizzard occasionally picks one out to be his sexual favorite, a role that includes sitting on the floor beneath his piano and pushing the pedals when his musical reverie requires it. This role ultimately goes to Rose (Ethel Grey Terry), a secret service agent who falls in love with Blizzard and blows her mission. Even as Rose is succumbing to Blizzard's dubious charms, Blizzard kidnaps Dr. Ferris's daughter, Barbara (Claire Adams), an ambitious sculptress who has been using him as the model for her anticipated masterwork, "Satan—after the fall." This New Woman too appears to be on the way to becoming enthralled with Blizzard. When her father confronts him, the latter demands that the doctor graft the legs of Barbara's stalwart fiancé onto his own body. Instead, Dr. Ferris realizes the perversely charismatic Blizzard is the child he mutilated so many years before.

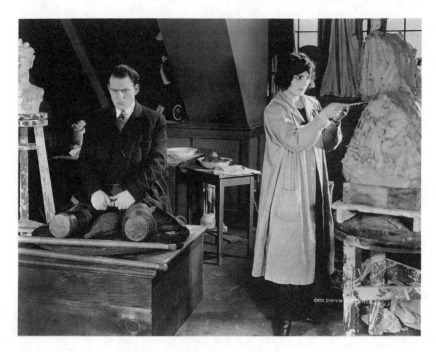

Perversely charismatic to the New Woman: Lon Chaney and Claire Adams in
The Penalty

This time, the doctor correctly chooses to operate on his patient's brain.
"Blizzard—that cripple from hell," awakens from the anesthesia a
reformed man, freed of his mania. He marries Rose and settles into normality, but is killed by a drug-crazed former underworld ally. Blizzard dies
calmly, noting that he finds death "interesting." In the film's last glimpse
of the heavenly realm, Blizzard is reunited with his legs—a scene that supposedly brought cheers from audiences of the time.

In *The Penalty*, as in *The Shock*, the camera lingers over Chaney's ability
to manipulate his body, strapped into a harness to make it appear as if his
legs are amputated at the knees. He hops up onto the sweatshop table,
slides down a pole like a fireman to his apartment, and pulls himself up a
pulley from his underground cache of guns. One reviewer noted: "We have
him in the Capitol Theatre screen this week in Gouverneur Morris's *The
Penalty* where he is somewhat of an actor as well as a contortionist. The
producer did not overlook the chance to prove that Mr. Chaney's loss of

"Something of an actor as well as a contortionist" (Charles Clary and Lon Chaney in *The Penalty*)

legs was purely acrobatic, for we have pictures [in the last, heavenly scene] of the actor as a sound bi-ped."[77]

Reviewers of the time were unanimous in finding the film repulsive yet fascinating. In what could serve as a summary of reviewers' opinions, Burns Mantle, writing in *Photoplay*, told his readers:

Here is a picture that is about as cheerful as a hanging—and as interesting. You can't, being an average human and normal as to your emotional reactions, really like *The Penalty*, any more than you could enjoy a hanging. But for all its gruesome detail, you are quite certain to be interested in it.[78]

In targeting the film's exhibition appeal, a trade magazine review suggested that Chaney's acrobatic tricks in *The Penalty* in his "no legs outfit" should be reproduced at the theater in a freak show-like promotion stunt: "As a prologue suggestion we offer the plan of obtaining the services of a man with no legs to be presented in a series of stunts similar to those which Chaney does in the picture. Or better still an imitation of Chaney by a contortionist."[79] Chaney was now a star. Contortionists were imitating him. He had become the ultimate blowoff whose acrobatic feats did not make him Douglas Fairbanks but were reminiscent of the combination of disability and compensating ability often employed in freak show performances.

The Star as "Ten in One"

The revelation of the freak may be, as Leslie Fiedler suggests, a sexually metaphorical unveiling of "the final forbidden mystery," but that revelation was carefully centered on the platform performance, not on the freak's appearance away from it. The freak off the platform was of no interest or, more accurately, was an interest that could not be exploited as "amusement" because it could not be properly constructed. The mystery of the freak needed to be preserved. That necessity was exemplified in how certain freak acts carefully controlled their venues or their frequency of appearances.

Chaney's film promotion also cultivated mystery in a similar fashion as freak show publicity. Advertisements for *The Monster* (1925) featured an ugly man (Chaney?) pointing to a door marked with a question mark. The tag line asks: "What lies beyond the door?" Similarly, for *A Blind Bargain* (1922), advertisements featured the tag, "The Most Amazing Mystery Play of the Year! What dark Fate, cruel, monstrous, lay behind the door of the secret underground chamber? Every moment of this picture will thrill and surprise you." The advertisement features a drawing of two women clasping their hands in fear as they look at a man with twisted legs coming through the door. Advance publicity for *The Phantom of the Opera* never revealed Chaney's face so that the revelation of his death's mask makeup would be saved for the film's most famous moment. Trade magazines often suggested that Chaney's films had "teaser possibilities" for drawing audiences.[80]

As if the star were the final blowoff who had to be carefully protected from view, the studio pressbook for *The Big City* (1928) makes this suggestion to exhibitors:

The secret of Lon Chaney's remarkable drawing power is the inability of your patrons to anticipate in advance just what form of characterization he will attempt next. He is forever performing the weird, the unusual or the unexpected. Just what shape this will take and how the picture will develop is the lure which brings them back to your box office time and again. Preserve this air of mystery in all your

"Teaser possibilities" for drawing an audience to the freak show "blowoff"
(Lon Chaney and Mary Philbin in *The Phantom of the Opera*)

advertising and promotion activities. . . . Keep them guessing. . . . Don't say too
much—and your patrons' money will talk at the box office.[81]

Of course, *The Big City* featured Chaney au naturel, so the air of mystery
encouraged by MGM may have been required to keep from disappointing
fans who expected him to play with multiple disguises. In keeping with
freak show presentation as well, advertisements for *The Unholy Three*
(1930) revealed the multiple "faces" of Chaney, but also shifted interest to
his "five different voices" as the teaser for his first talkie.

A career based on self-effacing impersonation certainly is not unknown
in Hollywood, as demonstrated by such impersonator-artistes as Paul
Muni. Nevertheless, one might argue that acting stars who disappear into
their roles are never stars for long. The Hollywood system appears too
dependent on the extratextual as well as textual overvaluation of star faces
and bodies as recognizable commodities. The star is made into a physical

Multiple voices plus the multiple faces of the "ten-in-one"
show (Advertisement for *The Unholy Three*, 1930)

spectacle set into play to be admired, emulated, and even envied.[82] While
it is not unknown for stars to transform themselves physically in the process
of creating the codes of character (such as Robert DeNiro's weight gain
for *Raging Bull*), it is generally acknowledged that making your star
unrecognizable is dangerous. This is because the value of stardom is most
frequently measured in audience anticipation at seeing—and recogniz-
ing—their favorite box-office attraction.

Chaney did not really disappear into his roles, and his stardom as a self-
effacing actor appears unusual, for his popularity was not really linked to
the variety of his impersonations. On the contrary, as this chapter has
shown, his films suggest a startling confirmation of sameness. In fact, studio exploitation seemed to expect that the viewers of Chaney's films in
the 1920s anticipated the actor's specialization in representing the physically grotesque much as they later anticipated the appearance of stars who
sang or danced in talkies. A feature in the exploitation guide for *Mockery*
notes that "patrons marvel at his results [in impersonation] and look forward to his next picture with a great deal of expectancy." The banner illustration accompanying this article offers a visual panorama of a dozen
Chaney impersonations that creates a striking similarity to posed photographs of many sideshows, including Sells-Floto's "complete Congress
of Strange People."[83] In spite of his characters' physical differences, there
was consistency to his roles in the sense that Chaney was a star for a
decade using deliberately exaggerated theatrically based effects that rendered him into figures who paralleled the different modes of freak show
presentation.

Exploitation of the exotic mode of difference
(Advertisement for *Mr. Wu*, c. 1927)

Chaney's face and his body were overvalued like those of most other stars but in a different form—as the movies' best palette for the grotesque, the horrible, the ugly, the weird—the stuff of the freak show. In contrast to the codification of the talents of Hollywood stars as an illusion of the natural rather than of the theatrically or filmically constructed, Chaney was constructed as a star whose stardom was pitched to his audience as rooted in his willingness to be constructed, each time anew, for his films. In spite of his apparent versatility in presenting himself (hence the saying, "Don't step on it, it might be Lon Chaney"), he was never unrecognizable in the sense of being mistaken for other than Lon Chaney because the theatrical means of altering his body and face were limited.[84] Also, he often returned to the same bodily distortions (legless, armless, unable to walk). In addition, he was featured in films made almost identical through their revenge-redemption theme or through their insistence on giving him multiple disguises. The latter mode included his dual character roles for *Treasure Island* (1921), *Outside the Law* (1921), *Mr. Wu*, *The Monster*, and *The Black Bird*.

In keeping with the era's marked fascination with the Orient, Chaney was, like Valentino, a familiar figure in the "exotic mode." However, in contrast to Valentino's association with dance exoticism, Chaney's representations were aligned with the freak show's particular exploitation of the phenomenon as a spectacle with connotations of grotesque physical or behavioral difference.[85] He would portray Asians in a notable number of films including *Bits of Life* (1921), *Flesh and Blood* (1922), *Shadows* (1922), and *Mr. Wu* (1927). Many other of his films are set in exotic

Exotic, but still typically Chaney—a vengeful father protecting his daughter: Lon Chaney and Renee Adoree in *Mr. Wu*

locales or have criminal characters, such as Wilse Dilling in *The Shock* and Blizzard in *The Penalty*, who are part of an underworld orientalized by location (San Francisco's Chinatown).

While conjuring up stereotypes about ethnic criminality and oriental mystery, his films also bring into play questions of identity in relation to the differences figured by ethnicity. Some Chaney vehicles in the exotic mode, such as *Mr. Wu*, follow the typical Chaney formula of a vengeful protagonist/father seeking to protect his daughter through actions described by one racially toned review as "the weird traditions of his ancestors."[86] However, a film such as *Shadows* (1922) offers a less formulaic picture of the social stigmatization of ethnic minorities in Anglo communities. Echoing *Broken Blossoms*, the film tells the story of Yen Sin, a "Chink" who endures an isolated life as the one "pagan" in a pious, Christian fishing village. He proves his moral superiority by saving a young minister from ruin. Emotionally overcome by the minister's ability to forgive the man who tried to ruin him, Yen Sin converts to Christianity, then dies in self-imposed exile on the stormy waters that once washed him ashore.

Turning an oppressed ethnic into an Asian Quasimodo: Lon Chaney, John Malden, and Marguerite De La Motte in *Shadows* (1922)

Although the film condemns racial hatred, Chaney's portrayal (including intertitles in pidgin English) sustains every imaginable racial stereotype that turns the main character into a kind of Asian Quasimodo. In similar fashion as *Hunchback*, *Shadows* works hard to aggrandize the character through his physical sufferings.

From the benign oriental exotic of *Shadows*, to the half man, half beast of *The Monster*, to the self-made freaks of *The Black Bird* and *The Unknown*, to the *mutiles* of *West of Zanzibar*, *Where East Is East*, and *The Penalty*, Chaney offered a shocking spectacle of difference, whether constructed through cultural exoticization or through anomalous physicality. He offered all the possibilities of the freak show under "one tent"—the umbrella of his star-centered impersonations. This "versatility" is not out of line with a liminality in the process of constructing freaks that was particularly evident in shifting modes of freak presentational style.

In freak show tradition, an African giant might be presented in an exotic mode as a wild Watusi (Watutsi) king during one phase of his career and as

Aggrandizing the stigmatized exotic through physical suffering: Lon Chaney as Yen Sin in *Shadows*

a colonialized, even "civilized" military man in another.[87] John Robinson, who was promoted as the world's heaviest man, was photographed (in an aggrandized mode) in vaguely military attire with a medal pinned to his broad chest. He also appeared in exotic drag, as a South Seas woman, complete with cascading black wig, Hawaiian style shift, and Japanese fan.[88] While it is impossible to know whether Robinson put his drag presentation into his act, such portraits were made to be sold, so we can assume this portrait circulated among freak show patrons.

Robinson's shifting presentation demonstrates that, in many respects, freaks were a class of actors who were typecast into particular roles because, like Chaney, their platform appearance traded on interest in deviance and in the grotesque. They did not necessarily limit themselves to one unchanging performative persona unless that persona was unequivocally successful. As in the case of Zip, even the most successful sideshow persona was subject to discursive modification and adjustments to cater perhaps to changing audience interests, although, as in the case of Chaney (and Zip), the symbolic force of the performer's perceived difference may have remained fundamentally unchanged.

"Why must he always suffer?"

In numerous fan magazine articles throughout the 1920s, film promotion and Hollywood publicity cultivated Chaney's image as a "mystery" man through strategies that paralleled many of those employed by the freak show. He was depicted as the only star who refused involvement in the Hollywood scene and could or would not be recognized offscreen, even by others in the Hollywood community. Such a strategy runs counter to Richard deCordova's astute analysis of the beginnings of the star system and the extratextual systems it set into place: deCordova argues that the intrigue of the star image always alluded, ultimately, to the promise of a sexual secret to be revealed.[89] Nevertheless, a public identity was constructed for Chaney as a "monomaniacal" working actor who had a peculiar talent developed from a peculiar background (deaf-mute parents). Although it was present from the beginning of Chaney's stardom, the stigma of that origin was combined with an aggrandizing of his mastery of performance-centered craft and his willingness to suffer for it.

Richard Schickel has suggested that Lon Chaney was actually "a man with no face at all . . . [with] no recognizable traits of personality, even of face or body, with which [his audience] . . . could identify."[90] Schickel's assessment echoes that of commentators in the 1920s. Although they did not discuss audience identification, they tended to agree that the star did elicit audience sympathy for his characters; they often suggested, as does Ivan St. Johns, that Lon Chaney the actor had "lost his own identity": "In fact, it doesn't seem to me he has a personality. . . . He has submerged himself so long in characterization, that to me he has become selfless, a channel for other personalities. . . . I couldn't find any Lon Chaney. He just IS whatever he's playing at the time."[91]

The cultivation of a Chaney who lacked a personality between characterizations would seem to run counter to the conventions of the "cult of personality" surrounding Hollywood stars and mark him as an anomaly in Hollywood's star-making process. However, it fit into the freak-show mode of constructing the personality of the performer as almost entirely performance-centered in its construction. Although photographs and brochures might promote the attraction, neither of these revealed very much about the freak's off-platform life. In this reticence, as in that surrounding Chaney, the mystery of the freak might be preserved and sustained. And, of course, the gaffed elements in the freak's construction would be safely guarded.

Although the story is likely apocryphal, it was reported many times that Chaney limited studio distribution of photos that depicted him without his performance makeup. Virtually every photo appearance of Chaney without makeup was touted in fan magazines as being the first photo of its kind. Such a strategy fits with the freak show/circus venue in which performance is seen as being central to the meaning of the star rather than the extratextual secret to be uncovered in the star/performer's life. The freak show cultivated a mystery that was not necessarily fathomed even in the final revelation of nudity in the blowoff, and could not be solved extratextually—away from the sideshow platform.

Especially toward the end of his career, extratextual material emphasized mystery as the defining truth to the star's identity. Ruth Biery tantalizingly told fan magazine readers that Chaney's "life is a mystery closed to publicity," but her interview at least has him explaining why he "feels his obligation to his public to preserve the tremendous illusion he has built up."[92] A fan magazine article of 1926 actually asserts that the star's "aversion to publicity is not modesty. It is business. To be interviewed, exposed and exploited in the wrong manner is like pulling the beard off Santa Claus."[93] In reality, it may have been closer to pulling the beard off the bearded lady or the ape-suit off Zip.

But having a star persona rooted in onscreen inscriptions rather than through an extratextual discourse did not mean that Chaney's fans had nothing to anticipate in the construction of his star subjectivity. He was not personality-centered; rather, like freak show and circus performers, he was performance-centered. The audience's anticipation was constructed to be more on the order of those who paid ten cents to enter the sideshow tent in response to the talker's ballyhoo, to the imaginative extratextual spiel that led to anticipation, suspense, and the promised payoff of the revelation of the freak's mystery. Fan magazines attempted to create, if not a personality, then at least a professional history for the actor, a history that emphasized his use of his body as well as his makeup box as expressive tools for creating extraordinary images of human suffering.

As in freak show brochures, Chaney's domestic life might be mentioned in the most general terms (he had a wife and son), but his personal life was subordinated to the imperative of creating the performance. Extratextual emphasis on Chaney's makeup mysteries fit into this scheme,[94] but in order to extract some narrative from his extratextual enigma as a person, the development of his bizarre characterizations were often discussed in ways that recall the freak show's strategies for aggrandizing and normalizing their stigmatized subjects.

Thus, if the audience could not identify with Chaney as a recognizable star personality, extratextual discourses would provide a star who identified with his audience and with their experience of him in his films. Over the years, fan magazine discourse regularly attempted to normalize him as a disinterested observer of human wreckage who borrowed from real life to construct his onscreen characterizations. In *Motion Picture Classic*'s "The Most Grotesque Moment of My Life," Chaney (or a ghostwriter) tells readers of the fan magazine that his "grotesque and different" characterizations are the result of his "natural gift for the art of make-up," one that allows him to give his public "a number of horrifying hours." He relates that he has a "hobby of wandering about the slums of the bigger cities" and observing "beggars, gunmen and dopefiends"; these unfortunates provide the models for his disguises. He recounts one occasion when he returned to his hotel from walking through San Francisco's Chinatown. In his room, he says, he was confronted by six disfigured men whose awful presence caused him to break out in a cold sweat even though they just wanted to honor him as "King of the Cripples." Like a platform talker inventing stories of freak origination, Chaney recalls the exotic tales they told of a war injury, a steeplejack fall, a log-rolling accident, and a near-fatal squeezing by a boa constrictor. He reassures fan magazine readers that his experience with these men was a "nightmare of reality"; by doing this, he affirms his identification with his audience and their feelings of horror when confronted with his screen roles.[95]

As part of this attempt to normalize Chaney, extratextual discourse painted a picture of the actor as the victim of an industry that exploited his high sense of professionalism and his desire for "realism." In an early fan magazine article (1921), he recounts how the director of *The Miracle Man* "wanted me to crawl through dozens of scenes with my body twisted beyond recognition." The suffering he experienced in that film, he notes, was "child's play" in comparison with what was demanded of him in the role of Blizzard in *The Penalty*:

"I was condemned to wear [a] special harness, my legs strapped back behind me to give the effect of limbs amputated at the knee. Talk not to me of the trials of a film actor's life. The wearing of the harness caused me exquisite agony of pain being so acute that I was unable to hold the position for more than a few minutes at a time.

... I don't want to play any more cripple roles yet awhile. . . . Still, it's all in a movie day's work."[96]

Ultimately, Chaney was constructed as an actor whose craft went beyond the normal limits of stardom and beyond actorly self-effacement. Toward the end of his career there was a growing convergence between his off-screen and onscreen roles. He became a legend as the "martyr to the movies."[97] The masochism of his roles was conflated with his offscreen persona. One fan magazine suggested: "There is something morose, tragic and grim about him. . . . He suffers much physical pain in achieving his histrionic ends."[98] It was frequently noted, years after their production, that "he was forced to suffer great physical pain" as Quasimodo and sustained lasting injuries from filming *The Penalty* and *The Road to Mandalay*.[99]

Nevertheless, Chaney's film roles were not attributed to his own masochistic desires, but to Hollywood's demands on his acting talent. Pain became a testament of his mastery of his craft and his devotion to his audience. His status as willing victim, as in his films, was normalized by reference to a family discourse of sacrifice. An obituary article entitled "Lon Chaney Raised 2 Fingers to Signal That He Was Dying" recounts how the "beloved martyr of movie-land" left his hospital bed to finish his last film; this was claimed to be in keeping with a career that "was a living martyrdom" in which "every role cost him untold agony in mind and body." The physical debilitation caused by his commitment to acting was a testament to his family, to his support of the wife "whom he worshipped."[100]

What emerges in this discourse is a perverse negotiation of onscreen and offscreen Lon Chaney to bring the offscreen personality (and the actor's death) in line with the masochistic triumph so frequently used to end his films. Yet, interestingly, this attribution of martyrdom to Chaney in his assumption of his roles also has precedent in the freak show. Such a strategy follows the promotional tactics of the freak show, which consistently downplayed choice in the matter of freakdom and portrayed self-made freaks such as tattooed people as victims of adventures in foreign lands. Tattooed people were frequently promoted as having been captured and unwillingly decorated in ritual torture by exotic peoples. Mortado, "The Human Fountain," had holes drilled in his hands and feet and forced water through them to make the spectacle of his mutilation obvious; he was imaginatively advertised as "the only living man captured by savages and actually crucified."[101] After all, these freak promotions and Chaney's extra-textual promotion seem to say, what man would choose to be a freak?

Lon Chaney's performance specialization was a disturbing and curious one, one that might seem virtually inexplicable within a system whose effects have until recently been associated almost exclusively with the viewer's desire to identify with stars as ego ideals in their power and physical perfection. His stardom might seem doubly beyond explanation in the context of 1920s America and its cultural ideals of masculine beauty and prowess that seemed so persuasively articulated by Hollywood. Obviously, Chaney did not elicit identification with his contortionist's athleticism in the same manner as Douglas Fairbanks elicited admiration for his physical prowess; nor did he elicit admiration for his manly beauty and his love-making on the order of a Valentino or a Barrymore. His screen work did not depend upon the same generic traditions that shaped these stars even if his characters, like theirs, share in a fundamental affirmation of the transformative capacities of masculinity. Instead, Chaney's work depended upon the audience's familiarity with the freak show spectacle as the precursor to, and frequent overt intertext of, the star's films. Within this context, Chaney existed as a curiosity, but a distinctly masculine one whose grotesque lacks and/or pathetic differences were those identified with being male, and whose redemption through sacrifice foregrounds the transformative paradigm underscoring so much of the era's discussion of masculinity.

Although he occasionally essayed "straight" roles, such as the hard-bitten sergeant in *Tell It to the Marines* (1926), Chaney was most consistently presented across his film career as a "monstrous" figure. However, his monstrosity was not associated with the supernatural world, but one made familiar through the world of the freak show. In this respect, Chaney created a grotesque cinematic fetish whose specularization depended upon an older noncinematic tradition. Thus, the figuration of Lon Chaney as the 1920s' most famous cinematic freak drew upon several traditional modes of freak presentation, all with significant cultural implications for the representation of masculinity as Otherness.

If the human body always must function as a sign within a historically bound cultural economy, one might conjecture that the preoccupation with certain distortions of the human body evidenced in Chaney's films must certainly have had historically specific connotations that are difficult to reconstruct. From the evidence that his films and extratextual discourse offer, we can conjecture that his symbolic Otherness reverberated with the concerns about masculinity and identity that found numerous other avenues for expression, including eugenics commentary, the political discourse of racial chauvinism, and character-building. In an era in which the perfection of masculinity was preached as an achievable goal, Chaney's films voice uncertainties about the masculine ideals advanced by character-builders. While there are many possible readings of Chaney's rich films, it appears that, for his many male fans, he might have functioned as an expiation of male anxiety and self-loathing directed toward the male body in its imperfectability at a time when society exalted—and seemed to sincerely believe—in its perfection. As a corollary to this, the containment of Chaney's freakdom in narratives of revenge and redemption seems symbolically expressive of uncertainties regarding the paternal role at a time when the American family was undergoing tremendous change. With Chaney, the vulnerability of the male body is inscribed in a grotesque and obsessive way that suggests the force field of masculine crisis. In this respect, Chaney's stardom suggests a subversion of masculine norms that makes Barrymore's woman-made androgyny and Valentino's ethnic Otherness (and feminized expressiveness through dance) pale by comparison.

Chaney has been considered to be one of the most unwholesome and inexplicable star phenomenons of film in the late 1910s and 1920s. Reviewers of the time were clearly skeptical of the social value of his films, even as a growing part of the American public were beginning to doubt the propriety of the freak show. Chaney's stardom raises questions not only about the available range of inscriptions of masculinity during a specific historical period but about spectators' relationship to Hollywood illusionism and the pleasure of encountering anew with each film a star whose anticipated *performance* of a grotesque and suffering identity is the very reason for viewing. Chaney was the opposite of a "natural" star. When he is not playing a man who is pretending to be disabled, the very explicitness of Chaney's performance recalls the freak show's tacit agreement that everything is constructed—nothing is what it seems. In their weird pleasures and even weirder depiction of masculine Otherness, Chaney's films suggest that in the star's cinematic sideshow, nothing on the "platform" should be taken at face value. Gaffed freaks abound, the most horrible spectacle is an illusion, and the whole mystery of masculine masquerade may turn out to be mere ballyhoo.

Conclusion

Film pioneer Thomas Ince defined stardom very simply. He said that stardom occurs when "some actor or actress . . . can portray a certain type better than any other actor or actress—some player who has an individuality, or a personality, if you like it better that way—some actor or actress whose work 'gets over' the footlights or appears on the screen so as to make that particular player seem to dominate the scene."[1] Ince's simple definition is convergent with this rather complex study, which has attempted to historically analyze "certain types" of masculinity represented by particular stars who seemed to portray those types "better" than anyone else.

This has been a study which has foregrounded masculinity—and stardom—as cultural constructions that move through time, with structures and purposes that change because neither is autonomous from history. They both are intensely reactive to forces "outside" themselves. Thus, my emphasis on the importance of cultural intertexts has served the purpose of addressing why these stars came to embody specific masculine types, how these modes of masculinity were formulated in social discourse, and why these stars exercised a certain hold over the collective imagination. In this study I have sought to reveal the necessity of the fullest possible examination of the cultural framework in analyzing how stardom comes to represent anything—especially gender.

All the stars discussed—Fairbanks, Barrymore, Valentino, and Chaney—reveal the significant tensions that underscored American notions of masculinity during the late 1910s and 1920s. Those tensions were negotiated differently in the construction of each of these stars. The various guises of masculinity revealed in these stars may indicate just how reactive notions of masculine identity were to perceived social upheaval, especially to that associated with women. In keeping with the era's dominant discoveries on masculine development, they all appear to reveal the underlying assumption that men were made—not born. From their most normative to their most transgressive embodiments of transformative masculinity, these stars seem to confirm an intertitle from Barrymore's *Dr. Jekyll and Mr. Hyde* that echoes character builders: "What we want most to be, we *are*."

These stars reveal America's self-conscious struggle in the first part of the century to come to grips with perceived problems in its constructions of masculinity. That revelation leads us to suggest that the films and stars of this era have been too long neglected as a social discourse with important implications for the study of gender. As such, they yield important insights into the relationship between mass media and the perception of gender identity and sexual subjectivity within a given historical period. In view of this, even the vehicles of an "obvious" and apparently "light-weight" star personality such as Douglas Fairbanks becomes amazingly suggestive when analyzed within a fully formulated sense of historically specific notions of masculinity (and femininity).

The 1910s and 1920s have proven particularly rich for a consideration of masculinity because of the self-consciousness with which masculine development was approached on a number of fronts. The pressures of modernity and the nostalgic pull of traditional, "antimodernist" masculinity associated with the past are evidenced in the films of all these stars, albeit in different ways. Whether this trend indicates a general pattern in the star system's construction of gender in the twenties should be explored through further research. As I have discussed elsewhere, there is some evidence that popular constructions of screen femininity in the 1920s often attempted to steer a similar mediating course between archetypal new and old social/sexual identities so that the "very modern girl" could emerge as an ideal compromise between the passive Victorian ideal and the sensation-seeking flapper.[2] As the chapter on Valentino suggests, modernism was forcefully linked in the popular press to the New Woman and her "radical" assertions of female desire. In films that inscribe women's "modern" desire, masculinity is often depicted as a counterforce that brings female sexual rebellion in line with this compromise.[3] Nevertheless, even in this function, normative masculinity does not necessarily assert only the values of antimodernism.

Do the stars discussed here provide a representative range of options for male stardom in the 1920s? My tentative answer would be "yes," but more research needs to be done in how movies negotiated masculinity across the decade in a number of genres. I do not presume that the stars discussed in this book present the only possible formulations of movie masculinity during the era.[4] Certainly Fairbanks, Barrymore, and Valentino created trends in representing masculinity which ultimately seem to converge in a vision of manhood that would rather not negotiate gender identity in modern dress (i.e., contemporary) settings. However, we need to remember that there are still considerable differences in the historically based costume films of these stars, and the numerous swashbucklers and Ruritainian romances of other stars (such as John Gilbert and Ronald Colman) in the late twenties would need to be looked at before we make assumptions about the meaning of the figuration of masculinity solely on the basis of genre. Needless to say, the connection between stardom and genre seems to be an important one, and the temporary decline of the Hollywood costume film in the early thirties in the wake of talkies may be one event that requires further investigation.

Ironically, if we look beyond the 1920s, Chaney's representation of masculinity is not as singular as it might appear. Of all the stars discussed, his mode of anguished, alienated, perversely aggressive masculinity seems to prefigure important screen types of masculinity that had particular currency in the Depression-era 1930s. We may regard the horror film of the 1930s as obviously indebted to Chaney's depiction of masculinity as a grotesque Otherness, but Chaney's au naturel depictions of a hard-bitten criminal type in many of his films (including *Outside the Law*, *The Shock*, *The Big City*, and some sideshow films such as the two versions of *The Unholy Three*) appear connected to the "realistic" gangster types that gained a foothold in the late 1920s in crime films such as *Thunderbolt* (1929) and *Underworld* (1927) and that took off in popularity in the early 1930s.

Also, the underworld or working-class milieu of many of the Star Sinister's films anticipates the shift in the 1930s that undercut the heady romanticism of many films in the silent years with more down-to-earth settings for more down-to-earth heroes.[5] The latter ranged from stars such as Wallace Beery, who specialized in ne'er-do-well roles, to regular guy romantic heroes such as Clark Gable and Joel McCrea. Perhaps, had he lived beyond his first talkie, Chaney may have become an important transitional figure of aggressive, alienated masculinity extending into the sound era.[6] By way of contrast, Fairbanks and Barrymore found only mixed success in the 1930s. Attempting everything from *The Taming of the Shrew* (1929) with wife Mary Pickford as Kate to an updated version of Robinson Crusoe (*Mr. Robinson Crusoe*, 1932), Fairbanks never seemed comfortable with sound or with acting his age. Early retirement put a stop to the handful of Fairbanks sound films that were not particularly successful with the critics or the public. Slipping into premature mental and physical degeneracy, Barrymore's star status as a romantic lead dimmed, though he did give wonderful performances in a number of important

A hard-bitten, criminal type that takes on new life in the 1930s: Lon Chaney as Black Mike Sylva in *Outside the Law* (1921)

films—for example, as a debonair baron in *Grand Hotel* (1932), as a gentle academic coping with ruthless capitalists in *Topaze* (1933), and as the outrageous theatrical producer, Oscar Jaffe, in *Twentieth Century* (1934).

This study has tried to suggest how, in the creation of individual stars, the cultural system that is the framework for film comes into play in complicated ways that reveal a nuanced process of negotiating and sustaining the star phenomenon. I believe that process has not been fully appreciated in its complexity. The field of film studies is just beginning to investigate stars and stardom to a commensurable degree as it has other film phenomena such as genre, narrative, technology, directors, film style, and studio practice. In this book I have attempted to suggest that we should rethink our preconceptions about stardom in the late 1910s and 1920s. This may lead us to regard the representation of masculinity in the Hollywood star vehicles discussed here as a model for the unexpected and important insights into the interrelationship between culture and popular cinema's approach to gender identity that remain to be discovered through the films and stars of other eras. I have tried to answer as many questions as possible about the four stars who have served as the focus of this study, but many, many questions remain unanswered. I must leave it to other scholars to give us authoritative accounts of those stars and star-centered issues of the Jazz Age that remain unexamined here.

The historical and cultural specificity of stardom demands attention even as our fascination with stars defies time and place. Although any detailed analysis such as this book tends to demystify its subject, I hope that in some sense Norma Desmond is right when, in her movie-driven madness at the end of *Sunset Boulevard*, she whispers: "Stars never age. . . . Stars are eternal."

Introduction

1. See, for example, Frederick Lewis Allen, *Only Yesterday* (New York: Harper, 1931), William E. Leuchtenburg, *The Perils of Prosperity, 1914–1932* (Chicago: University of Chicago Press, 1958), Dorothy M. Brown, *Setting a Course: American Women in the 1920s* (Boston: Twayne, 1987), Stanley Cohen, *Rebellion Against Victorianism: The Impetus for Cultural Change in 1920s America* (New York: Oxford University Press, 1991), Paul A. Carter, *Another Part of the Twenties* (New York: Columbia University Press, 1973), and Paula S. Fass, *The Damned and the Beautiful: American Youth in the 1920s* (New York: Oxford University Press, 1977).

2. Richard deCordova, *Picture Personalities: The Emergence of the Star System in America* (Urbana: University of Illinois Press, 1990), 45.

3. Thomas H. Ince, "The Star Is Here to Stay," *Munsey's Magazine* 65, no. 2 (November 1918): 337–46 (the quotations are from p. 337).

4. DeCordova, *Picture Personalities*, 87.

5. Ibid., 136.

6. On the public's interest in scandals involving stars, see DeCordova, *Picture Personalities*, 219–24. For a discussion of Hollywood's family discourse within the context of fan magazines in the 1920s see Gaylyn Studlar, "The Perils of Pleasure? Fan Magazine Discourse as Women's Commodified Culture in the 1920s," *Wide Angle* 13, no. 1 (January 1991): 10–12.

7. For example, see Jackie Stacey, *Star Gazing: Hollywood Cinema and Female Spectatorship* (New York: Routledge, 1994); Dennis Bingham, *Acting Male: Masculinities in the Films of James Stewart, Jack Nicholson, and Clint Eastwood* (New Brunswick, N.J.: Rutgers University Press, 1994); Christine Gledhill, ed., *Stardom: Industry of Desire* (London: Routledge, 1991); Robert Sklar, *City Boys: Cagney, Bogart, Garfield* (Princeton: Princeton University Press, 1992).

8. After the star's death, various Valentino fan clubs, including the "Rudolph Valentino Memorial Committee," were reputed to be in the process of raising money for an appropriately stellar memorial to their idol, but nothing ever came of this other than a modest statue (called "Inspiration" and placed in DeLongpre Park in West Hollywood).

9. Miriam Hansen, "Pleasure, Ambivalence, Identification: Valentino and Female Spectatorship," *Cinema Journal* 25, no. 4 (Summer 1986): 6–32.

10. Gaylyn Studlar, "Discourses of Gender and Ethnicity: The Construction and De(con)struction of Rudolph Valentino as Other," *Film Criticism* 13, no. 2 (Winter 1989): 18–35.

11. My title is derived from an advertisement for Allan Leigh's *Women Like Men* (New York: Macaulay, 1926) that appeared in the *New York Times* (April 4, 1926): "This powerful novel reveals the struggle made by a woman to overcome the age-

long handicap of her sex. She tries to live the codeless existence of the male in this mad masquerade . . ."

12. Gaylyn Studlar, *In the Realm of Pleasure: Von Sternberg, Dietrich, and the Masochistic Aesthetic* (Urbana: University of Illinois Press, 1988).

13. For the most convincing adaptations of the psychoanalytic notion of "masquerade" as applied to male stars, see Steven Cohan, "Masquerading as the American Male in the Fifties: *Picnic*, William Holden and the Spectacle of Masculinity in Hollywood Film," *Camera Obscura* 25–26 (January–May 1991): 43–72; and Chris Holmlund, "Masculinity as Multiple Masquerade,"in Steven Cohan and Ina Rae Hark, eds., *Screening the Male: Exploring Masculinities in Hollywood Cinema* (London: Routledge, 1993), 213–44.

14. Cohan, "Masquerading as the American Male in the Fifties," 68.

15. Judith Butler, *Gender Trouble: Feminism and the Subversion of Identity* (New York: Routledge, 1990), 136.

16. DeCordova, *Picture Personalities*, 20.

17. Peter Lehman, *Running Scared: Masculinity and the Representation of the Male Body* (Philadelphia: Temple University Press, 1993), 104.

18. The term *woman-made* is found in many contexts within popular discourse of the period. See, for example, Anna Steese Richardson, "A Woman-Made Season," *McClure's* 46 (April 1916): 22; and Lorine Pruette, "Should Men Be Protected?" *The Nation* 125 (August 31, 1927): 200–201.

19. See deCordova, *Picture Personalities*, 141–43.

20. Truman B. Handy, "Masquerade," *Motion Picture Magazine* (December 1922): 43.

1. Building Mr. Pep: Boy Culture and the Construction of Douglas Fairbanks

1. C. R. H. Jackson, "The Moral Value of Physical Activities," in C. B. Horton, ed., *Reaching the Boys of an Entire Community* (New York: Association Press, 1909), 77–78.

2. Arthur Hornblow, Jr., "Douglas Fairbanks, Dramatic Dynamo: An Interview with a K.O. Athlete Who Has Just Left the Triangle Company and Joined the Artcraft," *Motion Picture Classic* (March 1917): 48.

3. "Mr. Roosevelt Asks for 'Real' Defence Programme; Calls the President a 'Shadow,'" *New York Tribune*, November 12, 1915, 4.

4. As Roberta Pearson astutely points out in her excellent study of silent film acting, *Eloquent Gestures*, the movies had long recruited stage-trained actors, but primarily from the minor ranks of stock companies. Such actors were not worried about ruining their reputations. At the same time, however, this class of actors lacked exploitation possibilities. The movies could not trade on their preestablished fame as actors. In contrast, Broadway theatrical stars had a presold celebrity value to a middle-class patronage that often expected, but was not given, stage stars in road shows. In addition to their celebrity, Broadway actors were thought to bring to film the "fine acting" and polished characterizations that movie producers assumed would appeal to the middle class. They also appeared perfectly suited to

feature films, a longer storytelling format that could more easily accommodate adaptations of star-centered stage vehicles. See Roberta E. Pearson, *Eloquent Gestures* (Berkeley: University of California Press, 1992), 135–36, 162; and Richard deCordova, *Picture Personalities: The Emergence of the Star System in America* (Urbana: University of Illinois Press, 1990), 43. On the relationship between audiences, the movies, and theatrical road companies, see Walter Prichard Eaton, "What's the Matter with the Road?" *American Magazine* 74 (July 1912): 359–68. On the attraction of film for "speaking stage" celebrities, see Thomas H. Ince, "The Star Is Here to Stay," *Munsey's Magazine* 65, no. 2 (November 1918): 337–46.

5. "Triangle's Auspicious Opening," *Moving Picture World* 26 (October 9, 1915): 233. In an unusual move, the *New York Times* reported on the film's special screening as a news event. "Triangle Debut," the *New York Times*, September 24, 1915, sec. 2, p. 2.

6. "Triangle's Auspicious Opening," 233. *Photoplay* declared him to be "one of the foremost screen acquisitions of the season" (photograph caption), *Photoplay* 9 (March 1916): 63. See also the review for *The Lamb* in *Variety*, October 1, 1915, p. 18, reprinted in *Variety Film Reviews, 1907–1980*, vol. 1 (New York: Garland, 1983), n.p.

7. This point was affirmed and reaffirmed in terms that suggest the powerful relationship between male identity and the era's mythically loaded representations of the American landscape. An article in *Motion Picture Classic* typically suggested in 1917: "Fairbanks was already popular, though the stage never gave him the elbow room he needed. His joyous personality was 'cramped, cabined and confined' in the narrow limits of the playhouse. He needed, not knowing it, the wide sweep of mountain and plain." Marjorie Gleyre Lachmund, "Douglas Fairbanks Discourses on Work and Play," *Motion Picture Classic* (December 1917): 54.

8. This has often been attributed to Griffith, but without confirmation of source. See, for example, Richard Schickel, *Douglas Fairbanks: The First Celebrity* (London: New Elm Books, 1976), 37.

9. Quoted in an advertisement in *Moving Picture World* (October 7, 1916): 127.

10. From an advertisement for *Reaching for the Moon* in the *Exhibitor's Trade Review* 3 (December 15, 1917): 82. In spite of warnings that producers and exhibitors had to stick together and prevent escalating performer costs, Triangle was not shy in promoting Douglas Fairbanks's films as star vehicles that almost exclusively focused on their new sensation. They told potential exhibitors of the Fairbanks feature *Flirting with Fate*: "The popularity of Fairbanks is unquestioned, many exhibitors have proved that the prominent display of Fairbanks' name will do more to increase box office receipts than almost any other one thing. That irresistible 'pep' and personality of the star so long famous on Broadway is intensified in motion pictures" (from an advertisement in *Moving Picture World* 29 [July 15, 1916]: 553).

Triangle would not be able to control the growing power of stars, including Fairbanks. In 1917 Fairbanks switched from Triangle to the Artcraft division of Paramount. Artcraft was devoted to high-quality productions, and there, with his own production company, and with scenarios either written or shaped by him, he now made films "of Fairbanks, by Fairbanks, and for Fairbanks," as an advertisement for *The Man from Painted Post* proudly asserted, in *Exhibitor's Trade Review* 2 (October 6, 1917): 1376.

11. During these years, the relatively new phenomenon of "stardom" was regarded as a two-edged sword to filmmakers and exhibitors. For industry commentary on the negative effects of stardom, see W. Stephen Bush, "Gouging Stars," *Moving Picture World* 29 (August 5, 1916): 645.

12. This phrase was often used. See, for example, the caption for an illustration of Fairbanks imitator William Russell, *Motion Picture Classic* (November 1917): n.p. For more on Russell, see n. 31, below.

13. George Creel, "A 'Close-Up' of Douglas Fairbanks," *Everybody's Magazine* 35, no. 6 (December 1916): 733.

14. Teddy Roosevelt, as quoted in Richard M. Abrams, *The Burdens of Progress, 1900–1929* (Glenview, Ill.: Scott, Foresman, 1978), 104. Roosevelt's Americanism was blatantly belligerent in seeking the heroic regeneration of adventure through physical confrontation—even in war. Of interest in this regard is Roosevelt's classic antipacifist statement: "It would be a mistake to nominate me for President, unless the country has as its mood something of the heroic" (quoted in G. Edward White, *The Eastern Establishment and the Western Experiment* [New Haven: Yale University Press, 1968], 199). Fairbanks's "Americanism" as "restless endeavor, energetic ambition, indefatigable energy" is discussed from a surprisingly cynical point of view by Hazel Naylor in "The Fairbanks Scale of Americanism," *Motion Picture Magazine* (February 1919): 30–32.

15. Advertisement for *The Man from Painted Post* in *Exhibitor's Trade Review* 2 (October 6, 1917): 1376.

16. Review of *Arizona* (1918) in the *New York Times*, December 16, 1918, reprinted in *The New York Times Film Reviews* (New York: New York Times, 1970): n.p.

17. An advertisement shamelessly declared that "Douglas Fairbanks steals the show from the Grand Canyon—that's just how good *he* is." Advertisement for *A Modern Musketeer* in *Exhibitor's Trade Review* 3 (February 2, 1918): 713.

18. Hornblow, Jr., "Douglas Fairbanks, Dramatic Dynamo," 48.

19. Marguerite Sheridan, "The Lass Eileen," *Motion Picture Classic* (April 1918): 27. See also *Motion Picture Classic* (July 1917), p. 10: "Douglas Fairbanks needs no introduction—his smile has made him famous. The electric comedian's pet motto reads: 'Smile and the world smiles with you; cry and you get the gate'" (caption).

20. "Two Triangles," review of *The Matrimaniac* in the *Moving Picture World* 30 (December 16, 1916): 1653.

21. Review of *Knickerbocker Buckaroo* in the *New York Times*, May 26, 1919 (reprinted in *New York Times Film Reviews*, n.p.).

22. Review of *American Aristocracy* in the *New York Times*, November 6, 1916 (reprinted in *New York Times Film Reviews*, n.p.).

23. See, for example, Creel, "A 'Close-Up' of Douglas Fairbanks," 738.

24. "The Shadow Stage," *Photoplay* 11 (March 1917): 117. The "demi-tasse" phrase no doubt refers to Loos's small stature (under five feet).

25. Nutritional reform was part of the broader physical culture movement and included much emphasis on the role of "rational living" for health. The film *The Road to Wellville* (1994), directed by Alan Parker, satirizes this period's health food fads and myriad commodity cures.

26. Lary May's comments regarding this film are very much in error. In fact, the film becomes virtually unrecognizable in his attempt to use it as an example of how "flowing from the new approach to leisure was a major economic and political reorientation." For example, May suggests of Pete: "Although his parents [*sic*] disapprove, these shady actions [eating steak, boxing, and so on] make him attractive to women who are trying to be morally emancipated as well. . . . As reporters ask him for the secret to his strength, his answer is "Pringle Products." . . . Soon the goods move off the shelf. . . . The boy becomes a success by showing manufacturers how to capitalize on the needs of the new generation. . . . The message, then, is that the discontent with work and loss of power can be alleviated through consumption." May goes on to suggest, erroneously I believe, that the Fairbanks hero is an advocate for consumerism and "expanding the necessities of life." May, *Screening Out the Past: The Birth of Mass Culture and the Motion Picture Industry* (Chicago: University of Chicago Press, 1980), 116–17.

27. Per copy in an advertisement for the House of Kuppenheimer in *The Youth's Companion* magazine (June 1915): 320.

28. "Fairbanks Was an Old Man in '96," *Photoplay* 11 (May 1917): 34.

29. For a personal account of such antics see Robert Parrish, *Growing Up in Hollywood* (Boston: Little, Brown, 1976), 3–8. See also Herbert Blumer, *Movies and Conduct* (c. 1933; rpt., New York: Arno, 1978), 243, 254. Blumer cites adolescent girls who recalled identifying strongly with the star's screen adventures: "Douglas Fairbanks in *The Mark of Zorro* . . . so appealed to my childish adventurous instincts that I saw the picture four different times and would have seen it more if I had had the time. His grace in dueling always made me want to some day learn to fence, but this childish day-dream and illusion of mine had to be spoiled, because, you know, ethics (and now I am sarcastic) state that little ladies must not handle dangerous weapons, must not even dream of acting so tomboyish" (254).

30. Advertisement in the *Exhibitor's Trade Review* 2, no. 17 (September 29. 1917): 1284.

31. Also following suit was George Walsh, "The Smiling Athletic All 'Round Good Fellow.'" Walsh, a Fox player, has his 'peppiest punch'" (*This Is the Life*, advertised in *Moving Picture World* 34 [October 27, 1917]: 482). O'Malley is advertised in the May 13, 1916, issue of *Exhibitor's Trade Review* as the "complete and decided expression" of Americanism. William Russell's vehicles were often unabashed ripoffs of Fairbanks's, as in the case of *Snap Judgment*, in which Russell exploited the typical Fairbanks plot device of the cultural (East/West) "dual personality." In *Leave It to Me* (1920), Russell plays Dickey Derrickson, a wealthy idler who is scorned by his girlfriend until he proves himself a hero. Even established stars such as J. Warren Kerrigan were promoted to exhibitors with Fairbanks-like flair: "Will entertain any human being with red blood in his veins" (advertisement for *A Man's Man* in *Moving Picture World* 34 [November 3, 1917]: 649).

32. Photo caption for "William Russell," *Motion Picture Classic* (November 1917): n.p.

33. Alistair Cooke, *Douglas Fairbanks: The Making of a Screen Character* (New York: Museum of Modern Art, 1940). In 1919 Ince suggested that William S. Hart, Mary Pickford, Charlie Chaplin, and Fairbanks were the "'Big Four' of the films." See Ince, "The Star Is Here to Stay," 341.

34. Charles K. Taylor, "The Most Popular Man in the World," *The Outlook* 138 (December 24, 1924): 683. The ability to make such a statement, in defiance of Chaplin's long-touted status as the world's most popular cinematic actor, may have been influenced by the growing disillusionment in the late 1920s with Chaplin's personal life. In 1927 Chaplin was described in passing as "the whimsical, bitter, moody, genius." See Adela Rogers St. Johns, "The Married Life of Doug and Mary," *Photoplay* 31 (February 1927): 134. For an illuminating and perceptive study of the ongoing construction of Chaplin's image in the United States, see Charles Maland's *Chaplin and American Culture: The Evolution of a Star Image* (Princeton: Princeton University Press, 1989). Although predictably sentimental, the Pickford Company documentary *Birth of a Legend* provides newsreel footage of huge crowds (at Liberty Bond rallies featuring Chaplin, Pickford, and Fairbanks; at various sites throughout the Pickford/Fairbanks European honeymoon; and during the couple's visit to Russia) that still impressively confirms the extent of Fairbanks's and Pickford's celebrity.

35. Review of *The Good Bad Man* in the *New York Times*, April 22, 1916 (reprinted in *New York Times Film Reviews*, n.p.).

36. Untitled clipping (c. 1917), 96–98, Hoblitzelle Theatre Arts Library, Harry Ransom Center, University of Texas.

37. Frederick James Smith, "Roping Doug Fairbanks into an Interview," *Motion Picture Classic* (September 1917): 46.

38. See, for example, the full-page photo captioned, "The Two Douglas Fairbanks—Father and Son," that offers an uncharacteristically passive Doug smoking a pipe and sitting on porch steps next to a sailor-suited (and chubby) Douglas Junior who, it is claimed, "can climb trees and jump fences and perform other athletic stunts almost as well as his wonderful father." Douglas Fairbanks, "Combining Play with Work," *American Magazine* (July 1917): 35.

39. "The One and Only 'Doug' Himself," *Woman's Home Companion* 46 (July 1919): 52 (clipping file, New York Public Library for the Performing Arts, Theatre Collection, hereafter cited as NYPL-TC).

40. Contributor's Afterward to Douglas Fairbanks, "'Kind of Crazy,'" *Motion Picture Magazine* (March 1923): 86.

41. St. Johns, "The Married Life of Doug and Mary," 35.

42. "The business of ranching has, for some occult reason, [maintained] a special charm for the gilded youth of the Eastern states; and Mr. Roosevelt seems to have followed it . . . for some years before his fancy led into politics." Untitled article in *The Dial* 15 (September 16, 1893): 149.

43. Howard Mumford Jones, *The Age of Energy* (New York: Viking, 1971), 229.

44. For a helpful discussion of the importance of these years in shaping Roosevelt's view of masculinity in relation to American lifestyles, see G. Edward White, *The Eastern Establishment and the Western Experience*, 65–66, 79–93.

45. An adviser said of Roosevelt: "You must remember, the president is about six years old." Quoted in Richard Hofstadter, *The American Political Tradition* (New York: Knopf, 1948), 236. Boy Scout executives mourned Roosevelt's death in 1919 as a blow to their cause and, more specifically, as the sad end to the former president's enthusiastic association with, and symbolic representation of, their movement. Roosevelt's grave at Oyster Bay became a site for a yearly pilgrimage by Boy Scouts.

46. William Allen White, "Roosevelt: A Force for Righteousness," *McClure's* 28, no. 4 (February 1907): 389.

47. An advertisement for Fairbanks's *The Man from Painted Post* plays on this image of him: "He is just a big-hearted citizen who will tickle your sense of humor and make you glad you're alive." *Exhibitor's Trade Review* 2 (September 22, 1917): 1201.

48. Creel, "A 'Close-Up' of Douglas Fairbanks," 730, 738.

49. "The Shadow Stage," *Photoplay* 11 (March 1917): 116. In the future, the article declared, "He is going to grow right along with camera-craft, and . . . he will crown his career with a man of maturity who will be not only a triumph of acting but *a national expression*" (116–17).

50. In a postobituary reappraisal of Fairbanks in the *New York Times* in 1939, Frank Nugent suggested: "Doug Fairbanks was make-believe at its best, a game we youngsters never tired of playing, a game . . . our fathers secretly shared. He was complete fantasy, not like Disney's, which has an overlay of whimsey and sophistication, but unabashed and joyous. Balustrades were made to be vaulted, draperies to be a giant slide, chandeliers to swing from, citadels to be scaled. There wasn't a small boy in the neighborhood who did not, in a Fairbanks picture, see himself triumphing over the local bully, winning the soft-eyed adoration of whatever ten-year-old blonde he had been courting, and wreaking vengeance on the teacher who made him stand in the corner that afternoon." Quoted in Gary Carey, *Doug and Mary* (New York: Dutton, 1977), 224.

51. James E. West, "Preface" (1923) to Douglas Fairbanks, *Youth Points the Way* (New York and London: Appleton, 1924), vii–viii (emphasis added).

52. Jeffrey P. Hantover, "Sex Role, Sexuality, and Social Status: The Early Years of the Boy Scouts of America" (Ph.D. diss., University of Chicago, 1976), 288.

53. Ernest Thompson Seton, letter to Robert Baden-Powell, June 24, 1910, in collection of Mrs. Dee Seton Barber, quoted by Michael Rosenthal, *The Character Factory: Baden-Powell and the Origins of the Boy Scout Movement* (New York: Pantheon, 1986), 80.

54. The most balanced and broadly defined discussion of the role of all these men in boy culture reform is David I. Macleod's *Building Character in the American Boy* (Madison: University of Wisconsin Press, 1983).

55. Readers of Lary May's work will recognize that he also uses the term *revitalization* to characterize Fairbanks's role in American culture, which May sees as

operating to achieve "a new urban middle-class ideal . . . that might solve the problems of alienating work and social conflict" (*Screening Out the Past*, 99). It should be at once obvious that our notions of what required revitalization and the dynamics of such a process with regards to Fairbanks are very different. See ibid., 96–119.

56. Joe L. Dubbert, "Progressivism and the Masculinity Crisis," in Joseph H. Pleck and Elizabeth H. Pleck, eds., *The American Man* (Englewood Cliffs, N.J.: Prentice-Hall, 1980), 306–7.

57. For such an interpretation, see Dubbert, "Progressivism and the Masculinity Crisis," in Pleck and Pleck, eds., *The American Man*, 303–19; Hantover, "Sex Role, Sexuality, and Social Status"; and also Michael S. Kimmel, "Consuming Manhood: The Feminization of American Culture and the Recreation of the Male Body, 1832–1920," *Michigan Quarterly Review* 33, no. 1 (Winter 1994): 7–36.

Challenging the notion of a specific "turning point" in the phenomenon, Clyde Griffen argues that "it remains unclear when this crisis began, how long it lasted, and when it was resolved if at all" (Griffen, "Reconstructing Masculinity from the Evangelical Revival to the Waning of Progressivism: A Speculative Synthesis," in Griffen and Mark C. Carnes, eds., *Meanings for Manhood: Constructions of Masculinity in Victorian America* (Chicago: University of Chicago Press, 1990), 183–204 (quotation from p. 184). As he rightfully says, we "really don't know yet how deep or widespread the concern was" about masculine identity during the Progressive years (200). It seems to have been a preoccupation, but the degree of satire in Fairbanks's films suggests the ability, at least by some, to step back from the problem with a measure of emotional distance. By way of contrast with Griffen, Michael S. Kimmel tends to overdramatize these anxieties, especially with regard to "sexual panic."

58. Theodore Roosevelt, *The Strenuous Life* (New York: Century, 1901), 1–7.

59. Theodore Roosevelt, quoted in Michael T. Isenberg, *John L. Sullivan and His America* (Urbana: University of Illinois Press, 1988), 63.

60. Macleod's works suggests the need to distinguish between these sometimes almost indistinguishable crosscurrents existing between Britain and the United States in character-building theories and organizations. The shared solutions for the "boy problem" between the two countries may tend to obscure differences in the impetus for each country's concern with boys—Britain's being linked to "upper-class fear of rival empires," as Macleod suggests, and America's caused by more internalized dangers. Macleod, *Building Character in the American Boy*, 45.

61. The best recent works on the organization of boy culture in response to adult anxiety are Macleod, *Building Character in the American Boy*; E. Anthony Rotundo, *American Manhood: Transformations in Masculinity from the Revolution to the Modern Era* (New York: Basic Books, 1993), esp. 30–74; and Rosenthal, *The Character Factory*.

62. Seton, quoted from "History of the Boy Scouts," cited in Rosenthal, *The Character Factory*, 65.

63. E. Anthony Rotundo, "Boy Culture: Middle-Class Boyhood in Nineteenth-Century America," in Griffen and Carnes, eds., *Meanings for Manhood*, 15–17.

64. Kimmel, "Consuming Manhood," 14.

65. Hantover suggests that the collapse in gendered spheres of work meant that the traditional institutional anchors of masculinity were undercut, and this put into crisis "essential elements in the definition of manliness" (Hantover, "Sex Role, Sexuality, and Social Status," 288). However, it should be pointed out that increased heterosociality in the middle class in the late and post-Victorian eras was very much welcomed by some reformers who saw the patriarchal model of the family as antiquated. This increase in heterosociality among the middle class helped break down barriers between the gender-defined spheres.

66. On the general effort to control urban social problems in the late nineteenth century and changes in attitude surrounding the urban middle class, see Paul Boyer, *Urban Masses and Moral Order in America, 1820–1920* (Cambridge: Harvard University Press, 1978). For a helpful discussion of the many social anxieties that led to boy reform, see Macleod, *Building Character in the American Boy*, 1–59.

67. See Hantover, "Sex Role, Sexuality, and Social Status," 91, 194.

68. See C. Wright Mills, *White Collar: The American Middle Classes* (New York: Stokes, 1951). Cindy Aron claims that the heterosocial middle-class workplace was "a new kind of middle-class culture—one that began to dissolve the barriers between the separate spheres of nineteenth-century middle-class America." See Aron, *Ladies and Gentlemen of the Civil Service: Middle-Class Workers in Victorian America* (New York: Oxford University Press, 1987), 188.

69. See, for example, Seton's remarks regarding the "growth of immense cities" and the concurrent creation of a generation "strained and broken by the grind of the over-busy world." See Seton, *Boy Scouts of America: A Handbook of Woodcraft, Scouting, and Lifecraft* (1910; rpt., New York: Doubleday (for the Boy Scouts of America), 1944), xi, xii, 1, 2.

70. For a general discussion of the politicization of these feelings in late nineteenth-century America, see John Higham, *Strangers in the Land: Patterns of American Nativism, 1860–1925* (1963), 2d ed. (New Brunswick, N.J.: Rutgers University Press, 1988).

71. On the wilderness cult as a response to this view of urbanization and immigration, see Roderick Nash, *Wilderness and the American Mind*, rev. ed. (New Haven: Yale University Press, 1973), 144.

72. See Calvin Coolidge, "Whose Country Is This?" *Good Housekeeping* 72 (February 1921): 14; and George Creel, "Close the Gates," *Collier's* (May 6, 1922): 9–11.

73. Norman E. Richardson and Ormond E. Loomis, *The Boy Scout Movement Applied by the Church* (New York: Scribner's, 1915), 25–26.

74. Rotundo, *American Manhood*, 256–57.

75. Women were regarded as more innately attuned to civilization than men, especially in boy culture literature. J. Adams Puffer is typical in his comment: "One notes incidentally how much better fitted for civilization, both in mind and body, women are than men." Puffer, *The Boy and His Gang* (Boston: Houghton Mifflin, 1912), 84.

76. For one discussion of the "masculine primitive" as an extolling of animal energy and primitive passion in late nineteenth-century America, see Rotundo,

American Manhood, 227–32. For a discussion of the fear (and labeling) of feminization during this period, see Hantover, "Sex Role, Sexuality, and Social Status," 289. For a comprehensive account of the feminization of Victorian society through the "sentimental forces" of female writer-reformists that worked to redefine mass culture, see Ann Douglas, *The Feminization of American Culture* (New York: Anchor Books, 1977).

77. Praised as "one of the most perfectly built men in existence," Sandow was among the performers brought to Edison's Black Maria studio in its early days to be captured on film.

78. A hugely successful cycle of boxing films came to the screen at the turn of the century. See Dan Streible, "A History of the Boxing Film, 1894–1915," *Film History* 32 (1989): 235–52.

79. Richardson and Loomis, *The Boy Scout Movement Applied by the Church*, 49–50.

80. Quoted in Pleck and Pleck, eds., *The American Man*, 2.

81. Luther H. Gulick, "The High Tide of Physical Conscience," *World's Work* 16, no. 2 (June 1908): 10384.

82. Bernarr MacFadden, *Manhood and Marriage* (New York: Physical Culture Publishing, 1916), 259. Not only was the spiritual man expected to be physically forceful, but "the vigorously sexed man is usually hard and rugged" (ibid., 147). On this issue see also R. Warren Conant, *The Virility of Christ: A New View: A Book for Men*, 2d rev. ed. (Chicago, 1915); and James R. McGovern, "David Graham Phillips and the Virility Impulse of the Progressives," *New England Quarterly* 39 (1966): 98.

Many reformers and organizations (including the Boy Scouts of America) were extremely worried about sexual "self-abuse" among boys and preached for vigorous play to help boys retain their "purity." MacFadden's comments on marrying early (perhaps to avoid masturbation or other abuses of the "sexual capacity") are echoed by Fairbanks's *Wedlock in Time* (New York: Britton, 1918), in which he is says that one sign of the "manly man" is love of children and that "it is a happy idea to marry while we are young . . . when both are at an age when adjustment is natural. . . . The waiting game is a hard one and it makes us worldly. What once seemed like a rose now seems like a hollyhock" (7–8).

83. Gulick, "The High Tide of Physical Conscience," 10385.

84. As Donald J. Mrozek has suggested of the era: "To say that the body was at its most beautiful and its most perfect is also to say that it attained fulfillment in the very process of experience that formed it, as it was performing the specific actions that set out the practical limits of one's being and character." Mrozek, *Sport and American Mentality, 1880–1910* (Knoxville: University of Tennessee Press, 1983), 224.

85. William Forbush, *A Manual of Boys' Clubs*, 6, quoted in Hantover, "Sex Role, Sexuality, and Social Status," 48.

86. Edgar Allen Forbes, "The Y.M.C.A. Around the World," *World's Work* (July 1908): 10467. Forbes makes particular note of the fact that the YMCA's work "is not done by ministers but by the young men themselves," and goes on to suggest that this has cemented the place of the organization "as an American rather than as a religious institution"(10467). In keeping with most other character-builders,

Gulick believed that motor behavior, the primary agency for shaping moral reflexes, was instinctual in its source, yet required nurturing. See Macleod, *Building Character in the American Boy*, 150.

87. See Douglas, *The Feminization of American Culture*, 8–11.

88. Most boy reformers valorized the impact of a perfected physicality on the entire character of boys and men as including the spiritual and conceived of as a dynamic, physically bound process. On early twentieth-century views on the relationship between physical activity and morality see Mrozek, *Sport and American Mentality*, esp. "Toward a New Image of the Body," 189–225.

89. Conant, *The Virility of Christ*, 14. On morality and goodness in boys and men see Rotundo, *American Manhood*, 227–32.

90. Richardson and Loomis, *The Boy Scout Movement Applied by the Church*, 74. It was also suggested that, under the right influence, the boy would build on his feelings for the gang and "yield his supreme loyalty to Jesus Christ." James Franklin Page, *Socializing for the New Order: Or, Educational Values of the Juvenile Organization* (Rock Island, Ill.: Augustana College, 1919), 53.

91. Griffen, "Reconstructing Masculinity," 199.

92. Ibid., 183.

93. Charles Rosenberg, "Sexuality, Class, and Role in Nineteenth-Century America," in Pleck and Pleck, eds., *The American Man*, 219–54.

94. See Griffen, "Reconstructing Masculinity," 203.

95. Roosevelt, quoted in E. Anthony Rotundo, "Manhood in America, 1770–1910" (Ph.D. dissertation, Brandeis University, 1982), 335.

96. Rafford Pyke, "What Men Like in Men," *Cosmopolitan* 33 (May 1902): 402, 405. Michael S. Kimmel cites this article to suggest that "most terrifying to men, and most indicative of this fear of cultural feminization, was the specter of the sissy" (Kimmel, "Consuming Manhood," 19).

97. John Dewey, quoted in William A. McKeever, *Training the Boy* (New York: Macmillan, 1919), 204.

98. Puffer, *The Boy and His Gang*, 78. Prof. George Walter Fiske similarly suggested that "the savage is a child and the child a savage . . . [and] they know little of the conventions of society." Fiske, *Boy Life and Self-Government* (New York: Association Press, 1911), 11.

99. Richardson and Loomis offer a partial rebuttal to the recapitulation theory (see *The Boy Scout Movement Applied by the Church*, 66–75). See also G. Stanley Hall, *Adolescence* (New York: Appleton, 1904).

100. Fiske, quoted in Page, *Socializing for the New Order*, 30–31.

101. Macleod, *Building Character in the American Boy*, 54. Most boy reformers steadfastly denied that there were class differences or biases in their work, though middle-class ideals were dominant. See Richardson and Loomis, *The Boy Scout Movement Applied by the Church*, 44. See also Thomas H. Russell, *Stories of Boy Life: A Book of Stories About Boys for Boys* (N.p.: Fireside, 1914).

102. McKeever, *Training the Boy*, 111.

103. Page, *Socializing for the New Order*, 92, 94.

104. U.S. Census Bureau, *Religious Bodies (1916)* (Washington, D.C.: GPO, 1919), vol. 1, 40–41.

105. Puffer, *The Boy and His Gang*, 165.

106. Anonymous, quoted in Dominick Cavallo, *Muscles and Morals: Organized Playgrounds and Urban Reform, 1880–1920* (Philadelphia: University of Pennsylvania Press, 1981), 244. The first annual convention of the Playground Association of America took place in 1907.

107. Pyke, "What Men Like in Men," 404. Although Pyke goes into great detail regarding the physical characteristics of the sissy, he concludes, in typical character-building fashion, that the type "represents a certain intellectual and spiritual incompleteness, in the presence of which the normal man experiences a most intense repulsion" (405).

108. Louis Reeves Harrison, "*Double Trouble,*" *Moving Picture World* 26 (December 5, 1915): 1319.

109. Ernest Thompson Seton, "The Boy Scouts in America," *The Outlook* 95 (July 23, 1910): 632.

110. On the rise of the playground movement, see Boyer, *Urban Masses and Moral Order in America*. See also Clarence E. Rainwater, *The Play Movement in the United States* (Chicago: University of Chicago Press, 1922). On democracy and character-building, see Richardson and Loomis, *The Boy Scout Movement Applied by the Church*, 43–44.

111. Richardson and Loomis, *The Boy Scout Movement Applied by the Church*, 43–44.

112. Ernest Thompson Seton, "The Scouting Mind" (manuscript, c. 1910–11), in Ernest Thompson Seton Papers, Seton Memorial Library and Museum; quoted in Macleod, *Building Character in the American Boy*, 32.

113. On the balance of expression and repression of instincts, see Carl Werner, *Bringing Up the Boy: A Message to Fathers and Mothers from a Boy of Yesterday Concerning the Man of To-morrow* (New York: Dodd, Mead, 1913), 20. This matter was approached differently by different organizations. While the Knights of King Arthur and organizations aimed at the lower class generally stressed the suppression of instinct and the encouragement of chivalry or the values of the "Christian gentleman," other organizations such as the Boy Scouts emphasized wilderness experience for the release of instinctual behavior. However, the latter also placed great emphasis, at least in "The Scout Law," on curbing childish cruelty, attributed to childhood's savage instinct.

114. Booth Tarkington, "Booth Tarkington Sends Us This Word About Douglas Fairbanks," insert in Fairbanks, "Combining Play with Work," *American Magazine* (July 1917): 33.

115. Thornton W. Burgess, "Making Men of Them," *Good Housekeeping* 59 (September 9, 1914): 10.

116. See, for example, *Knights of the Square Table* (Alan Crosland, 1917).

117. Ralph D. Blumenfeld, "The Boy Scouts," *The Outlook* 95 (July 23, 1910): 621; and Burgess, "Making Men of Them," 12.

118. Review of *The Good Bad Man* in the *Moving Picture World* 28 (April 22, 1916): 643.

119. Williams, quoted in Douglas Fairbanks, Jr., *The Fairbanks Album* (Boston: New York Graphic Society, 1975), 91.

120. Russell, *Stories of Boy Life*, 171.

121. Photo caption in Fairbanks, "How I Keep Running on 'High,'" *American Magazine* 94 (August 1922): 38.

122. Hornblow, Jr., "Douglas Fairbanks, Dramatic Dynamo," 47.

123. Creel, "A 'Close-up' of Douglas Fairbanks," 734.

124. See, for example, L. E. Eubanks, "The Screen Apollo," *Motion Picture Classic* (June 1917): 19–22. See also Barbara Beach, "The Gladiator of the Cinema," *Motion Picture Classic* (August 1919): 18–19, 85; and Truman B. Handy, "He Who Plays Hero," *Motion Picture Classic* (August 1922): 52–54. In the Beach article George Walsh is also constructed as the balanced Boy Scout ideal. He "regards all other women as he would his mother and sister. . . . A woman's request is a command to George Walsh. . . . He will spend hours trying to entertain people who have no vital connection with his life, but who he knows have had some affliction."

125. For *Down to Earth*'s alternate title see Patricia King Hanson, ed., *The American Film Institute Catalog of Motion Pictures Produced in the United States: Feature Films, 1911–1920, Film Entries* (Berkeley: University of California Press, 1988), 227.

126. Holmes, quoted in Gulick, "The High Tide of Physical Conscience," 10384.

127. "It is all a question of the amount of nerve-strain involved. Late hours and excitement are among the very worst of dissipations." MacFadden, *Manhood and Marriage*, 147.

128. Luther H. Gulick, "The Will to Be Cheerful," *World's Work* 16, no. 3 (July 1908): 10498. Conant echoes the discourse of character-building positivism also taken up by Fairbanks's books: "If you wish to retain youth and effectiveness, never let go enthusiasms and ideals. Think of pleasant things. . . . Unpleasant thoughts have a way of obtruding themselves uninvited, it takes a strong effort of will to shut the door on them" (*The Virility of Christ*, 314).

129. Ernest Thompson Seton, *How To Play Indian* (Philadelphia: Curtis, 1903). Seton, like many of the other boy reformers, appealed to American mothers to recognize the need for masculine influence. His Woodcraft Indian movement got its first national acclaim with a series of articles in *Ladies' Home Journal* in 1902.

130. Seton, "The Boy Scouts in America," 630. Seton blamed urban growth, the industrialization of work, and spectator sports for the weakness in and perversion of masculinity.

131. Puffer, *The Boy and His Gang*, 84.

132. Seton, *Boy Scouts of America: A Handbook*, xi, xii, 1, 2.

133. Quotation from Page, *Socializing for the New Order*, 78–79. Gulick believed most sports would not bring girls to womanhood, and it was just as "fatuous as to expect a boy to acquire a self-controlled spine by cooking and sewing, to learn how to say 'yes' and 'no' and to stick to it, by darning stockings or dressing dolls" (Luther Gulick, address to the National Education Association in 1912, quoted in Page, ibid., 79). On Gulick's cofounding of the Camp Fire Girls with its "womanly" symbol of the "domestic fire," see Macleod, *Building Character in the American Boy*, 50–51. See also Helen Buckler et al., *WO-HE-LO: The Story of Camp Fire Girls, 1910–1960* (New York: Holt, Rinehart and Winston, 1961), 22.

For a contrarian view of women and sports, see Bliss Carmen, "Physical Freedom for Women," *Harper's Weekly* 58 (September 13, 1913): 12.

134. Describing the "joys of camp," *The Outlook* encouraged its young readers "to join this army of country-loving boys and girls" who were "dreaming of camp fires and fishing, of hiking and sleeping out under the stars, of basket-ball and base-ball in the open" by earning vacation money by selling subscriptions to their magazine. "Boy and Girl Campers Ahoy!" *The Outlook* 137 (July 2, 1924): 368.

135. "When Your Boy Goes Camping," *The Outlook* 137 (June 18, 1924): 125.

136. Fairbanks, "How I Keep Running on 'High,'" 37, and Fairbanks, "If I Were Bringing Up Your Children," *Woman's Home Companion* 46 (July 1919): 24, 88.

137. Most biographers of Fairbanks seem to agree that these books were written by Kenneth Davenport, who is identified by Richard Schickel as Fairbanks's secretary and a former actor whose health was questionable. Fairbanks biographies all tend to relate a similar story regarding Davenport: that he contracted tuberculosis when he loaned Fairbanks his overcoat and was subsequently put on the Fairbanks payroll. See Schickel, *Douglas Fairbanks*, 51, and also Booton Herndon, *Mary Pickford and Douglas Fairbanks* (New York: Norton, 1977), 166.

138. Schickel, *Douglas Fairbanks*, 52.

139. Fairbanks, *Youth Points the Way*, 26–27.

140. Fairbanks, *Youth Points the Way*, 16–17, 20. Seton suggested: "This is a time when the whole nation is turning toward the outdoor life, seeking in it the physical regeneration so needful of continued national existence." Ernest Thompson Seton, *The Birch-bark Roll of Woodcraft Indians* (New York: Doubleday, 1906), 5. See also Edgar M. Robinson, "Boys as Savages," *Association Boys* 1 (1902): 129.

141. Douglas Fairbanks, *Taking Stock of Ourselves* (New York: Britton, 1918), 14.

142. Fairbanks, *Wedlock in Time*, 18.

143. Ibid., 22–23.

144. Fairbanks, *Taking Stock of Ourselves*, 13.

145. Fairbanks, "How I Keep Running on 'High,'" 39. This statement is repeated almost verbatim in Fairbanks, "If I Were Bringing Up Your Children," 24.

146. Ibid., 138. In a claim disputed by later biographers, George Creel also claims that Fairbanks never used a double ("A 'Close-up' of Douglas Fairbanks," 734).

147. Hector Ames, "Always Up Against It Is Douglas Fairbanks," *Motion Picture Classic* (July 1916): 18, 64.

148. Fairbanks, quoted in Carey, *Doug and Mary*, 58.

149. Russell, *Stories of Boy Life*, 171.

150. Ibid., 177.

151. Lee, quoted in Boyer, *Urban Masses and Moral Order in America*, 242. In 1906 Lee, Luther Gulick, Henry Stoddard Curtis, and others founded the Playground Association of America. See also Luther Gulick, "Play and Democracy," *Charities and the Commons* 18 (August 3, 1907): 481–86.

152. Russell, *Stories of Boy Life*, 9.

153. Rotundo, *American Manhood*, 259, 262.

154. Quote from Creel, "A 'Close-up' of Douglas Fairbanks," 734.

155. I wish to thank Kate Fowkes for sharing with me her unpublished paper, "An Introductory Analysis of Dialogue Titles in *Wild and Woolly*: An Anita Loos Screenplay," Society for Cinema Studies Conference, New Orleans, May 2, 1992.

156. Kristin Thompson has called attention to some of the unusual stylistic qualities of Fairbanks's comedies of the 1910s in her useful article, "Fairbanks Without the Moustache: A Case for the Early Films," in Paolo Cherchi Usai and Lorenzo Codelli, eds., *The Path to Hollywood, 1911–1920* (Rome: Edizioni Biblioteca dell'Immagine, 1988), 156–92.

157. I cannot agree with Lary May, who claims that the Fairbanks hero fears "that pleasure will endanger the frontier spirit" or that "he is not up to the task." May says that the films characteristically offer a hero who is "loaded with the worries of modern middle-class existence" (*Screening Out the Past*, 110). Although we assume that Fairbanks appealed to middle-class men, it was not because he represented their concerns and fears onscreen in such a literal way. Only in *Reaching for the Moon* (1917) is Fairbanks's character thoroughly enmeshed in the kind of middle-class culture (i.e., work) that was associated with male social anxiety, and his escape (via dream) is ultimately so unpleasurable that he learns to rechannel his energies toward reality via the character-building maxims of his boss. He ends up with wife and son in an idyllically depicted suburban (i.e., New Jersey) housing tract.

158. For a helpful discussion of the machine ethos in modern America, see Cecelia Tichi, *Shifting Gears: Technology, Literature, Culture in Modernist America* (Chapel Hill: University of North Carolina Press, 1987).

159. T. J. Jackson Lears, *No Place of Grace: Antimodernism and the Transformation of American Culture, 1880–1920* (New York: Pantheon, 1981), 57.

160. Burgess, "Making Men of Them," 8. As Tichi notes, the image of the "human engine" became a cliché during the early twentieth century (*Shifting Gears*, 37).

161. Fairbanks, "How I Keep Running on 'High,'" 37.

162. Unsourced newspaper article (c. 1918), cited in David Carroll, *The Matinee Idols* (New York: Arbor House, 1972), 96, 98.

163. Tichi, *Shifting Gears*, 34.

164. Burgess, "Making Men of Them," 3.

165. Anonymous children's rhyme, characterized by Daniel Carter Beard as the "most wanton and wicked song" that he knew as a child. Quoted in his autobiography, *Hardly a Man Is Now Alive* (New York: Doubleday, Doran, 1939), 111.

166. C. P. Seldon, "The Rule of the Mother," *North American Review* 161 (November 1895): 638–39.

167. Seldon, "The Rule of the Mother," 637.

168. Ibid., 639.

169. Quote from Puffer, *The Boy and His Gang*, 177. For a typical assessment of the middle-class situation, see Werner, *Bringing Up the Boy*. "Unfortunately, the father, not eager to invade what he believes to be the mother's sphere, usually is

content to leave the management of the boy in the mother's hands, while the mother, not recognising the deficiency of her position, labours on patiently, lovingly, untiringly, but in many cases blindly, and often with poor success. . . . There are no sex distinctions to the average mother" (8–9).

170. Puffer, *The Boy and His Gang*, 120–21. Puffer makes this statement in reference to female teachers, but his attitude toward mothers is the same. See also G. Stanley Hall, "Feminization in School and Home," *World's Work* 16 (May 1908): 10237–10244. Fairbanks addresses mothers directly on the subject of raising their sons in "If I Were Bringing Up Your Children," 24, 88.

171. Puffer, *The Boy and His Gang*, 110.

172. Werner, *Bringing Up the Boy*, 37. We should not ignore contrarian discourse of the time that idealizes the mother-son relationship and denounces those who blame mothers for weak sons. See, for example, Albert Beveridge, *The Young Man and the World* (New York: Appleton, 1906). Several scholars have observed just how many of those men involved in boy reform (such as Robert Baden-Powell and Dan Beard) were unusually devoted to their own mothers long into adulthood. See Rosenthal, *The Character Factory*, 16–17, 20–21, 50.

173. Puffer, *The Boy and His Gang*, 146. For a classic statement on how the "manly boy" should act, see Theodore Roosevelt, "What We Can Expect of the American Boy," *St. Nicholas* 27 (May 1900): 570–74.

174. George Fiske, quoted in Page, *Socializing for the New Order*, 49.

175. *Little Lord Fauntleroy* (1886) was a novel by Frances Hodgson Burnett. In *Bringing Up the Boy*, Werner notes: "Why some mothers persist in Little-Lord Fauntlery-ing their boys within an inch of their lives is to me a profound mystery. Can any mother enlighten me on the long-curls cruelty? Is it selfish vanity? Could any mother, for the mere gratification of an egoistic desire, be so unfeeling as to send her helpless boy out into the scene of humiliation and actual physical torture of which the boy with the long curls becomes the pitiable centre as soon as he turns the corner?" (13).

A review of the 1921 film version of the Burnett novel attributes to Fairbanks the primary influence on the realistic boyishness of Pickford's performance as Cedric Errol (Little Lord Fauntleroy): "The boy instincts, however, true to very young life, are permitted expression . . . especially during Fauntleroy's fight with Francis Marion. This fight is distinctly Fairbankesque. 'Doug' is written all over it, especially in the flying leap." See the review of *Little Lord Fauntleroy* in *Exhibitor's Trade Review* 30 (October 1, 1921): 1237.

176. David Bergman, "Strategic Camp: The Art of Gay Rhetoric," *Camp Grounds* (Amherst: University of Massachusetts Press, 1993), 93.

177. Michael Monahan, "The American Peril," *The Forum* 51 (June 1914): 878.

178. Daniel Carter Beard, *The Buckskin Book of the Boy Pioneers of America* (New York: Pioneer Press, 1912), 3.

179. Puffer, *The Boy and His Gang*, 180–81.

180. For a review of the nineteenth-century origins of the cult of the bad boy, see Macleod, *Building Character in the American Boy*, 54. The most interesting first-person account of "that beautiful, forgotten land" of mid-nineteenth-century

boyhood is Daniel Carter Beard's surprisingly engaging *Hardly a Man Is Now Alive*.

181. "The Cult of the Bad Boy," *The Independent* 92 (October 6, 1917): 3592.

182. Werner, *Bringing Up the Boy*, 7–8, 113. In fact, boy reformers were united in asserting that women's influence undid the natural masculinity in boys. According to Werner, by the age of five "the boy reaches the age of recognisable and indisputable masculinity." Women might admire the essential manly ideals promoted by character-builders but inadvertently repressed them by raising boys like girls. See Burgess, "Making Men of Them," 3. On boys' need to escape the "'pink cotton wool' of an overindulgent home," see Edgar M. Robinson, "Boys as Savages," *Association Boys* 1 (1902): 129.

183. An impressive list of these is provided by Page, *Socializing for the New Order*, 103.

184. Theodore Roosevelt, *An Autobiography*, vol. 22 in the *Complete Works of Theodore Roosevelt* (New York: Macmillan, 1925), 17. Roosevelt, quoted in E. Morison, *Letters* 1:33, as cited in G. Edward White, *The Eastern Establishment and the Western Experience*, 63.

185. Werner, *Bringing Up the Boy*, 7–8.

186. Nelson W. Aldrich, Jr., *Old Money: The Mythology of America's Upper Class* (New York: Vintage, 1988), 113.

187. Aldrich, Jr., *Old Money*, 111–13. Ellen H. Richards suggests that during this era, "feminine" qualities defined as fragility, ease, and indulgence in comfort were believed to reflect the "debilitating effect of luxuries." By way of contrast, wise investments in the home and savings led to "true manliness of character." Ellen H. Richards, *The Cost of Living as Modified by Sanitary Science* (New York: John Wiley, 1899), 126, 134.

188. See Daniel Horowitz, "Frugality or Comfort: Middle-Class Styles of Life in the Early Twentieth Century," *American Quarterly* 37 (Summer 1985): 239–59.

189. Burgess, "Making Men of Them," 5.

190. Quoted in Rosenthal, *The Character Factory*, 164. This point is echoed in Fairbanks's book, *Taking Stock of Ourselves*, in which he emphasizes the need for preparedness: "Go about the program of life cheerfully and stout of heart—for now we are in a state of preparedness" (10).

191. Rosenthal, *The Character Factory*, 164.

192. Donald Mrozek, *Sport and the American Mentality*, 207. Many reformers emphasized instinct. Ernest Thompson Seton refers to the "well-known stages of race development" in his introduction to John L. Alexander's *Boy Training* (New York: Association Press, 1911), 2.

193. Puffer, *The Boy and His Gang*, 112, 121.

194. Page, *Socializing for the New Order*, 23.

195. "When Your Boy Goes Camping," *The Outlook* 137 (June 18, 1924): 17. See also, Puffer, *The Boy and His Gang*, 173. Puffer complains of camp life advertised in magazines as being "altogether too much an affair *de luxe* to be of much real value. . . . [They] lose all the training . . . which a proper camp ought to give.

Worst of all, they have little chance to 'endure hardship.' Life is nearly as soft as in the city; and for all the primitive manliness that the camp puts into them, they might as well have stayed at home" (173).

196. Stewart Edward White, *The Forest* (New York: The Outlook Co., 1903), 5.

197. Joseph Knowles, *Alone in the Wilderness* (Cambridge: Harvard University Press, 1914; London: Longmans, Green, 1914), 4. Knowles spends much of his book aligning himself with the work of the Boy Scouts of America: "It is useless for me to tell the Boy Scouts how to build a fire, without any matches. They know already. . . . The more experience a boy has in the woods the more his instinct will be developed" (249, 251).

198. Nash, *Wilderness and the American Mind*, 202.

199. Ibid., 46–54.

200. G. Edward White, *The Eastern Establishment and the Western Experience*, 108.

201. See ibid., 109. On Remington's reaction to immigration and for Roosevelt's Anglo-Saxon elitism, see 174–75, 190, 197.

202. Review of Theodore Roosevelt's *The Wilderness Hunter* in the *New York Times*, August 6, 1894, 1.

203. John Muir, "The Wild Parks and Forest Reservations of the West," *Atlantic Monthly* 88 (1898): 19.

204. As Russell suggests in *Stories of Boy Life*, "Healthy, manly boys become manly men" (56).

205. George S. Evans, "The Wilderness," *Overland Monthly* 43 (1904): 33.

206. G. Edward White, *The Eastern Establishment and the Western Experience*, 108.

207. Puffer, *The Boy and His Gang*, 117.

208. Review in the *New York Times*, July 22, 1917 (reprinted in *New York Times Film Reviews*, n.p.).

209. Lears, *No Place of Grace*, 117.

210. Walter Bytell, review of *Wild and Woolly* in *Variety*, June 22, 1917 (reprinted in *Variety Film Reviews, 1907–1980*, n.p.).

211. Washington Irving, *Tales of a Traveller: A Tour on the Prairies* (1835; rpt., New York: Century, 1909), 43.

212. Song written by Doug Fairbanks, cited in "News of the Producing Centers," *Exhibitor's Trade Review* 2 (May 6, 1916): "Doug Fairbanks has written a song entitled, 'I'm so Gosh Darn Tuft,' and it is now being featured by Raymond Hitchcock in London" (58).

213. As late as 1932 a *New York Times* review of one of his last films, *Mr. Robinson Crusoe*, seems to be caught up in wishful thinking when it declares: "The star, as always, creates an atmosphere of surging good health, of a youthful ardor which refuses to be dimmed and should communicate itself to the audience in a manner to assure a hearty reception." Review in *New York Times Film Reviews*, n.p.

214. Nash, *Wilderness and the American Mind*, 151.

215. Fairbanks, *Youth Points the Way*, 17.

216. On boys' wanderlust, see Puffer, *The Boy and His Gang*, 114–15, and also Beard, *Hardly a Man Is Now Alive*.

217. Puffer, *The Boy and His Gang*, 50, 115.

218. Smith, "Roping Doug Fairbanks into an Interview," 46.

219. Fairbanks, "Combining Play with Work," 33.

220. Fairbanks, *Youth Points the Way*, 66–67.

221. Ibid., 50.

222. Review of *The Half Breed* in the *New York Times*, July 10, 1916 (reprinted in *New York Times Film Reviews*, n.p.).

223. Evans, "The Wilderness," 33.

224. In *Down to Earth* Billy Gaynor (Fairbanks) is seen on portage next to the Amazon. Coincidentally, the jungles of South America were one of T.R.'s last sites for thrills.

225. Macleod, *Building Character in the American Boy*, 227.

226. For a lucid, thorough survey of what the author defines as the "historical adventure movie," see Brian Taves's *The Romance of Adventure* (Jackson: University of Mississippi Press, 1993).

227. David B. Pratt notes in his excellent study of the reception of Ernst Lubitsch's films in the United States that "the entire post-World War I cycle of costume epics has suffered from a general neglect." Pratt, "'O Lubitsch, Where Wert Thou?': *Passion*, the German Invasion, and the Emergence of the Name 'Lubitsch,'" *Wide Angle* 13, no. 1 (1991): 34, 35.

228. See Cecil B. DeMille, "The Public Is Always Right," *Ladies' Home Journal* 44 (August 1927): 73. Although the German costume films are now regarded as watershed films that had a crucial influence on filmmakers like Fairbanks, the American film industry was reluctant to acknowledge their influence. DeMille, commenting on why Fairbanks's *Robin Hood* (1922) was successful, says: "The Theater owners then turned to the producers and demanded to know why the costume pictures had been so long kept off the screen, forgetting that they had been partly responsible for keeping them from the public" (73). On the reception of the German films, see David B. Pratt, "'Fit Food for Madhouse Inmates': The Box-Office Reception of the German Invasion of 1921," *Griffithiana* 48–49 (October 1993): 96–157.

229. For a survey of all the literature popular with boys in the late nineteenth century within the context of British culture, see Joseph Bristow, *Empire Boys: Adventures in a Man's World* (London: HarperCollins Academic, 1991).

230. Seton, "The Boy Scouts in America," 630. Seton decided a more American figure was needed and settled on the American Indian warrior for his Order of Woodcraft Chivalry (see Macleod, *Character Building in the American Boy*, 143). See also Beard, *Hardly a Man Is Now Alive*: "In both these organizations, the Sons of Daniel Boone and the Boy Pioneers, I confined myself to the United States for my inspiration. I did not summon to my aid King Arthur and his Round Table . . . the Black Prince or Saladin of the Saracens. No, not even Robin Hood, though he was my type of man. In place of the lance and buckler was the American long rifle and buckskin clothes, in place of the shining plumed helmet was the American coonskin cap" (353–54).

231. For an account of the direct influence of Fairbanks on the creation of Superman, see Dennis Dooley, "The Man of Tomorrow and the Boys of

Yesterday," in Dooley and Gary Engle, eds., *Superman at Fifty: The Persistence of a Legend* (Cleveland, Ohio: Octavia Press, 1987), 30.

232. Karl K. Kitchner, "Celebrities Join in Viewing New Screen Features," *Cleveland Plain Dealer*, December 15, 1920, n.p. (clipping, NYPL-TC).

233. "World's Record Made by *Mark of Zorro* in New York Showing," December 18, 1920 (unsourced clipping, NYPL-TC).

234. "Fairbanks in Picturesque Role," *Morning Telegraph*, November 30, 1920, n.p. (clipping, NYPL-TC).

235. Fairbanks biographer Booton Herndon offers a psychobiographical explanation of Fairbanks and his films that focuses on the actor's problematic, early loss of his biological father, Jewish attorney Hezekiah Charles Ulman, to desertion. Ulman's relationship to his famous, illegitimate son was a carefully guarded Fairbanks family secret. Herndon, *Mary Pickford and Douglas Fairbanks*, 12–23.

236. "United Artists: *Black Pirate*," *Moving Picture World* (November 29, 1926): 305.

237. Lears, *No Place of Grace*, 170–71.

238. Ibid., 146. The review of the film in *Exhibitor's Trade Review* suggested that it was "a mad but intensely interesting jumble" and that "one senses that he [Fairbanks] thoroughly enjoys the strenuous life of the part." See "'The Mark of Zorro' Another Fairbanks Success," *Exhibitor's Trade Review* 9, no. 2 (1920): 109.

239. Lears, *No Place of Grace*, 146.

240. Advertisement in the *Ladies' Home Journal* (March 1923): n.p.

241. Douglas Fairbanks, "A Huge Responsibility," *Ladies' Home Journal* 41 (May 1924): 37.

242. Taylor, "The Most Popular Man in the World," 685.

243. Fairbanks, as quoted in the "Prefatory" of the souvenir program issued for the March 3, 1924, premiere at the Liberty Theatre. *The Thief of Bagdad* clipping file, Margaret Herrick Library, Academy of Motion Picture Arts and Sciences Center (hereafter cited as AMPAS).

244. For an extended discussion of the influence of modern dance and dance design on the film, see Studlar, "Douglas Fairbanks: Thief of the Ballets Russes," in Ellen Goellner and Jacqueline Shea Murphy, eds., *Bodies of the Text: Dance as Theory, Literature as Dance* (New Brunswick, N.J.: Rutgers University Press, 1994), 107–24.

245. There is a bathing scene in *The Half Breed* (1916) in which Fairbanks appears clad only in a thong.

246. Untitled clipping from *Motion Picture News*, March 5, 1924, 1554 (*The Thief of Bagdad* clipping file, AMPAS). The financial success of the film is disputed. Implying an access to new research on box-office figures, Richard Koszarski suggests it made money despite its unusually high production costs (over two million dollars, by some reports). Koszarski, *An Evening's Entertainment: The Age of the Silent Feature Picture, 1915–1928* (New York: Scribner's, 1990), 270, 349.

247. Vachel Lindsay, "*The Thief of Bagdad*," *Michigan Quarterly Review* 31 (Spring 1992): 231, 240 (reproduced from Lindsay, "The Greatest Movies Now

Running," unpublished manuscript in Clifton Waller Barrett Collection, Alderman Library, University of Virginia).

248. Taylor, "The Most Popular Man in the World," 684. More than any other male star of the time, Fairbanks had achieved a seamless convergence between his onscreen and offscreen selves, between character-building artist-filmmaker and energetic hero. When Charles K. Taylor praised Fairbanks in 1924 as "the Most Popular Man in the World," he wrote that "he does not act at all. He simply portrays himself. He acts in his natural manner. . . . You behold on the screen the real Douglas Fairbanks. It is his real personality with which the vast motion-picture audience has become acquainted" (Taylor, "The Most Popular Man in the World," 684). One unimpressed movie fan suggested that Fairbanks was incapable of "subordinating his own personality to the personality of the character he is portraying" ("Letters to the Editor," *Motion Picture Magazine* [November 1922]: 46).

249. Fairbanks, as quoted in the souvenir program, Liberty Theatre (*The Thief of Bagdad* clipping file, AMPAS).

250. Quoted in Carnes, *Meanings for Manhood*, 106.

251. Macleod, *Building Character in the American Boy*, 54.

252. Charles K. Taylor, "Doug Gets Away with It," *The Outlook* 142 (April 14, 1926): 561–62.

253. Lears, *No Place of Grace*, 144–45.

254. Anthony Ludovici, *Woman: A Vindication* (New York: Knopf, 1923), 10, 291.

255. Ludovici, *Woman: A Vindication*, 290–91.

256. James R. Quirk, "Speaking of Pictures," *Photoplay* 31 (December 1926): 27.

257. Marquis Busby, "Overtime Acting: How the Screen's Peerage Stages Elaborate Scenes for Interviewers," *Motion Picture Classic* (August 1928): 17.

258. G. Stanley Hall, "Notes on Early Memories," *Pedagogical Seminary* 6 (December 1899): 496–97.

2. *"Impassioned Vitality": John Barrymore and America's Matinee Girls*

1. Elizabeth M. Gilmer, "The Art of Wooing," *Cosmopolitan* 38 (February 1905): 441–47.

2. Julia Dean, "What Women Like Best in the Plays of Today," *Green Book* (June 1914): 961–65.

3. Helen Carlisle, "The Movie Fan," *Motion Picture Magazine* (November 1922): 50.

4. In 1918 it was discovered that Francis X. Bushman was not only married with children but was divorcing his wife in order to marry his frequent costar, Beverly Bayne. It was suggested also that he had beaten his wife and children. In response to this news, some theaters refused to show his films.

5. Mary Ann Doane, *The Desire to Desire: The Women's Film of the 1940s* (Bloomington: Indiana University Press, 1987), 32; see also 2, 5, 31, 66–69.

6. Doane, *The Desire to Desire*, 1–2, 12–13.

7. Ibid., 1.

8. Anthony Ludovici, *Woman: A Vindication* (New York: Knopf, 1923), 290–91. See also Louis E. Bisch, "Are Women Inferior or Are They Trying to Sidetrack Nature?" *Century* 113 (April 1927):674–81.

9. Ludovici, *Woman: A Vindication*, 291, 265. See also Michael Monahan, "The American Peril," *The Forum* 51 (June 1914): 882, and "Literature and Art," *Current Opinion* 55, no. 4 (October 1913): 269.

10. Martin Pumphrey, "The Flapper, the Housewife, and the Making of Modernity," *Cultural Studies* 1 (May 1987): 184.

11. On consumerism during this era, see William Leach, "Transformations in a Culture of Consumptions: Women and Department Stores, 1890–1925," *Journal of American History* 71 (September 1984): 321–35; and also Simon J. Bronner, ed., *Consuming Visions: Accumulation and Display of Goods in America, 1880–1929* (New York: Norton, 1989). For a film-industry-related view of the female consumer, see "Women: The Greatest Buyers in the World," *Shadowland* (January 1923): 4.

12. For one prewar attempt at such enumeration, see Michael Davis, *The Exploitation of Pleasure* (New York: Department of Child Hygiene of the Russell Sage Foundation, 1911).

13. See Beth Brown, "Making Movies for Women," *Moving Picture World* (March 26, 1927): 342; Frederick James Smith, "Does Decency Help or Hinder?" *Photoplay* 26 (November 1924): 36. Leo Handel's 1950 study suggests that Hollywood's declarations of a female majority might not have been a disingenuous consumer ploy. He says that the industry often operated "under the impression" that women were a majority of the American film audiences and notes that "it is even possible, though not probable, that this proportion (of 65–70% women) held true at some time in the past." See Handel, *Hollywood Looks at Its Audience* (Urbana: University of Illinois Press, 1950), 90.

14. *Exhibitors Herald/Moving Picture World* (March 1928), cited in Charlotte Herzog, "'Powder Puff' Promotion: The Fashion Show-in-the-Film," in *Fabrications* (New York: Routledge, 1990), 157. I have not been able to find the original trade magazine citation, which Herzog quotes from Jeanne Allen, "The Film Viewer as Consumer," *Quarterly Review of Film* 5, no. 4 (1980): 486, but which does not appear in Allen's notes.

15. Obviously, the film industry had a great stake in promoting itself as a female-dominated (or interested) industry because of consumer tie-ins as well as box-office attendance. Kathryn Fuller blames film industry and industry-related promotion (such as fan magazines) for creating the "stereotypical picture of movie audiences filled with women, female teenagers, and children." To support her observation, Fuller quotes "box-office tallies" from an uncited source that reports that only one-third of the movie audience consisted of adult men, while "the other two-thirds were composed of adult women and young people of both sexes." Thus, even Fuller's unnamed source is still intriguing in its suggestion that the industry was not far from wrong in insisting on the critical role women and, especially, young women played in forming movie audiences. Kathryn Helgesen Fuller, "Shadowland: American Audiences and the Moviegoing Experience in the Silent Film Era" (Ph.D. diss. Johns Hopkins University, 1992), 230.

Russell Merritt, in arguing for the early (pre-1914) presence of the middle class in nickelodeons, forcefully discounts the notion of women's importance in early filmgoing: "Although women and children were still the most discussed groups of patrons, adult males statistically outnumbered both groups combined; Frederic C. Howe estimated that 75% of the national movie audience was adult male" (Russell Merritt, "Nickelodeon Theaters, 1905–1914: Building an Audience for the Movies," in Tino Balio, ed., *The American Film Industry* [Madison: University of Wisconsin Press, 1976], 98). Unfortunately, Merritt appears to misquote Howe, who actually says that men are taking their wives and children to movies (413) and that "possibly twenty-five per cent of the total motion picture audience is made up of children under sixteen" (415). Frederic C. Howe, "What to Do with the Motion-Picture Show: Shall It Be Censored?" *The Outlook* 107 (June 20, 1914): 412–16.

16. "The Scarlet Streak," *Exhibitors Herald*, December 5, 1925, 29.

17. Lorine Pruette, "Should Men Be Protected?" *The Nation* (August 31, 1927): 200. For discussions of women's new sexual license and changing expectations of marriage, see Joseph Collins, "Woman's Morality in Transition," *Current History* 27 (1927): 33–40; and Edward Sapir, "The Discipline of Sex," *American Mercury* 16 (April 1929): 413–20. See also Dorothy Bromley, "Feminist–New Style," *Harper's Magazine* 155 (1927): 552.

18. Beatrice Hinkle, "The Chaos of Modern Marriage," *Harper's Magazine* 152 (December 1925): 4.

19. Kate Gannett Wells, "The Transitional American Woman," *Atlantic Monthly* 46 (December 1880): 817–23. Wells discusses American women's "restlessness," their embracing of missions (suffrage, temperance, etc.) and concurrent disillusionment with marriage and domestic duties. The label of "the New Woman" is often applied both to those women involved in suffrage and social reform in the 1900s and 1910s as well as to flappers of the 1920s who were associated with hedonism rather than social activism. Among the many historical discussions of these feminine types are Paula S. Fass, *The Damned and the Beautiful: American Youth in the 1920s* (Oxford: Oxford University Press, 1977); Nancy Woloch, *Women and the American Experience* (New York: Knopf, 1984); and Estelle B. Freedman, "The New Woman: Changing Views of Women in the 1920s," *Journal of American History* 56 (September 1974): 372–93.

20. See Miriam Hansen, "Pleasure, Ambivalence, Identification: Valentino and Female Spectatorship," *Cinema Journal* 25, no. 4 (Summer 1986): 6, 19.

21. See Hansen, "Pleasure, Ambivalence, Identification," and Gaylyn Studlar, "Discourses of Gender and Ethnicity: The Construction and De(con)struction of Rudolph Valentino as Other," *Film Criticism* 13, no. 2 (Winter 1989): 18–35. Hansen provides a valuable attempt to complicate the psychoanalytic models that have couched the discussion of female spectatorship, and her expanded analysis of Valentino in *Babel and Babylon* (Cambridge: Harvard University Press, 1991) usefully offers an intelligent consideration of some extratextual materials associated with him. Her work is of considerable value on both counts, but I would suggest that the net has to be cast wider in terms of male stars and in terms of culture in order to fully understand Valentino's impact within the fascinating historical framework of the 1920s. Graciously citing my 1989 article on Valentino, Hansen cor-

rects her claim, made in 1986, regarding Valentino's status as the first film matinee idol for women (*Babel and Babylon*, 254). In her original article she stated: "For the first time in film history, women spectators were perceived as a socially and economically significant group, female spectatorship was recognized as a mass phenomenon; and the films were explicitly addressed to a female spectator, regardless of the actual composition of the audience." Ben Singer's meticulous work on the serial queen has offered a corrective to such assumptions as well. See Singer, "Female Power in the Serial Queen Melodrama: The Etiology of an Anomaly," *Camera Obscura* 22 (January 1990): 93.

22. Richard Koszarski, *An Evening's Entertainment: The Age of the Silent Feature Picture, 1915–1928* (New York: Scribner's, 1990), 301. By 1924 a reviewer in *Variety* was noting that Barrymore's *Beau Brummel* was "another of the long run of costume screen plays" (review in *Variety*, April 2, 1924; reprinted in *Variety Film Reviews, 1907–1980* [New York: Garland, 1983], n.p.).

23. For commentary that places Valentino within the context of male stardom see, for example, Frederick James Smith, "Does Decency Help or Hinder?" 36.

24. Leo Ditrichstein, "Why the Matinee Idol Was Shattered," *Green Book* (October 1914): 738.

25. "Will This Keep Jack Barrymore from Marrying?" *Toledo Times*, June 5, 1910, n.p.: Barrymore Scrapbooks, Robinson Locke Collection (New York Public Library for the Performing Arts, Theatre Collection; hereafter, NYPL-TC).

26. *Vanity Fair* (March 1908): n.p. (clipping file, NYPL-TC).

27. Quote from untitled newspaper clipping, no source (August 12, 1910): n.p. For a confirmation of the nationwide publicity surrounding Barrymore's matinee idol status, see this and other entries in the Barrymore Scrapbooks, Robinson Locke Collection, NYPL-TC.

28. "'The Dawn of Tomorrow,' 'Kitty Grey, a Stubborn Cinderella,'" *New York Times*, January 31, 1909; reprinted in *The New York Times Theater Reviews* (New York: Arno Press and the New York Times, 1975): n.p. The reviewer notes: "As one of the best of the younger comedians it is to be regretted, perhaps, that he has not found better opportunities for his talents, and it is to be hoped that a season of the girls-and-music type of thing will satisfy any ambitions he may have in that direction."

29. Amy Leslie, quoted in Margot Peters, *The House of Barrymore* (New York: Knopf, 1990), 112.

30. H. I. Brock, "American Hamlets Rare Visitors to London," *New York Times Magazine*, March 8, 1925, 6.

31. Alexander Woollcott, "Second Thoughts on First Night," *New York Times*, September 18, 1919; reprinted in *New York Times Theater Reviews*, n.p.

32. "Movies Get Barrymore: There Goes Another to Motion Pictures," *Toledo Blade*, December 26, 1913, n.p. (Barrymore Scrapbooks, Robinson Locke Collection, NYPL-TC).

33. In a 1907 review Amy Leslie had told her readers that Barrymore's stage vehicles didn't capture how interesting he was in person: "He was applauded for nothing. . . . [He] shall be adored no matter how inaccurate or how slipshod his artistic efforts may be at anytime. . . . He is immeasurably more seductive in a draw-

ing room or at one's right at a slow dinner, because his own lines and lazy wit, his own ideas of being interesting are vastly superior to anything of the same sort rising young lady playwrights can provide." Amy Leslie, review of *The Boys in Company B*, July 20, 1907, n.p. (untitled, unsourced clipping, Barrymore Scrapbooks, Robinson Locke Collection, NYPL-TC).

34. Quotation from Brock, "American Hamlets Rare Visitors to London," 6.

35. Maria Sermolino, "John Barrymore's Barber," *Theatre Magazine* (July 1919): n.p. (clipping, NYPL-TC), emphasis in original.

36. Untitled clipping, n.d., n.p. (clipping file, NYPL-TC), emphasis in original.

37. Review of *The Test of Honour* in *Photoplay* 15 (June 1919): n.p. (clipping file, NYPL-TC).

38. Ditrichstein, "Why the Matinee Idol Was Shattered," 735–38.

39. With direct competition from the movies for its middle-class audience outside of key urban centers, it is not surprising that the number of companies on tour in 1915 dropped to less than half of what it had been in 1912 and continued to decline precipitously. Especially ready to accept feature films with stars from the stage (like those produced by Adolph Zukor's Famous Players) were those audiences in the hinterlands accustomed to road-show theatricals. Like the new feature films, road shows often heavily advertised their star-centered-ness. Unfortunately, the latter also had a reputation for untruthfulness: audiences were forewarned by experience not to expect the stars advertised. Thus, prerecorded movies seemed to promise reliability as well as a heretofore unprecedented availability to the great players of the stage. See Jack Poggi, *Theater in America: The Impact of Economic Forces, 1870–1967* (Ithaca, N.Y.: Cornell University Press, 1968), 33–34. For the responses of towns to false road-show advertising, see Walter Prichard Eaton, "What's the Matter with the Road?" *American Magazine* 74 (July 1912): 360.

40. A. S. [Anna Steese] Richardson, "A Woman-Made Season," *McClure's* 46 (April 1916): 22.

41. Richardson, "A Woman-Made Season," 22.

42. Charles W. Collin, "The Woman's New Plaything—Motion Pictures," *Green Book* (July 1914): 29–30. Matinee idol King Baggott's 1913 *Dr. Jekyll and Mr. Hyde* was but one of several early film versions of the play. And one female theatergoer was quoted in 1913 as expressing a typical response to the new medium's appeal: "Why, we used to go to the theatre one night a week. Now we go to the pictures nearly every night. We don't think of the theatre anymore." George Blaisdell, "At the Sign of the Flaming Arcs," *Moving Picture World* 15 (January 4, 1913): 34.

43. Widely bemoaned in theater-oriented commentary, this shift of both players and audience interest was regarded as showing the true "menace" of the movies, which was "the snowball of the amusement world, rolling over the country and growing bigger and bigger as it annexes theatres, managers, actors, and authors." See, for example, Harold Edwards, "The Menace of the Movies," *The Theatre* 22 (October 1915): 176. Edwards refuses to equate movie fans with theatergoers; instead, he says the term *fans* is appropriate because "the word implies an indiscriminate devotion" (177).

Some theater folk were in deep denial about the impact of the movies on the theater. See, for example, Daniel Frohman, "Do Motion Pictures Mean the Death of the Drama?" *The Theatre* 22 (December 1915): 310. Frohman says: "As for motion picture [*sic*] being a menace to the theatre . . . that is manifestly impossible. . . . As long as civilization endures, the stage will form one of its chief sources of amusement." Legitimate theater had rarely admitted to feeling the pressure of the growing movie industry before the solidification of the feature film during the years 1912–1915. It was sometimes asserted that the early cinema rivaled only "lower" forms of entertainment in attempting to capture a shared working-class audience. Current film history suggests that these class (and gender) divisions of audience were not as strict as we might be tempted to assume by such commentary, but the relationship between stage and screen obviously changed when movie companies like Adolph Zukor's aptly named Famous Players Film Company began to court stage stars and to present them in those "famous plays" which had, of course, made them famous. James K. Hackett filmed *The Prisoner of Zenda* (1913) with Edwin S. Porter, directing, for Zukor. See Robert McLaughlin, *Broadway and Hollywood: A History of Economic Interaction* (New York: Arno, 1974), 7–19. For stage actors' reactions to their movie experience, see Anna Steese Richardson, "'Filmitis': The Modern Malady—Its Symptoms and Its Cure," *McClure's* (January 1916): 14. For an excellent general view of the beginnings of the star system in film, see Richard deCordova, *Picture Personalities* (Urbana: University of Illinois Press, 1990).

44. Review of *The Jest* in *Variety* (February 27, 1920): n.p. (clipping file, NYPL-TC).

45. "Cerline Boll Sketches the Cinema Artist—John Barrymore [caption]" in *Motion Picture Magazine* (March 1922): 43.

46. Although the Clyde Fitch play from which it was adapted seems to have been called *Beau Brummell*, and spelling of the film's title varies in trade magazines and reviews, the title of the film on a print with what appear to be the original title and intertitles is *Beau Brummel*.

47. Review of *"Don Juan"* in *Variety*, August 11, 1926; reprinted in *Variety Film Reviews, 1907–1980*, n.p.

48. Clipping, *Film Daily*, March 20, 1927, unpaginated (clipping file, NYPL-TC).

49. Released in the same year, these two films have amazing similarities: the hero's masquerade, the father-daughter alignment, the presentation of the villain, the "wooing" sequences, and even the rescue-action sequences. While Mix's film includes romance, *The Son of the Sheik* (1926), as the next chapter discusses, was Valentino's most "male-aimed" film, and its production was accompanied by publicity that suggested Valentino's (or United Artists') attempt to appeal more to men. The film is also quite obviously indebted to Fairbanks's *Don Q, Son of Zorro* (1925) as well as more generally to the action-oriented, oedipal machinations typical of Fairbanks costume films in the 1920s.

50. Gilmer, "The Art of Wooing," 441.

51. Ibid.

52. For a discussion of this see Pearson, *Eloquent Gestures*, 8–16, 136.

53. "Women and the American Theatre," *The Nation* 106, no. 2761 (June 1, 1918): 665. Critic Walter Prichard Eaton echoes many other commentaries when he notes, "It is estimated by the theatrical managers that almost seventy-five percent of theater audiences in this country are women." See Eaton, "Women as Theater-Goers," *Woman's Home Companion* 37 (October 1910): 13.

54. Benjamin McArthur, *Actors and American Culture, 1880–1920* (Philadelphia: Temple University Press, 1984), 11. See also Ben Graf Henneke, "The Playgoer in America, 1752–1952" (Ph.D. diss., University of Illinois, 1953), 78–81.

55. Eliot Gregory, "Our Foolish Virgins," *Century* 63 (November 1901): 9.

56. Edward Bok, "The Young Girl at the Matinee [editorial]" *Ladies' Home Journal* 20 (June 1903): 16.

57. Gregory, "Our Foolish Virgins," 9.

58. See "As an Actor Sees Women," *Ladies' Home Journal* 25 (November 1908): 26. On the obsessed, independent movie fan, see Fuller, "Shadowland," 229.

59. Lary May, *Screening Out the Past* (Chicago: University of Chicago Press, 1980), 16–21. As is typical of May, he tends to dramatize and simplify what occurred with the advent of the movies. In order to see it as "a profound event," the divisions between film and the theater are subjected to exaggeration.

60. For an example of how such an uninterrogated broad periodization is incorporated into an analysis of the representation of women in film, see Leslie Fishbein, "The Demise of the Cult of True Womanhood in Early American Film, 1900–1930: Two Modes of Subversion," *Journal of Popular Film and Television* (Summer 1984): 67–72. Fishbein argues that the version of femininity advanced in the "cult of true womanhood" (à la 1820–1860) was evidenced in American film from 1900 to 1930. The main source for her definition of this cult is Barbara Welter's "The Cult of True Womanhood, 1820–1860," *American Quarterly* 18 (Summer 1966): 155–74.

61. Because of their relative scarcity and their sharing of much of the same work as men, women in rurally based Western states, logically, were in the forefront of the expansion of American women's participation in the public sphere. American women of all ages, but especially younger women, were regarded as being much bolder than their European counterparts in claiming their place in public life.

62. Ben Singer's excellent study of the serial queen phenomenon persuasively argues for the impact of these changes on film's depiction of women. See Singer, "Female Power in the Serial Queen Melodrama," 91–129.

63. T. J. Jackson Lears, *No Place of Grace: Antimodernism and the Transformation of American Culture, 1880–1920* (New York: Pantheon, 1981), 160.

64. David Carroll, *The Matinee Idols* (New York: Arbor House, 1972), 38 (and William Brady, quoted in Carroll, ibid., 38).

65. Carroll, *The Matinee Idols*, 42. Twenty-five years later, his New York City funeral at "the Little Church Around the Corner" was still being referenced in a fan magazine-like book on male matinee idols, Gustav Kobbe's *Famous Actors and Their Homes* (Boston: Little, Brown, 1903), 197.

66. The *San Francisco Chronicle* noted that "members of the procession and ladies in the hotel" provided the huge number of floral tributes. When Montague was laid out in a hotel suite, an actress in the company of his current play, *The*

Diplomat, threw herself against the casket's faceplate. Then an actor, Mr. Carroll, "showed similar emotion, and it required the earnest entreaties of his friends to induce him to leave the place." See "Obsequies of Harry Montague," *San Francisco Chronicle*, August 13, 1878, 3.

67. Reported in "Obsequies of Harry Montague," 3.

68. "Montague's Funeral Services at the Little Church Around the Corner," *New York Sun*, August, 22, 1878, n.p. (reprinted in the *San Francisco Chronicle*, August 31, 1878, 4).

69. "Thousands in Riot at Valentino Bier," *New York Times*, August 25, 1926, 1, 3. Newspaper reports noted (with some incredulity) that fans "suffered discomfort and rough handling for hours for whatever satisfaction it gave them to be hustled by the dead screen star's coffin" (1). The public demonstration over Valentino's death has been read as proof of Valentino's status as a unique "fetish" for women within the Hollywood star system of this period. In keeping with such a reading, his female fans' funereal excess is taken as a sign of their rebellion against the blockage of feminine desire in a patriarchal society. See Hansen, "Pleasure, Ambivalence, Identification," 6–32. On the ethnic makeup of the crowd and the "lipstick and powder puff" fans, see "Valentino Shielded: Public Display of Body Ended," *Los Angeles Times*, August 26, 1926, 2.

70. "Montague's Funeral Services at the Little Church Around the Corner," *New York Sun*, August, 22, 1878, 4. In response to Valentino's death, female fans brought flowers, not in tribute, implied the *New York Times*, but with a calculated interest in being granted access to Campbell's Funeral Church, where many fainted dead away on reaching the coveted place in front of the star's casket. Valentino's manager, George Ullman, closed the proceedings because the crowds "showed the most gross irreverence." See "Public Now Barred at Valentino's Bier," *New York Times*, August 26, 1926, 1, 5. The *Times* implied that the crowds at the funeral chapel should not be called mourners because "they were merely curious, and looked it" ("Thousands in Riot at Valentino Bier," *New York Times*, August 25, 1926, 3).

71. "Thousands in Riot at Valentino Bier," *New York Times*, 3.

72. Emma Kaufman, "Mr. Kyrle Bellew and the Matinee Girl," n.p., c. December 1901 (newspaper clipping, Bellew Scrapbooks, Robinson Locke Collection, NYPL-TC).

73. For a full account of this see Winifred Black, "Kyrle Bellew Is Back at the Old Stand," unsourced clipping, n.p., c. 1900 (Bellew Scrapbooks, Robinson Locke Collection, NYPL-TC). Black's rather sarcastic article was written around the time of Bellew's return to the United States: "What a swath he did cut in the ranks of the matinee girls. . . . You couldn't get within ten yards of the stage door on matinee days. The girls fairly swirled in the offing. When he sailed for England the dock was one weeping mass of femininity. It was a craze, like the dancing mania of the fifteenth century or the hysteria fad in a fashionable boarding school."

74. Carroll, *The Matinee Idols*, 40.

75. Ibid., 42–44. On his invented biography, see also untitled clipping, n.p., c. March 1893 (NYPL-TC). The newspaper article notes: "Some of the papers have

recently been telling stories about the life of Kyrle Bellew, the actor, most of which are pure inventions."

76. Review of Bellew in *A Gentleman of France* in untitled clipping, *New York Sun*, December 31, 1901 (Bellew Scrapbooks, Robinson Locke Collection, NYPL-TC).

77. Bok, "The Young Girl at the Matinee," 16.

78. See, for example, Brandon Tynan, "Concerning Audiences," *Drama* 10, no. 9 (June 1920): 291. Tynan echoes numerous others in his remarks: "It is to women that the drama for the most part must make its appeal. Matinee audiences are composed almost entirely of women, and evening audiences of women and the men they have brought with them."

79. "The American Girl's Damaging Influence on the Drama," *Current Opinion* 43 (December 1907): 673. For another condemnation of women's negative influence on the quality of acting and playwriting see, "A Warning to Matinee Girls," *New York Morning Telegraph*, February 27, 1901, 6. The number of musicals did go up during the years 1901–1914, as McLaughlin notes in *Broadway and Hollywood*, 271.

80. "As an Actor Sees Women," *Ladies' Home Journal* (November 1908): 26.

81. "Women and the American Theatre," *The Nation* (June 1, 1918): 665. By the 1910s American film was orienting its consumer appeal squarely through its own star system, which borrowed marketing techniques from that of the stage. However, the popularity of stage actresses in the 1910s was rivaled by the growing popularity of film actresses who, through the movies, had the opportunity to appeal to a truly mass audience, broader and less class-specific than was possible for any stage "personality" to reach through touring and theatrical promotion. As has previously been mentioned, the marketing of the movie performer's personality was used to sell not only films but also an array of tie-in merchandise. This effort was supported by a sophisticated film industry that churned out a myriad variety of promotional materials for nationwide consumption. These ranged from "objective" news items in local newspapers, fan magazine publicity articles and interviews, and exhibition stunts promoted in trade magazines and adapted to the local level by the movie industry's exhibition sector.

82. For a discussion of this, see David Grimstead, *Melodrama Unveiled* (1968; rpt., Berkeley: University of California Press, 1987), 93.

83. Mrs. Olive Logan, *Before the Footlights and Behind the Scenes* (Philadelphia: Parmelee, 1870), 387.

84. "As an Actor Sees Women," *Ladies' Home Journal* (November 1908): 26.

85. Echoing numerous other commentators, Walter Prichard Eaton claimed to have "heard a matinee audience of women applaud the actress' gowns as she lifted them up to pack her trunk" even though the character was involved in a "situation as tense and grave as can be imagined" (Eaton, "Women as Theater-Goers," 13). A similar situation in which "a certain pink silk lined hood" causes the audience to stop the play's action to applaud Billie Burke's "ravishing" appearance in said hood is recounted by Ada Patterson in "Has the Costume Play Come Back?" *Theatre Magazine* 33 (December 1919): 358.

86. One writer blamed the cultish admiration of matinee girls for Ethel Barrymore's "shallow and trivial" vehicles. See "Women and the American Theatre," *The Nation* 106 (June 1, 1918): 665.

87. Charles Cherry, "When There Were Matinee Idols," *Theatre Magazine* (May 1919): 290–92. This kind of denial was continued in film stardom/fandom as well. Valentino was quoted as saying, "My mash notes—they're very lovely. Of course, they're really a means of expressing admiration for my acting." Quoted in Henry Harrison, "Rudolph Valentino Talks About His Poetry, Mash Notes, and Sheiks," *Brooklyn Eagle*, September 21, 1924, 8 (clipping file, NYPL-TC).

88. *The Theatre* (1903), quoted in Carroll, *The Matinee Idols*, 15–16.

89. Gregory, "Our Foolish Virgins," 9.

90. Michael Strange, *Who Tells Me True* (New York: Scribner's, 1940), 164.

91. In 1899 a twenty-one-year-old female stalker pulled a gun on Bellew. His response was to run away ("show the white feather"), which led to much mirthful derision of him in the popular press. It was gleefully noted that the matinee idol who was so athletic and heroic on stage was too cowardly to do what the box-office ticket-taker calmly accomplished: taking the gun away from a "harmless imbecile." See "Kyrle Bellew's Beauty: Turns the Head of a Young Girl Who Followed Him from New York to Boston," undated newspaper clipping (n.p., c. 1899); and untitled clipping, n.p., c. February 1899 (Bellew Scrapbooks, Robinson Locke Collection, NYPL-TC). A Barrymore performance was disrupted by a "large blonde person . . . [who] began shouting at the top of her voice that she was engaged to marry Jack Barrymore, but he didn't know it" (see untitled clipping, *New York Sun*, May 8, 1907, n.p. [Barrymore Scrapbooks, Robinson Locke Collection, NYPL-TC]).

92. Untitled clipping, June 18, 1910, n.p. (Barrymore Scrapbooks, Robinson Locke Collection, NYPL-TC).

93. James Metcalfe, review of *Raffles, the Amateur Cracksman* in *Life* (November 19, 1903): 486; reprinted in Anthony Slide, ed., *Selected Theatre Criticism*, volume 1, *1900–1919* (Metuchen, N.J.: Scarecrow Press, 1985), 232–33.

94. "'Shakespeare Well Acted Pays,' Says Lewis Waller," *The Theatre* (November 1912): 159. See Rudolph Valentino, "An Open Letter from Valentino To the American Public," in which he responds to criticism of his fight with Paramount. He [or a ghostwriter] says: "The newspaper reports of the court proceedings were for the most part unfair and ridiculous. I was pictured as highly temperamental, as grasping for money" (*Photoplay* 23 [January 1923]: 34). A newspaper article of 1924 is subtitled: "Screen Idol Says He Hopes to Make a Million Dollars Before He Retires from the Movies." See also Harrison, "Rudolph Valentino Talks About His Poetry, Mash Notes, and Sheiks," 8.

95. "'Shakespeare Well Acted Pays,' Says Lewis Waller," *The Theatre* (November 1912): 159. As noted, such a description prefigures the discourse on Valentino, in particular that associated with the film star's appearance in a 1924 film version of *Monsieur Beaucaire*, which was advertised with a line that seems rather disingenuous considering the play's long life: "Only Valentino could be Booth Tarkington's *Monsieur Beaucaire*, the most romantic figure in American literature." Valentino was cast in the role after resolving his battle with Paramount

over his salary and control of his material. Advance publicity suggested that the actor was going to appear in "satin knee panties [in caption to photo]," but Valentino is praised elsewhere in the same publication as "a gorgeous and picturesque figure in the laces and satins of Beaucaire." See "Rudolph Valentino as Monsieur Beaucaire," *Photoplay* 25 (April 1924): 78.

96. Walter Jones, "The Beautifullest Boy in America," *Green Book* 13, no. 2 (February 1915): 231–57.

97. Untitled newspaper clipping, February 2, 1899, n.p. (Bellew Scrapbooks, Robinson Locke Collection, NYPL-TC).

98. Untitled clipping, June 18, 1910, n.p. (Barrymore Scrapbooks, Robinson Locke Collection, NYPL-TC).

99. "John Barrymore on Still [*sic*] Hunt for Arnold Daly," *New York Review*, December 5, 1914, n.p. (clipping, Barrymore Scrapbooks, Robinson Locke Collection, NYPL-TC). "Embryo" quote from untitled clipping, *New York Telegraph*, May 25, 1901, n.p. (Barrymore Scrapbooks, Robinson Locke Collection, NYPL-TC).

100. "Mr. Barrymore and Mr. Drew," *Collier's* (October 30, 1914): n.p. (clipping, Barrymore Scrapbooks, Robinson Locke Collection, NYPL-TC).

101. " 'Uncle Sam,' New Farce at Liberty," *New York Times*, October 31, 1911; reprinted in *New York Times Theater Reviews*, n.p.

102. Review of *The Affairs of Anatol* in *Everybody's Magazine* (c. 1913), n.p. (untitled clipping, Barrymore Scrapbooks, Robinson Locke Collection, NYPL-TC).

103. See "John Barrymore on Still Hunt for Arnold Daly," *New York Review*, December 5, 1914, n.p. See also Peters, *The House of Barrymore*, 132.

104. "John Barrymore on Still Hunt for Arnold Daly," *New York Review*, December 5, 1914, n.p. Daly was reported to have apologized before "blood was shed."

105. "John Barrymore Manages to Lick Someone at Last," *New York Review*, August 2, 1912, n.p.

106. Sermolino, "John Barrymore's Barber," n.p.

107. Ibid., n.p.

108. Review, "A Gentleman of Leisure," in the *New York Times*, August 25, 1911; reprinted in *New York Times Theater Reviews*, n.p.

109. This is the only reference to a British equivalent to the matinee girls that I have found. American commentators of the 1870s and 1880s thought the matinee girl thoroughly and uniquely American, but she seems to have caught on elsewhere by the 1900s–1910s, the years to which this article seems to refer. As late as 1901, Bellew claimed that "the matinee girl is purely an American product. She exists nowhere else. In England she would be impossible." See Kaufman, "Mr. Kyrle Bellew and the Matinee Girl," n.p. (clipping, NYPL-TC); and Ivor Brown, "Edwardian Idols of My Youth," in Anthony Curtis, ed., *The Rise and Fall of the Matinee Idol* (New York: St. Martin's, 1974), 33.

110. James Metcalfe, review of *Beaucaire* in *Life* (December 12, 1901): 518; reprinted in Slide, ed., *Selected Theatre Criticism* 1:21.

111. Anna Steese Richardson, "Wanted: A Little Love," *McClure's* 46 (February 1916): 68. On the versatility of these players during a "transitional" era

in the theater, see Garff B. Wilson, *A History of American Acting* (Bloomington: Indiana University Press, 1966), 200–37. Richardson's "'Filmitis': The Modern Malady—Its Symptoms and Its Cure" describes the theatrical matinee idol as depending upon the appeal of "modes, monocles, and manners," at least in reference to William Faversham (14).

112. Ada Patterson, *Theatre Magazine* (1908): 160–61, cited in William Young, *Famous Actors and Actresses* (New York: Bowker, 1975), 895.

113. Followings existed for both male and female stars, though the ones associated with male stars seem (at least in documentation) to have been more vigorous in their idolization. This quotation is in reference to the Ethel Barrymore "cult." James L. Ford, "The Ethel Barrymore Following," *Appleton's Magazine* (November 1908): 548.

114. Ford, "The Ethel Barrymore Following," 550.

115. "As an Actor Sees Women," *Ladies' Home Journal* (November 1908): 26.

116. "The Brutality of the Matinee Girl," *Lippincott's Monthly Magazine* (December 1907): 687–88.

117. Carroll, *The Matinee Idols*, 52. There may have been more male fans on the order of the matinee girl, but if there were, their existence was not publicized in popular discourse. Occasionally, newspapers reported on the eccentric male who made a lifelong fetish of a particular stage or musical star. See, for example, the account of "Boots" Van Steenberg's obsession for Jenny Lind in "Crazed By Love," *San Francisco Chronicle*, August 5, 1878, 1. Women's star worship was implicated in creating generations of stagestruck girls who took radical measures (leaving kin and kith) to take to the stage rather than be satisfied with being a normal, "gentle, home-loving maid." See Gregory, "Our Foolish Virgins," 15.

There was a documentable increase in the number of women who were actresses and, to a much lesser extent, playwrights and managers. Between the years of 1890 and 1920, a startling upturn occurred in the numbers of "artistic actresses" around whom stage vehicles and even theatrical companies revolved. As the object of fan emulation, female stars like Maude Adams and Ethel Barrymore could entice a girl into the stage life by example. One researcher notes a fourfold increase from 4,000 to 16,000 actresses in the years 1890–1910 (Albert Auster, *Actresses and Suffragists: Women in the American Theater, 1890–1990* [New York: Praeger, 1984], 45).

118. Gregory, "Our Foolish Virgins," 3.

119. Richardson, "'Filmitis,'" 13. It was believed that an impressionable girl might abandon home and hearth to become an actress in an attempt to be near her idol. Barrymore's first wife, Katherine Corri Harris, was a stagestruck debutante.

120. As Auster notes, the growing importance of women in the theatrical scene in the post-Victorian years also stirred up controversy about the long-standing view that the stage as a profession virtually guaranteed a girl's fall from purity (see Auster, *Actresses and Suffragists*, 43). The growing numbers of women on the stage during these years seem obvious confirmation of *The Theatre*'s assertion that "the matinee girls form an army of neophytes, for whom it would take very little push to find themselves behind the footlights instead of in front of them" (Henry P.

Mawson, "The Truth About Going on the Stage," *The Theater* 2 [August 1902]: 11). For another of the many attempts to warn girls away from the stage, see Charles Belmont Davis: "The Girl and the Stage: The Truth Which Lies Behind the Footlights,"*Collier's* 44 (October 1909): 21–30.

121. Cherry, "When There Were Matinee Idols," 290. In a view of matinee idols glimpsed, he admits, through "roseate glasses," Cherry suggests that the relationship between stage idols and the matinee girls was one of "pleasant intimacy" that had disappeared with film stars and the "strange young women who worshipped them." He questioned whether these new devotees were "true progeny of a past idolatry" (290–91).

122. Joan Bennett and Lois Kibbee, *The Bennett Playbill* (New York: Holt, Rinehart and Winston, 1978), 5, 6. Bennett also notes how the matinee idol's "handsome features . . . impeccable wardrobe . . . and thrilling voice" figured as being more important than his acting skills. She also confirms that her father was yet another matinee idol who "hated the label 'matinee idol'" (10).

123. Strange, *Who Tells Me True*, 164–65.

124. See E. Anthony Rotundo, *American Manhood: Transformations in Masculinity from the Revolution to the Modern Era* (New York: Basic Books, 1993), 128–66. See also Stephen Kern, *The Culture of Love: Victorians to Moderns* (Cambridge: Harvard University Press, 1992), 281–95, 336–46.

125. Quoted in Carl N. Degler, *At Odds: Women and the Family in America from the Revolution to the Present* (New York: Oxford University Press, 1980), 259.

126. Rotundo, *American Manhood*, 156. For primary research material on attitudes, see Clelia Duel Mosher, *The Mosher Survey: Sexual Attitudes of Forty-five Victorian Women*, edited by James MaHood and Kristine Wenberg (Albany: State University of New York, [1980]).

127. Kern, *The Culture of Love*, 101.

128. Lears, *No Place of Grace*, 5.

129. H. Rider Haggard, "About Fiction," *Contemporary Review* 51 (1887): 177; quoted in Joseph Bristow, *Empire Boys: Adventure in a Man's World* (London: HarperCollins Academic, 1991), 116.

130. Unidentified clipping, n.p. (NYPL-TC).

131. Alexander Woollcott, review of *Peter Ibbetson* in the *New York Times*, April 22, 1917; reprinted in *New York Times Theater Reviews*, n.p. Barrymore would repeat this flower-kissing to good effect at the finale of a key scene in his romance film *Tempest* (1928).

132. Alexander Woollcott, quoted in "'Dreaming True' on the Stage," *Literary Digest* 54 (June 2, 1917): 1700.

133. Woollcott, review of *Peter Ibbetson*, *New York Times*, 1.

134. Marsden Hartley, "John Barrymore's Ibbetson," *The Dial* 64 (March 1918): 227.

135. Woollcott, quoted in "'Dreaming True' on the Stage," 1700. For Woollcott on the play's potential for provoking laughter, see "At Richard III" in the *New York Times*, March 21, 1920; reprinted in *New York Times Theater Reviews*, n.p.

136. Hartley, "John Barrymore's Ibbetson," 227. On the ending see Channing Pollock's review in *Green Book* (July 1917): n.p. (clipping file, NYPL-TC); and Richard Henry Little (pseudonym), "John Barrymore and *Peter Ibbetson*," *Chicago Herald*, April 21, 1918, n.p. (Barrymore Scrapbooks, Robinson Locke Collection, NYPL-TC).

137. "An Acting Edition of *Peter Ibbetson*," *New York Times*, c. 1918, n.p.; and "*Ibbetson* Charms at Lyric," clipping (c. 1918), n.p. (both articles in *Peter Ibbetson* clipping file, Museum of the City of New York).

138. Strange, *Who Tells Me True*, 154.

139. Adele Ade, "Barrymore Off Stage," c. 1918, n.p. (*Peter Ibbetson* clipping file, Museum of the City of New York).

140. John Barrymore, *Confessions of an Actor* (Indianapolis: Bobbs-Merrill, 1926), n.p.

141. Carroll, *The Matinee Idols*, 147.

142. Reviews in *Variety*, May 11, 1917, n.p., and *Variety*, June 15, 1917, n.p. (clippings, NYPL-TC). *Peter Ibbetson* was adapted to film in 1921 as *Forever* starring Wallace Reid, and again in 1935, under its original title, with Gary Cooper starring.

143. Interview with Constance Collier in untitled clipping, c. 1918 (*Peter Ibbetson* clipping file, Museum of the City of New York).

144. Review of *Peter Ibbetson* by Amy Leslie, c. 1919 (untitled clipping, NYPL-TC).

145. Charlotte Fairchild, "Mr. John Barrymore as St. Francis of Assisi: A Photographic Study of the Well-Known Actor," *Theatre Magazine* 26 (December 1917): 362.

146. Nina Auerbach, *Woman and the Demon* (Cambridge: Harvard University Press, 1982), 48–52.

147. Untitled clipping from *Woman's Home Companion* (December 1919): n.p. (clipping file, NYPL-TC).

148. Strange, quoted in Peters, *The House of Barrymore*, 163.

149. William James, cited in Robert N. Bellah et al., *Habits of the Heart* (New York: Harper and Row, 1985), 120. See also Henry Childs Merwin, "On Being Civilized Too Much," *Atlantic Monthly* 79 (June 1897): 220–22.

150. Rafford Pyke, "What Men Like in Men," *Cosmopolitan* 33 (May 1902): 406.

151. For a discussion of changing representations of the "sad young man" as a stereotype of homosexuality, see Richard Dyer, *The Matter of Images* (London: Routledge, 1993), 73–92.

152. Eve Kosofsky Sedgwick, *Epistemology of the Closet* (Berkeley: University of California Press, 1990), 167.

153. Sedgwick, *Epistemology of the Closet*, 164.

154. Hartley, "John Barrymore's Ibbetson," 227.

155. Julian Johnson, "The Art of John Barrymore," *Photoplay* 15 (February 1919): 55.

156. Hartley uses the term "spiritual" five times. The *New York Tribune* reviewer is typical: "There was a notable spirituality in his [Barrymore's] live per-

formance that gave the play its tone" (quoted in "'Dreaming True' on the Stage," 1701).

157. Johnson, "The Art of John Barrymore," 55.

158. John Kobel, *Damned in Paradise: The Life of John Barrymore* (New York: Atheneum, 1977), 126. Barrymore's fears of being viewed as effeminate also may have figured in his famous comment that he wanted Hamlet to be so masculine that "when I come out on the stage they can hear my balls clank."

159. Strange, *Who Tells Me True*, 155. It was later suggested that he secretly wrapped one calf to improve his legs' symmetry, and that the visual effect, more crucially, relied also on his stuffing the costume's codpiece.

160. One spectator noted: "I have seen *The Jest* a number of times and on each occasion I have been amazed at the murmurs of surprise which invariably greet Giannetto's sudden entrance" (see "To the Dramatic Critic," *New York Times*, January 11, 1920, n.p. [clipping, Barrymore clipping files, Museum of the City of New York]). George Oppenheimer quipped in retrospect: "Strong women fainted, and if they didn't, they should have" (Oppenheimer, "The Great Days of Broadway," in Curtis, ed., *The Rise and Fall of the Matinee Idol*, 113).

161. Burns Mantle, review of *The Jest* in the *Chicago Tribune*, c. 1919, n.p. (clipping file, NYPL-TC). John Corbin described Giannetto as a "young artist of sensitive fibre and kindly nature [who] is goaded by intolerable persecution to retaliation in kind. He pursues his revenge . . . and, in so doing, destroys his own soul" (John Corbin, "The Brothers Barrymore," *New York Times*, April 10, 1919; reprinted in *New York Times Theater Reviews*, n.p.).

162. Dorothy Parker, untitled clipping, *Vanity Fair* (June 1919): n.p. (Barrymore Scrapbooks, Robinson Locke Collection, NYPL-TC).

163. Gilbert W. Gabriel, "John Barrymore as Hamlet," *World's Work* 90, no. 1 (September 1925): 500.

164. Corbin, "The Brothers Barrymore," *New York Times*, reprinted in *New York Times Theater Reviews*, n.p.

165. Brock, "American Hamlets Rare Visitors to London," 6.

166. Strange, *Who Tells Me True*, 155. In support of her view she offers an anecdote. She tells of meeting a "very handsome distinguished priest" who raged against the play and demanded to know how could "'any woman in her senses marry a man who played *The Jest* as Mr. Barrymore played it?'" Her husband asked if the priest had seen the play; Strange recalls: "'Five times! Five times!' shouted our visitor, in a vast excess of disgruntled fury, directed I thought at us and himself, and the buoyant magnetism of forbidden fruit" (156).

167. Strange, *Who Tells Me True*, 155.

168. [T.H.], "A Tragedy of Blood," *The Nation* 108 (April 19, 1919): 619.

169. The "effeminate youth" quote is from Burns Mantle, "Pondering Mr. Barrymore, *Variety*, December 26, 1919, n.p. (clipping NYPL-TC). See also Woollcott, "Second Thoughts on First Nights," *New York Times*, September 27, 1919.

170. George Oppenheimer recalls a 1931 revival: "Years later another actor, not nearly as attractive or as able as John, revived *The Jest*, claiming that he would outdo John in the part. On his first entrance he was dressed in tights with a wig

like John's and all the other costume appurtenances. There was a pause. Then from the back of the house there could be heard a man's voice that said, 'My God, it's Ethel'" (Oppenheimer, "The Great Days of Broadway," 113).

171. Peters, *The House of Barrymore*, 132.

172. Monahan, "The American Peril," 878–82.

173. Mercedes de Costa discusses the marriage in *Here Lies the Heart* (1960; rpt., New York: Arno, 1975), 103. See also James Kotsilibas-Davis, *The Barrymores* (New York: Crown, 1981), 29.

174. Robert Benchley, quoted in Peters, *The House of Barrymore*, 219. The climax of the play involves a wanton duchess's attempted seduction of the hapless, disfigured hero, Gwymplaine (Barrymore): "Talk [to me] with the savage pulsating words of your clown language. Talk to me as if you held a whip in your hand." Michael Strange, *Clair de Lune: A Play in Two Acts and Six Scenes* (New York: Putnam's, 1921), 91.

175. Winifred S. Merrick (letter) in "Brickbats and Bouquets," *Photoplay* 31 (April 1927): 92.

176. Busnell Diamond, "Heights and Depths, and the Films: New Scope and New Standards Disclosed in John Barrymore's Photo-Play of Jekyll and Hyde," *Boston Transcript*, April 3, 1920, n.p. (Barrymore Scrapbooks, Robinson Locke Collection, NYPL-TC).

177. Diamond, "Heights and Depths," n.p.

178. "The Jekyll-Hyde Work," c. 1920, n.p. (anonymous newspaper clipping, Barrymore file, Hoblitzelle Theatre Arts Library, Harry Ransom Center, University of Texas).

179. Sedgwick, *Epistemology of the Closet*, 172.

180. Some reviewers noted all these changes and blamed them on the movies: see "The Jekyll-Hyde Work," c. 1920, n.p. (anonymous newspaper clipping, Barrymore file, Hoblitzelle Theatre Arts Library, Harry Ransom Center, University of Texas). Jekyll's use of Gina's "Italian" ring (designed as a vial for poison) was copied from the first act of *The Jest* (see Diamond, "Heights and Depths," n.p.). Several years later, Barrymore (or a ghostwriter) attempted to justify the radical changes in *The Sea Beast*, his film adaptation of *Moby Dick*: "Of course for the movies it was necessary to add a love story and though this did not please the people who love the book very much, the picture made a great hit with almost everyone except those who knew a great deal about the sea" (John Barrymore, "Hamlet in Hollywood," *Ladies' Home Journal* [June 1927]: 61).

181. They also suggest the iconography of the "cadaverously beautiful young man" made conventional and sentimental in nineteenth-century Romantic painting present in film images attributed to covert male eroticism in the work of gay director F. W. Murnau in the 1920s (see Dyer, *The Matter of Images*, 77–79). On Murnau and homoeroticism see Janet Bergstrom, "Sexuality at a Loss: The Films of F. W. Murnau," *Poetics Today* 6, nos. 1–2 (Spring 1985): 185–203.

182. Hansen dismisses Barrymore's screen appeal, along with that of Richard Barthelmess, as not being attributable to their bodies. Hansen says that these two stars "seemed to owe their good looks to a transcendent spirituality rather than

anything related to their bodies and sexuality." Hansen, "Pleasure, Ambivalence, and Identification," 23.

183. Steven Neale, "Masculinity as Spectacle," *Screen* 24, no. 6 (November–December 1983): 14–15.

184. Peter Lehman and Paul Smith have also taken issue with Neale's remarks. See Lehman, *Running Scared: Masculinity and the Representation of the Male Body* (Philadelphia: Temple University Press, 1993), 32–33, and Paul Smith, "Action Movie Hysteria: Or, Eastwood Bound," *Differences* 1, no. 3 (1989): 93.

185. Nancy Pryor, "The Sheik Stuff Is Out: Hugh Allen Says It Leaves Him Cold," *Motion Picture Classic* (June 1928): 26.

186. Perhaps to help stifle the implication that he is unredeemable or is so polymorphous as to indulge in same-sex desire, it is not male sexual insatiability that must be curbed in some of these films but the desire for revenge. Both *Beau Brummel* and *Don Juan* offer revenge as the motivating force for the hero's intransigent sexuality.

187. The Prince of Wales tells her that "The Beau's false chivalry has deceived many a woman" and proceeds to demonstrate this by repeating one of Beau's techniques, kissing the palm of the woman's hand, as he echoes the Beau's most intimate utterance to her: "I place my heart in the hollow of your little hand."

188. Charles Darton, "They Love Barrymore," *Screen Secrets* 6 (November 1928): 40.

189. This point has been made by Miriam Hansen, "Pleasure, Ambivalence, Identification," 13.

190. Neale, "Masculinity as Spectacle," 14–15.

191. Ibid., 8.

192. Hansen, "Pleasure, Ambivalence, Identification," 18–20.

193. Georges Bataille, *Eroticism* (San Francisco: City Lights Books, 1986), 24.

194. Bellew's *A Gentleman of France* was adapted for the stage from the same source and drew at least one reviewer's praise at the expense of the Barrymore version. *Variety* noted: "In watching this scene progress one could not fail to think back to the days of "A Gentleman of France" and recall the manner in which the late Kyrle Bellew handled himself in that famous stair duel scene. Such a comparison is not favorable to Mr. Barrymore." Review of *When a Man Loves* in *Variety*, February 9, 1927; reprinted in *Variety Film Reviews, 1907–1980*, n.p.

195. Bataille, *Eroticism*, 2.

196. Also, as *The Jest* shows, the link between the male body, violence, and male suffering appears to have a precedent in the theatrical construction of the theatrical matinee idol, as well as in the requirements of stage melodrama. From another perspective, the eroticized male body's association with violence can also be explained as a textual remnant, a holdover from the generically and spectatorially hybrid origins of these films, i.e., from the layering of romantic conventions and spectatorial structures aimed at women superimposed over male structures/ "male" genres such as the action-adventure swashbucklers.

197. In *Loving with a Vengeance* Tania Modleski suggests that the superior position of knowledge possessed by readers of Harlequin romances vis-à-vis the books' heroines results in a "schizophrenic" or "apersonal" reading analogous to the

symptomatology of hysteria. Tania Modleski, *Loving with a Vengeance* (New York: Methuen, 1984), 57.

198. Janice Radway, *Reading the Romance* (Chapel Hill: University of North Carolina Press, 1984), 148–49.

199. Hansen, "Pleasure, Ambivalence, Identification," 12.

200. "*Love* [review]" in *Variety*, August 15, 1927, 17; reprinted in *Variety Film Reviews, 1907–1980*, n.p.

201. Letter in "Brickbats and Bouquets," *Photoplay* 32 (June 1927): 84.

3. "Optic Intoxication":· Rudolph Valentino and Dance Madness

1. Ethel Watts Mumford, "Where Is Your Daughter This Afternoon?" *Harper's Weekly* 58 (September 17, 1914): 28.

2. Louise Closser Hale, "At the Back of the Cabaret," *McClure's* (January 1914): 30.

3. See, for example, review] of *A Sainted Devil* (1924) in *Variety*, November 26, 1924; reprinted in *Variety Film Reviews, 1907–1980* (New York: Garland, 1983), n.p.: "Maybe it'll satisfy the Valentino rooters. Most of them are women, and this is a woman's film." Also the review of *Monsieur Beaucaire* (1924) in *Variety*, August 13, 1924; reprinted in *Variety Film Reviews, 1907–1980*, n.p.: "The women will 'go' for this one by the thousands. The girls made up three-quarters of a sweltering house when this feature was reviewed."

4. N.E.A. Service, "A Love Recipe That Is Almost Sure to Start a Controversy," *Evening Examiner–New Era*, September 29, 1921 (unpaginated clipping, New York Public Library for the Performing Arts, Theatre Collection; hereafter, NYPL-TC).

5. Barrymore's defensiveness about his "manliness" continued in his film career. In 1928 he is quoted as saying of his thwarted appearance in *The Last of Mrs. Cheney*: "As for 'Mrs. Cheney' having a feminine slant, as you are all doubtless thinking, I can not see where it would have been more ladylike than 'Don Juan,' in which I looked like a female impersonator." See Ruth Waterbury, "Barrymore Ballyhoo," *Photoplay* 34 (August 1928): 73.

6. Michael Monahan, "The American Peril," *The Forum* 51 (June 1914): 878–79.

7. See Freeman Tilden, "Flapperdames and Flapperoosters," *Ladies' Home Journal* (May 1923): 10. See also Monahan, "The American Peril," *The Forum* 51 (June 1914). Monahan manages to connect women's influence with the tastes of immigrants. He argues that the "sexual themes" of sensational journalism "have been made possible largely by the immense immigration from Eastern Europe during the past twenty years. The taste is indeed rather Eurasian than American . . . and a decline of true journalistic power . . . seems closely related to the rise of women to influence in this field" (881).

8. Randolph Bartlett, "Speaking of Love," *Photoplay* 15 (February 1919): 71. By 1921 another male fan magazine writer complained of the prevalence of "young and pretty heroes" in motion pictures. See Bert Lytell, "A Lesson in Love," *Photoplay* 19 (February 1921): 43.

9. "Plain Mary" (pseudonym), "All for the Ladies," *Variety* (November 14, 1913): 13. This gossip column alludes to a married woman from "the Avenue" being but one among many who is engaged in an affair with a Latin dancer from one of the Broadway tango palaces.

10. Dan Beard, "Dan Beard's Own Page for Boys," *Woman's Home Companion* 34 (August 1907): 33.

11. Donald K. Pickens, *Eugenics and the Progressives* (Nashville, Tenn.: Vanderbilt University Press, 1968), 66–67. See also Paul J. Smith, *The Soul of Woman* (San Francisco: D. Elder, 1916), in which Smith says that women's "great task is to raise the level of racial quality" by being mothers who choose their "companions" carefully (60).

12. Louis Erenberg, *Steppin' Out* (Chicago: University of Chicago Press, 1984), 81–83.

13. John Wiley, *Triumph* (New York: Minton, Balch, 1926), 8.

14. Adela Rogers St. Johns, "What Kind of Men Attract Women Most?" *Photoplay* 25 (April 1924): 17.

15. The phrase "Valentino traps" is from Arthur Mayer, *Merely Colossal* (New York: Simon and Schuster, 1953), 178.

16. "Powder Puff," *Chicago Tribune*, July 18, 1926,10, reproduced in Kenneth Anger, *Hollywood Babylon* (1975; rpt., New York: Bell, 1981), 107.

17. Miriam Hansen, "Pleasure, Ambivalence, Identification: Valentino and Female Spectatorship," *Cinema Journal* 25, no. 4 (Summer 1986): 20–21. Although Hansen attempts to acknowledge historical factors in Valentino's construction in her expansion of this article for *Babel and Babylon*, she still seems to locate Valentino's "contradictions" as somehow outside the terms established intertextually and historically. See Hansen, *Babel and Babylon* (Cambridge: Harvard University Press, 1991), 256.

18. Sumiko Higashi, "Ethnicity, Class, and Gender in Film: DeMille's *The Cheat*," in Lester Friedman, ed. *Unspeakable Images: Ethnicity and the American Cinema* (Urbana: University of Illinois Press, 1991), 116.

19. Sigmund Spaeth, quoted in Marshall Stearns and Jean Stearns, *Jazz Dance: The Story of American Vernacular Dance* (New York: Macmillan, 1968), unidentified page (Tango File, Dance Collection, New York Public Library for the Performing Arts; hereafter cited as NYPL-DC).

20. Quoted in Elizabeth Kendall, *Where She Danced* (New York: Knopf, 1979), 75.

21. Quoted in Kendall, *Where She Danced*, 119.

22. Ibid., 80.

23. Olive Russell, "U.S. Below Par in Appreciation of Dancing," unidentified newspaper, Cleveland, Ohio: n.p. (Denishawn Dance Scrapbook, NYPL-DC).

24. Adolph Bolm, "The Future of Dance in America," *Shadowland* 7 (April 1923): 71.

25. Ellen Terry, quoted in "The Vital Art of the Russian Dancers," *Current Opinion* 55, no. 3 (August 1913): 173. She suggests that the presence of men in ballet both replaces "those feminine travesties of men known in our pantomimes as 'principal boys,'" and also makes ballet "far less sexual and far more beautiful" than the dancing of women.

26. Frederick Lewis Allen, quoted in Kendall, *Where She Danced*, 127. Kendall offers an extended discussion of the rise of these schools (116–31). See also Naima Prevots, *Dancing in the Sun: Hollywood Choreographers, 1915–1937* (Ann Arbor: UMI Research Press, 1987).

27. Vera Caspary, "The Twilight of the Dance Gods: Merely a Theory Regarding Masculine Arms and Feminine Ankles," *The Dance* 6, no. 2 (1926): 60.

28. Nesta MacDonald, *Diaghilev Observed by Critics in England and the United States, 1911–1929* (New York: Dance Horizons, 1975), 174–76 (quotation from unidentified clipping quoted in MacDonald, 178).

29. Unidentified clipping, quoted in MacDonald, *Diaghilev Observed*, 178.

30. Ibid., 179. Valentino's features, like those of the era's film "vamps," were often described as "Oriental," as in Willis Goldbeck, "The Perfect Lover," *Motion Picture Magazine* (May 1922): 40: "His eyes are intensely dark. . . . In make-up they are amazing. With a savor of the Orient, his lids are lost behind the smooth continuance of his brows, lending his countenance its inscrutable caste, its heightened mystery."

31. Henry T. Finck, "The Ballet Russe, Bakst, and Nijinsky," *The Nation* 101, no. 2652 (April 27, 1916): 464. Although he danced with the Ballets Russes and also formed his own company, Mordkin was best known as Anna Pavlova's dance partner.

32. The *New York Evening Post*, cited in *Musical America* April 4, 1916, and quoted in MacDonald, *Diaghilev Observed*, 174.

33. Peter Wollen, "Fashion/Orientalism/The Body," *New Formations* 1 (Spring 1987): 8.

34. It was noted in Milwaukee by the committee of city censors that there was "nothing shocking or even mildly wicked in dance, posture, costume or suggestion" in the Ballets Russes productions planned for the city, in spite of advance photos to the contrary (*Milwaukee Sentinel*, February 29, 1916, quoted in MacDonald, *Diaghilev Observed*, 161). It was also noted that Gertrude Hoffman's version of *Schéhérazade* a few years before had been considerably "rougher" in this regard (*Milwaukee Sentinel*, January 16, 1916, quoted in MacDonald, 161).

35. Lynn Garafola calls the faun's final masturbatory gesture "a declaration of war against the received conventions of ballet." Garafola, "Vaslav Nijinsky," *Raritan* 8, no. 1 (Summer 1988): 2–3.

36. Erenberg, *Steppin' Out*, 154. One example of the American reaction against the moral dangers of concert dance can to be found in the Catholic Theatre Movement, founded in 1913 and devoted to censoring. Members of the organization took a pledge to "avoid improper plays and exhibitions." This committee was, of course, very interested in the American premiere of *L'Après-Midi d'un Faune* (see MacDonald, *Diaghilev Observed*, 142). Kathy Peiss discusses dance madness in the context of working-class culture between 1880 and 1920 in *Cheap Amusements: Working Women and Leisure in Turn-of-the-Century New York* (Philadelphia: Temple University Press, 1986).

37. The quotation is from "New Reflections on the Dancing Mania," *Current Opinion* 55, no. 4 (October 1913): 263. See also Erenberg, *Steppin Out*, 81; and "Turkey Trot and Tango—A Disease or a Remedy," *Current Opinion* 55, no. 2 (August 1913): 187.

38. "The Revolt of Decency, " *New York Sun*, quoted in *Literary Digest* 46 (April 9, 1913): 894.

39. Ellis Loxley, "The Turkey-Trot and Dance America, 1900–1910," *Educational Dance* (December 1939): 8.

40. *The Standard*, quoted in "New Reflections on the Dancing Mania," *Current Opinion* 55 (October 1913): 264.

41. Fan magazines emerged as an extratextual form of promotion particularly enthusiastic in promoting the linkage between film and contemporary forms of dance. They included many photographs of actresses assuming dancelike costumes and poses, and also featured photo layouts and articles with exclusive emphasis on dance. This was logical because of their orientation to women, the same gender-specific audience that was known to fill dance matinees and tango tea palaces. See, for example, "Figures of the Dance," *Motion Picture Classic* 15, no. 6 (February 1923): 50–51. For a discussion of fan magazines' orientation to women in the 1920s see Gaylyn Studlar, "The Perils of Pleasure? Fan Magazine Discourse as Women's Commodified Culture in the 1920s," *Wide Angle* 13, no. 1 (1991): 6–23.

42. Kendall, *Where She Danced*, 136.

43. The dance scenes in the Babylon sequences of *Intolerance* (1916), of course, are the most infamous in Griffith's work because of their startling sensuality. See Kendall, *Where She Danced*, 137–44.

44. Pavlova made her screen debut in the 1916 feature, *The Dumb Girl of Portici*, directed by Lois Weber and Phillips Smalley and adapted from the opera, *La Muette de Portici*. Advertisements touted her as "the most wonderful, emotional actress of the decade." See ad in *Moving Picture World* 28 (April 1, 1916): 4–5. Michael Morris details some of Kosloff's various activities for the movie industry, including his work as a technical adviser teaching film stars how to move, in *Madame Valentino* (New York: Abbeville Press, 1991), 41–63.

45. William Marion Reedy, quoted in "Sex O'Clock in America [editorial]," *Current Opinion* 55, no. 2 (August 1913): 113.

46. Reedy, quoted in "Sex O'Clock in America," 113.

47. "Trotting Forward," *The Nation* 96, no. 2493 (April 10, 1913): 353. Griffith's *The Mothering Heart* (1913) is but one of a number of films that depict nightclub dancing.

48. Maurice Mouvet, *Art of Dancing* (New York: Schirmer, 1915), 35–46; Erenberg, *Steppin' Out*, 165.

49. Erenberg, *Steppin' Out*, 165.

50. Ted Shawn, *The American Ballet* (New York: Henry Holt, 1936), 47. Shawn also suggested a more mundane reason for the dance's decline, that "the tango died because it was impossible in a crowded room to do the figures."

51. Frederick Lewis Allen, "When America Learned to Dance," *Scribner's Magazine* 102, no. 3 (September 1937): 15.

52. Irene Castle, quoted in "Dancing Assisted Her," *Los Angeles Examiner*, October 8, 1916, n.p. (clipping, Castle Scrapbooks, Robinson Locke Collection, NYPL-TC).

53. Irene and Vernon Castle, *Modern Dancing* (New York: Harper Brothers, 1914), 87. Their version was known as the "Castle Innovation Tango." The

Castles made one film, a fictionalized autobiographical account of their lives together called *The Whirl of Life* (1915) In it they, like Valentino, are depicted as turning to dance because they are stranded in a foreign land (France) and have no other means of support. The film also includes a subplot revolving around the kidnapping of Irene by a rival theatrical producer. With the help of his dog, Vernon rescues Irene in the nick of time to go on with the show.

The relative lack of passion in the Castles' dancing has an ironic epilogue. Irene made the transition to movies, but met with public disfavor soon after Vernon's death. For months she kept up a demeanor of distraught widowhood (including pictorial fashion layouts in mourning outfits for *Vogue*), until it was found out that she had secretly married a few short weeks after Vernon's fatal accident. Editorial writers blasted her as a hypocrite who kept her second marriage secret to facilitate the sale of her book on a husband she apparently had never loved. Irene defended herself in statements that rather ungraciously imputed her dead husband's memory: she implied that she and Vernon had not slept together for years because he was disinterested. See untitled clipping, *New York Telegram*, August 20, 1919 (Castle Scrapbooks, Robinson Locke Collection, NYPL-TC).

54. Mumford, "Where Is Your Daughter This Afternoon?" 28.

55. Ibid. While most observers refused to separate the combination of dance, alcohol, and men that threatened the morals of tomorrow's mothers, *Harper's Weekly* suggested in an editorial that the real culprit was alcohol and that the much-maligned new dance "if danced in places where no liquor is served, is much less of a sex stimulant than the ordinary musical comedy." In response to an article by Pavlova, the editorial also suggested that social dancing, as an "active exercise," was "steadying and makes for normality of feeling whereas keeping quiet and taking in sensuous impressions makes in the opposite direction." See "Morals and Dancing," *Harper's Weekly* 58 (September 13, 1913): 3.

56. "Morals and Dancing [editorial]," 1.

57. Mumford, "Where Is Your Daughter This Afternoon?" 28.

58. Irene and Vernon Castle, *Modern Dancing*, 164.

59. Erenberg, *Steppin' Out*, 83.

60. William Inglis, "Is Modern Dancing Indecent?" *Harper's Weekly* 57 (May 17, 1913): 11. He described also the crowd as made up of women, debutantes, and "a great many slender, downy youths who were identified as college 'men.'"

61. Inglis, "Is Modern Dancing Indecent?" 11.

62. Knight Dunlap, *Personal Beauty and Racial Betterment* (St. Louis: C. V. Mosby, 1920), 87–89.

63. Charlotte Perkins Gilman, "Vanguard, Rear-Guard, and Mud-Guard," *Century* 104 (1922): 351, 353. See Erenberg for a discussion of the Eugenia Kelly case (1915) that crystallized public fears of how women from good families would be degraded by tango gigolos (*Steppin' Out*, 77–85).

64. John Higham, *Strangers in the Land: Patterns of American Nativism, 1860–1925*, 2d ed. (New Brunswick, N.J.: Rutgers University Press, 1988), 158–68.

65. George Creel, "Close the Gates," *Collier's* (May 6, 1922): 9–11.

66. Quoted in the *Congressional Record*, 63rd Cong., 2d sess., 2624.

67. Lothrop Stoddard, *The Rising Tide of Color Against White World Supremacy* (New York: Scribner's, 1920), 166. Griffith's *The Birth of a Nation* (1915) worked along the same lines as racist propaganda to mitigate against racial mixing.

68. Erenberg, *Steppin' Out*, 83.

69. Unidentified newspaper clipping, c. 1914, n.p. (Tango file, NYPL-DC).

70. For more on this, see Studlar, "Perils of Pleasure? Fan Magazine Discourse as Women's Commodified Culture in the 1920s."

71. Review of *The Four Horsemen of the Apocalypse* in the *New York World*, c. September 1921, n.p. (clipping, NYPL-TC).

72. "*Four Horsemen* Enthralls Viewers," *San Francisco Call*, June 28, 1921, n.p. (clipping, NYPL-TC).

73. Per caption for a photo of *Four Horsemen of the Apocalypse* in the *Newark American Tribune*, c. September 1921, n.p. (clipping file, NYPL-TC).

74. *Four Horsemen* advertisement, c. 1921, n.p. (clipping file, NYPL-TC).

75. Alexander Walker refers to this scene as "stunningly designed." See Walker, *Rudolph Valentino* (Harmondsworth, Eng.: Penguin, 1977), 22.

76. Judith Hanna, *Dance, Sex, and Gender* (Chicago: University of Chicago Press, 1988), 164–65.

77. The advertisement is for *The City of Dim Faces*, c. 1918 (unidentified clipping, n.p., NYPL-TC).

78. Hanna, *Dance, Sex, and Gender*, 14–15. Obviously, there are many reasons why patriarchal culture would encourage such a sensitivity to further its own aims.

79. Hansen, "Pleasure, Ambivalence, Identification," 20–21.

80. Carol Thurston, *The Romance Revolution* (Urbana: University of Illinois Press, 1987), pp. 38–39. The plot of *The Sheik* adheres with striking accuracy to the ideal romance described by Radway. Lady Diane, orphaned daughter of an English poet, initially appears to be the epitome of the "New Woman" since she is a boyish creature who has renounced marriage. But unlike the typical New Woman, she is resolutely chaste and, more precisely, has never been kissed. She is a headstrong adventurer but not an adventuress. The security of her asexual identity is destroyed when, during a trip to the Saudi Arabian desert, she is kidnapped by an Arab tribal chieftain, handsome but cruel, who proceeds to rape her (this is censored out of the film). He teaches her the meaning of submission (the meaning, she says later, of what it is to be a woman) and, as a consequence, she finds herself in love with him. She is ready to respond to him, but the presence of a European visitor interrupts their reconciliation, and she begins to fear his apparent cold indifference. She is captured by a rival tribe. The Sheik rescues her but is gravely wounded. Diane is told that her kidnapper/lover is not an Arab, but the son of an English lord and a Spanish aristocrat. Therefore, his barbaric behavior was not the result of the inbred cruelty of his race, but of his traumatic discovery that his long-dead mother suffered cruelly at the hands of his British father. In the book, when the Sheik recovers, he is filled with remorse and decides to send Diane back, but she convinces him that they cannot live without each other.

81. Janice Radway, *Reading the Romance* (Chapel Hill: University of North Carolina Press, 1984), 147.

82. Radway, *Reading the Romance*, 128, 70.

83. Ibid., 71–73.

84. Radway, *Reading the Romance*, 70–73.

85. Ibid., 147, 149. Similar scenes occur with Barrymore in *Tempest* (his cradling of the heroine's dying father) and, as the previous chapter noted, in *The Beloved Rogue* (Villon's interaction with his mother). The fan magazine's family discourse on the mothers of matinee idols was also used in Valentino's "My Life Story," serialized in *Photoplay* beginning in February 1923, and in "Moreno: How it Feels to Become a Star," in which "Tony" Moreno declares that he first shared his stardom (seeing his name on a marquee) with his mother (unidentified fan magazine clipping, NYPL-TC)

86. See *The Eagle* advertisement for the Rialto Theater, New York, c. November 1925, n.p. (clipping file, NYPL-TC).

87. Radway, *Reading the Romance*, 83.

88. Nanette Kutner, "Valentino's Own Version of the Tango," *Dance Lover's Magazine* 3, no. 5 (1925): 22.

89. Mary Winship, "When Valentino Taught Me to Dance," *Photoplay* 21 (May 1922): 45, 118. See also Gladys Hall, "'Women I Like to Dance With,' by Rudolph Valentino," *Movie Weekly*, January 27, 1923, 7 (clipping file, NYPL-TC). Valentino supposedly asked for the press to use the original Italian spelling of his name (as Rodolph) around this time. The star gave a "complete course of tango lessons" in the pages of the fan magazine *Screenland* starting in November 1921.

90. On the transformative capacity of dance see Francis Sparshott, *Off the Ground: First Steps to a Philosophical Consideration of Dance* (Princeton: Princeton University Press, 1988), 399.

91. Radway, *Reading the Romance*, 78.

92. Unsourced advertisements, c. 1921 (clippings, NYPL-TC).

93. Quoted in Peter Filene, "In Time of War," in Joseph H. Pleck and Elizabeth H. Pleck, eds., *The American Man* (Englewood Cliffs, N.J.: Prentice-Hall, 1980), 324.

94. Advertisement for *Moran of the Lady Letty* in unidentified newspaper, c. 1922, n.p. (clipping file, NYPL-TC).

95. The phrase "Love Story with a Viking Heroine" is how the narration (synopsis) of the film's scenario is advertised for its appearance in *Photoplay*. See Gene Sheridan, "*Moran of the Lady Letty*," *Photoplay* 21 (February 1922): 49–51.

96. Caption to Valentino photo in *Screenland* (1923): n.p. (clipping file, NYPL-TC).

97. Goldbeck, "The Perfect Lover," 40.

98. Ibid., 94.

99. Gladys Hall, "From Sanctimony to Serials," *Motion Picture Magazine* 28 (December 1919): 30–31.

100. Erenberg, *Steppin Out*, 85.

101. "Most Screen Stars Capable of Taking Up Other Professions," *Screenland* (Dallas, Texas) 1, no. 2 (1922): 12.

102. C. Sarason (letter), *New York Daily News*, September 9 1924, n.p. (clipping file, NYPL-TC).

103. In J. Winkler, "'I'm Tired of Being a Sheik,'" Valentino says, "Bonnie Glass and Joan Sawyer, in turn, took me as a partner" (*Collier's* 77 [January 16, 1926]: 18).

104. "Wedded, Found Spouse Broke?" *Los Angeles Times*, November 24, 1921 (unpaginated clipping, NYPL-TC).

105. Gladys Hall, "A Maker of Young Men," *Motion Picture Classic* 19 (March 1924): 21. On Mathis's power in the studio system and her status as "the most influential screenwriter of the day," see Richard Koszarski, *An Evening's Entertainment: The Age of the Silent Feature Picture, 1915–1928* (New York: Scribner's, 1990), 239.

106. The phrase "a Continental gentleman" is from Adela Whiteley Fletcher, "Across the Silversheet," *Motion Picture Magazine* (n.d.): 108 (clipping, NYPL-TC). Fletcher says of *The Sheik*: "Remembering censorship, we wondered why they ever bought the motion picture rights in the first place." See also "Do Women Like Masterful Men?" *Baltimore News*, October 22, 1921 (unpaginated clipping, NYPL-TC). Other Valentino comments on American women and the negative effects of their "liberation" can be found in "Is the American Girl Playing a Losing Game?" *Metropolitan*, January 1923 (unpaginated clipping, NYPL-TC).

107. Rudolph Valentino, "Woman and Love," *Photoplay* 21 (March 1922): 106.

108. Mildred R. Hut (letter to the editor), *Photoplay* 22 (October 1922): 117, cited in Janet Staiger, *Interpreting Films: Studies in the Historical Reception of American Cinema*, ch. 6, "'The Handmaiden of Villainy': *Foolish Wives*, Politics, Gender Orientation, and the Other" (Princeton: Princeton University Press, 1992), 132. Staiger focuses on the reception of "outrage" that greeted von Stroheim's *Foolish Wives*.

109. Letter in *Photoplay* 22 (November 1922): 76. Valentino admitted he had elevated himself from occupying a park bench by becoming a paid dance companion, "employed," as he later admitted, "to teach and dance with women patrons" at "one of the first dancing of the popular dance places in New York." Valentino, quoted in Winkler, "'I'm Tired of Being a Sheik,'" 28–29.

110. In the 1920s many plays and books took up this subject, including Booth Tarkington's *The Man from Home* (made into a film in 1922), which told the story of how "an Italian prince makes passionate love to a pretty American girl in an attempt to win her millions" (quotation from *Shadowland*'s June 1922 issue, describing the film [clipping, NYPL-TC, n.p.]). In Arthur Tuckerman, *Possible Husbands* (New York: Doubleday, 1926), the heroine says, "American women are too adaptable when contemplating a foreign marriage, especially if there's a title at stake" (8).

111. St. Johns, "What Kind of Men Attract Women Most?" 17.

112. Letter in "Brickbats and Bouquets," *Photoplay* 29 (February 1926): 118. In the late 1910s a star like Sessue Hayakawa (with even less recuperable origins than Moreno or Valentino) might play both sexy villain and tragic ethnic hero. Many of Hayakawa's films after his appearance in *The Cheat* (1915) treated the romance between white and the racial Other in a sympathetic light that marks Hayakawa's character as the hero. In this respect his films appear to rely on one of

two solutions to the dilemma of miscegenation: death for the Asian hero or the discovery of the heroine's mixed blood so that marriage may occur. Miriam Hansen gives the impression that Valentino was the first ethnic romantic hero and claims that Hayakawa "could only succeed in the part of a villain" (*Babel and Babylon*, 255). As a corrective to such a claim, Don Kirihara is doing important work on Hayakawa, who had his own production company, Haywood. See his "Sessue Hayakawa and the Functions of Race (1914–1922)," paper presented at the Society for Cinema Studies Conference, Syracuse, N.Y., March 1994, and his "Sessue Hayakawa, the Death of Asia, and Accommodationist Narrative," in Daniel Bernardi, ed., *The Birth of Whiteness* (New Brunswick, N.J.: Rutgers University Press, forthcoming).

113. Letter in "Brickbats and Bouquets," *Photoplay* 21 (May 1922): 117.

114. Goldbeck suggests of Valentino: "He has been called, with tentative reservations, 'the perfect lover.' . . . It is not his fault; so let him suffer for it" ("The Perfect Lover," 40). Hansen finds her psychoanalytic explanation for the unhappy endings to Valentino's films in "the deep affinity between eros and death drive" ("Valentino, Ambivalence, and Female Spectatorship," 29).

115. Tuckerman, *Possible Husbands* 214 and 182–83.

116. Theodore Roosevelt's views are discussed at length by Richard Slotkin, *Gunfighter Nation* (New York: HarperCollins, 1993), 36–62. See also John R. Commons, *Races and Immigrants* (New York: Macmillan: 1907), for a similar view of "race suicide."

117. Even movie stars who married so-called princes were not beyond criticism. Mae Murray's marriage to a "princelet" who regarded his occupation as being "Mae Murray's husband" is ridiculed in "Robbing the Cradle," *Motion Picture Classic* (August 1928): 78. Falling outside any criticism of European royalty because of his proper "Anglo-Saxon" lineage, the Prince of Wales was one of the most admired and discussed men in the society pages of American newspapers in the 1920s.

118. St. Johns, "What Kind of Men Attract Women Most?" 110–11.

119. Herbert Howe, "What Are Matinee Idols Made Of?" *Photoplay* 23 (April 1923): 41.

120. Edward Sapir, "The Discipline of Sex," *American Mercury* 16 (April 1929): 416–17, 419. On the sex-obsessed modern woman who was fashioning "the two sexes almost into one" (422) and destroying marriage as an institution, see Will Durant, "The Modern Woman; Philosophers Grow Dizzy as She Passes By," *Century* 113 (February 1927): 418–29.

121. "Letters to the Editor," *Photoplay* 23 (September 1922): 113.

122. Creel, "Close the Gates," 9. For a discussion of the dimensions of xenophobia in the United States during the 1920s, consult Higham, *Strangers in the Land*. Another article suggests that Valentino "epitomizes the feminine ideal of the amorous and romantic Prince Charming. . . . Valentino represents the world-old lure of sex and the ideal of perpetual romance" (untitled clipping, *Motion Picture Magazine* [September 1922], clipping file, British Film Institute).

123. Hansen, "Pleasure, Ambivalence, Identification," 32, 7.

124. Wollen, "Fashion/Orientalism/ The Body," 18–20.

125. Ibid., 5. This is a very persuasive and important article, but Wollen never really proves this point, nor does he take into consideration multiple factors at work in this redefinition outside of the work of Bakst, Paul Poiret, and Henri Matisse.

126. Richard Barthelmess's performance in *Broken Blossoms* (1919) evokes these same terms. It is interesting that Mouvet performed in a guise very similar to Barthelmess's in his "Opium Dance" (1920) and that a female vaudeville performer named Bessie McCoy Davis offered her version of Barthelmess's performance in a skit. See "Limehouse Nights Again," *Shadowland* (April 1920): 29.

127. Caspary, "The Twilight of the Dance Gods," 19

128. Wollen, "Fashion/Orientalism/The Body," 27.

129. Michael Morris argues that Valentino's alleged homosexuality is the result of unfounded insinuations of recent origin (*Madame Valentino*, 63–64). Although Miriam Hansen mentions "rumors" of the star's homosexuality circulating in the 1920s, I have not found any evidence of these in my research (see Hansen, "Pleasure, Ambivalence, Identification," 19). Fueled by Kenneth Anger's assertions of Valentino's homosexuality in *Hollywood Babylon*, there may be a temptation to read the star's sexuality retroactively. To a modern audience, Valentino's "sexual ambiguity" may seem self-evident in his films' textual inscription, but for his historical audience it may have been less evident or more centrally dependent on stereotyped assumptions about the sexuality of male dancers. See "Rudy's Rep" in Anger, *Hollywood Babylon*, 155–70.

130. Pearl Rall, "New Dance Music Ideal," *Los Angeles California Graphic*, June 9, 1917, n.p. (clipping, Denishawn Scrapbook, vol. 5, 1917–18, NYPL-DC).

131. Van Ryan, "Should Men Be Graceful?" *Physical Culture Magazine* (January 1921): 97.

132. "Who Are America's Favorite Dancers?" *The Dance* 5 (October 1925): 12–13. Valentino trailed Ted Shawn, Laurent Novikoff, and Buster West in the voting. The article notes: "Though Rudolph Valentino has not been seen dancing for two or three years, he still retains a following who loyally voted him the fourth most popular dancer in America and who put Mrs. Valentino's name on the gold star list. This is surprising since Mrs. Valentino has never sought fame as an individual artist." (64).

133. The most balanced version delineating this relationship is to be found in Morris, *Madame Valentino*.

134. Henry Harrison, "Rudolph Valentino Talks About His Poetry, Mash Notes, and Sheiks," *Brooklyn Eagle*, September 21, 1924, 8 (clipping file, NYPL-TC).

135. Radway, *Reading the Romance*, 76.

136. Ibid., 75.

137. Joseph Henaberry directed *Cobra* and also directed *A Sainted Devil*, the latter criticized by *Variety*'s reviewer: "The Henaberry direction is undistinguished and featured principally by the number of soft focus closeups which he gives the star, closeups which give full face, profile, ear, eye, nose and throat views of Rudy, which may be what the women want." See review of *A Sainted Devil* in *Variety*, November 11, 1924; reprinted in *Variety Film Reviews, 1907–1980*, n.p.

138. Photograph by Helen MacGregor in *Shadowland* (August 1923) (unpaginated clipping, NYPL-TC).

139. Walker, *Rudolph Valentino*, 51.

140. Adela Rogers St. Johns, "Why Do Great Lovers Fail as Husbands?" *Photoplay* 32 (1927): 29. Natacha's influence on Valentino continues to be portrayed in similar terms. David Gill's and Kevin Brownlow's *Hollywood* documentary television series attributes Valentino's faun photographs and one in which he posed in loin cloth as a Native American spirit guide ("Black Feather") to Natacha's "almost hypnotic influence" over her husband, who "submitted" to the photographs "because he loved and admired" his wife. The "Black Feather" study bears some resemblance to pictures that circulated of Ted Shawn from his ballet *Invocation of the Thunderbird*. For a sympathetic reevaluation of Natacha's impact on Valentino see Morris, *Madame Valentino*.

141. Herbert Howe, "Close-ups and Long Shots," *Photoplay* 29 (February 1926): 53.

142. Review of *The Son of the Sheik* in the *New York Times*, August 1, 1926; reprinted in *The New York Times Film Reviews* (New York: New York Times, 1970), n.p.

143. Arthur Brenton, "A Ladies' Man Who Is a Regular Guy," *Photoplay* 27 (December 1924): 132, 66.

144. "Rudolph Valentino to Change his Act?" *New York World*, November 22, 1925, n.p. (clipping, NYPL-TC).

145. Dick Dorgan, "I Hate Valentino," *Photoplay* 22 (June 1922): 26.

146. Valentino, quoted in Winkler, "'I'm Tired of Being a Sheik,'" 28. As if to emphasize Valentino's association with normative American masculinity (i.e., the middle-class businessman), a picture of Valentino accompanying the interview shows the star flourishing a smoking pipe. Roland Marchand notes that, in the 1920s, advertising for Edgeworth Smoking Tobacco "suggested that the growing number of women smokers had effeminized cigarettes; men should respond by turning to pipes. . . . Edgeworth proclaimed: 'A man looks like a man when he smokes a pipe.'" This was but one of the era's symbolic attempts to maintain the view of men as functional in contrast to women's decorative status. See Marchand, *Advertising the American Dream* (Berkeley: University of California Press, 1985), 191.

147. On July 18, 1926, the *Chicago Tribune* published what would come to be known in a few short months as the "Pink Powder Puff" attack. The attack consisted of an unsigned editorial that railed against the appearance of a pink powder machine in a men's washroom on the city's North Side. The blame for "this degeneration into effeminacy," this disturbing trend in the habits of American men, was laid at the feet of one person, Valentino, then currently appearing in the city to promote his latest film. Valentino promptly challenged the unknown journalist to a boxing match, but the latter never revealed his identity.

148. "The Office Roughneck Takes His Hat Off to Vernon Castle," *Detroit Journal*, February 19, 1918, n.p. (Castle Scrapbooks, Robinson Locke Collection, NYPL-TC).

149. "'Bury Capt. Castle with War Honors,'" n.p. (unidentified newspaper clipping, 1918; Castle Scrapbooks, Robinson Locke Collection, NYPL-TC). On

the tragic endings in films about dancers see Adrienne McLean, "The Image of the Ballet Artist in Popular Film," *Journal of Popular Culture* 25 (Summer 1991): 1–19. A fascinating and hilarious sound film called *Bolero* (1934) focuses on a fictional male cabaret dancer whose life seems to be a composite of aspects of the lives of Valentino, Mouvet, and Vernon Castle. The film foregrounds former dancer George Raft's amazing resemblance to Valentino (maintained as long as Raft's mouth is shut). Adding to the goofy fun is William Frawley as Raft's half brother and Carole Lombard as his sometime dance partner. Following the example of Vernon Castle and Julio Desnoyers, Raft's character goes off to fight in World War I. He survives just long enough to get in one more sexy tango before dying of a war-induced heart condition. Frawley's epitaph for him: "He was too good for this joint."

150. "A Dance Mappe of These U.S.: Culture Made Pleasant," *The Dance* 6 (October 1926): 25.

151. "Valentino Passes with No Kin at Side," *New York Times*, August 24, 1926, 1, 3.

152. "Native Town Forgets Actor," *New York Times*, August 26, 1926, 1, 5.

153. "Thousands in Riot at Valentino Bier," *New York Times*, August 25, 1926, 1, 3.

154. "Public Now Barred at Valentino's Bier," *New York Times*, August 26, 1926, 1, 5.

155. Ibid., 5.

156. Kendall, *Where She Danced*, 47.

157. Cecelia Tichi, *Shifting Gears: Technology, Literature, Culture in Modernist America* (Chapel Hill: University of North Carolina Press, 1987), 75.

4. Sideshow Oedipus: Lon Chaney and Film's Freak Possibilities

1. George Brinton Beal, *Through the Back Door of the Circus* (Springfield, Mass.: McLoughlin, 1938), 243.

2. "Amusement at the Abnormal," *The Nation* 86 (March 19, 1908): 254.

3. Robert Bogdan, *Freak Show* (Chicago: University of Chicago Press, 1988), 10. Modeled after P. T. Barnum's American Museum (founded in 1840), the country's numerous dime museums were credited with bringing the freak show to prominence.

4. In *Freaks: We Who Are Not as Others* (San Francisco: Re/Search Publications, 1990), Daniel P. Mannix notes: "In 1969, when World Fair Shows opened . . . the freaks were forbidden to appear, the prohibition being based on a 1921 state law that classed them with pornography" (49).

5. Milton Howe, "The Man Who Made Homeliness Pay," *Motion Picture Classic* (March 1926): 34.

6. Miriam Hansen also links Valentino to masochistic suffering although she seems to regard it as unique to the star and not culturally pervasive among either male stars or men in general during the 1920s. See Hansen, "Pleasure, Ambivalence, Identification: Valentino and Female Spectatorship," *Cinema Journal* 25, no. 4 (Summer 1986): 6–32.

7. T. J. Jackson Lears, *No Place of Grace: Antimodernism and the Transformation of American Culture, 1800–1920* (New York: Pantheon, 1981), 138.

8. Lears, *No Place of Grace*, 122.

9. A fan magazine article centers its discussion on the "startling fact" of Chaney's popularity. See Laura Louise Lowry, "Without Benefit of Ballyhoo: Lon Chaney Is Voted the Screen's Most Popular Star—Yet He Is Ever a Figure of Mystery," *Hollywood* (April 1929): n.p. (clipping file, British Film Institute, hereafter cited as BFI). Ruth Biery's "The Man Behind the Mask," *Screen Secrets* (June 1929), contrasts Chaney's ten years of unwavering star popularity to the "professional oblivion" his costars in *The Miracle Man* experienced: "Through all the years there had been no change in [Chaney's] box-office attraction—he had consistently topped the records" (n.p.; clipping file, BFI).

10. In *West of Zanzibar*, a sequence excised from the release version of the film showed Chaney's character as a sideshow performer who appears as a duck man. A photograph of Chaney in this suit (which gives the illusion that the actor is a mere two feet tall) appears in Michael Blake's detailed biography of the star, *Lon Chaney: The Man Behind a Thousand Faces* (New York: Vestal, 1990), 247.

11. Richard Koszarski includes a page and a half vignette about Chaney in *An Evening's Entertainment: The Age of the Silent Feature Picture, 1915–1928* (New York: Scribner's, 1990), 286–88. He locates the actor's appeal "in his traditional recourse to makeup and pantomime" and concludes that Chaney's specialization "in twisted minds and twisted bodies" provided "objective correlatives of evil unmatched onscreen before or since" (286, 288). Martin F. Norden discusses some of Chaney's films within a broad historical overview of Hollywood's representation of the physically disabled as a stereotyped minority group in *The Cinema of Isolation: A History of Physical Disability in the Movies* (New Brunswick, N.J.: Rutgers University Press, 1994), 82–99.

12. "The Star Sinister" is mentioned as a nickname for Chaney in a caption for a full-page photograph of Chaney printed in *Motion Picture Classic* (February 1923): n.p.

13. Dorothy Donnell, "A Martyr to the Movies?" *Motion Picture Magazine* (December 1930): 9. Herbert Howe asserts of Chaney: "He is a worker of screen miracles in characterizations built not only from the make-up box." Howe, "A Miracle Man of Make-Up," *Picture Play* (March 1920): n.p. (clipping file, BFI).

14. Review of *The Unholy Three* in *Variety*, August 5, 1925; reprinted in *Variety Film Reviews, 1907–1980* (New York: Garland, 1983), n.p.

15. Review of *The Black Bird* in the *New York Times*, February 1, 1926; reprinted in *The New York Times Film Reviews* (New York: New York Times, 1969), n.p.

16. Untitled clipping, February 3, 1916 [no source], n.p., *The Black Bird* file, Margaret Herrick Library, Academy of Motion Picture Arts and Sciences Center (hereafter cited as AMPAS).

17. Lon Chaney, "Why I Prefer Grotesque Characters," *Theatre Magazine* (October 1927): 58.

18. I wish to thank Tom Gunning for bringing this magazine and this phenomenon to my attention.

19. See, for example, Forest J. Ackerman, *Lon of a 1000 Faces!* (Beverly Hills, Calif.: Morrison, Ravel-Hill, 1983); Robert G. Anderson, *Faces, Forms, Films: The Artistry of Lon Chaney* (South Brunswick, N.J.: A. S. Barnes, 1971); and Blake, *Lon Chaney: The Man Behind the Thousand Faces.*

20. Mordant Hall, "A Slapstick Melodrama," review of *The Monster* in *Variety,* February 16, 1925; reprinted in *Variety Film Reviews, 1907–1980,* n.p.

21. Review of *The Hunchback of Notre Dame* in *Variety,* September 6, 1923, 22 (clipping, AMPAS).

22. "The Hideous Bell-Ringer," *New York Times,* September 3, 1923, 9 (clipping, AMPAS).

23. Undated clipping, *Motion Picture News,* n.p. (AMPAS).

24. "Straight from the Shoulder Reports," *Moving Picture World* (June 5, 1926): 487.

25. "Straight from the Shoulder Reports," *Moving Picture World* (December 11, 1926): 444.

26. Review in untitled clipping (trade magazine) dated June 30, 1926: n.p. (AMPAS).

27. "Straight from the Shoulder Reports," *Moving Picture World* (January 29, 1927): 373.

28. "Straight from the Shoulder Reports," *Moving Picture World* (March 12, 1927): 135.

29. "Straight from the Shoulder Reports," *Moving Picture World* (December 24, 1927): 34.

30. "Will Interest the Women!" (*Mr. Wu* pressbook), n.p. (AMPAS).

31. Photograph, Hertzberg Circus Collection and Museum, reproduced in Robert Lifson, *Enter the Sideshow* (Bala Cynwyd, Penn.: Mason Publishing, 1983), n.p.

32. Leslie Fiedler, *Freaks: Myths and Images of the Secret Self* (New York: Simon and Schuster, 1978), 31.

33. Fiedler, *Freaks,* 23.

34. While this was my initial thinking about Chaney's place in the cultural matrix of post-World War I, it is, I think, by itself too easy an explanation, especially when one considers that the flu epidemics of 1918–19 took many more American lives than the war and created tremendous national anxiety.

35. Lears, *No Place of Grace,* 122.

36. Ibid., 138.

37. David Rodowick, "Madness, Authority, and Ideology: The Domestic Melodrama of the 1950s," in Christine Gledhill, ed., *Home Is Where the Heart Is* (London: British Film Institute, 1987), 272.

38. My theoretical views on masochism are more fully developed in *In the Realm of Pleasure: Von Sternberg, Dietrich, and the Masochistic Aesthetic* (Urbana: University of Illinois Press, 1988). In keeping with Theodor Reik's views (*Masochism in Modern Man,* trans. Margaret H. Beigel and Gertrud M. Kurth [New York: Grove Press, 1941]), I would suggest that the masochism displayed in Chaney's films demonstrates that it is not suffering itself that is most important, but "what is bought by suffering" (318). In some measure, pleasure is not found

in suffering, but in the anticipation and enjoyment of the idea that the masochist will have the final triumph, "conquer all his enemies and then suppress them, that he is going to be acknowledged by the very society which neglects and rejects him now" (319). Masochistic revenge fantasies become explicit in Chaney's films and are accentuated, especially in films such as *The Unknown*, *Mr. Wu*, *West of Zanzibar*, and *He Who Gets Slapped*, as being capable of being acted out by the male character whose final triumph means his own death..

39. Chaney, "Why I Prefer Grotesque Characters," 58.

40. Pauline Kael, *Kiss Kiss Bang Bang* (Boston: Little, Brown, 1968), 330–31.

41. Alvin Harlow, *Old Bowery Days* (New York: Appleton, 1931), quoted in Michael Mitchell, *Monsters of the Gilded Age. The Photographs of Charles Eisenmann* (Toronto: Gage, 1979), 11.

42. Bogdan, *Freak Show* (Chicago: University of Chicago Press, 1988), 11.

43. Mitchell, *Monsters of the Gilded Age*, 76; see also Bogdan, *Freak Show*, 134–42. Like Valentino, Zip died in 1926 and lay "in state" at Campbell's Funeral Church in 1926, but in contrast to Valentino, his funeral cortege was reputed to have included a bevy of his friends as well as rivals from the sideshow. See "Many Circus Folk at Zip's Funeral," *New York Times*, April 28, 1926, 6.

44. See Beal, *Through the Back Door of the Circus*, 241.

45. By 1922 Frank Braden reflected on why Pinon fooled so many who were looking for fakery: "Newspaper men, educators, professional men and even show-men looked on this Mexican freak and did not scoff. They eyed the man carefully, viewing him from all sides, talked to him, puzzled, cogitated [*sic*]—and gave it up." Frank Braden, "The 'Wonders' of a Circus Sideshow," *Illustrated World* 36 (1922): 674.

46. "Facts Concerning Johnny Eck: The Only Living Half Boy," brochure photographically reproduced in Lifson, *Enter the Sideshow*, n.p.

47. Bogdan, *Freak Show*, 97–98.

48. "Millie Christine: The Two-Headed Lady" Eden Musee publication, c. 1874, unsourced clipping, 8 (Hertzberg Circus Collection and Museum, San Antonio, Texas).

49. Erving Goffman, *Stigma: Notes on the Management of Spoiled Identity* (1963; rpt., New York: Touchstone, 1986), 43 and 3. As Goffman suggests, stigma is an attribute that discredits, but what stigmatizes one person in a specific social context might be regarded as an enviable attribute in another (3). Thus, stigma emerges as "a special kind of relationship between attribute and stereotype" (4).

50. Goffman, *Stigma*, 44–45.

51. Mannix, *Freaks: We Who Are Not as Others*, 13; see also Lifson, *Enter the Sideshow*, n.p.

52. Claude Lecouteux, *Les monstres dans la litterature allemande du Moyen Age*, 3 vols. (Göppingen: Kummerle Verlag, 1982), 1:5.

53. The case of the "San Antonio Siamese Twins," the Hilton sisters, was the most widely publicized instance of "freak" abuse in the 1920s. See Bogdan, *Freak Show*, 169–73.

54. For a discussion of hybrids within historical taxonomies of the monstrously anomalous, see Peter Mason, "Half a Cow," *Semiotica* 85 (1991): 1–39.

55. Mannix, *Freaks: We Who Are Not as Others*, 85–86. Early in his career, in the 1860s, Zip was called "The Monkey-Man" and promoted as being the missing link between humans and apes to exploit current interest in Darwin's theories. In public he was never allowed to speak coherently (though he could), and his behavior was regarded as beneath that of any rational human being since he threw money back to onlookers.

56. Maternal impression during pregnancy and paternal degeneracy (from sexually transmitted disease, especially) were the most common explanations given for congenital birth defects or anomalous conditions.

57. Donald K. Pickens, *Eugenics and the Progressives* (Nashville, Tenn.: Vanderbilt University Press, 1968), 49. See also Mark H. Haller, *Eugenics: Hereditarian Attitudes in American Thought* (New Brunswick, N.J.: Rutgers University Press, 1963).

58. Pickens, *Eugenics and the Progressives*, 164.

59. Broughten Brandenburg, "How Shall We Make Our Immigration Laws More Effective?" *Proceedings of the National Conference of Charities and Correction* (1906): 1300.

60. Earnest A. Hooton, *Apes, Men, and Morons* (New York: Putnam's, 1939), 290. Hooton's eugenics-based theories of the racial causes of crime were widely published in the 1920s in American scholarly journals. See, for example, Hooton, "Progress in the Study of Race Mixture with Special Reference to Work Carried on at Harvard University," *Proceedings of the American Philosophical Society* 65 (1926): 312–25.

61. In *Monsters of the Gilded Age* Michael Mitchell, in the context of discussing the family portrait of Eli Bowen, a legless acrobat, echoes other freak show aficionados in asserting that freaks of the late nineteenth century "enjoyed a healthier social climate and better financial and social opportunities" than in the late twentieth century. He asserts that "publicity, travel and good wages made the dime museum stars attractive partners. Most married outside of the show world and a good many had children. Moreover, they lived where they pleased rather than in the show ghettos of Florida. . . . It is a mark of civilization . . . that Eli Bowen could present himself to the world as a father as well as a freak" (34).

62. Tom Gunning, "The Cinema of Attraction: Early Film, Its Spectator and the Avant-Garde," *Wide Angle* 8 (1986): 64.

63. Gunning, "The Cinema of Attraction," 68, 70.

64. Ibid., 66.

65. Herbert Howe, "A Miracle Man of Make-Up," 37.

66. Ibid., n.p., and Maude S. Cheatham, "Meet 'The Frog,'" *Motion Picture Classic* (March 1920): 38.

67. One publicity article on *The Hunchback of Notre Dame* again relies on the contortionist question posed to Lon Chaney, "who has played almost every known variety of cripple, often with gruesome realism." See "Lon Chaney Explains His Great Knot Trick," *Toledo Blade*, August 22, 1923, n.p. (Robinson Locke Collection Scrapbook, New York Public Library for the Performing Arts, Theatre Collection; hereafter cited as NYPL-TC).

68. Herbert Howe, "A Miracle Man of Make-Up," n.p..

69. Truman B. Handy, "Masquerade," *Motion Picture Magazine* (December 1922): 42.

70. Bogdan, *Freak Show*, 277.

71. "Circus and Museum Freaks, Curiosities of Pathology," *Scientific America Supplement* (April 4, 1908; reprinted from the *New York Medical Journal*), 222.

72. "Amusement at the Abnormal," *The Nation* 86 (March 19, 1908): 254.

73. Ibid.; see also Bogdan, *Freak Show*, 278–79.

74. "Circus and Museum Freaks," 222 (see note 72, above).

75. Perhaps it is these aspects of Chaney's films that resonate with adolescent male experience and partially explains his popularity in the 1950s among young males and the cult status accorded him in *Famous Monsters of Filmland*'s August 1958 issue.

76. Untitled clipping from *Exhibitors Herald* (December 11, 1920): n.p. (NYPL-TC); see also the review of *The Penalty* in *Variety* (November 19, 1920): 34.

77. "In Filmland," *New Jersey Mail*, November 16, 1923, n.p. ([?]Scrapbooks, Robinson Locke Collection, NYPL-TC).

78. Burns Mantle, review of *The Penalty* in *Photoplay* 19 (February 1921): 66. One reviewer called it "at times weirdly fascinating and at other times dangerously near the absurd" (untitled clipping, *Theatre Magazine* [February 1921]: n.p. [clipping, [?]Scrapbook, Robinson Locke Collection, NYPL-TC]). For yet another suggestion that "at first an attempt was made to get a crippled man for the part [in *The Penalty*]," see review in the *New York Sun*, February 28, 1920, n.p. (clipping, [?]Scrapbook, Robinson Locke Collection, NYPL-TC).

79. Trade magazine review of *The Penalty*, c. 1920, n.p. (clipping file, AMPAS).

80. Untitled clipping on *The Road to Mandalay*, unsourced trade magazine, n.p. (clipping file, AMPAS).

81. "Important Points to Remember," *The Big City* pressbook (AMPAS).

82. On these issues, see Barry King, "Articulating Stardom," *Screen* 26, no. 5 (September-October 1925): 27–50. For an in-depth analysis of the range of these emotions in relation to British female spectators of the 1940s and the Hollywood stars they watched, see Jackie Stacey, *Star Gazing* (New York: Routledge, 1993).

83. Metro-Goldwyn-Mayer's pressbook for *Mockery*, "Exploitation: The-Showman's [*sic*] Guide-For-Building-Bigger-Business," (c. 1927), 1

84. On the "*different* characterizations" (emphasis in original) that were being served up for Chaney as relief from his "super-morbid" roles, see Laurence Reid, "*Mockery* Not So Hot, But Chaney Puts It Over," *Motion Picture News*, September 2, 1927, n.p. (clipping, AMPAS). When he was not in disguise, he usually played hard-bitten men, often criminals.

85. Orientalist discourse cut across myriad forms of high and low art entertainment, including the cinema, dance, World's Fair architecture, museum displays of Asian art, advertisements for consumer goods, department store displays, fashion, etc. The fascination with an imaginary Orient was not limited to America. Scholarship that includes consideration of some of the venues for the exotic during this period includes Zeynep Celik, *Displaying the Orient: Architecture of Islam at Nineteenth-Century World's Fairs* (Berkeley: University of California Press,

1992); Rosalind H. Williams, *Dream Worlds: Mass Consumption in Late Nineteenth-Century France* (Berkeley: University of California Press, 1982); and Simon J. Bronner, ed., *Consuming Visions: Accumulation and Display of Goods in America, 1880–1929* (New York: Norton, 1989).

86. "Celestial Adventure," in "Weekly Film Pictorial Section: The Pre-view," *Los Angeles Sunday Times*, January 9, 1927, n.p. (clipping file, AMPAS).

87. Bogdan, *Freak Show*, 112–13.

88. Mitchell, *Monsters of the Gilded Age*, 102–3.

89. Richard deCordova, *Picture Personalities: The Emergence of the Star System in America* (Urbana: University of Illinois Press, 1990), 139.

90. Richard Schickel, *The Movies* (New York: Crown, 1972), 12.

91. Ivan St. Johns, "Mr. Nobody," *Photoplay* 31 (February 1927): 136.

92. Biery, "The Man Behind the Mask," n.p..

93. Milton Howe, "The Man Who Made Homeliness Pay," 34.

94. See, for example, Grace Kingsley, "'The Better I Get, the Worse I Look,' Says Lon Chaney," *Movie Weekly* (April 21, 1923): 21, 30.

95. Lon Chaney, as told to Walter Ramsey, "The Most Grotesque Moment of My Life," *Motion Picture Classic* (June 1930): 24–25, 84–85.

96. "A Master of Make-Up," *Picturegoer* (March 1921): 31.

97. Donnell, "A Martyr to the Movies?" 34–35, 90–92.

98. Joseph Henry Steele, "It Might Be Pagliacci," *Motion Picture Classic* (May 1928): 92–93.

99. Lowry, "Without Benefit of Ballyhoo," n.p..

100. Fred Caseen, "Lon Chaney Raised 2 Fingers to Signal That He Was Dying," *Philadelphia Inquirer*, c. 1930, n.p. (clipping, BFI).

101. Mannix, *Freaks: We Who Are Not as Others*, 119–20.

Conclusion

1. Thomas H. Ince, "The Star Is Here to Stay," *Munsey's Magazine* 65, no. 2 (November 1918): 346.

2. Gaylyn Studlar, "The Perils of Pleasure? Fan Magazine Discourse as Women's Commodified Culture in the 1920s," *Wide Angle* 13, no. 1 (January 1991): 17.

3. For a discussion of this see Studlar, "The Perils of Pleasure?" 16–22.

4. For example, Cecelia Tichi suggests the figure of the engineer became an archetype of industrial modernism in the 1920s (*Shifting Gears: Technology, Literature, Culture in Modernist America* [Chapel Hill: University of North Carolina Press, 1987]). Represented most prominently in national life by former engineer turned President of the United States, Calvin Coolidge, the engineer/businessman also found a home in many movies in films such as *The Winning of Barbara Worth* (1926) and *The Temptress* (1928), but no single star came to represent him as a type.

5. In 1928 one commentator suggested that romance and screen silence were synonymous and that "the minute you put words in the mouth of the screen lover" the illusion of the audience being "imaginary participants in the action" was "forever broken." Talkies had made film audiences "mere spectators." Hall K. Wills, "For Loving Out Loud," *Motion Picture Classic* 28 (December 1928): 55.

6. Some of Chaney's most exaggerated makeups, such as those for *The Hunchback of Notre Dame* and *The Phantom of the Opera*, did not permit him to talk clearly. Chaney was one of MGM's last stars to hold out against making a talkie (Garbo being the other). It is interesting to speculate whether the shift to talkies would have forced him to abandon his beloved makeup box and shift to his secondary specialty as a more "realistic" criminal type.

Index

311